FOOTBALL IN "QUOTES"

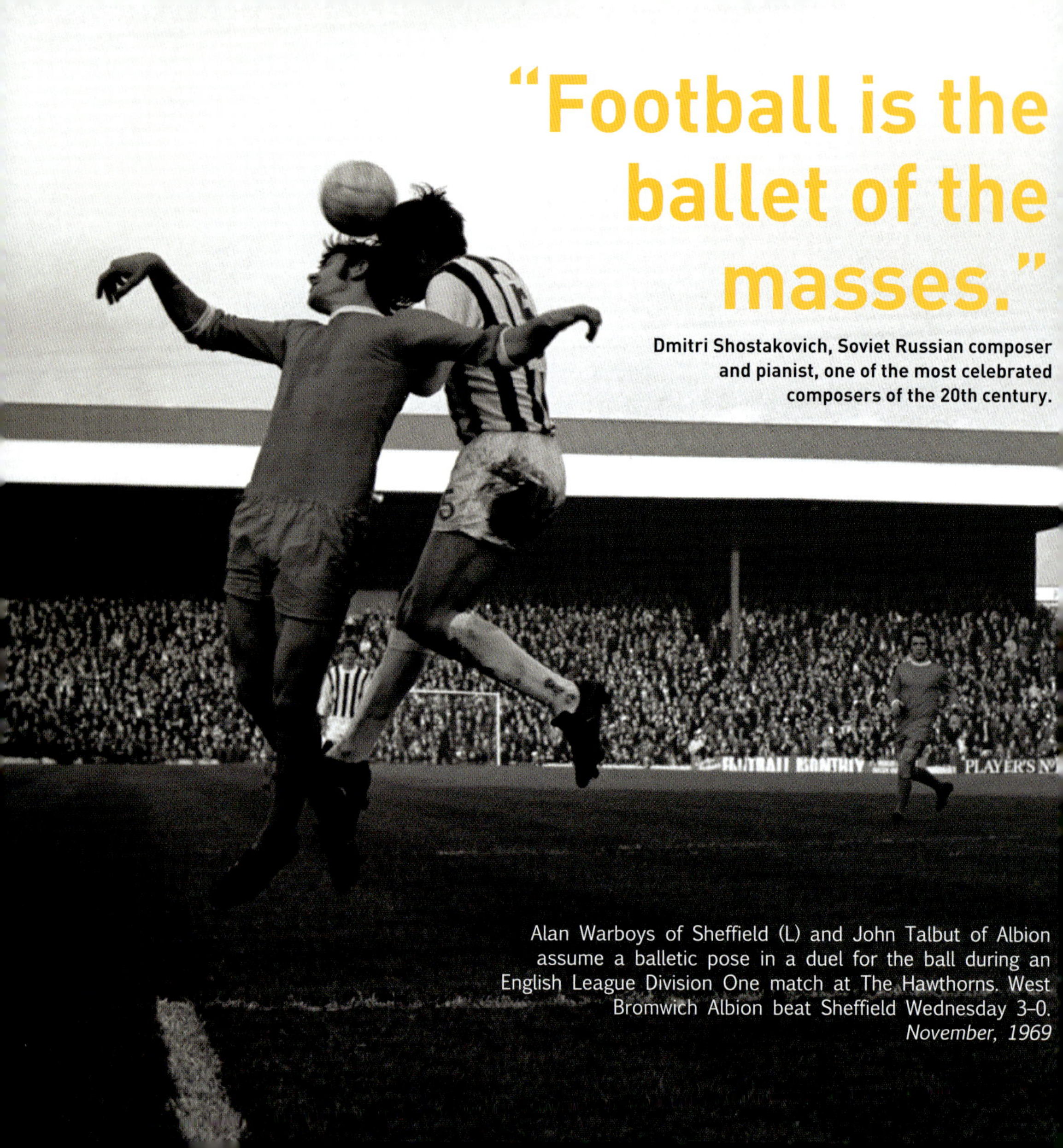

"Football is the ballet of the masses."

Dmitri Shostakovich, Soviet Russian composer and pianist, one of the most celebrated composers of the 20th century.

Alan Warboys of Sheffield (L) and John Talbut of Albion assume a balletic pose in a duel for the ball during an English League Division One match at The Hawthorns. West Bromwich Albion beat Sheffield Wednesday 3–0. *November, 1969*

FOOTBALL IN "QUOTES"

mirrorpix

AMMONITE
PRESS

First published 2012 by
Ammonite Press
an imprint of AE Publications Ltd,
166 High Street, Lewes, East Sussex, BN7 1XU

ISBN 978-1-90770-868-8

British Cataloguing in Publication Data. A catalogue record of this book is available from the British Library.

Editor: Ian Penberthy
Series Editor: Richard Wiles
Picture research: Mirrorpix
Design: Robin Shields

Colour reproduction by GMC Reprographics
Printed and bound in China by 1010 Printing International Ltd

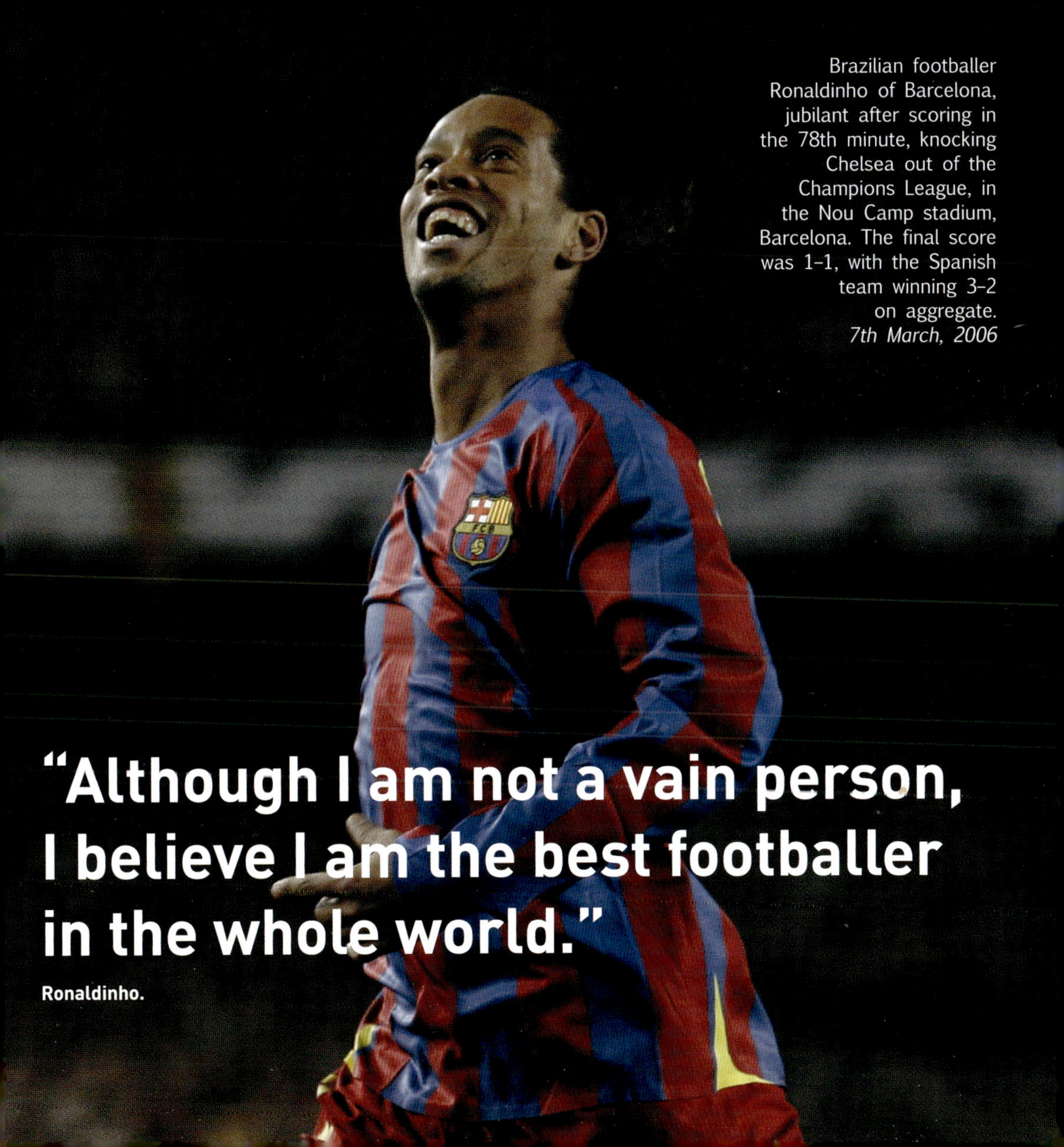

Brazilian footballer Ronaldinho of Barcelona, jubilant after scoring in the 78th minute, knocking Chelsea out of the Champions League, in the Nou Camp stadium, Barcelona. The final score was 1–1, with the Spanish team winning 3–2 on aggregate.
7th March, 2006

"Although I am not a vain person, I believe I am the best footballer in the whole world."

Ronaldinho.

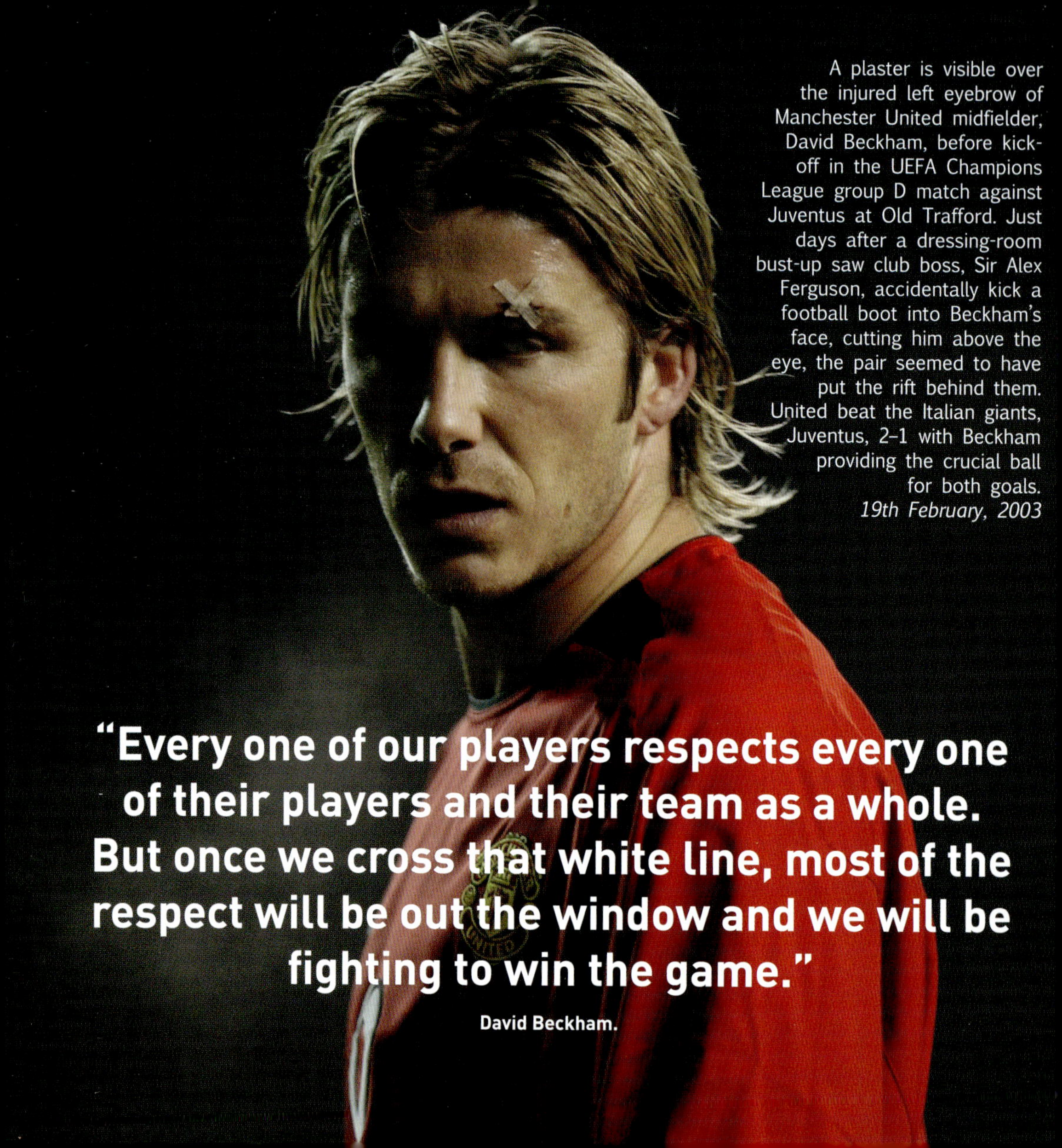

A plaster is visible over the injured left eyebrow of Manchester United midfielder, David Beckham, before kick-off in the UEFA Champions League group D match against Juventus at Old Trafford. Just days after a dressing-room bust-up saw club boss, Sir Alex Ferguson, accidentally kick a football boot into Beckham's face, cutting him above the eye, the pair seemed to have put the rift behind them. United beat the Italian giants, Juventus, 2–1 with Beckham providing the crucial ball for both goals.
19th February, 2003

"Every one of our players respects every one of their players and their team as a whole. But once we cross that white line, most of the respect will be out the window and we will be fighting to win the game."

David Beckham.

INTRODUCTION

"The Beautiful Game" has become the phrase universally quoted to describe football. Although the identity of its originator is widely disputed, some insist that Brazilian World Cup-winning star Valdir Periera (aka Didi) was the first to utter the three words, while British sports commentator Stuart Hall has also laid claim to its first use back in 1958. But whoever first coined the poetic idiom, undoubtedly it was Brazilian legend Pelé who was responsible for its worldwide dissemination, after incorporating it into the title of his 1977 autobiography, *My Life and the Beautiful Game*.

Evoking passion akin to religious fervour, football, a national obsession in Great Britain, has become a language spoken on an international level – yet frequently the garbled, unguarded or spontaneous utterances of footballers, commentators and media pundits are somewhat lost in translation. Words of inspiration and encouragement from managers and coaches can emerge from the mouths of these impassioned individuals, often in the heat of the moment, as misinformed, angry, antagonistic, obscene or pure gibberish – but invariably unintentionally hilarious.

Many players, paid enormous sums for their 90 minutes on the pitch, are idolised as heroes and held up as role models, sometimes doubling as fashion icons. While they might be revered for their athleticism and skill with a ball, their ability to string a few sentences together is frequently no match. Their off-pitch antics often see them tumble from grace, embroiled in tabloid scandal, victims to their own overblown egos. Others, known for their aggressive style of play or unsportsmanlike behaviour, vilified by press and supporters alike, are apt to be vociferous about the injustices afforded them.

Among this selection of wise words, team talk and tactics, for the purpose of critique and review, is a hotchpotch of crazy quips, witty anecdotes and slips-of-the-tongue, illustrated by more than 150 photographs from the vast archives of Mirrorpix. Their photographers have been at the touchline of most major football matches since the beginning of the 20th century, capturing images that range from cheeky, paparazzi-style snapshots, artfully frozen mid-air action and carefully posed portraits, to on-pitch scrambles for the ball that encapsulate the essence of The Beautiful Game.

"Winning isn't everything. There should be no conceit in victory and no despair in defeat."

Matt Busby.

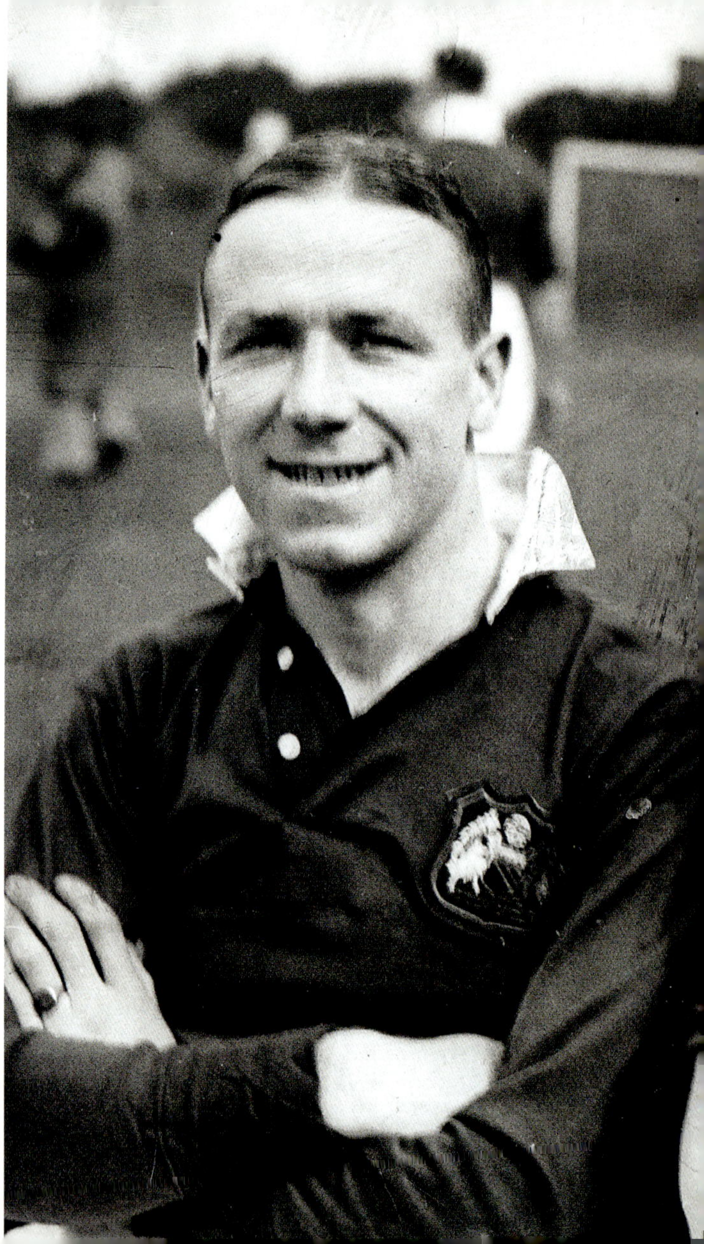

Twenty-five-year-old Scottish footballer Matt Busby of Manchester City FC, pictured two days after his team had beaten Portsmouth FC 2–1 in the 1934 FA Cup Final at Wembley Stadium, London. *30th April, 1934*

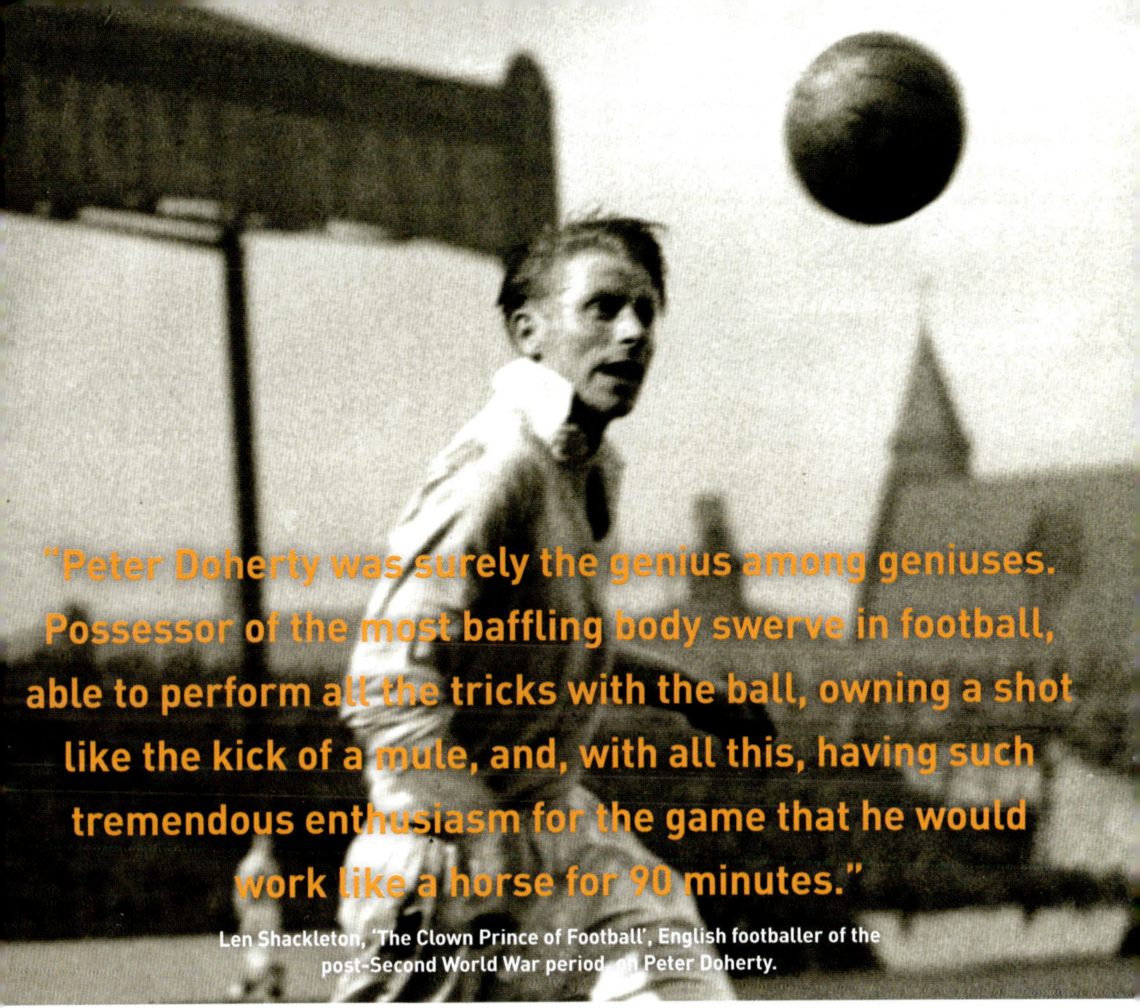

"Peter Doherty was surely the genius among geniuses. Possessor of the most baffling body swerve in football, able to perform all the tricks with the ball, owning a shot like the kick of a mule, and, with all this, having such tremendous enthusiasm for the game that he would work like a horse for 90 minutes."

Len Shackleton, 'The Clown Prince of Football', English footballer of the post-Second World War period, on Peter Doherty.

anchester City player Peter Doherty in 1936 after his transfer from Blackpool, where he had wished to remain. Of the transfer, he said: "My personal feelings counted for next to nothing in the transaction. I might as well have been a bale of merchandise."

1936

"I'm going for a pee. You coming?"

Dixie Dean, English footballer, one of the most prolific goal-scorers in English football history, scorer of 60 league goals during the 1927/28 season, to an over-enthusiastic marker.

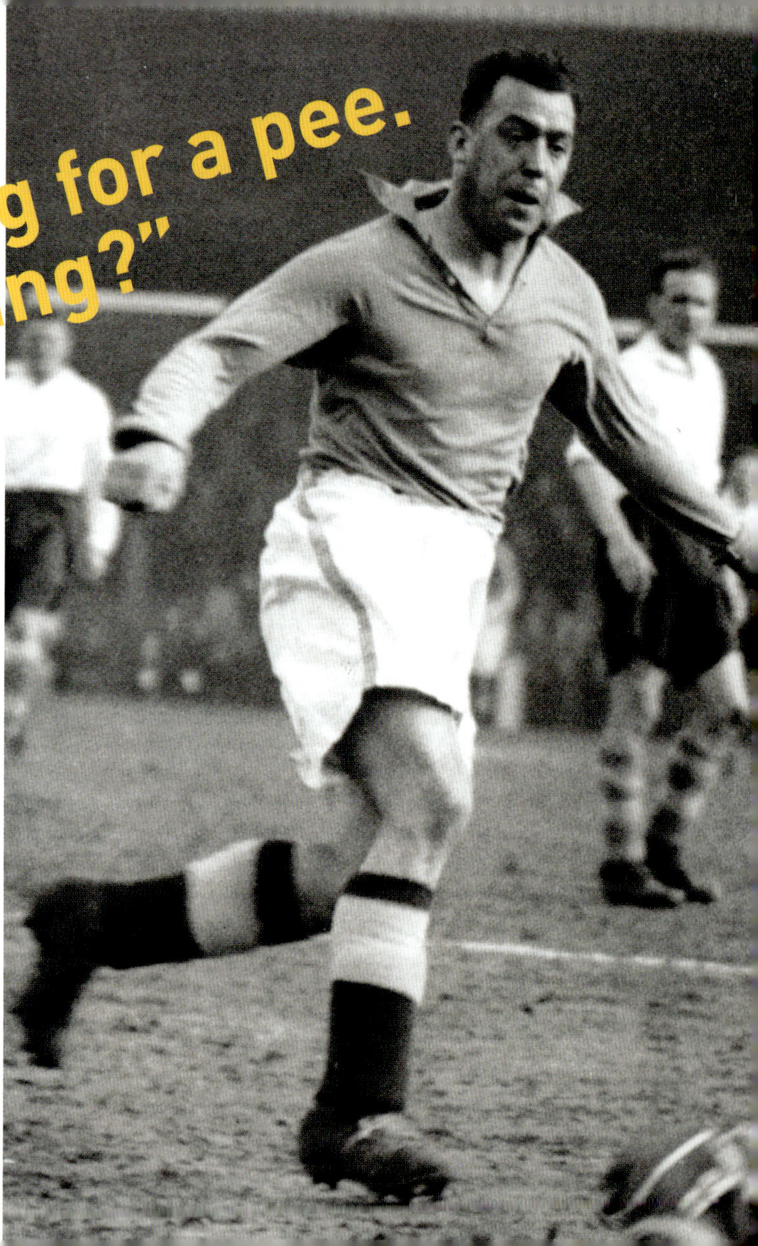

Thirty-year-old Dixie Dean in action as captain for Everton FC.
16th April, 1937

“He was the best header of the ball I ever saw in my life.”

Jack Charlton, on Welsh international footballer John Charles.

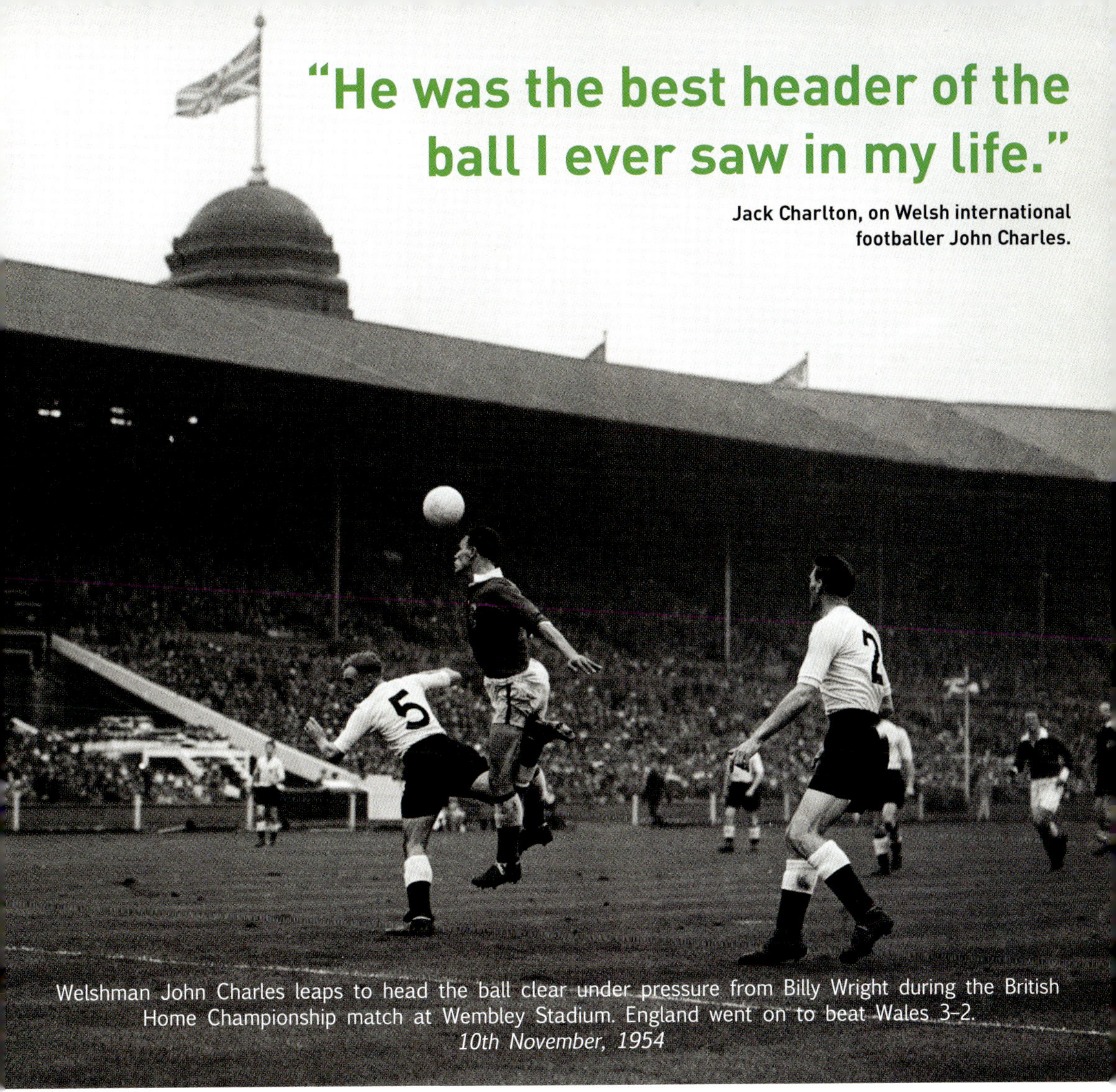

Welshman John Charles leaps to head the ball clear under pressure from Billy Wright during the British Home Championship match at Wembley Stadium. England went on to beat Wales 3–2.
10th November, 1954

"There was plenty of fellers who would kick your bollocks off. The difference was that at the end they'd shake your hand and help you to look for them."

Nat Lofthouse, English footballer; played 33 times in the English national team.

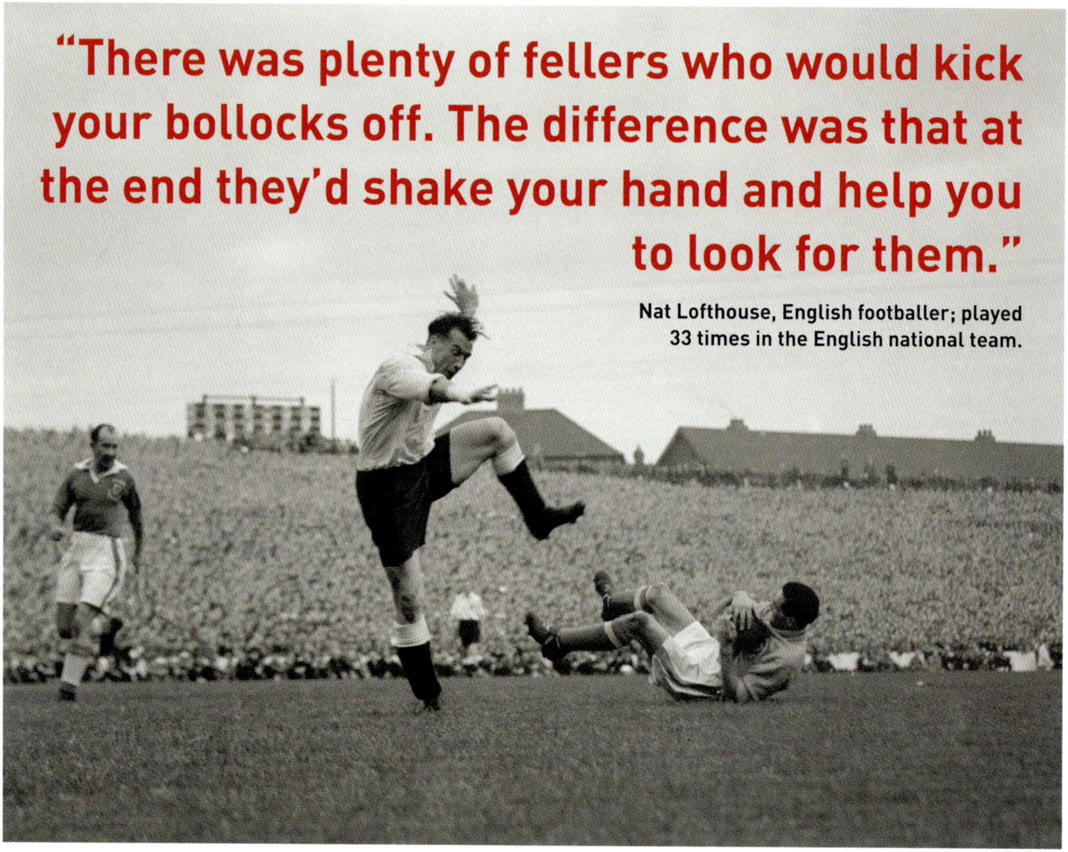

Welsh goalkeeper Jack Kelsey saves Nat Lofthouse's kick during the Home Championship International and 1954 World Cup qualifying match at Ninian Park, Cardiff, although England went on to beat Wales 4–1.
10th October, 1953

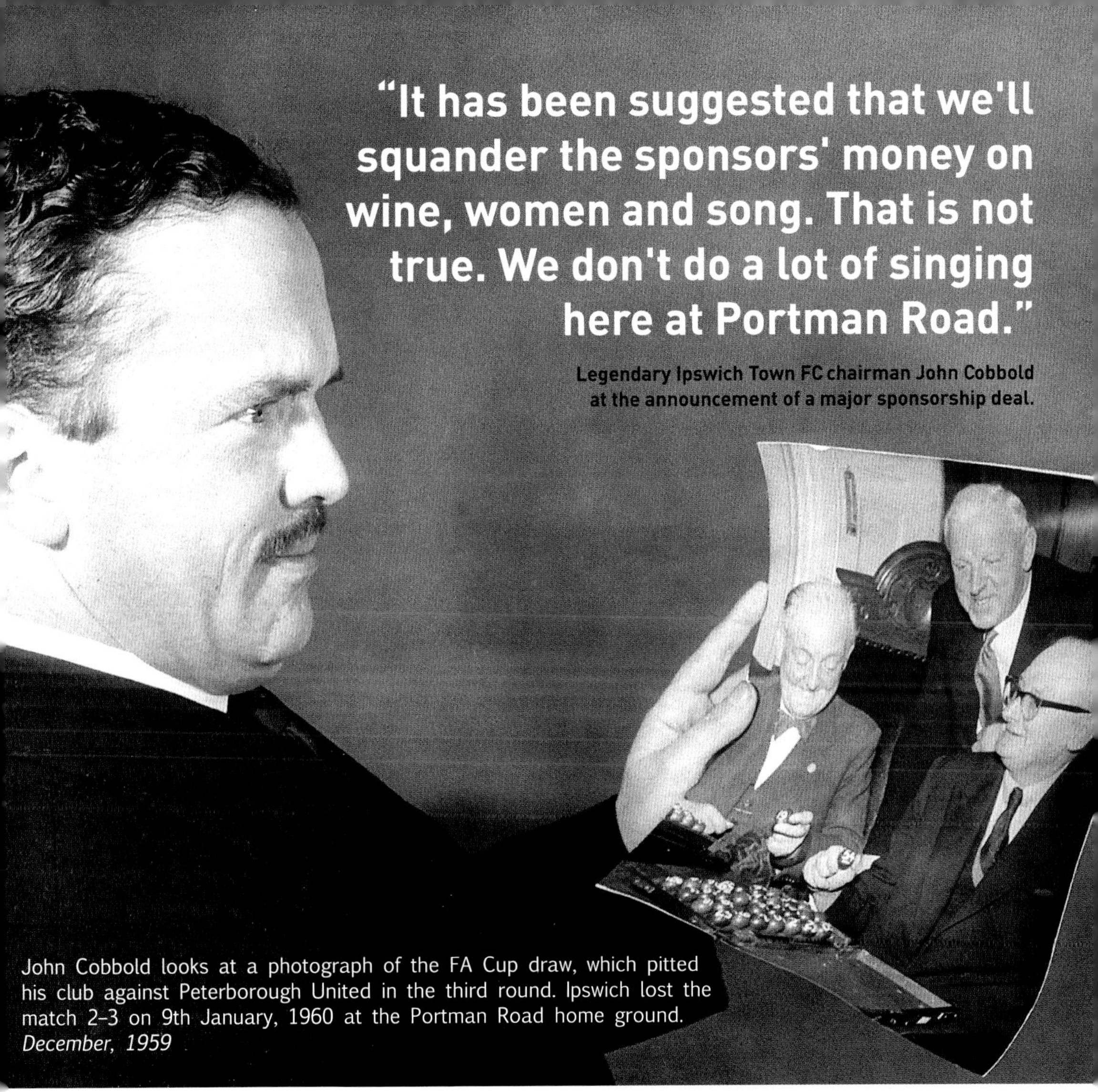

"It has been suggested that we'll squander the sponsors' money on wine, women and song. That is not true. We don't do a lot of singing here at Portman Road."

Legendary Ipswich Town FC chairman John Cobbold at the announcement of a major sponsorship deal.

John Cobbold looks at a photograph of the FA Cup draw, which pitted his club against Peterborough United in the third round. Ipswich lost the match 2–3 on 9th January, 1960 at the Portman Road home ground.
December, 1959

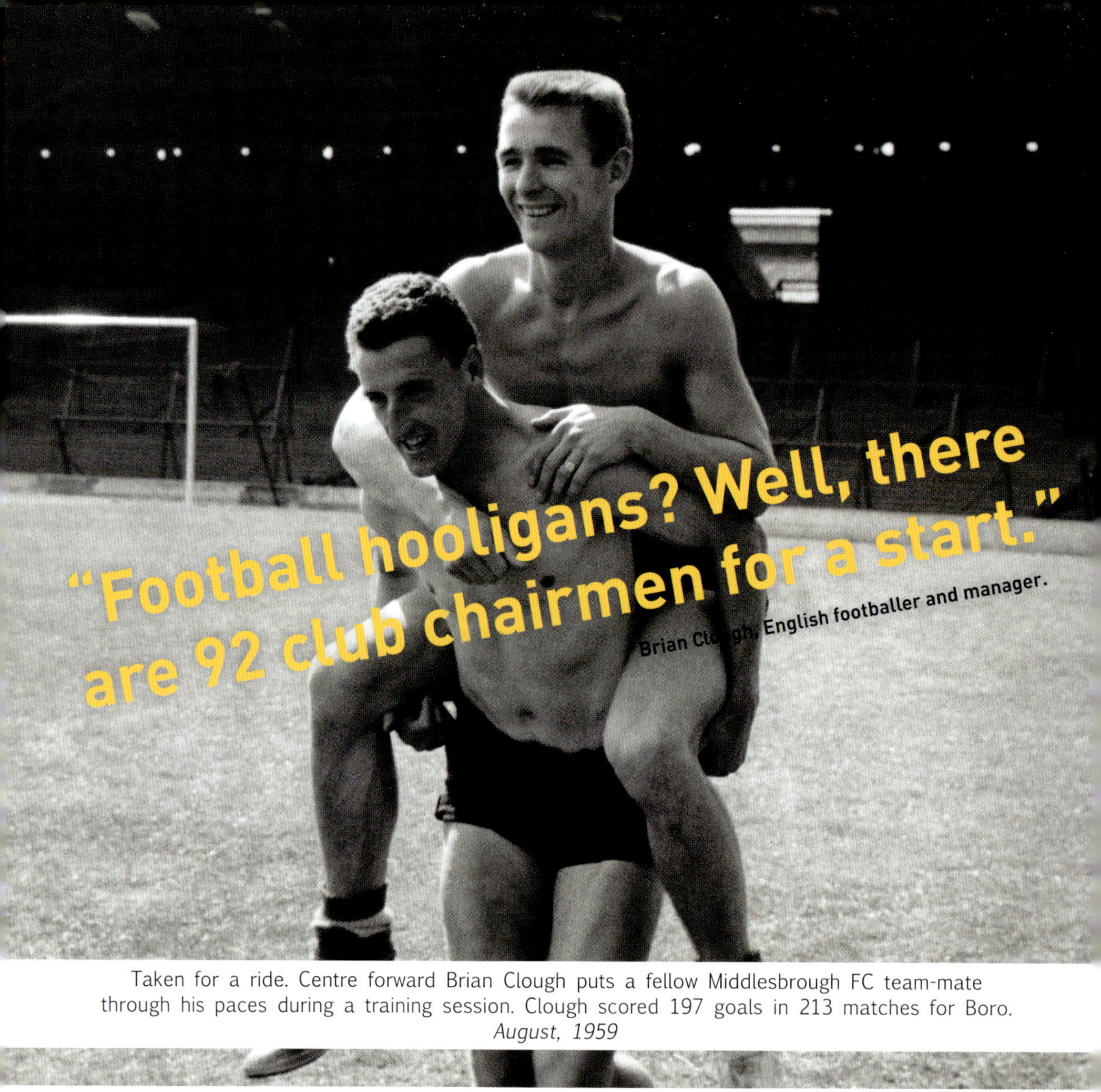

"Football hooligans? Well, there are 92 club chairmen for a start."

Brian Clough, English footballer and manager.

Taken for a ride. Centre forward Brian Clough puts a fellow Middlesbrough FC team-mate through his paces during a training session. Clough scored 197 goals in 213 matches for Boro.
August, 1959

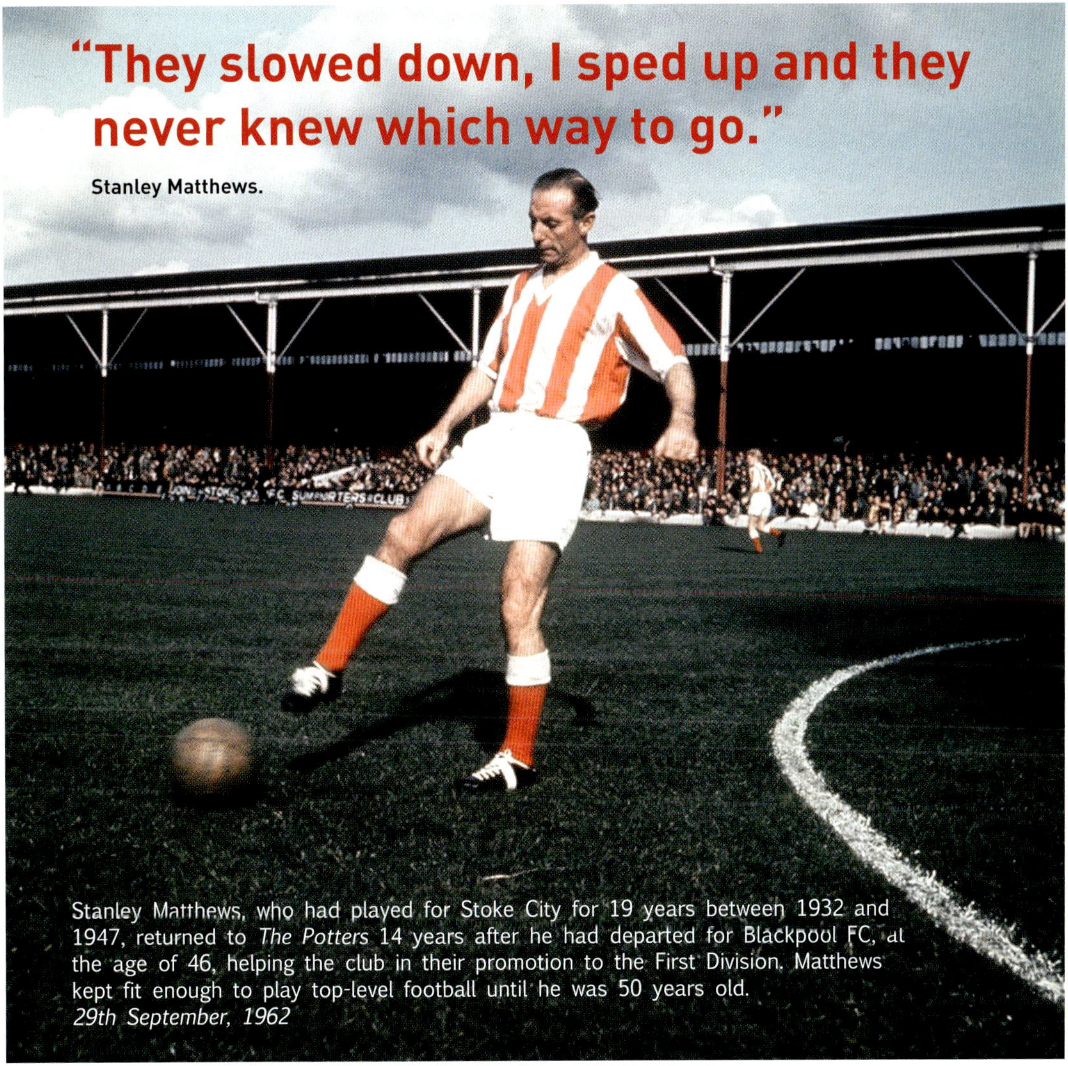

"They slowed down, I sped up and they never knew which way to go."

Stanley Matthews.

Stanley Matthews, who had played for Stoke City for 19 years between 1932 and 1947, returned to *The Potters* 14 years after he had departed for Blackpool FC, at the age of 46, helping the club in their promotion to the First Division. Matthews kept fit enough to play top-level football until he was 50 years old.
29th September, 1962

"Everything in our favour was against us."

Danny Blanchflower, Northern Ireland international footballer and manager, who captained Tottenham Hotspur during a double-winning season in 1961.

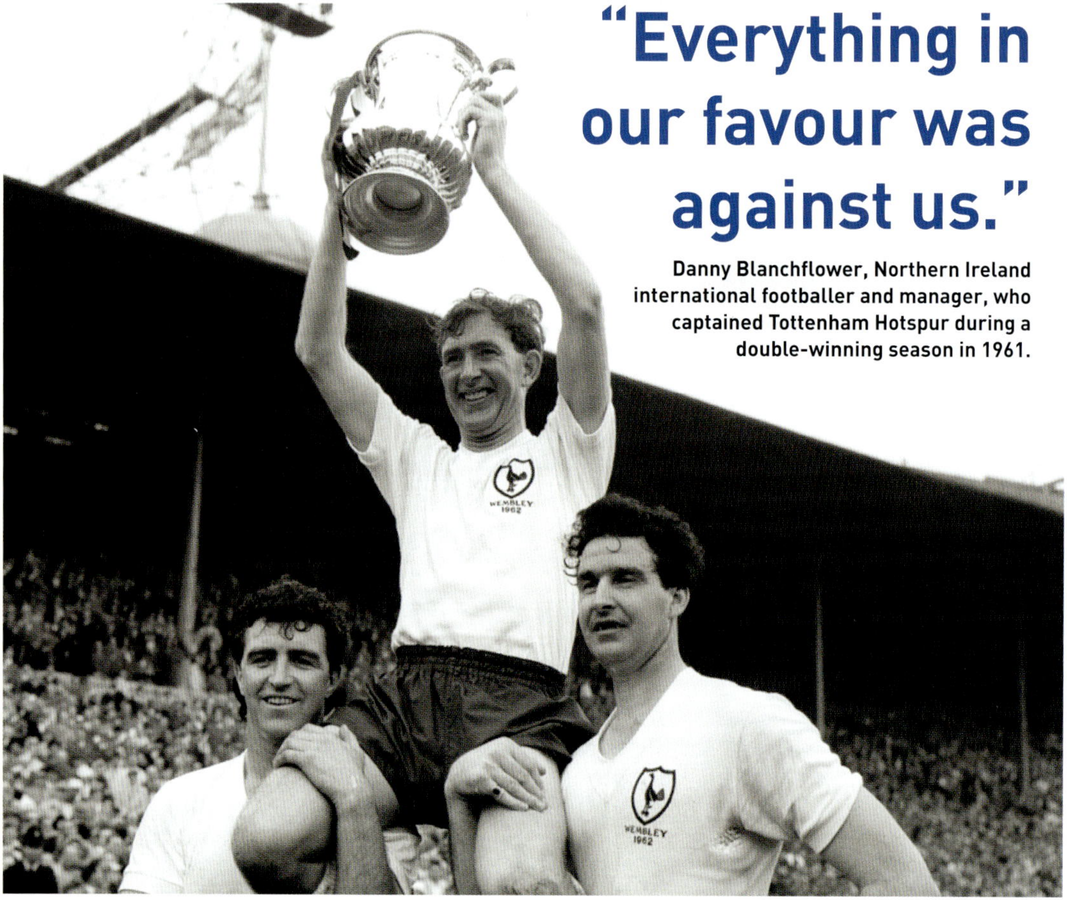

The 1962 FA Cup Final at Wembley Stadium was won by Tottenham Hotspur 3–1 over Burnley FC. Spurs captain Danny Blanchflower sits on the shoulders of team-mates Bobby Smith (L) and Maurice Norman (R) as he holds aloft the trophy.
5th May, 1962

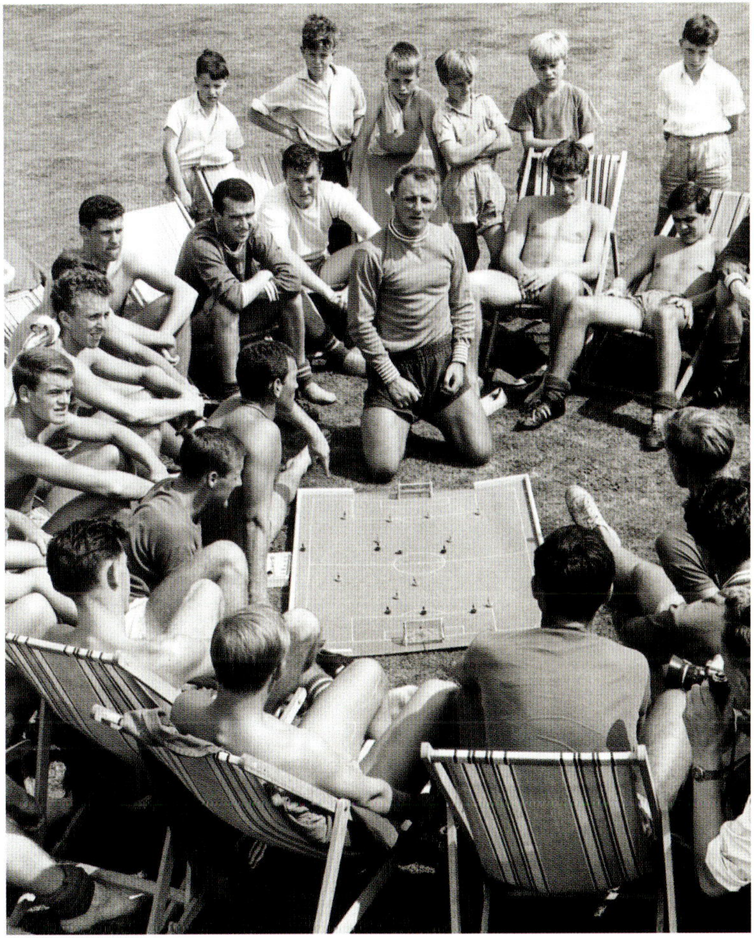

Chelsea players, preparing for their return to First Division football, listen to their manager, Tommy Docherty, at a training session in Ewell, Surrey. *31st July, 1963*

"The rules of soccer are very simple, basically it is this: if it moves, kick it. If it doesn't move, kick it until it does."

Phil Woosnam, Welsh former soccer player and manager.

“The fans are the heart of football.”

John Charles, Welsh international footballer, and great all-rounder, was never cautioned or sent off during his entire career, due to his principle of never intentionally hurting opposing players. Standing 6ft 2in tall, he was nicknamed The Gentle Giant.

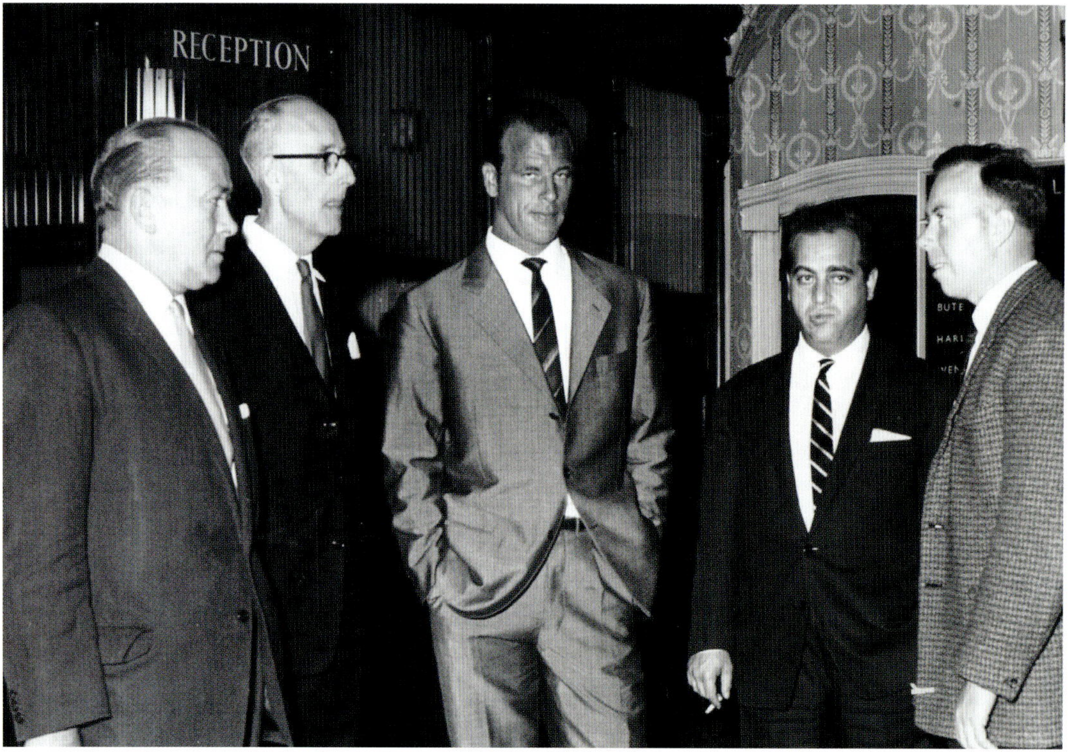

Dressed up. Suntanned Welsh footballing giant John Charles (C) cuts a suave figure between officials of Cardiff City and AS Roma, during his transfer from the Italian club, after a one-year tenure.
1963

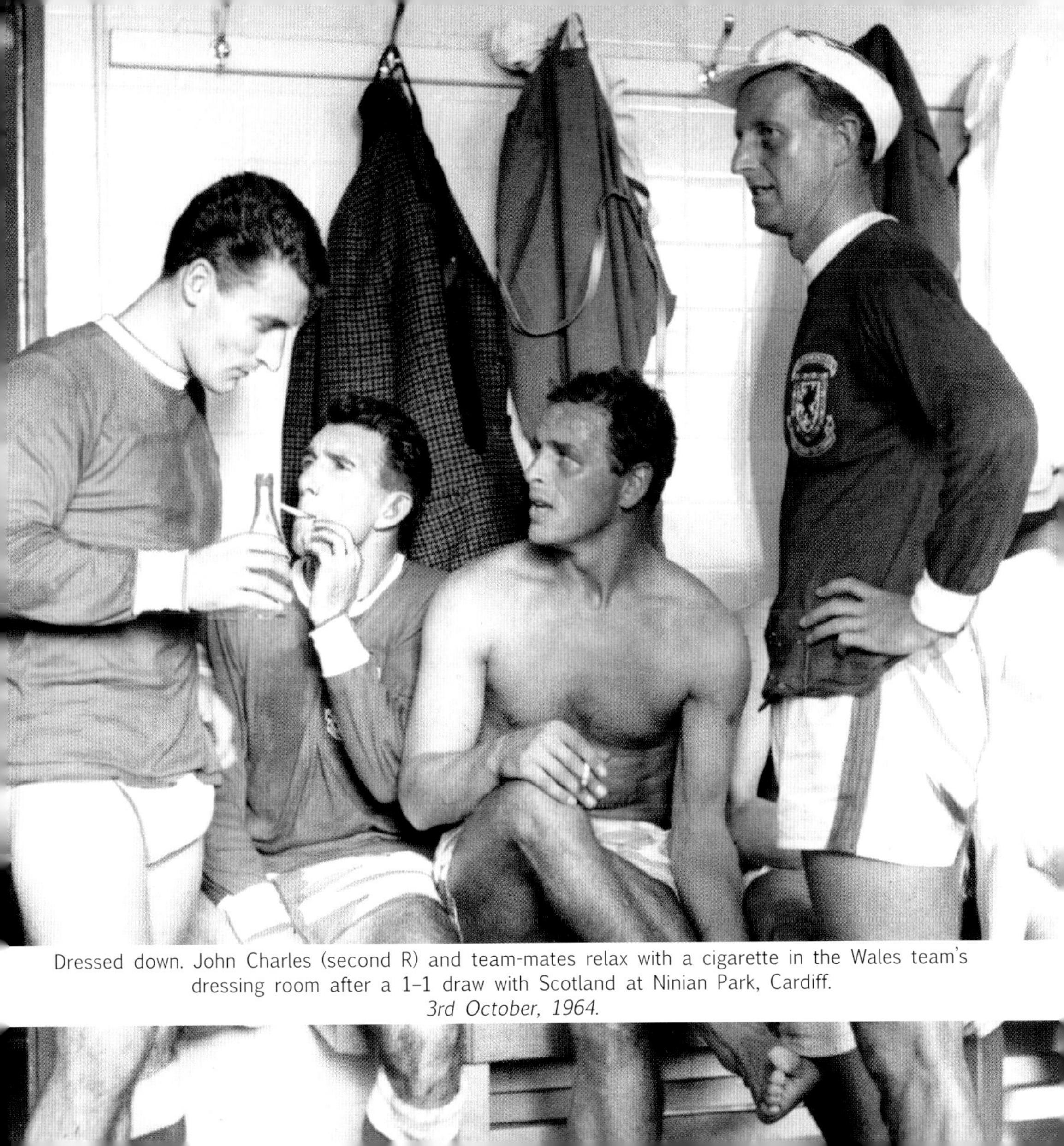

Dressed down. John Charles (second R) and team-mates relax with a cigarette in the Wales team's dressing room after a 1–1 draw with Scotland at Ninian Park, Cardiff.
3rd October, 1964.

"To be the ultimate team, you must use your body and your mind. Draw up on the resources of your team-mates. Choose your steps wisely and you will win. Remember, only teams succeed."

José Mourinho, Portuguese football manager.

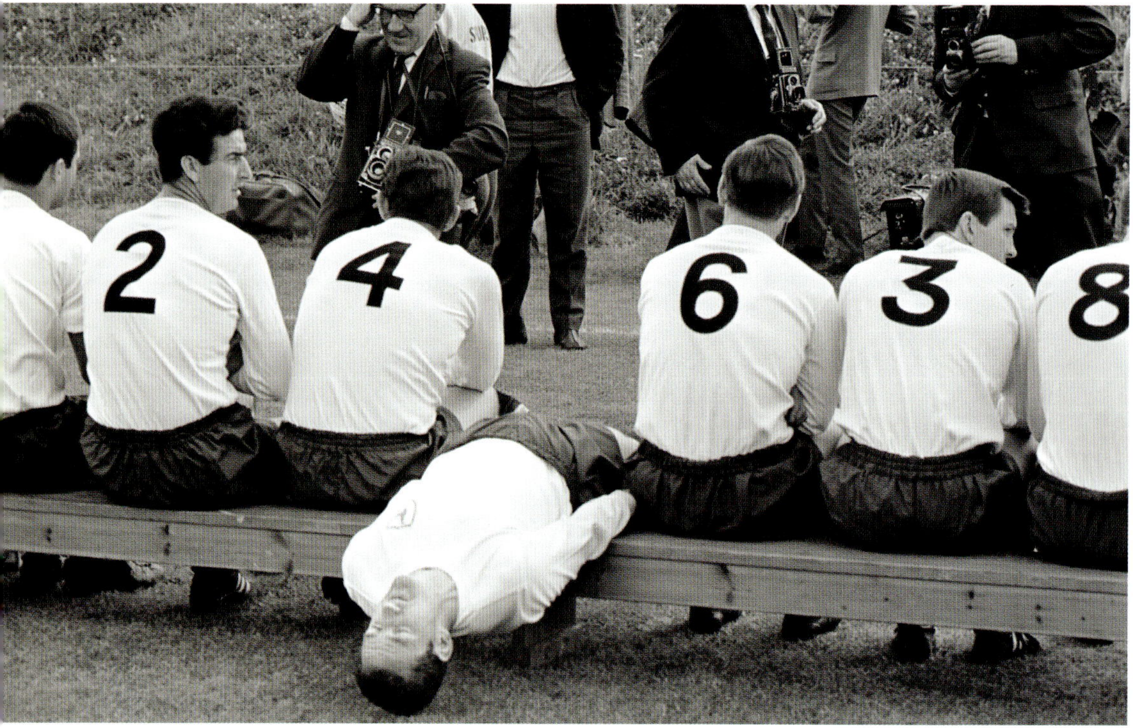

Posing or dozing? The Tottenham Hotspur team pose for press pictures before a training session. For left half Dave Mackay, the excitement proves too much. Mackay was a formidable force on the pitch. George Best of Manchester United, one of Tottenham's fiercest rivals in the 1960s, described the plucky Scot as "the hardest man I have ever played against – and certainly the bravest."

July, 1965

"I'm no hero. Doctors and nurses are heroes. Surgeons, people like that. We had a real hero born right here in Stoke-on-Trent: Reginald Mitchell, who designed the Spitfire. He saved Britain. Now that's what I call a hero."

Stanley Matthews.

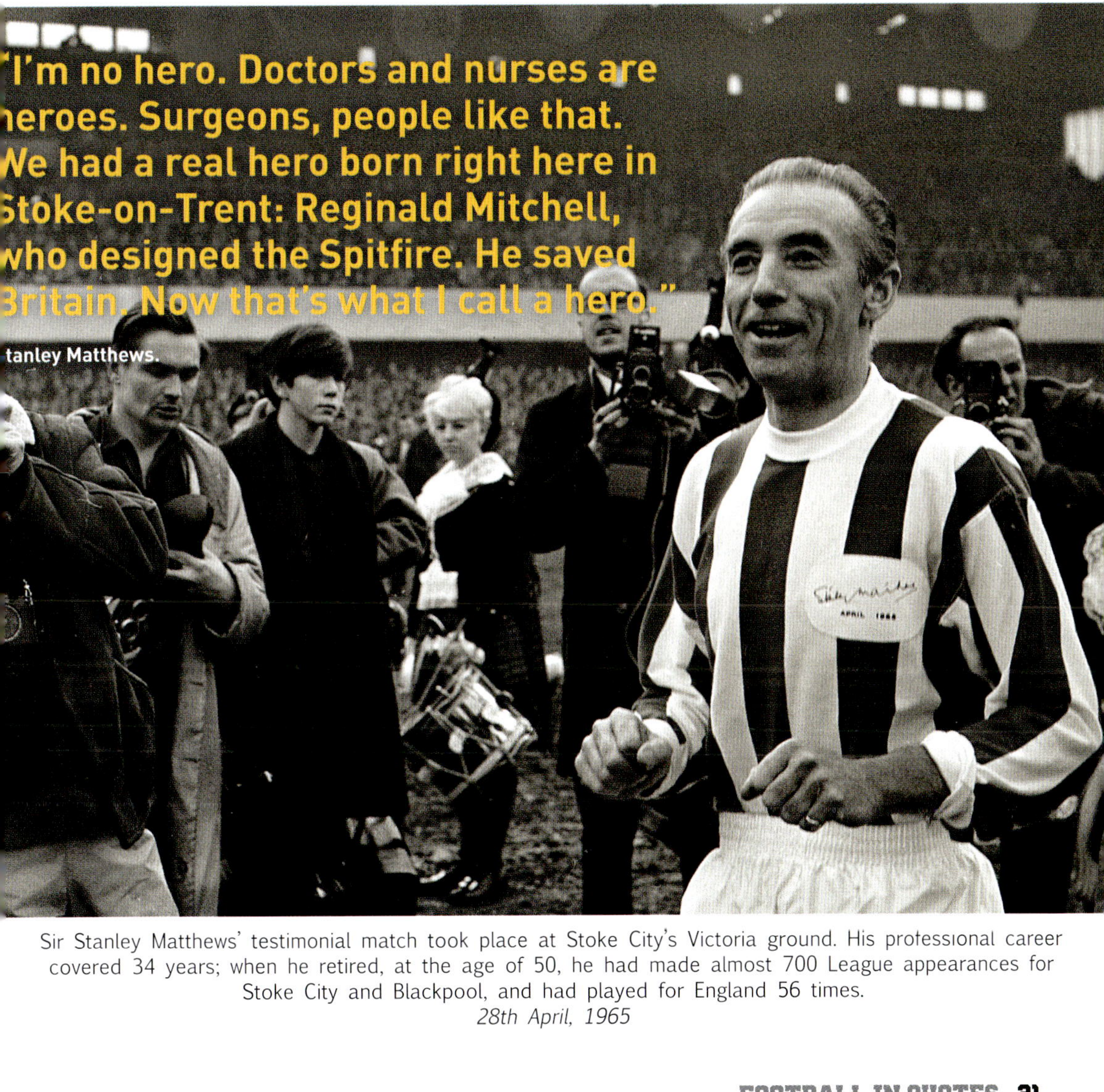

Sir Stanley Matthews' testimonial match took place at Stoke City's Victoria ground. His professional career covered 34 years; when he retired, at the age of 50, he had made almost 700 League appearances for Stoke City and Blackpool, and had played for England 56 times.

28th April, 1965

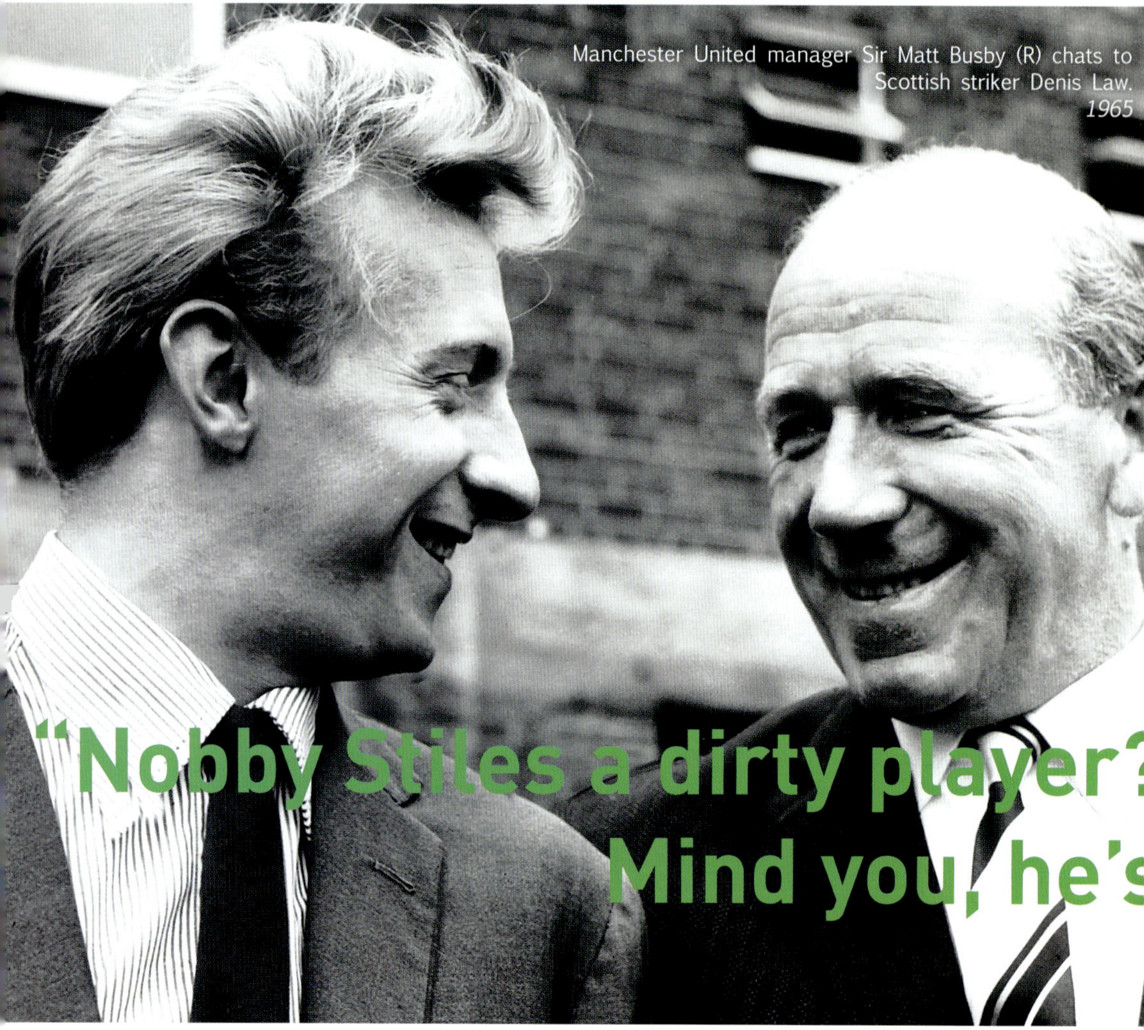

Manchester United manager Sir Matt Busby (R) chats to Scottish striker Denis Law.
1965

“Nobby Stiles a dirty player?
Mind you, he’s

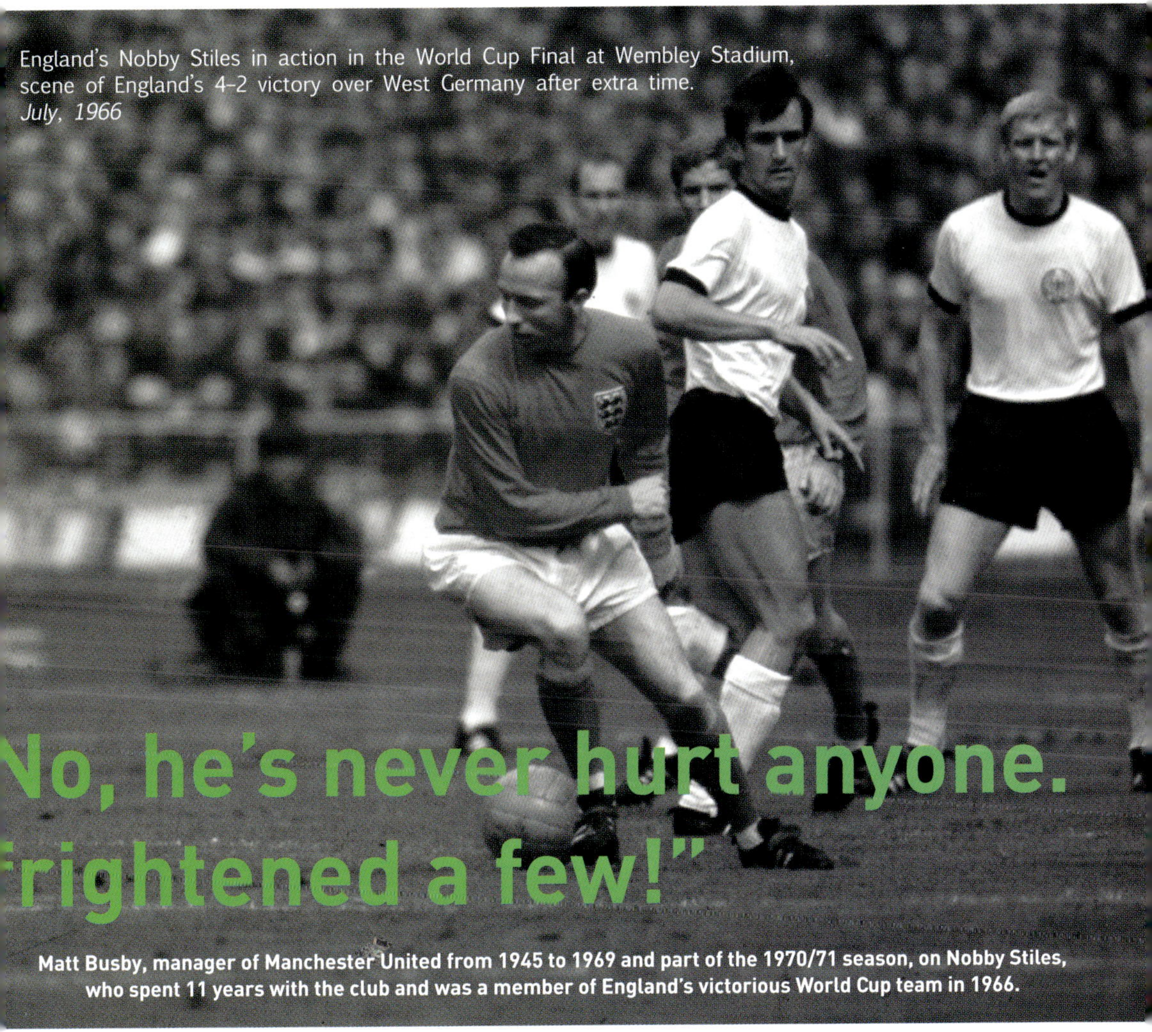

England's Nobby Stiles in action in the World Cup Final at Wembley Stadium, scene of England's 4–2 victory over West Germany after extra time.
July, 1966

"No, he's never hurt anyone. Frightened a few!"

Matt Busby, manager of Manchester United from 1945 to 1969 and part of the 1970/71 season, on Nobby Stiles, who spent 11 years with the club and was a member of England's victorious World Cup team in 1966.

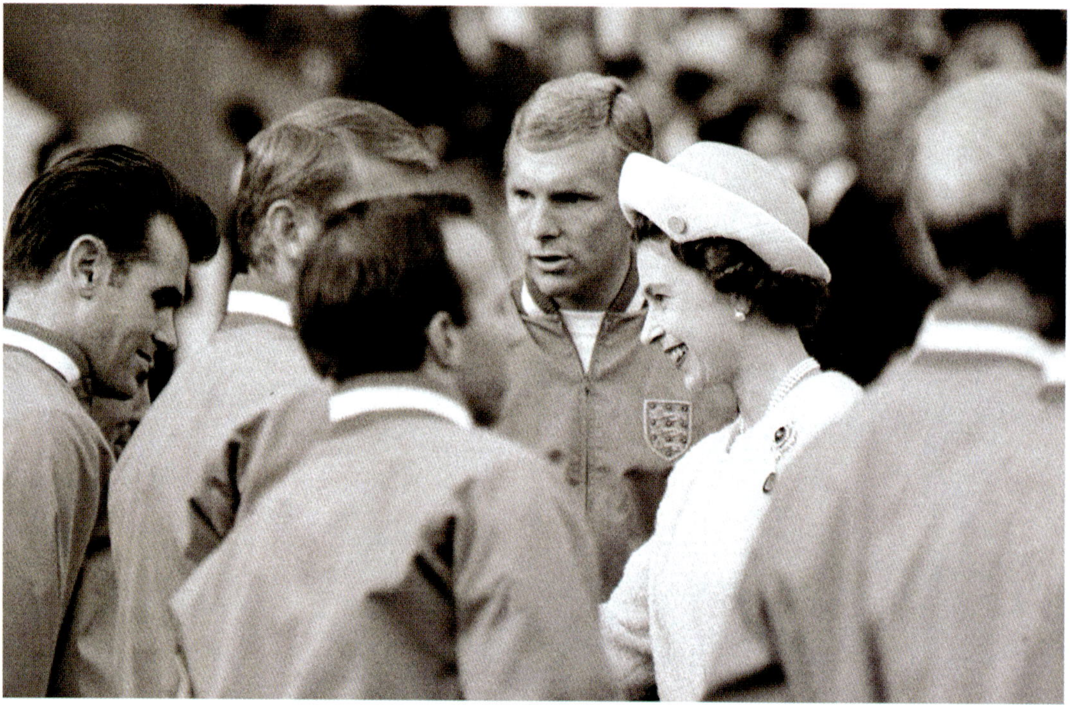

“Football’s a difficult business and aren’t they prima donnas?”

Queen Elizabeth II, giving her opinion to Premier League Chairman Sir David Richards, quoted in BBC News, 2nd January, 2007.

Captain Bobby Moore (C) presents the England team to Queen Elizabeth II prior to their opening qualifying match against Uruguay in the 1966 World Cup.
11th July, 1966

'WOOF!'

Pickles.

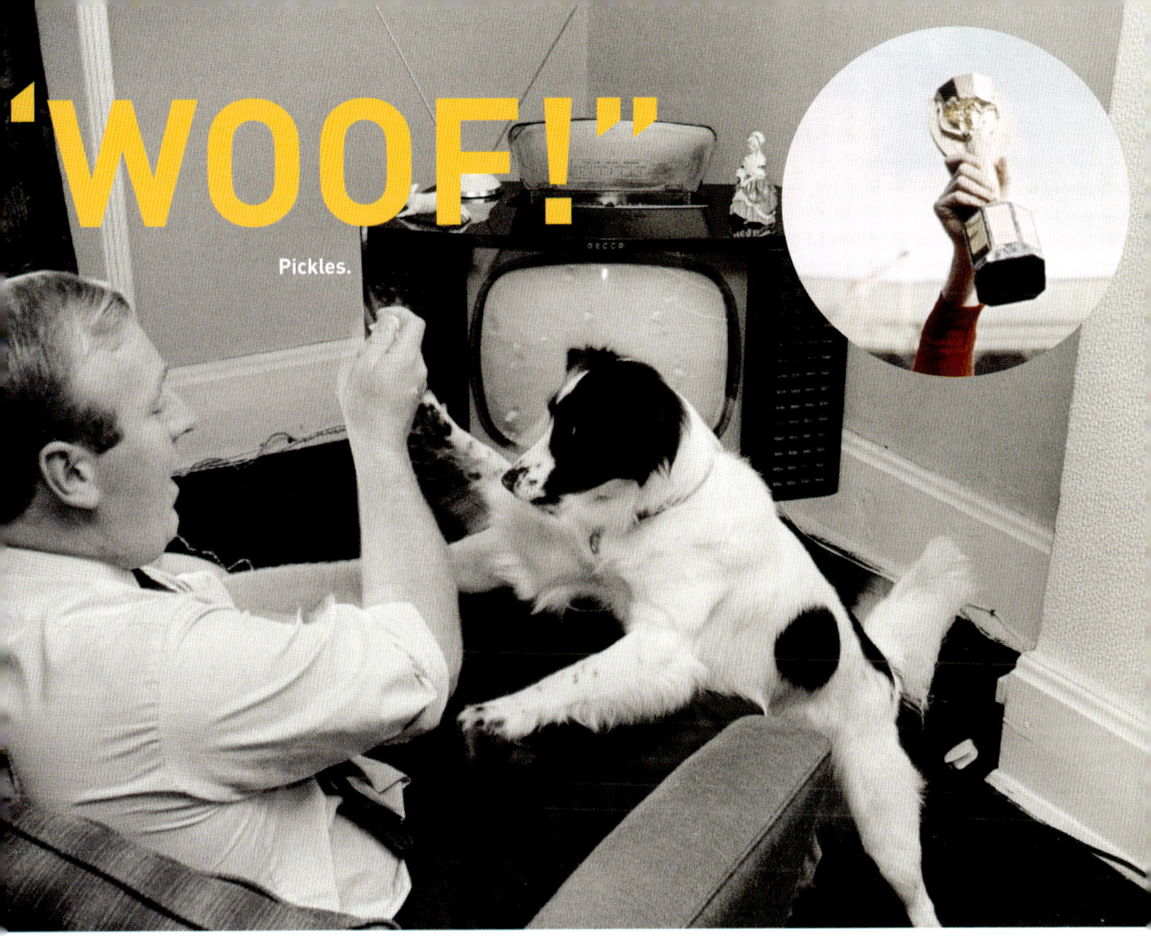

Pickles, the hero dog, who found the Jules Rimet Trophy (inset) after it had been stolen, at home with his owner, David Corbett, watching the World Cup Final on television. The trophy was found wrapped in newspaper beneath a suburban garden hedge in Beulah Hill, South London, by Pickles while taking a walk with his owner. The thief was never caught.

30th July, 1966

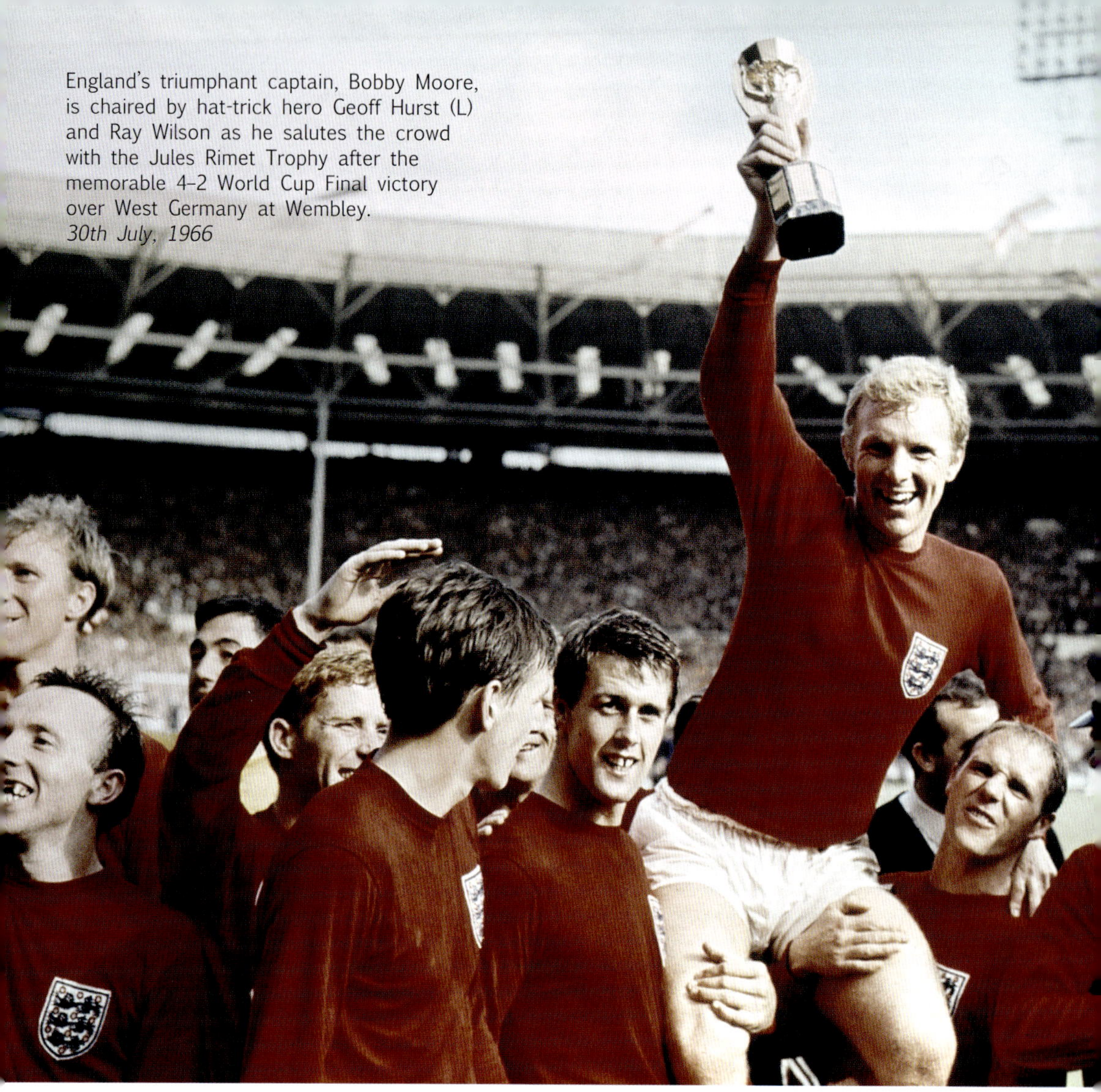

England's triumphant captain, Bobby Moore, is chaired by hat-trick hero Geoff Hurst (L) and Ray Wilson as he salutes the crowd with the Jules Rimet Trophy after the memorable 4–2 World Cup Final victory over West Germany at Wembley.
30th July, 1966

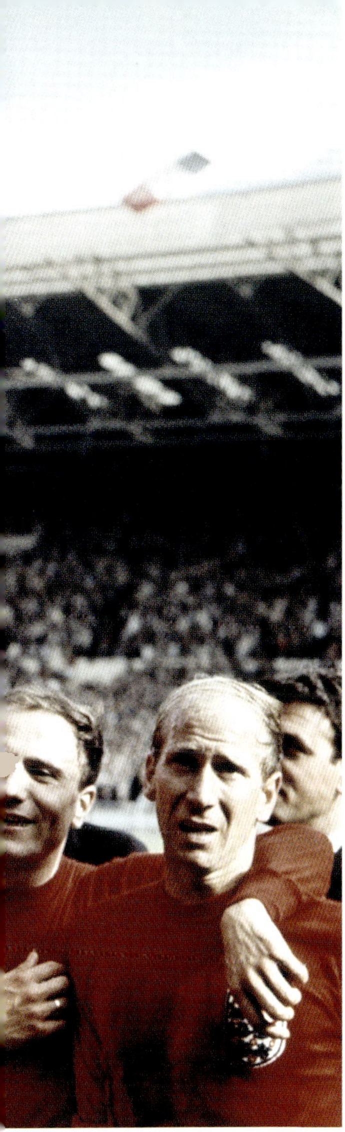

“If you never concede a goal, you’re going to win more games than you lose.”

Bobby Moore, English footballer, captain of the England team that won the World Cup in 1966, who made 106 appearances for the national team, captain of West Ham United for over 10 years, one of the greatest players ever.

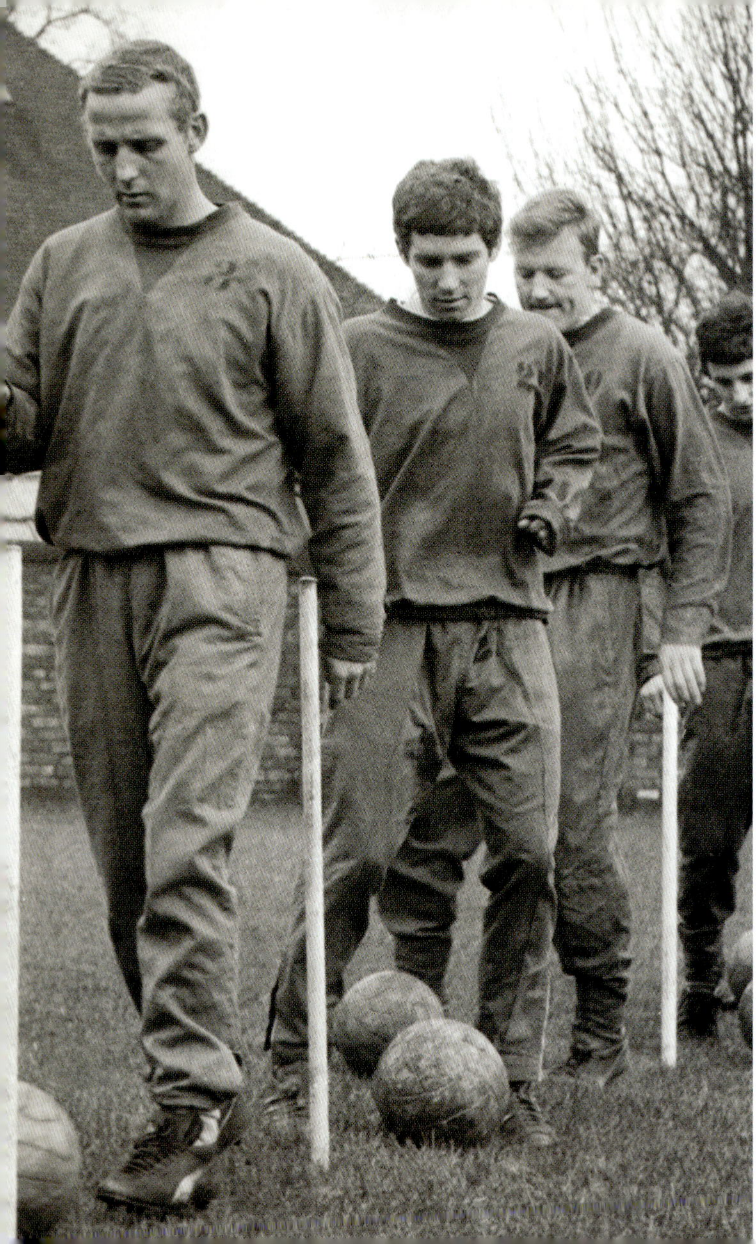

"In his early career he was a runner, a scrapper, a fighter, a workmanlike player. At the end of his career he became the best one-touch footballer in the game."

Lawrie McMenemy, football coach and manager, on his friend, the midfielder Alan Ball, the youngest member of the England side that won the World Cup in 1966, who went on to win 72 caps.

Everton footballers in dribbling practice at Bellefield ahead of their FA Cup fourth-round match against Wolves. L–R: Alex Young, Alan Ball, Jimmy Gabriel and Jimmy Husband.
14th February, 1967

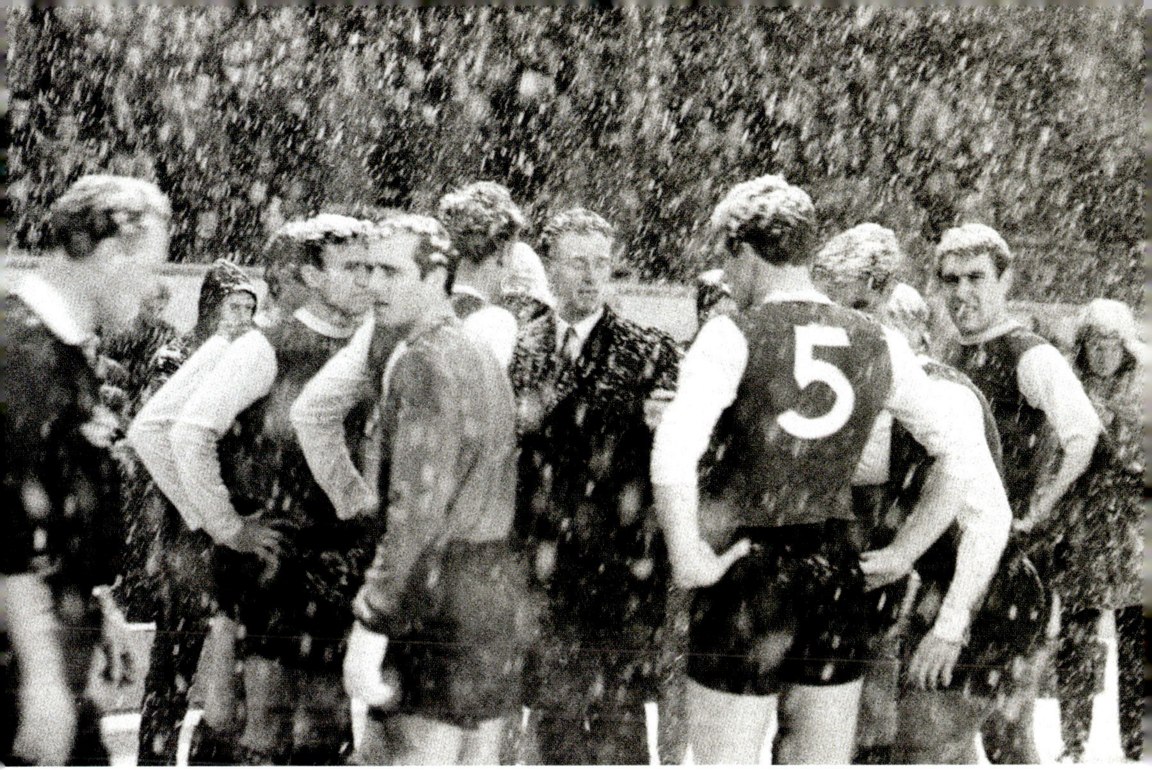

Snowballed. Sheffield Wednesday manager Alan Brown surrounded by his players as referee E.T. Jennings walks past to inspect the lines before abandoning the match against Arsenal,
9th December, 1967

"Soccer is the biggest thing that's happened in creation. It's bigger than any 'ism' you can name."

Alan Brown, footballer and manager, one of football's most inventive tactical minds, who was unfailingly passionate about the game, with a reputation for honesty among his peers.

"Those lucky enough to see him play will recall his boundless enthusiasm, 100% commitment and unrelenting passion for the club whenever he had the Liver Bird close to his chest."

Liverpool FC, on their website, praising Emlyn Hughes, former England and Liverpool captain, signed in 1967 by Bill Shankly. Larger-than-life Hughes, nicknamed 'Crazy Horse', earned 62 caps for the national team and led Liverpool to a string of honours while at the Anfield club.

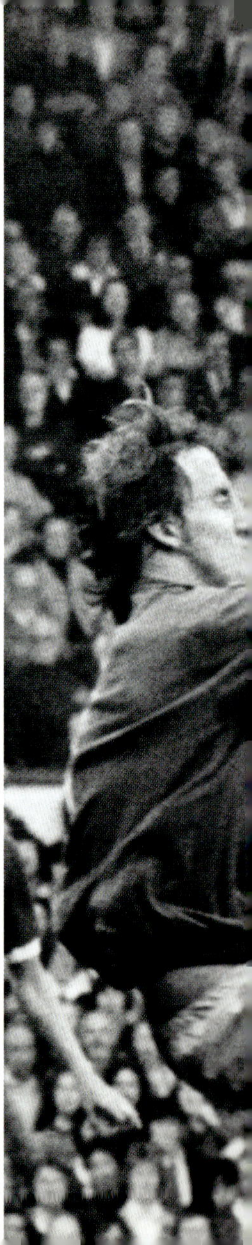

Feet first! Coventry City goalkeeper Jim Blyth throws in both arms as an airborne Emlyn Hughes thunderbolt blisters past. Liverpool beat Coventry 3–1 in the First Division match at Anfield.
4th September, 1976

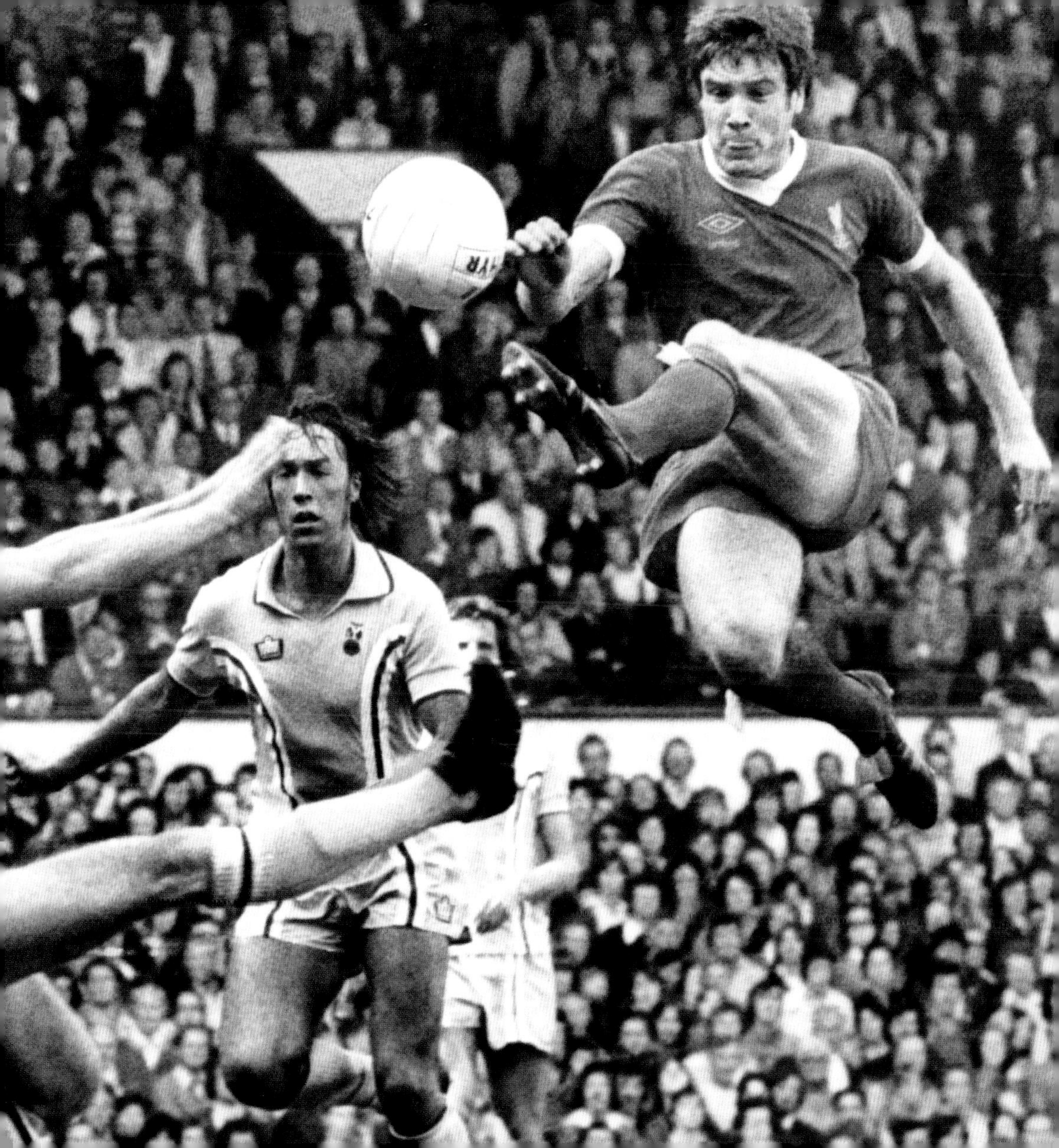

"On occasions I have been big headed. I think most people are when they get in the limelight. I call myself Big Head just to remind myself not to be."

Brian Clough, English footballer and manager, an outspoken and often controversial figure.

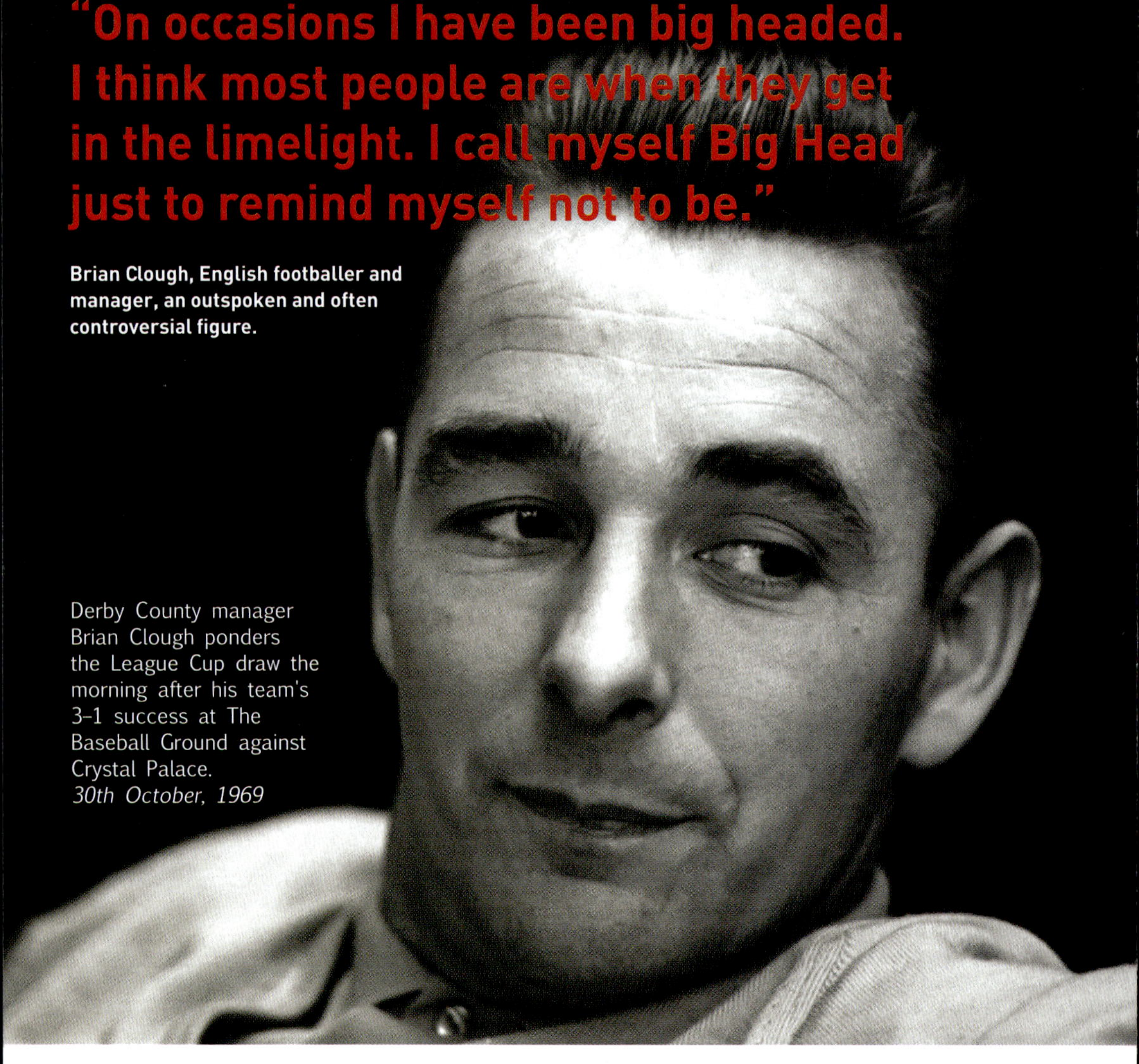

Derby County manager Brian Clough ponders the League Cup draw the morning after his team's 3–1 success at The Baseball Ground against Crystal Palace.
30th October, 1969

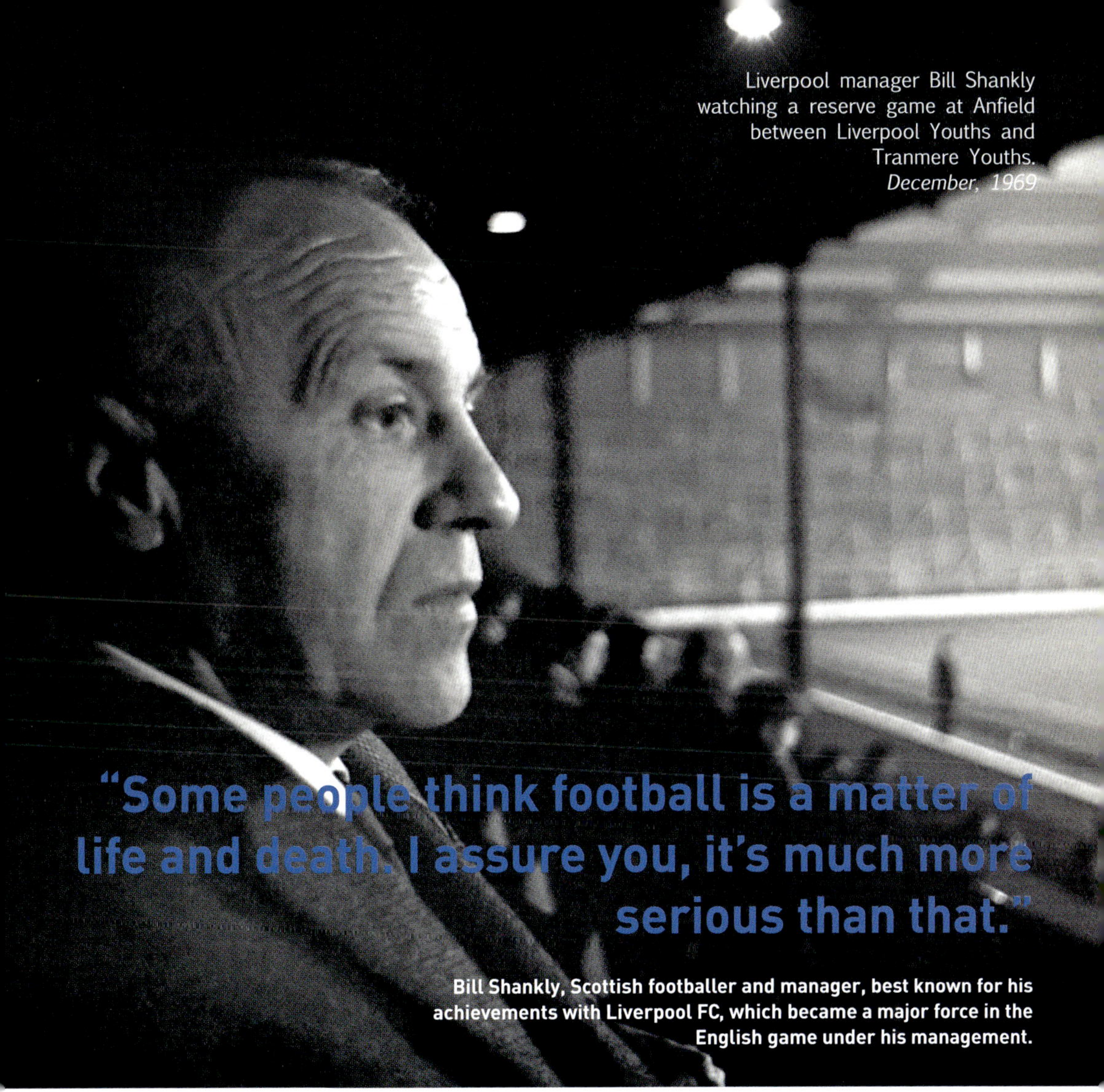

Liverpool manager Bill Shankly watching a reserve game at Anfield between Liverpool Youths and Tranmere Youths.
December, 1969

“Some people think football is a matter of life and death. I assure you, it’s much more serious than that.”

Bill Shankly, Scottish footballer and manager, best known for his achievements with Liverpool FC, which became a major force in the English game under his management.

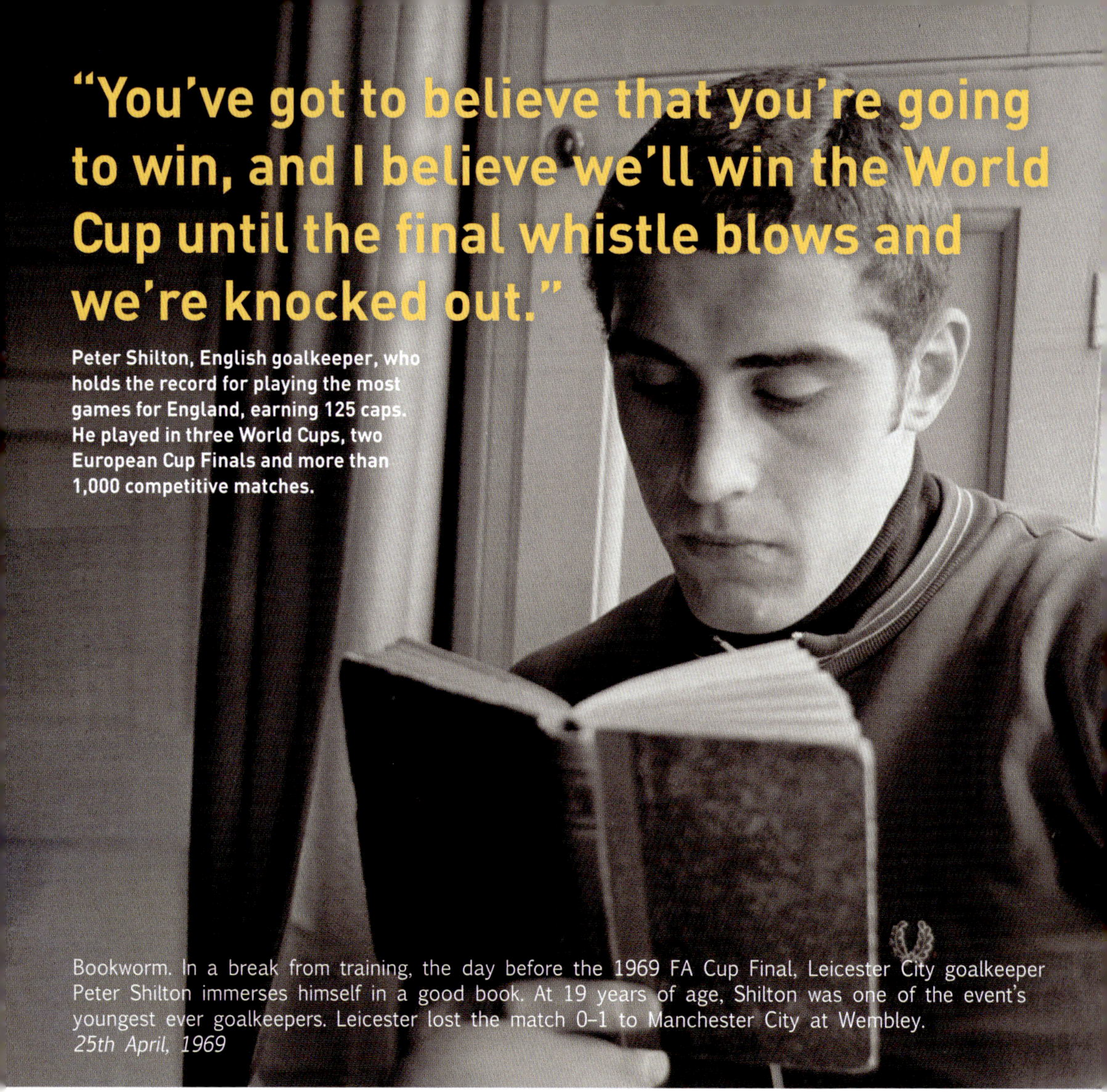

"You've got to believe that you're going to win, and I believe we'll win the World Cup until the final whistle blows and we're knocked out."

Peter Shilton, English goalkeeper, who holds the record for playing the most games for England, earning 125 caps. He played in three World Cups, two European Cup Finals and more than 1,000 competitive matches.

Bookworm. In a break from training, the day before the 1969 FA Cup Final, Leicester City goalkeeper Peter Shilton immerses himself in a good book. At 19 years of age, Shilton was one of the event's youngest ever goalkeepers. Leicester lost the match 0–1 to Manchester City at Wembley.
25th April, 1969

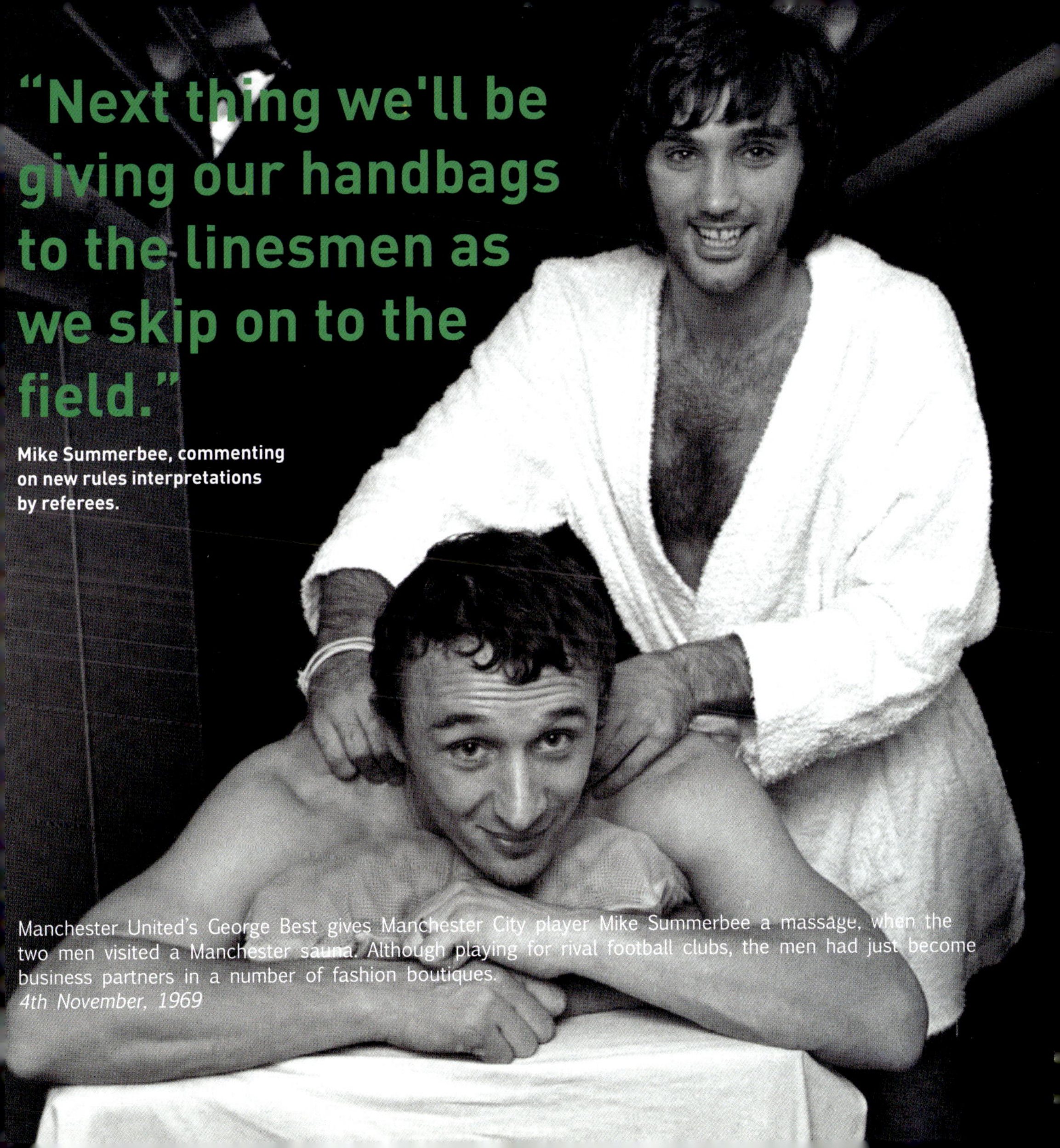

"Next thing we'll be giving our handbags to the linesmen as we skip on to the field."

Mike Summerbee, commenting on new rules interpretations by referees.

Manchester United's George Best gives Manchester City player Mike Summerbee a massage, when the two men visited a Manchester sauna. Although playing for rival football clubs, the men had just become business partners in a number of fashion boutiques.
4th November, 1969

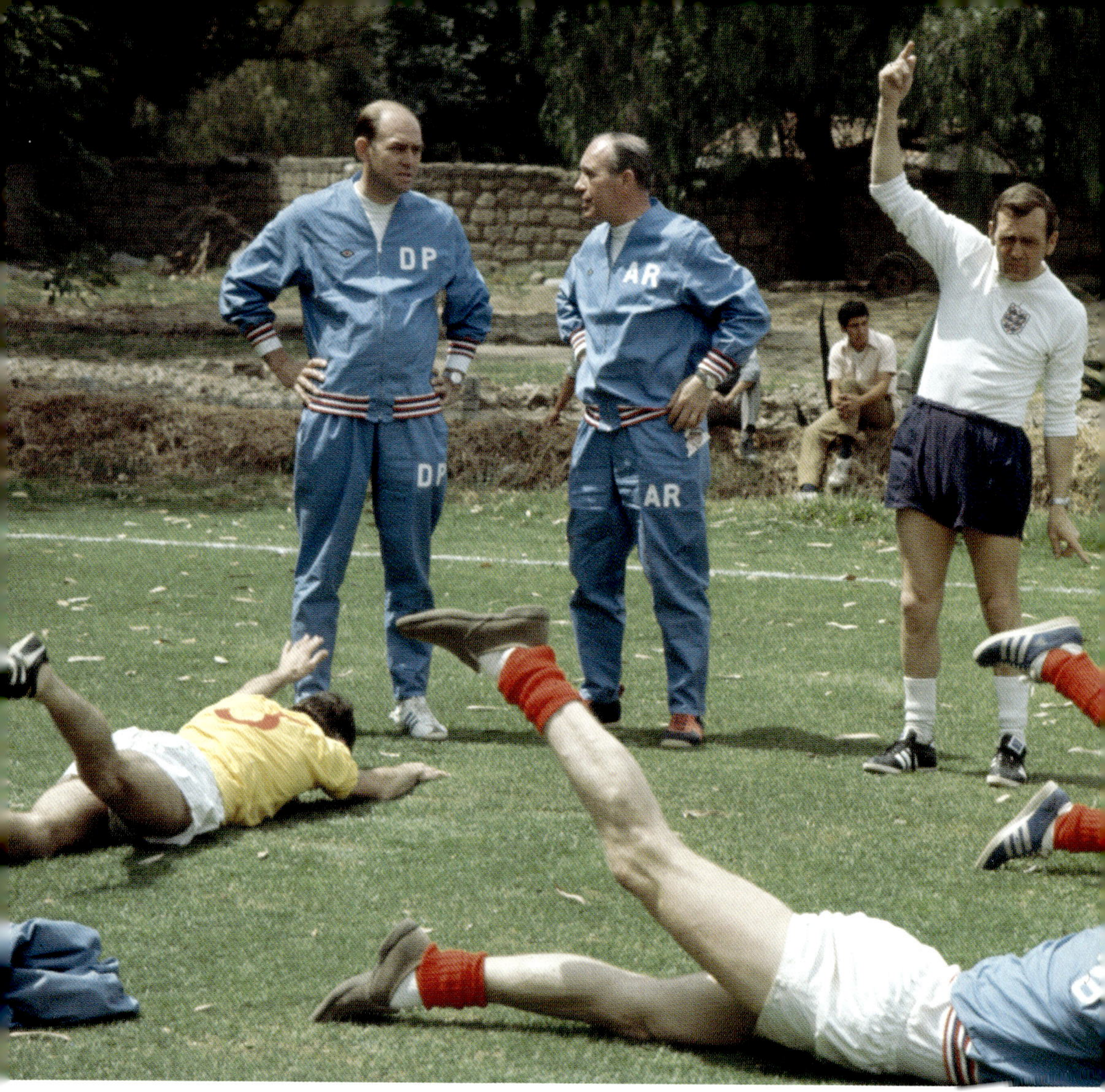
DP
AR
DP
AR

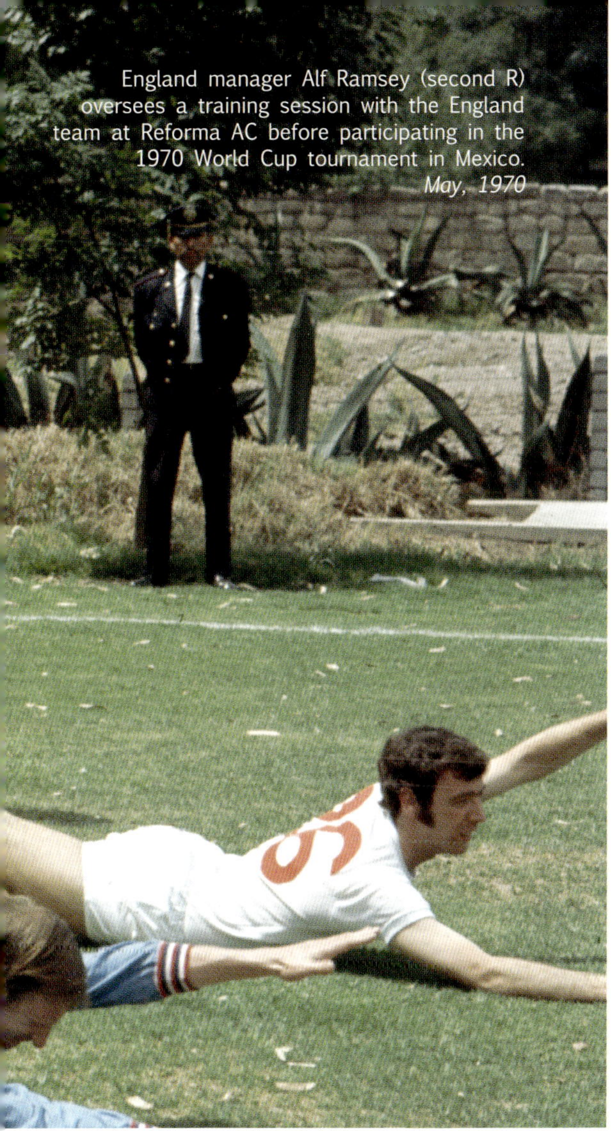

England manager Alf Ramsey (second R) oversees a training session with the England team at Reforma AC before participating in the 1970 World Cup tournament in Mexico. *May, 1970*

"...discipline was everything to him. He was not afraid of criticising you in front of the rest of the team. If he was giving a talk and somebody had given away a goal he would totally embarrass them in front of the rest of the team, so you knew what was there if you didn't do what he wanted."

Bobby Charlton, on Alf Ramsey.

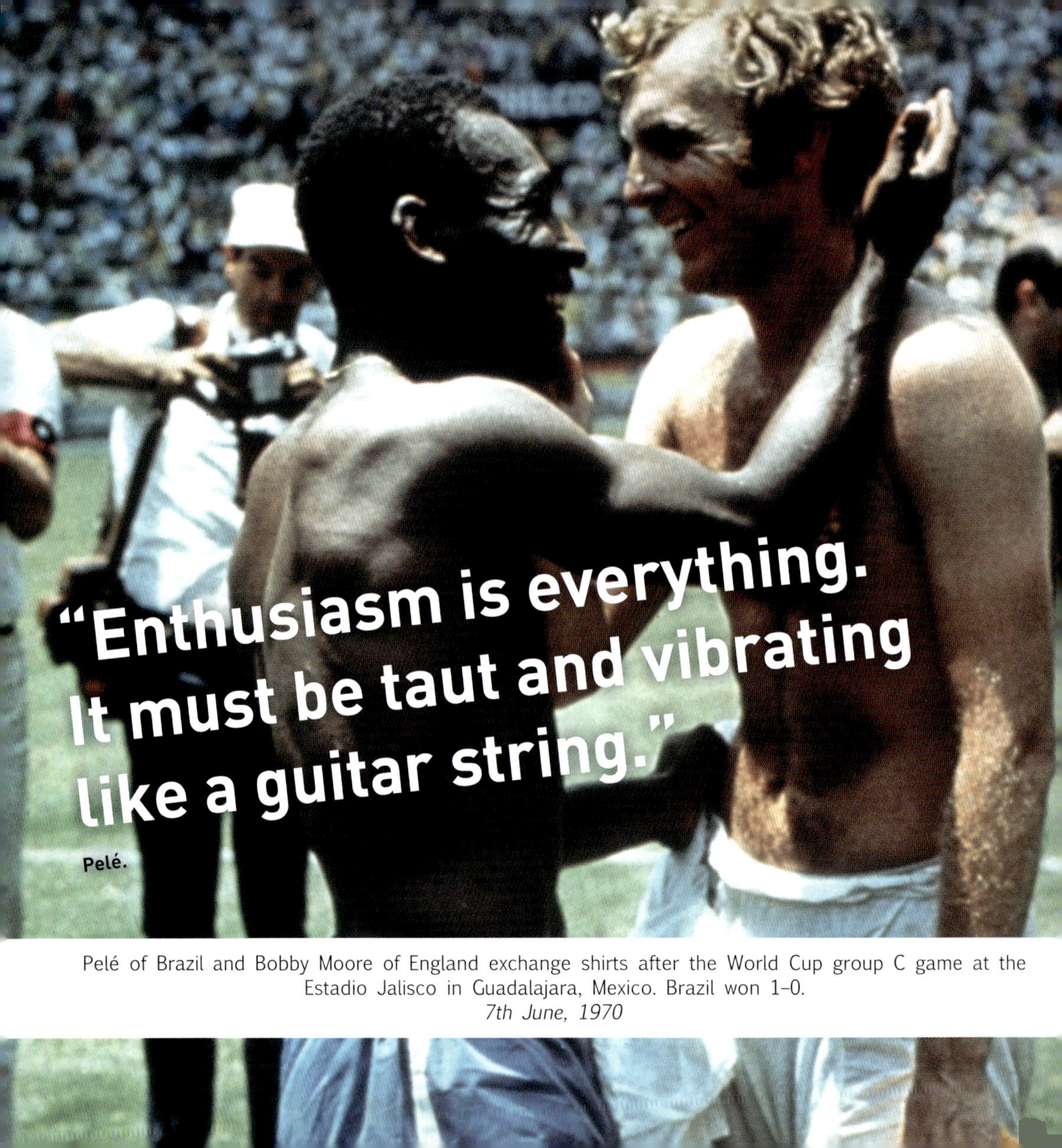

"Enthusiasm is everything. It must be taut and vibrating like a guitar string."

Pelé.

Pelé of Brazil and Bobby Moore of England exchange shirts after the World Cup group C game at the Estadio Jalisco in Guadalajara, Mexico. Brazil won 1–0.
7th June, 1970

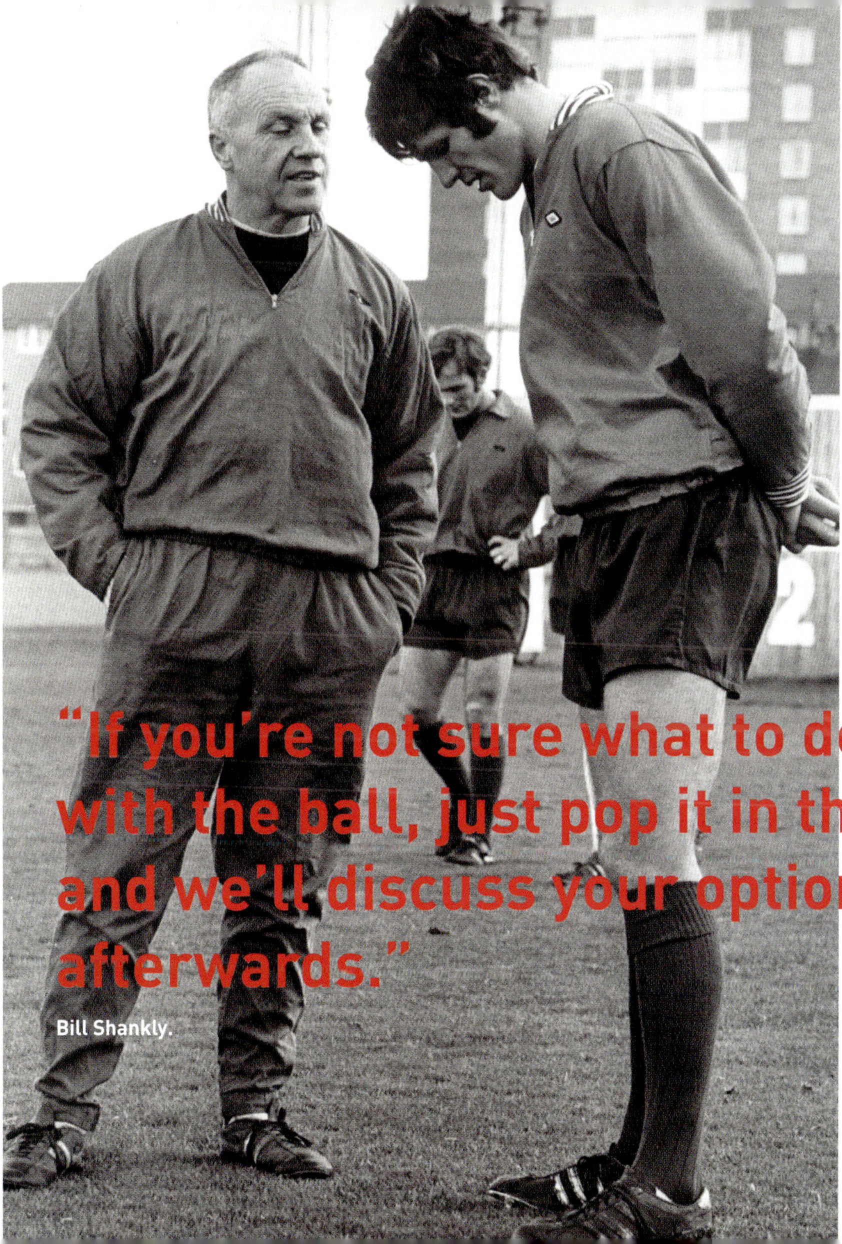

Liverpool manager Bill Shankly discusses tactics with striker John Toshack.
1970

“If you’re not sure what to do with the ball, just pop it in the net and we’ll discuss your options afterwards.”

Bill Shankly.

"I was born with a great gift, and sometimes with that comes a destructive streak. Just as I wanted to outdo everyone when I played, I had to outdo everyone when we were out on the town."

George Best, after being sent to prison for drink-driving.

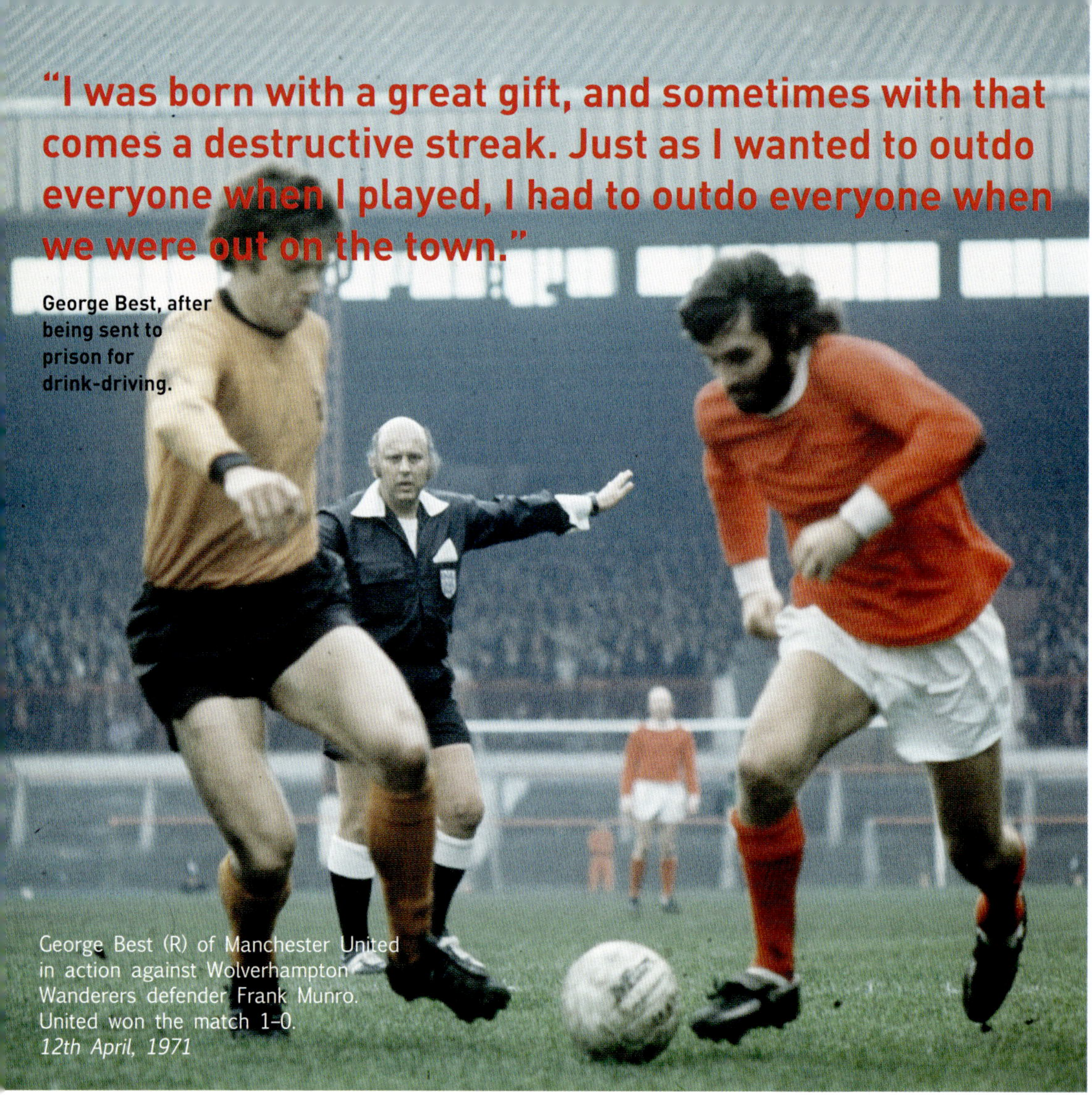

George Best (R) of Manchester United in action against Wolverhampton Wanderers defender Frank Munro. United won the match 1–0.
12th April, 1971

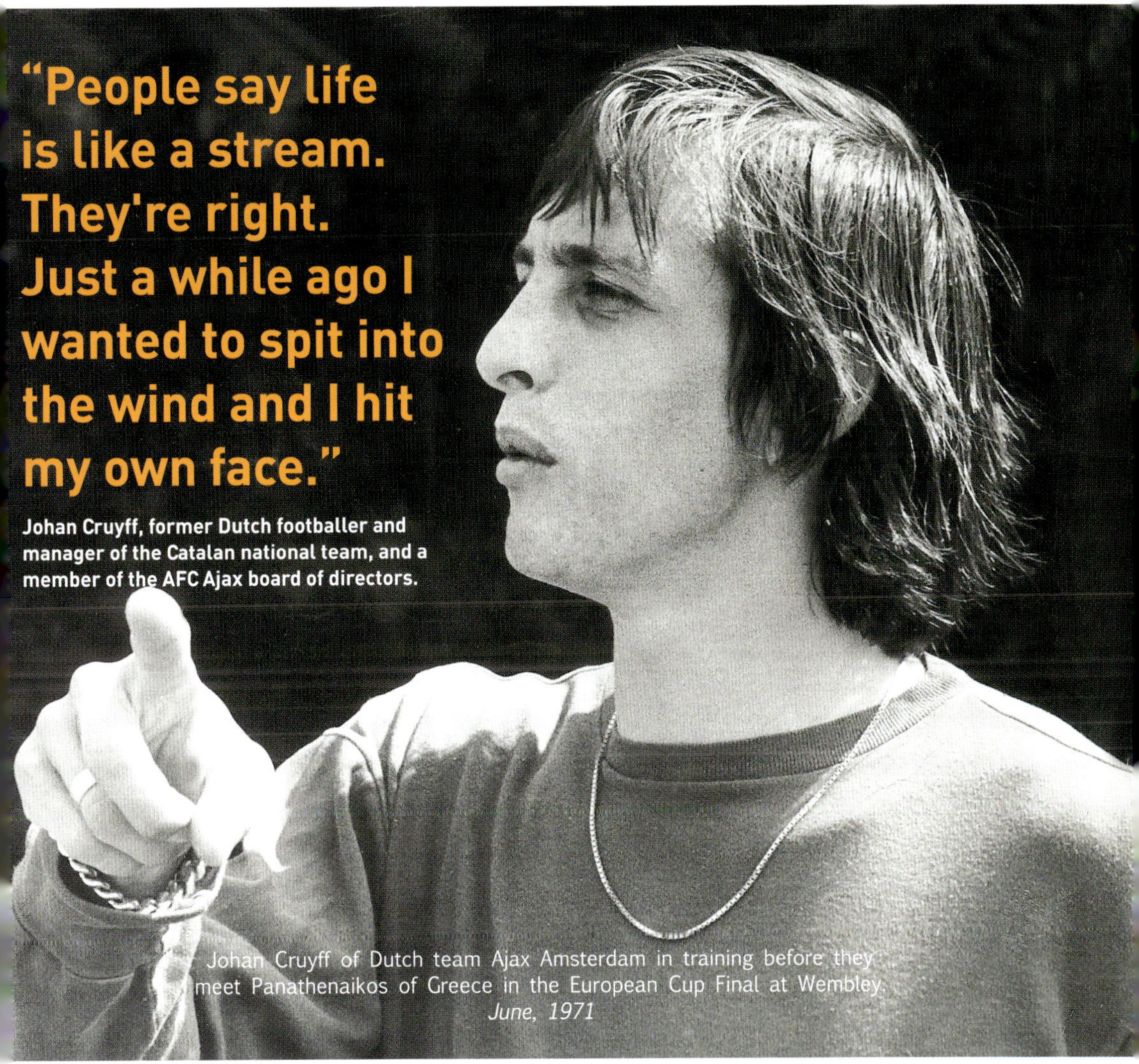

"People say life is like a stream. They're right. Just a while ago I wanted to spit into the wind and I hit my own face."

Johan Cruyff, former Dutch footballer and manager of the Catalan national team, and a member of the AFC Ajax board of directors.

Johan Cruyff of Dutch team Ajax Amsterdam in training before they meet Panathenaikos of Greece in the European Cup Final at Wembley.
June, 1971

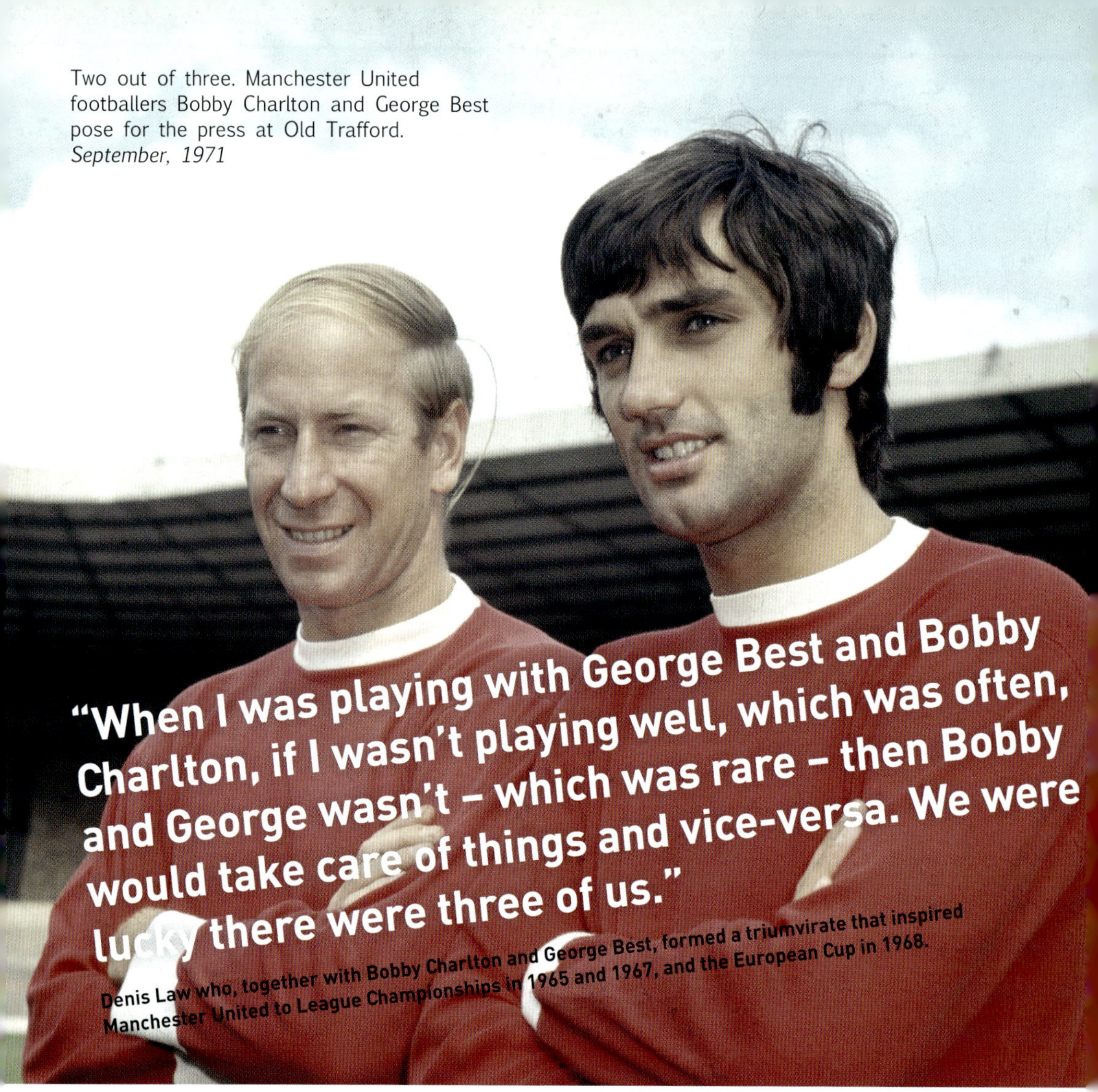

Two out of three. Manchester United footballers Bobby Charlton and George Best pose for the press at Old Trafford. *September, 1971*

"When I was playing with George Best and Bobby Charlton, if I wasn't playing well, which was often, and George wasn't – which was rare – then Bobby would take care of things and vice-versa. We were lucky there were three of us."

Denis Law who, together with Bobby Charlton and George Best, formed a triumvirate that inspired Manchester United to League Championships in 1965 and 1967, and the European Cup in 1968.

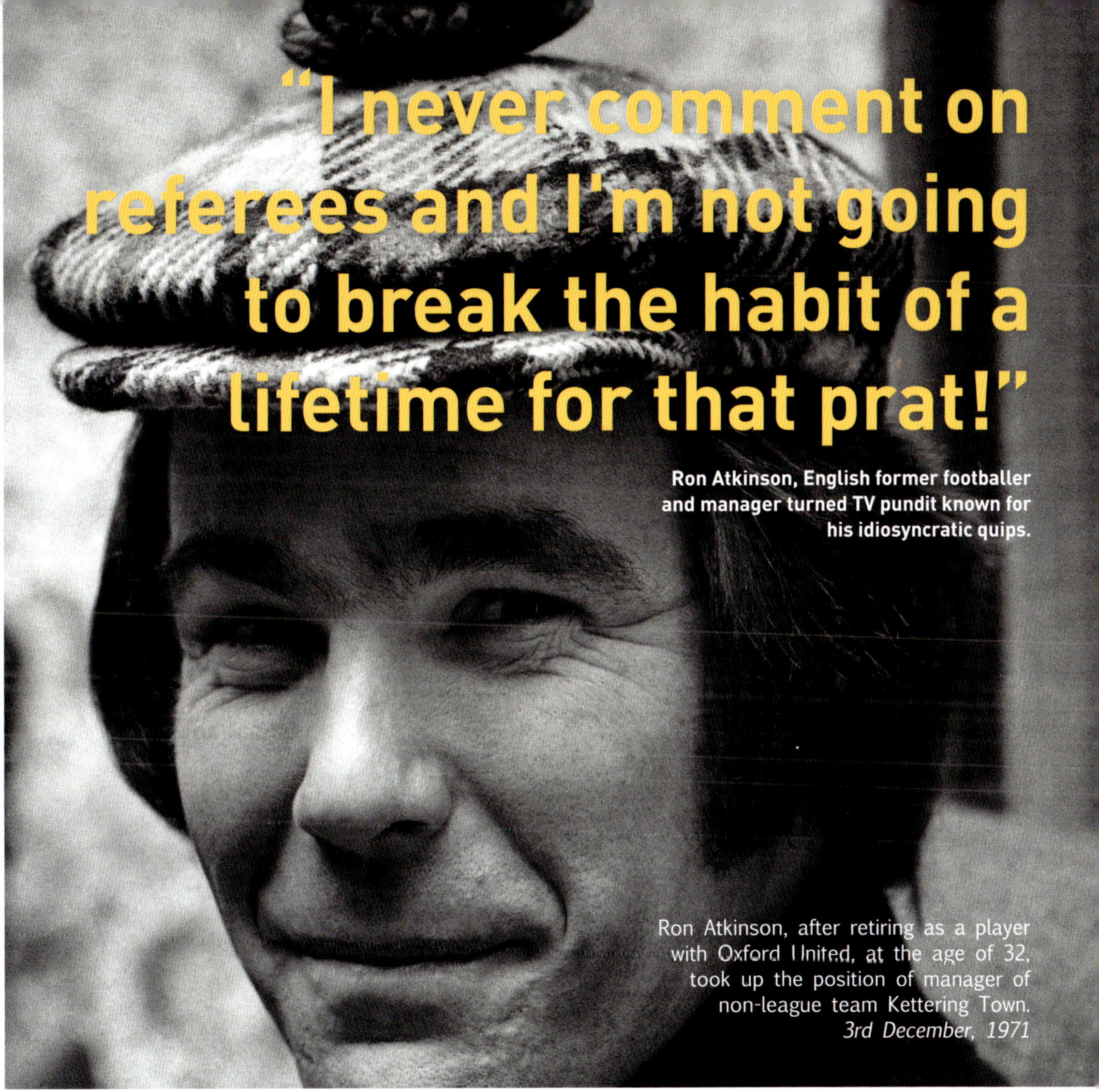

"I never comment on referees and I'm not going to break the habit of a lifetime for that prat!"

Ron Atkinson, English former footballer and manager turned TV pundit known for his idiosyncratic quips.

Ron Atkinson, after retiring as a player with Oxford United, at the age of 32, took up the position of manager of non-league team Kettering Town.
3rd December, 1971

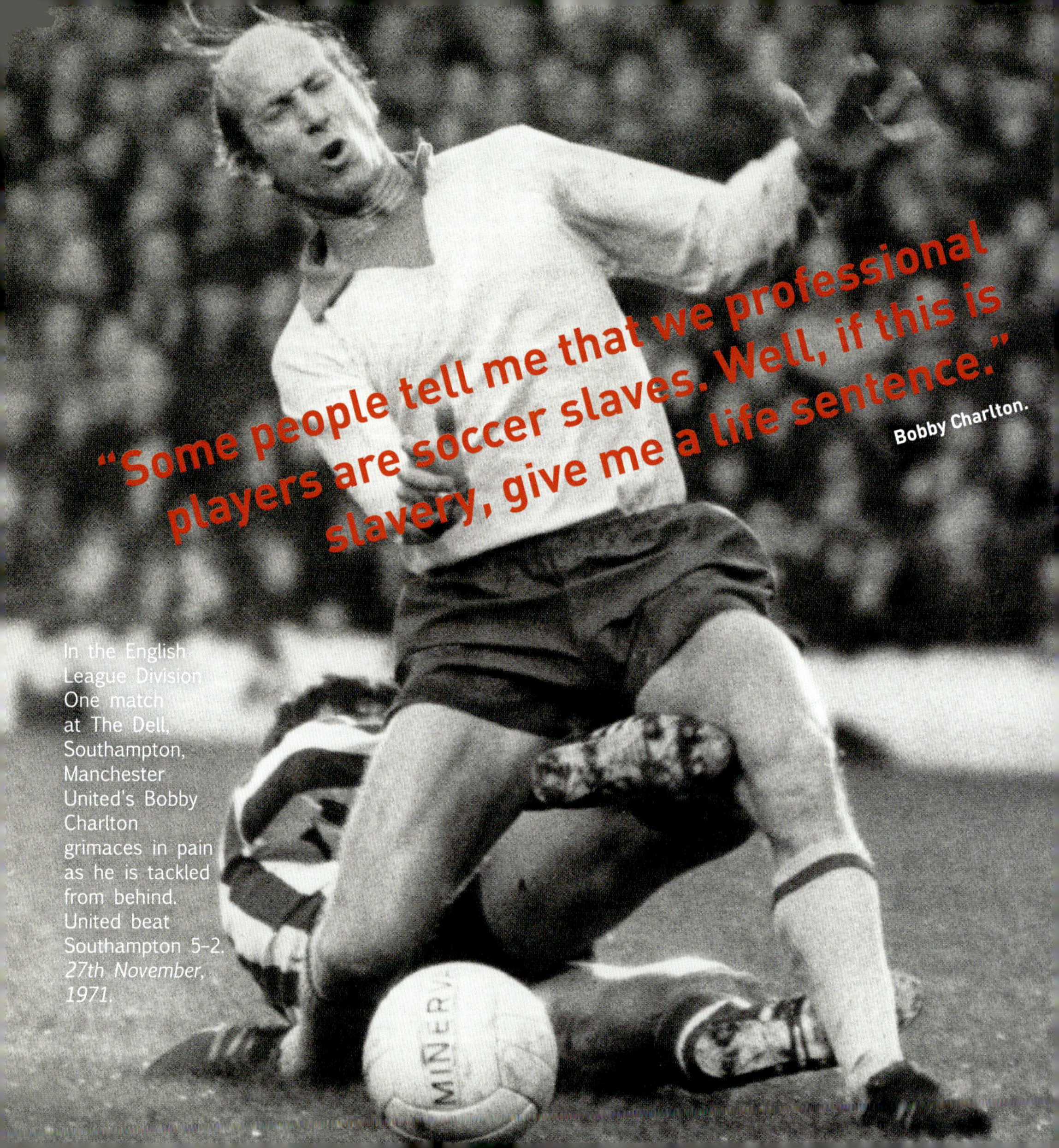

"Some people tell me that we professional players are soccer slaves. Well, if this is slavery, give me a life sentence."

Bobby Charlton.

In the English League Division One match at The Dell, Southampton, Manchester United's Bobby Charlton grimaces in pain as he is tackled from behind. United beat Southampton 5-2. *27th November, 1971.*

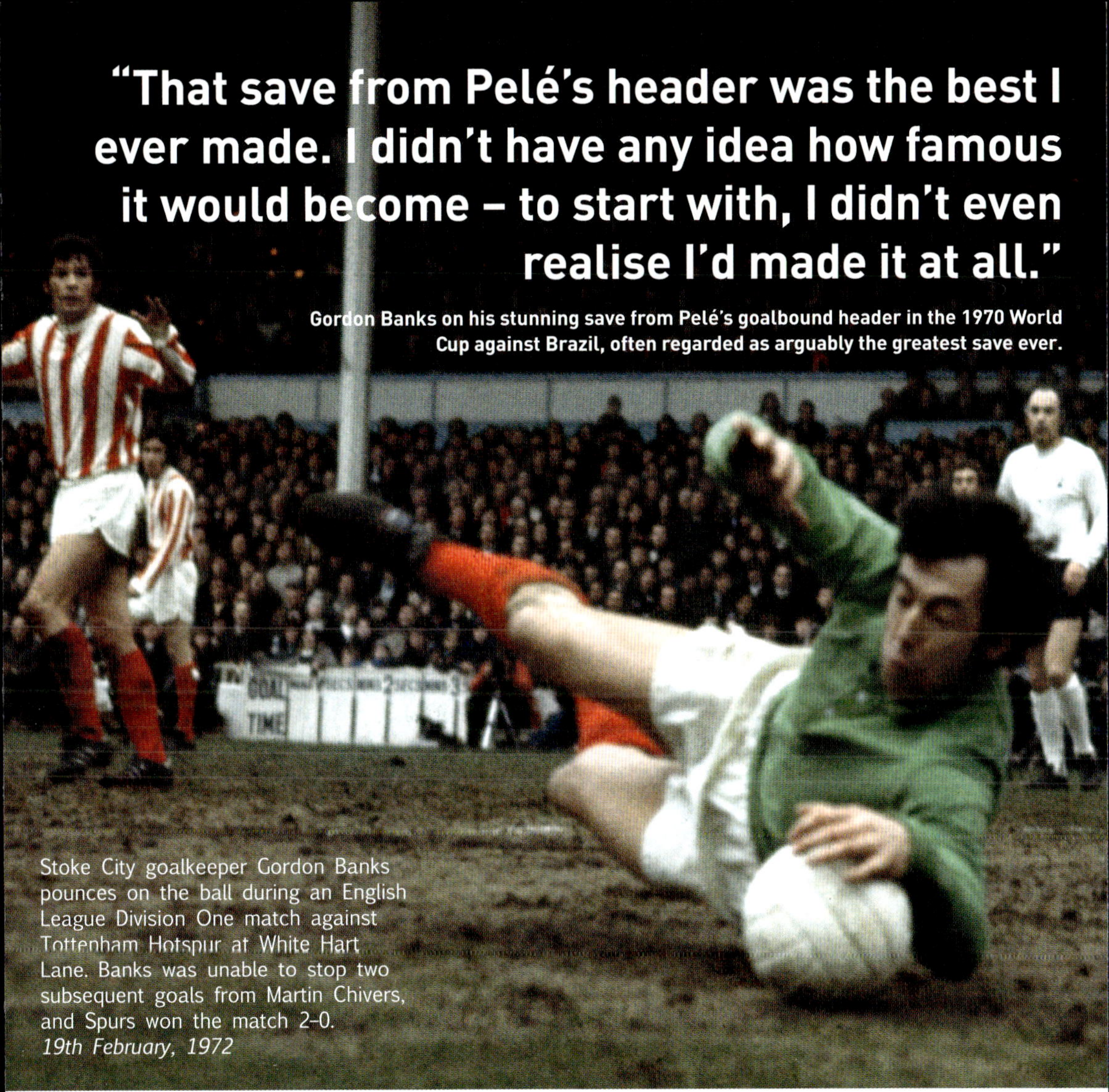

"That save from Pelé's header was the best I ever made. I didn't have any idea how famous it would become – to start with, I didn't even realise I'd made it at all."

Gordon Banks on his stunning save from Pelé's goalbound header in the 1970 World Cup against Brazil, often regarded as arguably the greatest save ever.

Stoke City goalkeeper Gordon Banks pounces on the ball during an English League Division One match against Tottenham Hotspur at White Hart Lane. Banks was unable to stop two subsequent goals from Martin Chivers, and Spurs won the match 2-0.
19th February, 1972

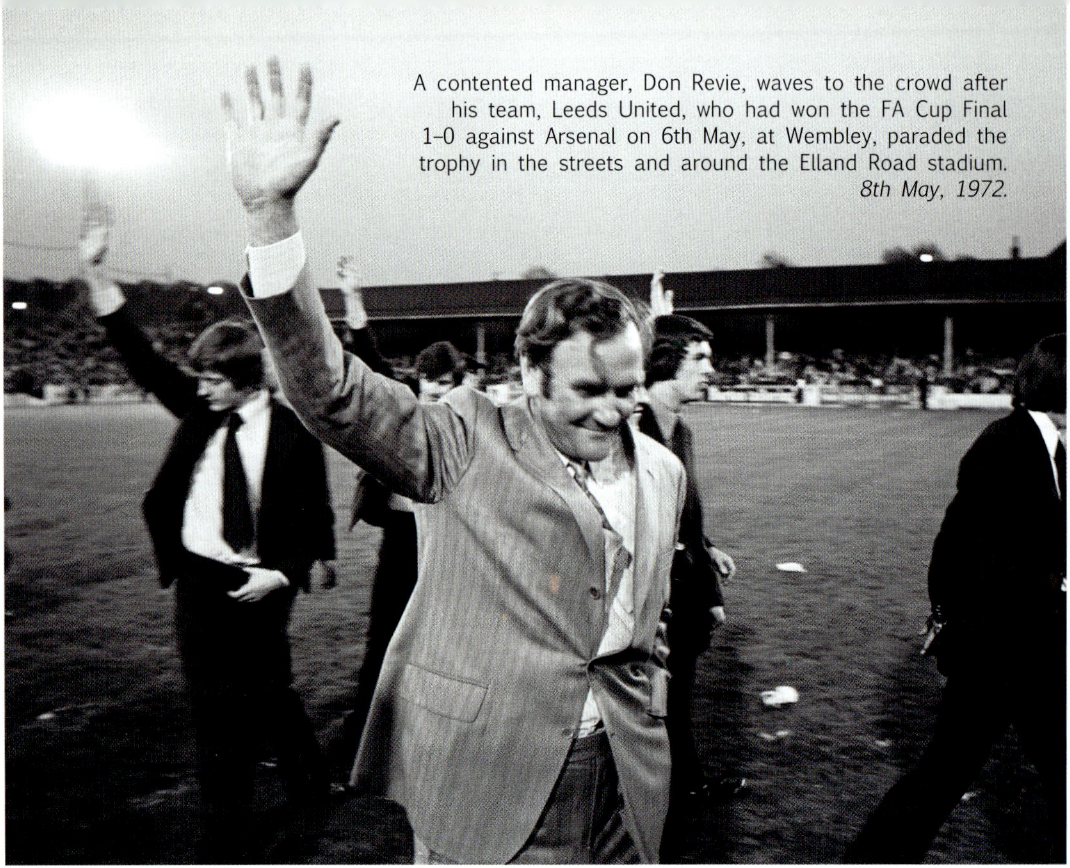

A contented manager, Don Revie, waves to the crowd after his team, Leeds United, who had won the FA Cup Final 1–0 against Arsenal on 6th May, at Wembley, paraded the trophy in the streets and around the Elland Road stadium. *8th May, 1972.*

"You get nowt for being second."

Don Revie, the English footballer who played for Leicester City, Hull City, Sunderland, Manchester City and Leeds United, as a deep-lying centre forward, and later managed Leeds United (1961–74) and England from 1974 until 1977.

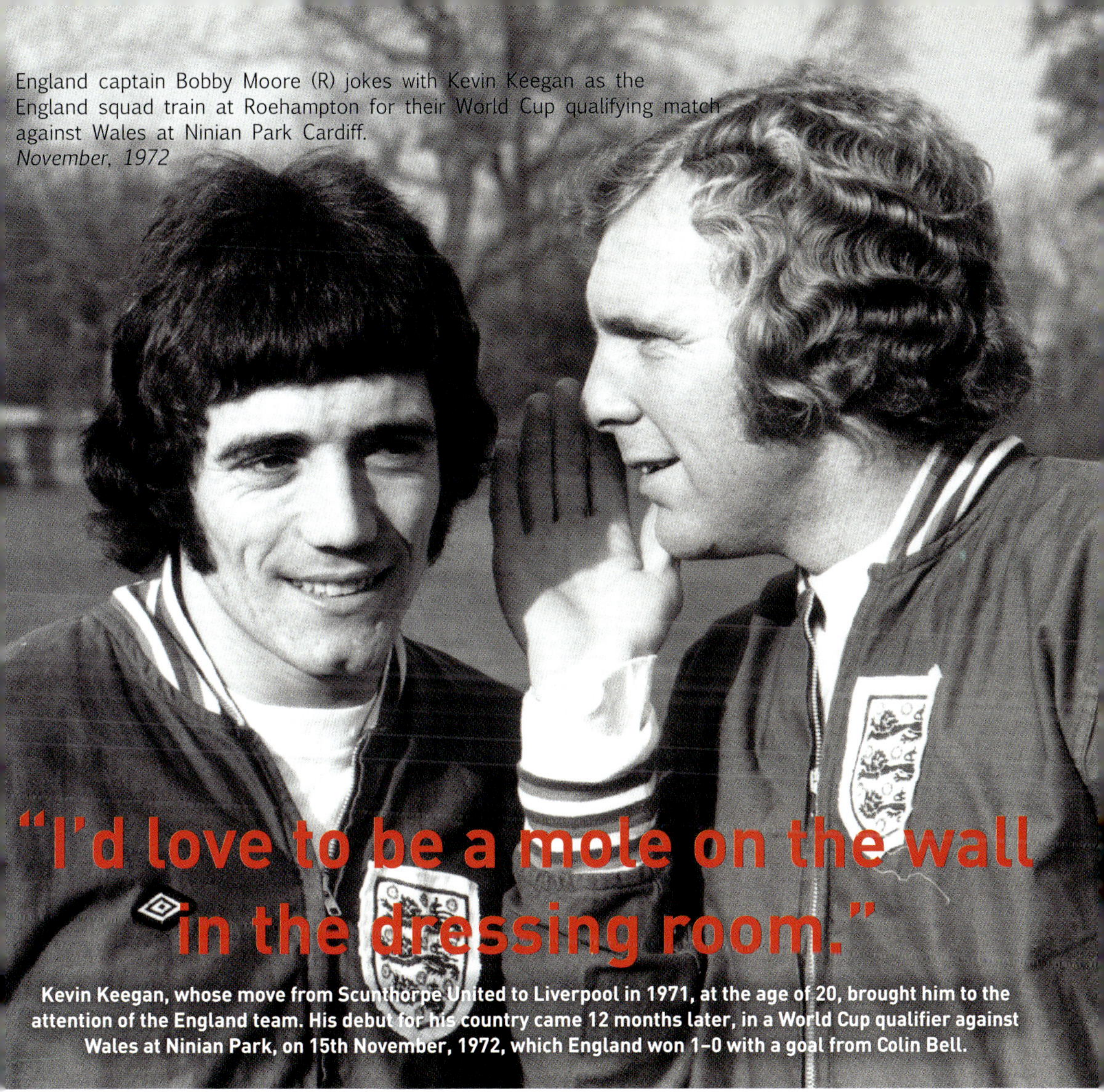

England captain Bobby Moore (R) jokes with Kevin Keegan as the England squad train at Roehampton for their World Cup qualifying match against Wales at Ninian Park Cardiff.
November, 1972

"I'd love to be a mole on the wall in the dressing room."

Kevin Keegan, whose move from Scunthorpe United to Liverpool in 1971, at the age of 20, brought him to the attention of the England team. His debut for his country came 12 months later, in a World Cup qualifier against Wales at Ninian Park, on 15th November, 1972, which England won 1–0 with a goal from Colin Bell.

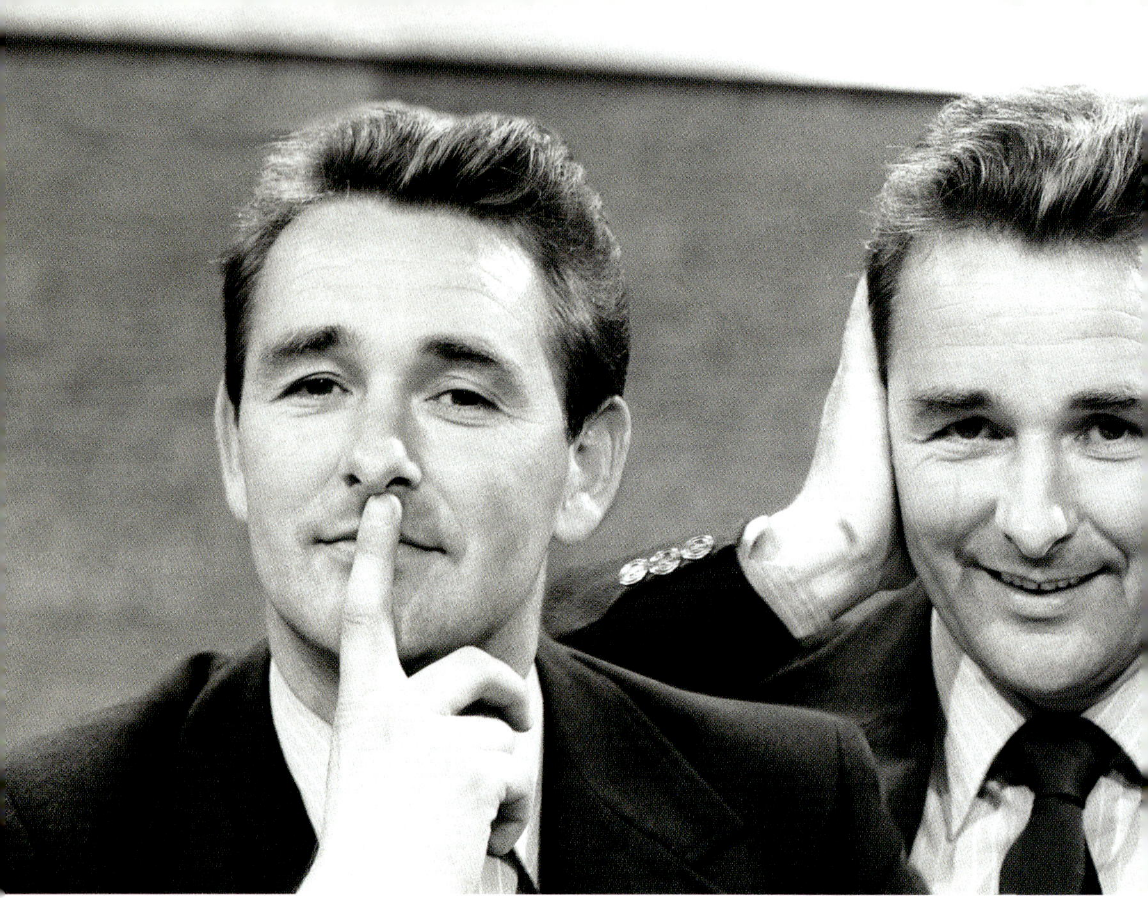

“Players lose you games, not tactics
tactics by people who barel

Brian Clough.

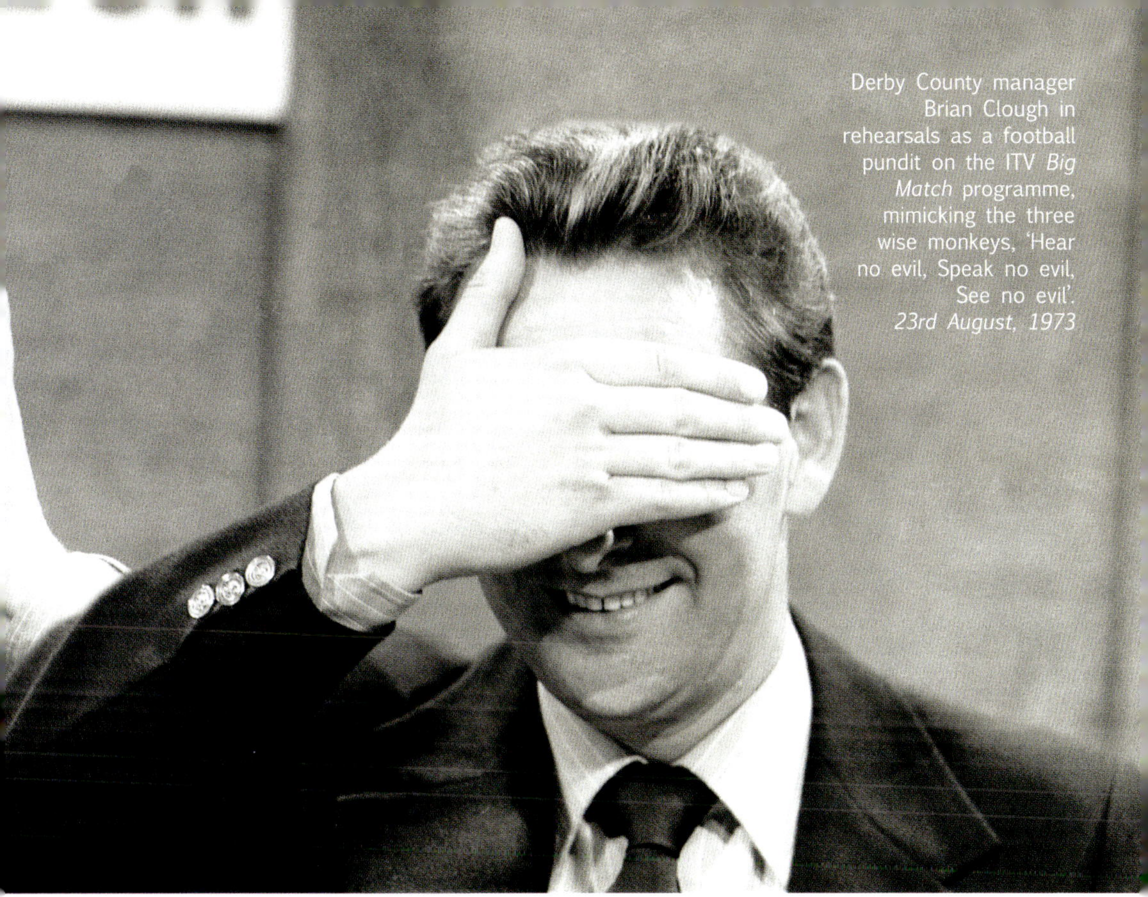

Derby County manager Brian Clough in rehearsals as a football pundit on the ITV *Big Match* programme, mimicking the three wise monkeys, 'Hear no evil, Speak no evil, See no evil'. *23rd August, 1973*

here's so much crap talked about
now how to win at dominoes."

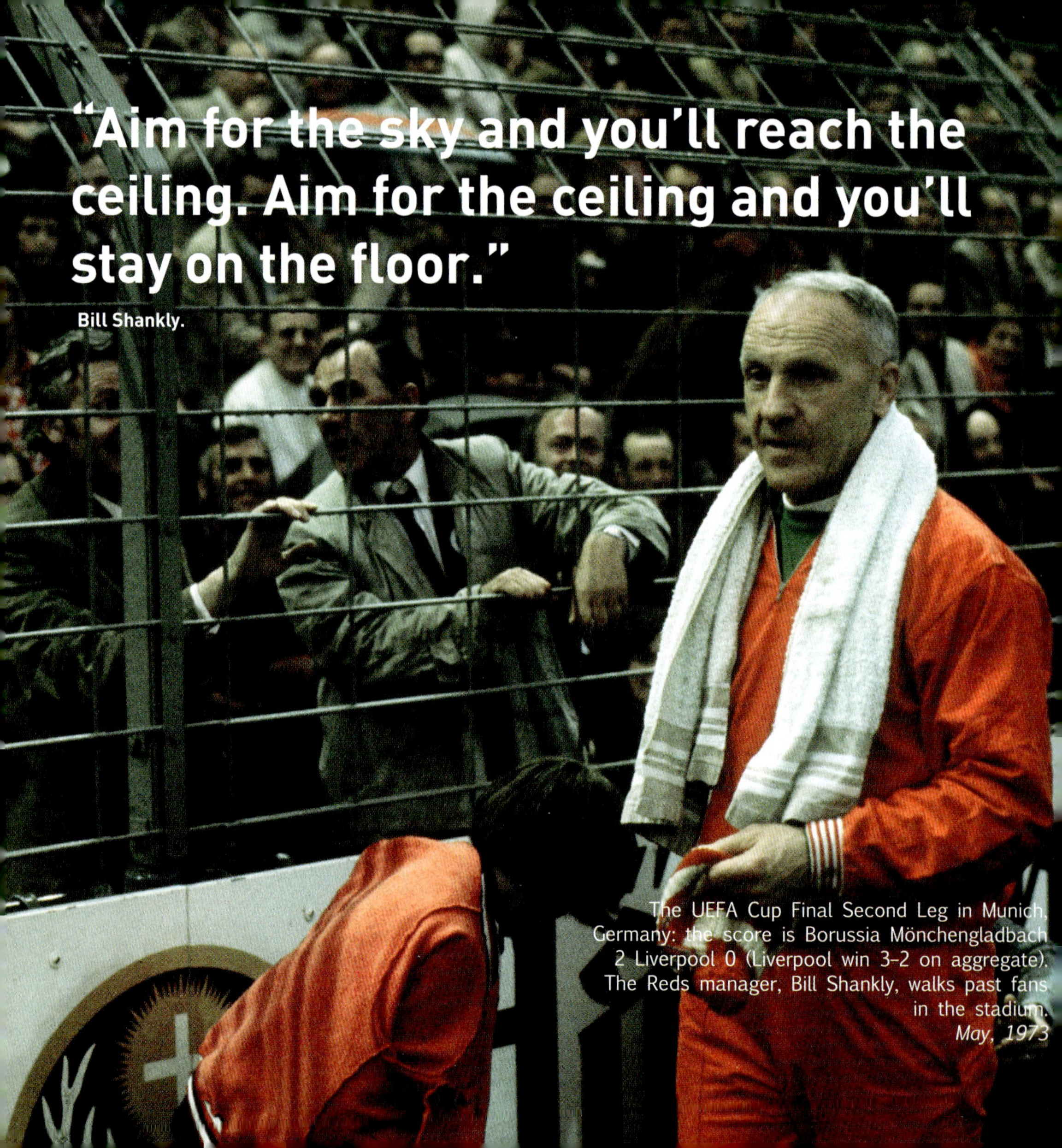

"Aim for the sky and you'll reach the ceiling. Aim for the ceiling and you'll stay on the floor."

Bill Shankly.

The UEFA Cup Final Second Leg in Munich, Germany: the score is Borussia Mönchengladbach 2 Liverpool 0 (Liverpool win 3–2 on aggregate). The Reds manager, Bill Shankly, walks past fans in the stadium.
May, 1973

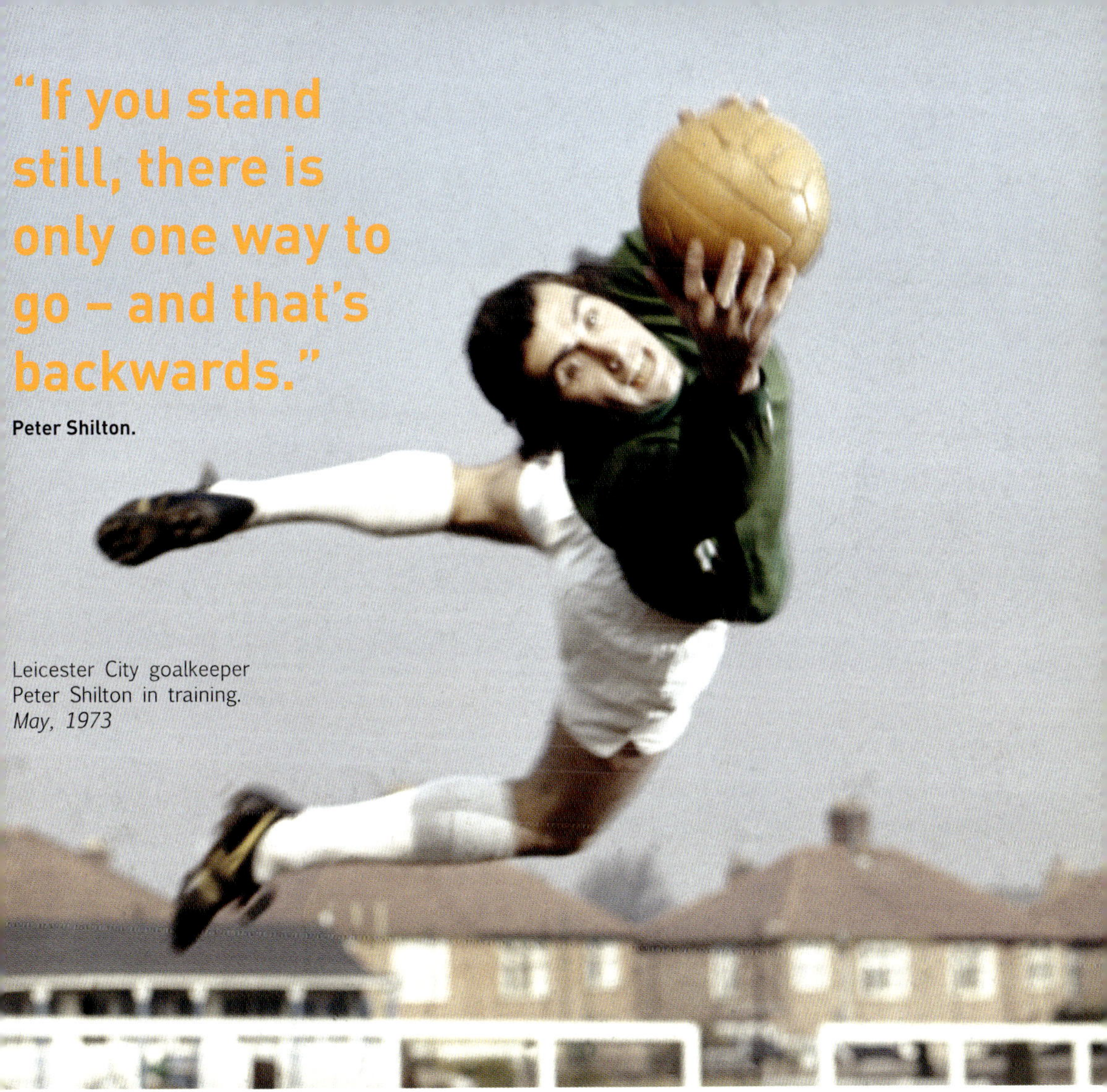

"If you stand still, there is only one way to go – and that's backwards."

Peter Shilton.

Leicester City goalkeeper Peter Shilton in training.
May, 1973

"Once an Arsenal man, always an Arsenal man."

Bob Wilson, former Scotland international goalkeeper and later broadcaster. As a player, Wilson made almost 300 appearances for Arsenal between 1963 and 1974.

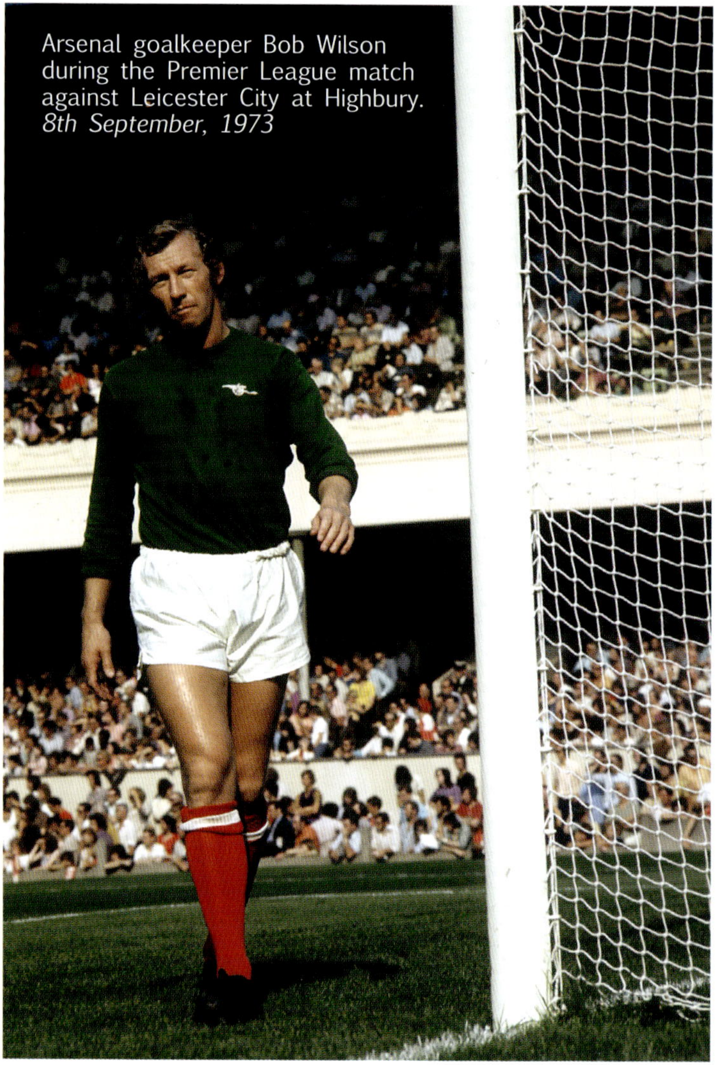

Arsenal goalkeeper Bob Wilson during the Premier League match against Leicester City at Highbury. *8th September, 1973*

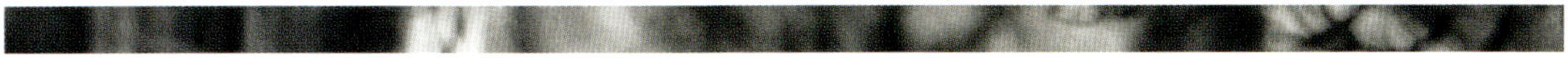

Terry Venables, Queens Park Rangers player and Professional Footballers' Association chairman, arrives at a Christmas party dressed as Santa Claus.
17th December, 1973

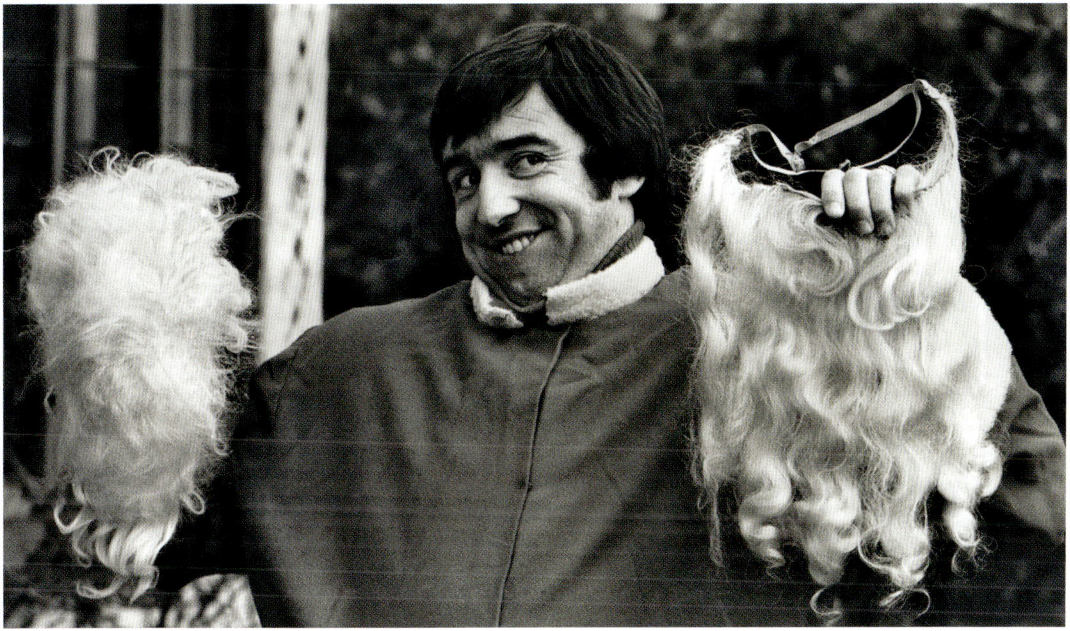

"If history repeats itself, I should think we can expect the same thing again."

Terry Venables, former football player and manager turned media pundit. During the 1960s and 1970s, 'El Tel' played for clubs including Chelsea, Tottenham Hotspur and Queens Park Rangers, gaining two caps for England. He was the national team manager of England, 1994–1996, and of Australia, 1997–1998.

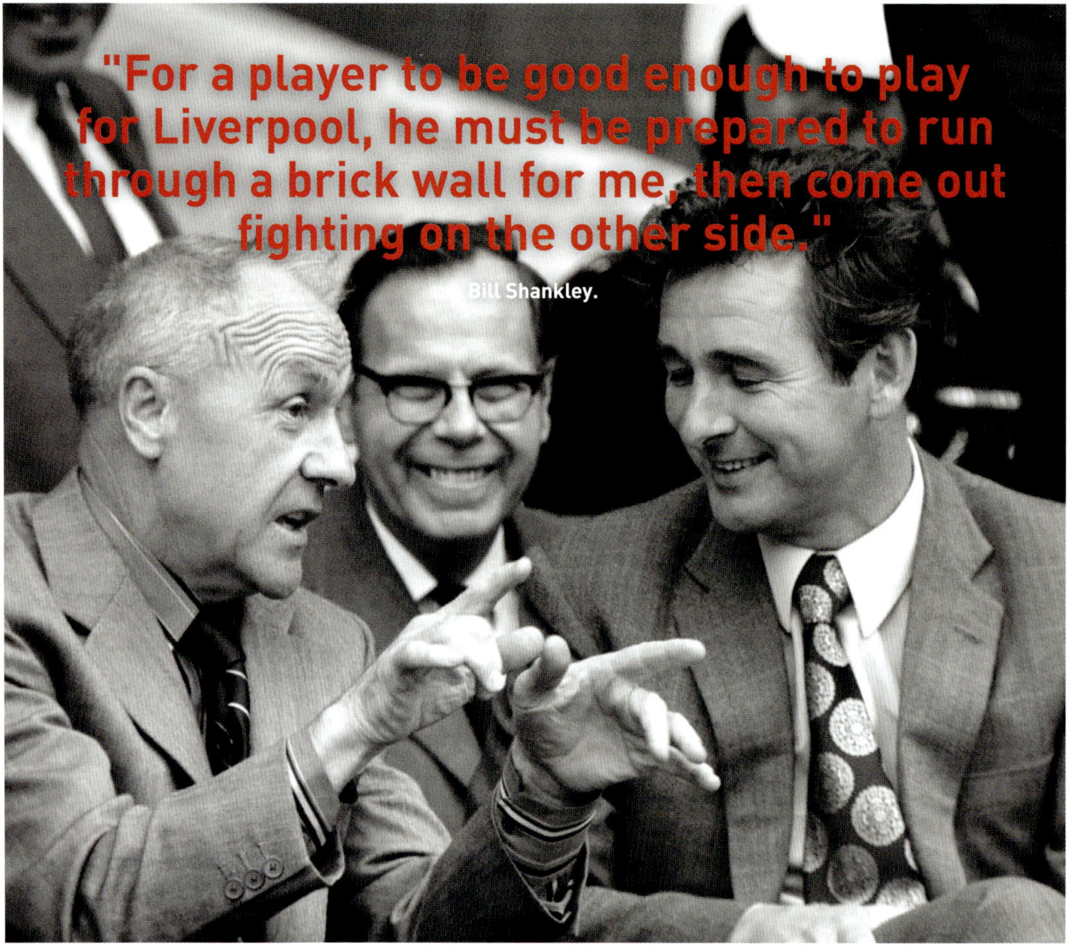

Liverpool manager Bill Shankly (L) watches penalties with Brian Clough (R) in the FA Charity Shield match at Wembley Stadium. It was Shankly's last game in charge before Clough took the helm after Don Revie left. The final score had been a 1-1 draw, with Liverpool winning 6-5 on penalties.
10th August, 1974

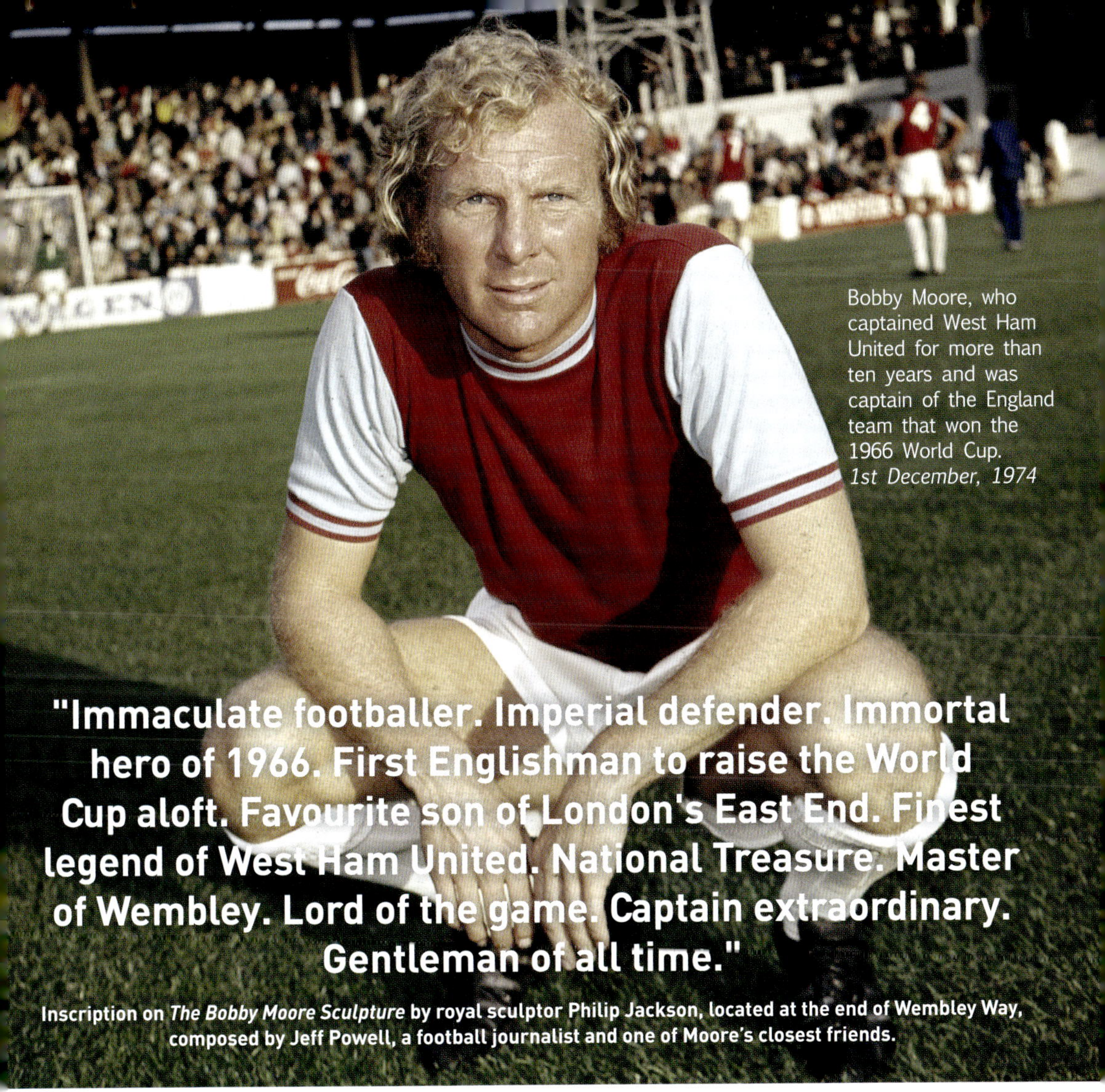

Bobby Moore, who captained West Ham United for more than ten years and was captain of the England team that won the 1966 World Cup.
1st December, 1974

"Immaculate footballer. Imperial defender. Immortal hero of 1966. First Englishman to raise the World Cup aloft. Favourite son of London's East End. Finest legend of West Ham United. National Treasure. Master of Wembley. Lord of the game. Captain extraordinary. Gentleman of all time."

Inscription on *The Bobby Moore Sculpture* by royal sculptor Philip Jackson, located at the end of Wembley Way, composed by Jeff Powell, a football journalist and one of Moore's closest friends.

"He was one of the greatest players I have seen – very much the linchpin of the 1966 team. Early in my management I knew I had to find a role suitable to Bobby's unique talents. He wasn't just a great goal scorer, with a blistering shot using either foot. Bobby was a player who could also do his share of hard work."

Alf Ramsey
on Bobby Charlton.

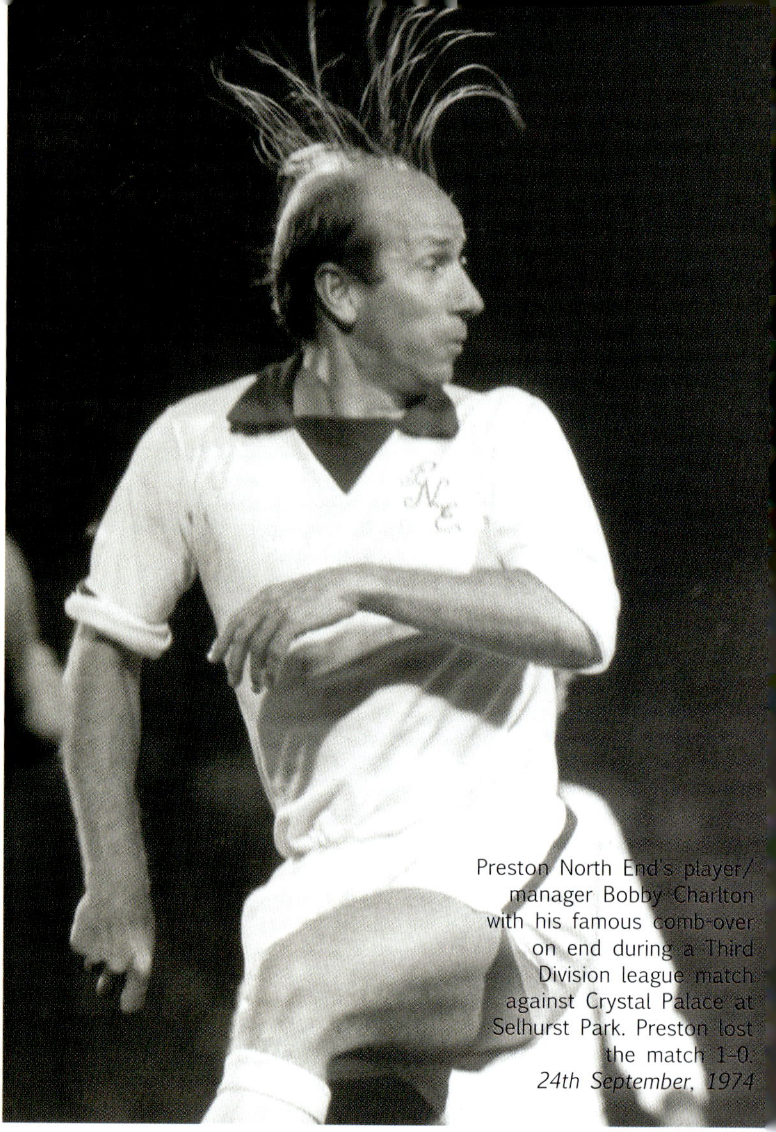

Preston North End's player/manager Bobby Charlton with his famous comb-over on end during a Third Division league match against Crystal Palace at Selhurst Park. Preston lost the match 1-0.
24th September, 1974

"Little Billy Bremner is the captain of the crew
For the sake of Leeds United he would break himself in two
His hair is red and fuzzy and his body's black and blue
But Leeds go marching on."

A verse from the Leeds United club song, to the tune of 'Glory Glory', referring to Bremner's role at the club.

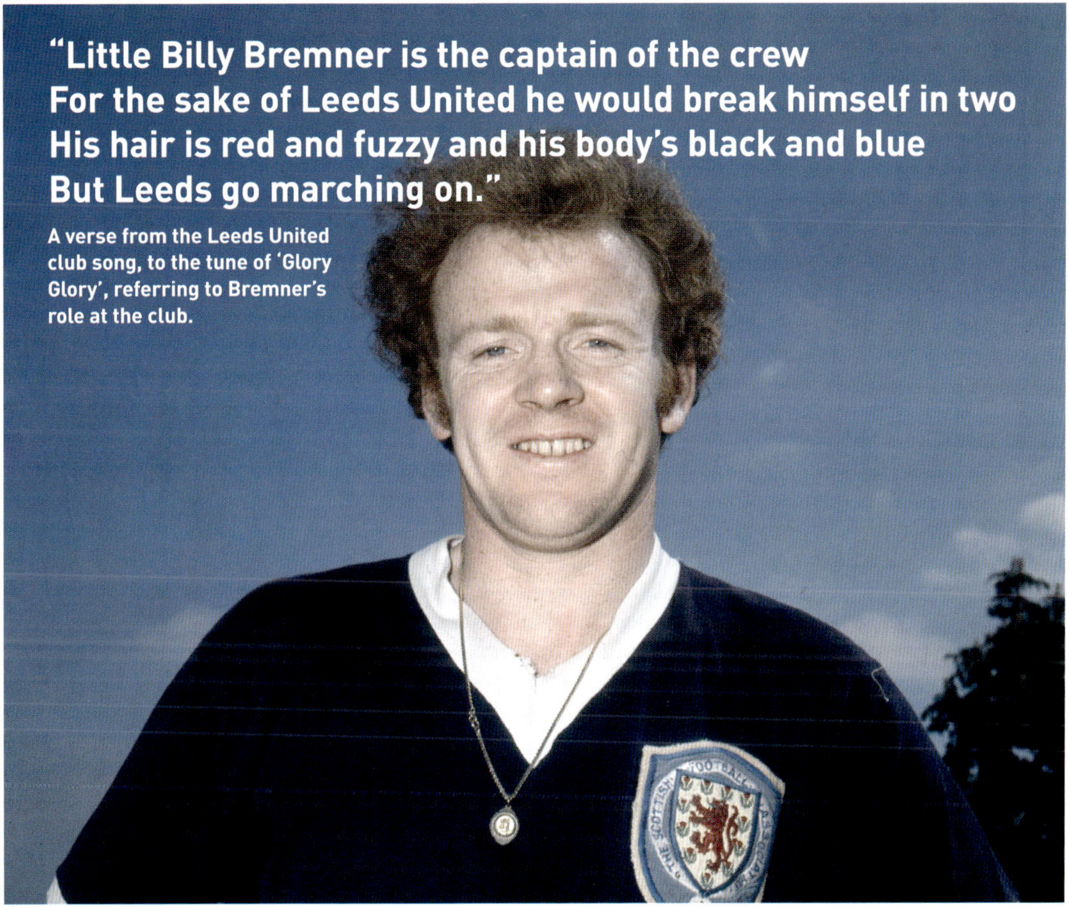

Billy Bremner, Scottish professional footballer and captain of the Leeds United team during the 1960s and 1970s, voted Leeds United's greatest player of all time. A statue dedicated to the plucky player stands outside the south-east corner of Elland Road.
1974

"In my early days, a goal against us was shrugged off. Nobody liked conceding a goal, but once the ball had gone into the net it was accepted as 'one of those things' and everybody in the team would concentrate on trying to get the goal back. But once the maximum wage had been lifted and win bonuses became all-important, it was suddenly considered a crime to concede a goal."

Gordon Banks.

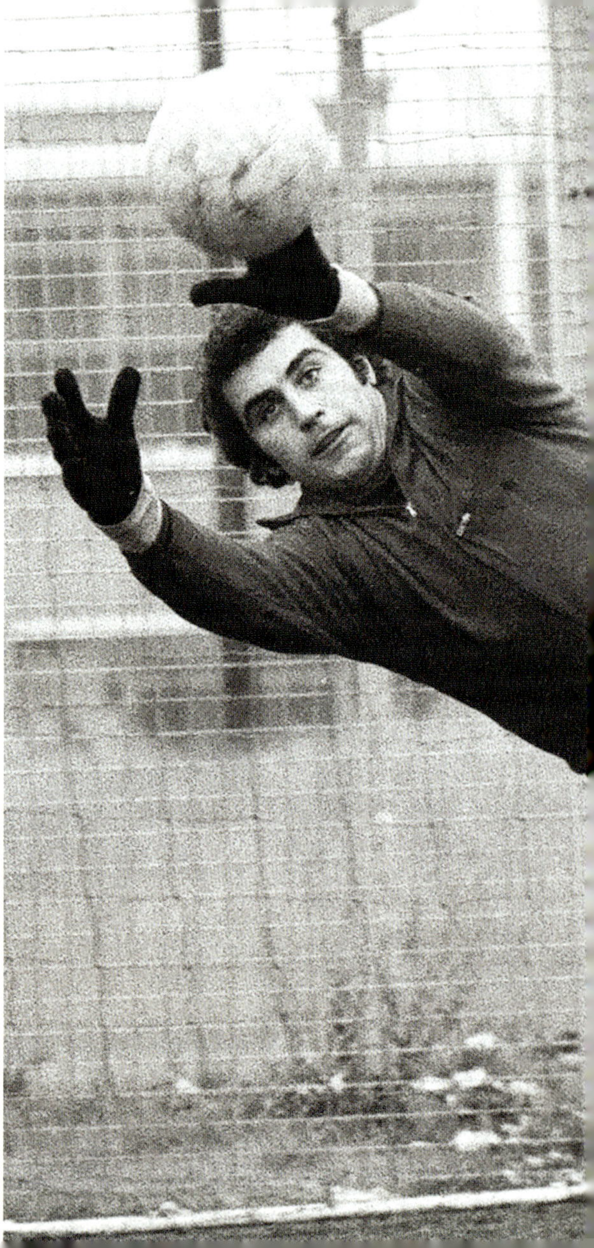

Peter Shilton (L), Tony Waddington's record signing, reported to Stoke FC ground for the first time as a Stoke player. First to greet him was Gordon Banks (R) and then it was down to some serious training, including a flying duet to a ball bound goalward.
24th November, 1974

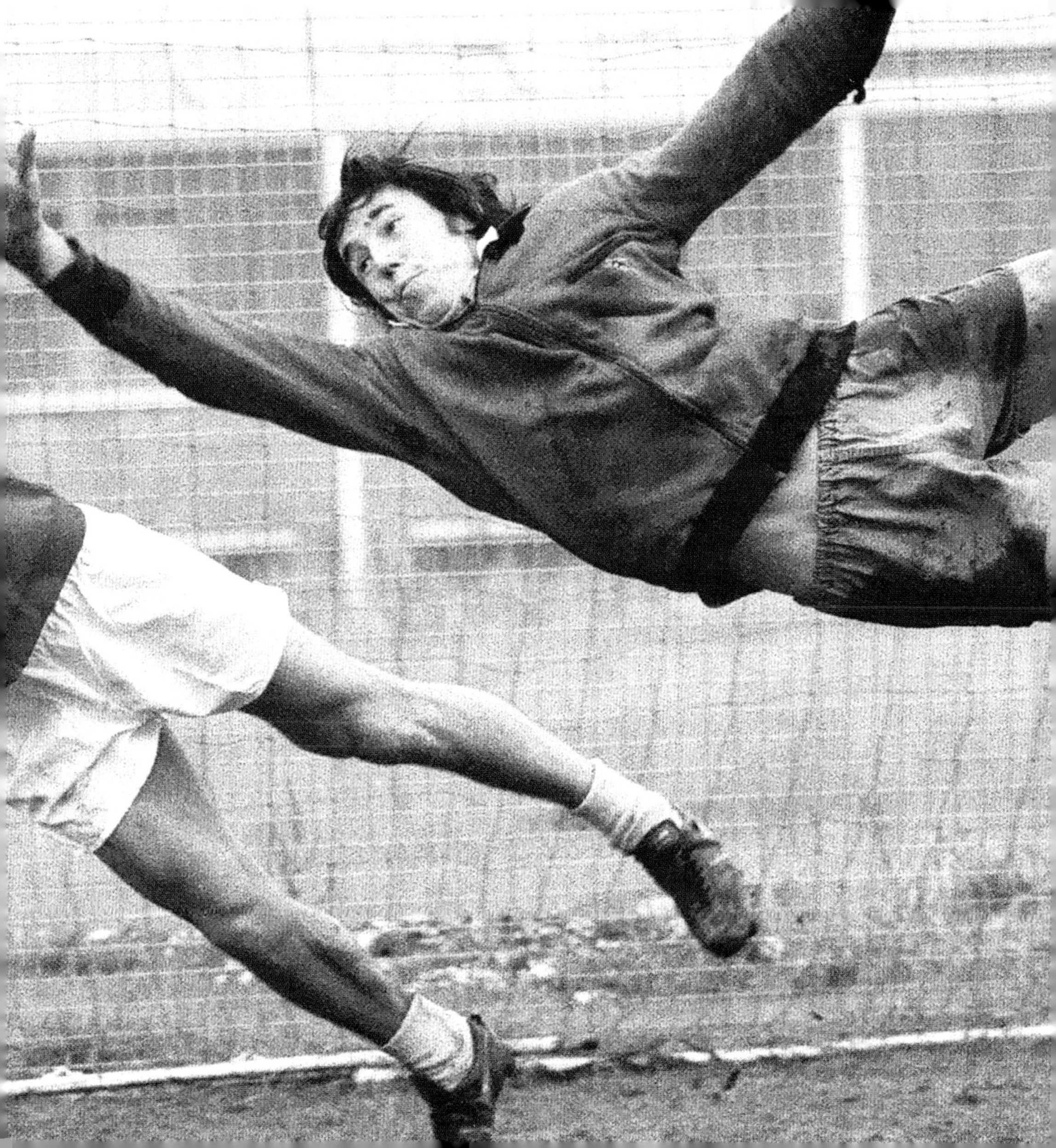

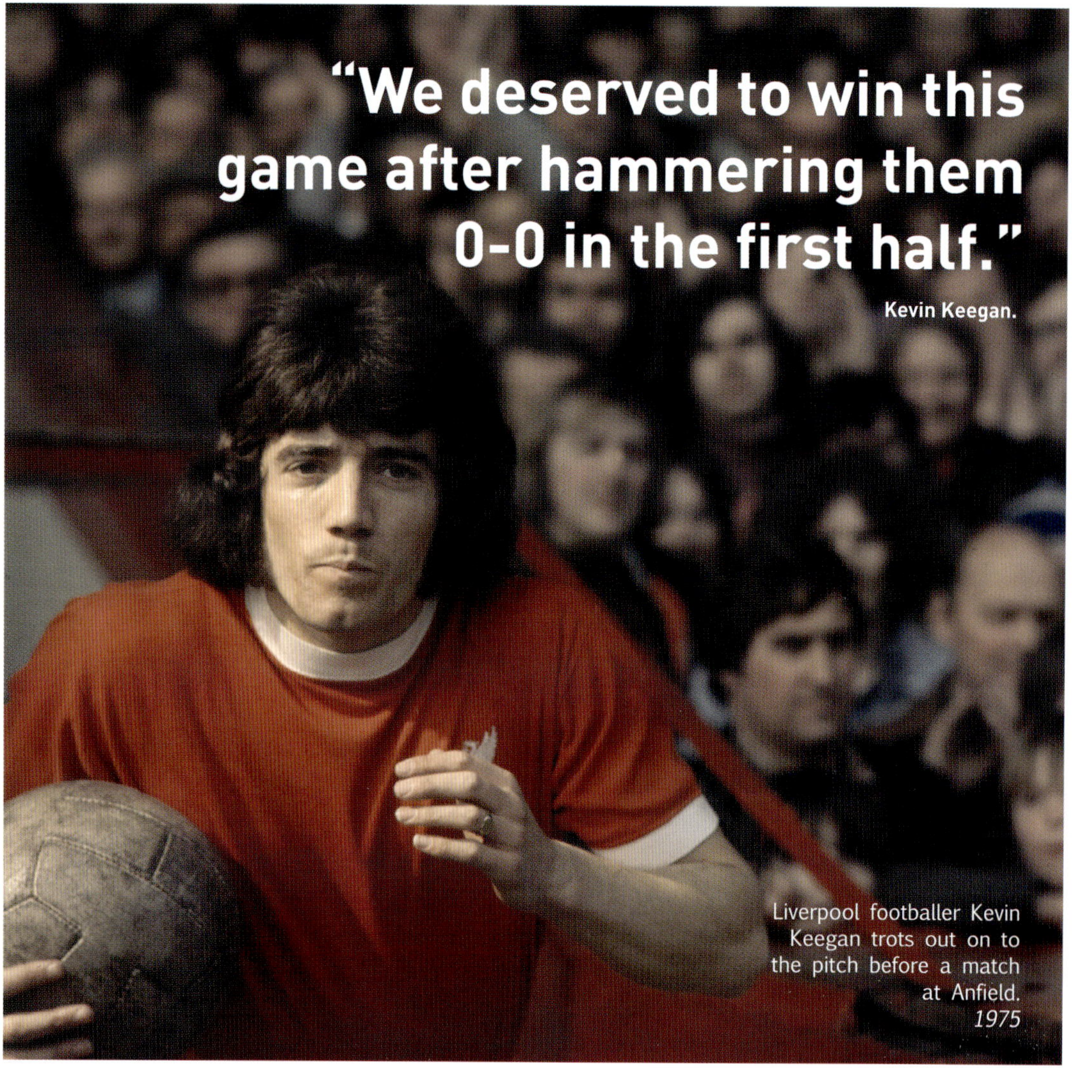

"We deserved to win this game after hammering them 0-0 in the first half."

Kevin Keegan.

Liverpool footballer Kevin Keegan trots out on to the pitch before a match at Anfield.
1975

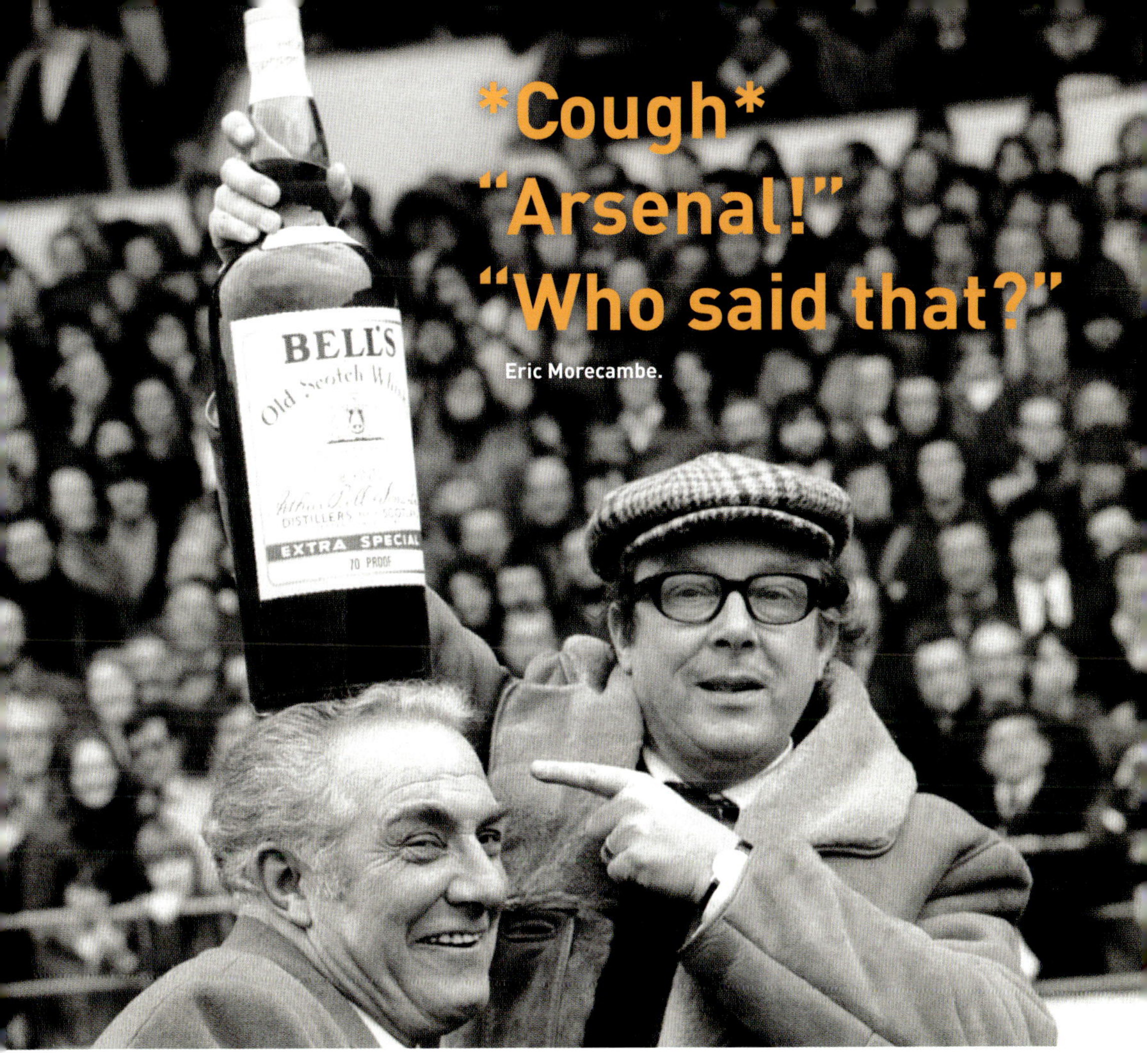

Cough "Arsenal!" "Who said that?"

Eric Morecambe.

Luton Town manager Harry Haslam has his 'Manager of the Month' Scotch balanced on his head by Eric Morecambe, a director of the club, after a 1–1 draw with Chelsea. The comedian often told the story of how once, when the team was 2–0 down at half time, the Luton fans chanted the Morecambe & Wise catchphrase "What do you think of it so far?" to which Eric replied, "Rubbish!"

11th January, 1975

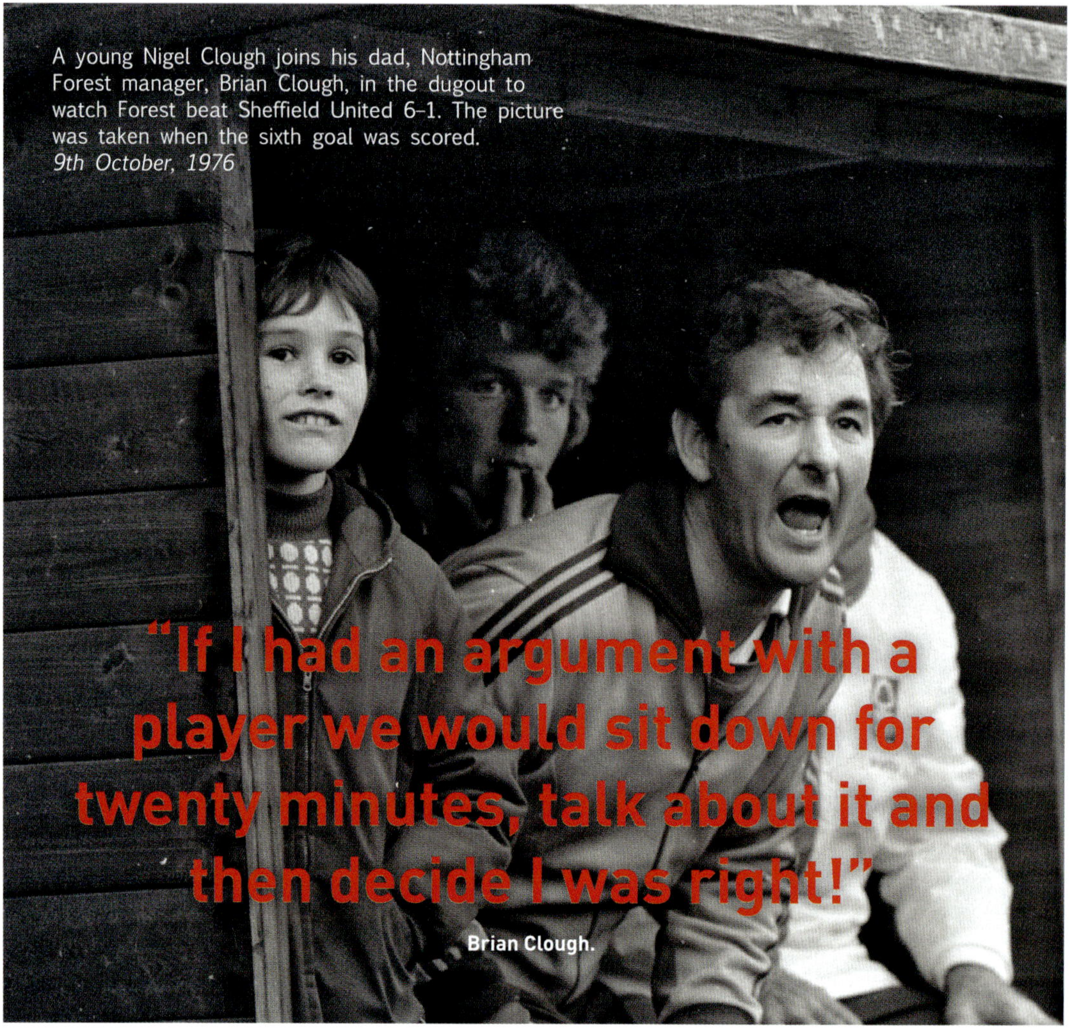

A young Nigel Clough joins his dad, Nottingham Forest manager, Brian Clough, in the dugout to watch Forest beat Sheffield United 6–1. The picture was taken when the sixth goal was scored.
9th October, 1976

"If I had an argument with a player we would sit down for twenty minutes, talk about it and then decide I was right!"

Brian Clough.

“A lot of hard work went into this defeat.”

Malcolm 'Big Mal' Allison, one of English football's most flamboyant and outspoken characters noted for his panache, fedora and cigar, on John Bond, who succeeded him as manager of Manchester City in 1980.

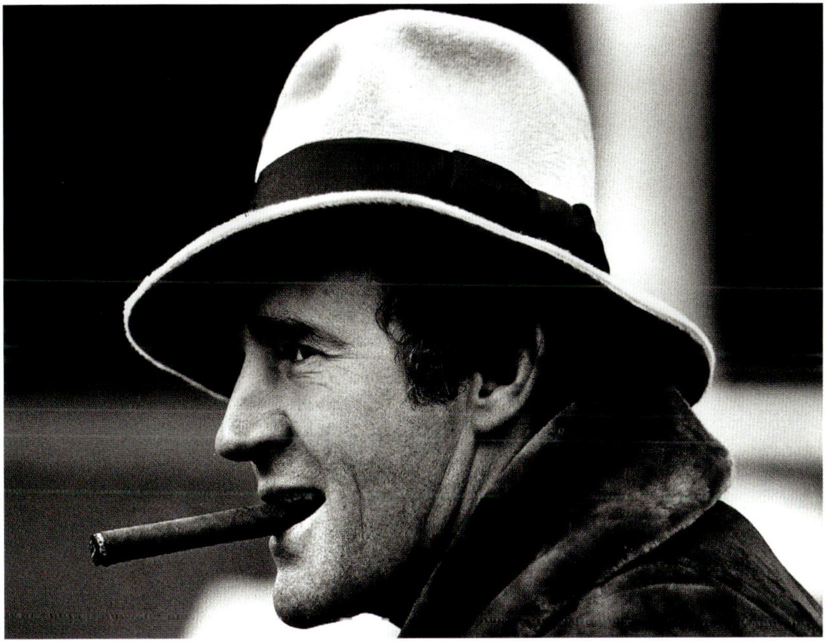

Malcolm Allison, former footballer, coach and manager of Manchester City and Crystal Palace, prior to his tenure at Galatasaray, Turkey. Allison's own playing career had been cut short in 1958 when, suffering from tuberculosis, he had a lung removed.
11th March, 1976

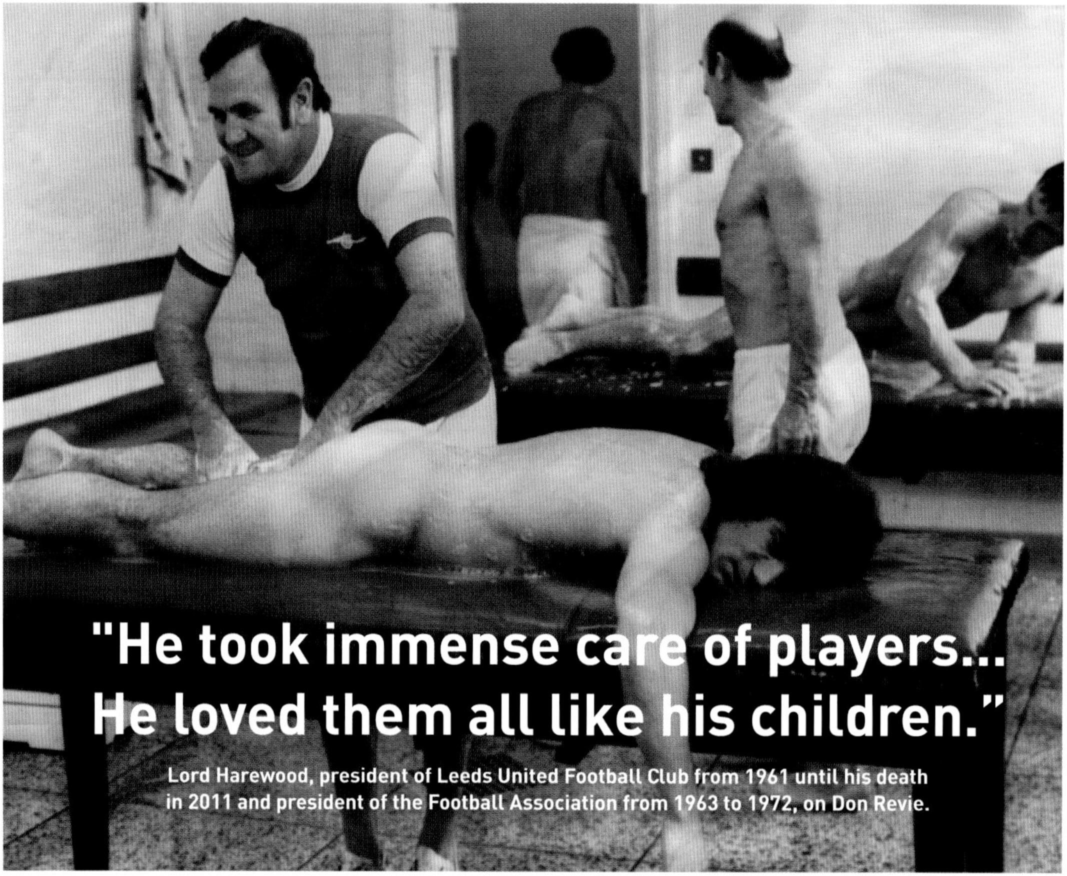

Don Revie, England manager from 1974 to 1976, gets to grips with Kevin Keegan's thigh. In the 1976 European championships, the team failed to get through the qualification group and progress to the finals. In 1977, while still under contract to the English FA, Revie quit as manager to coach the United Arab Emirates.

16th November, 1976

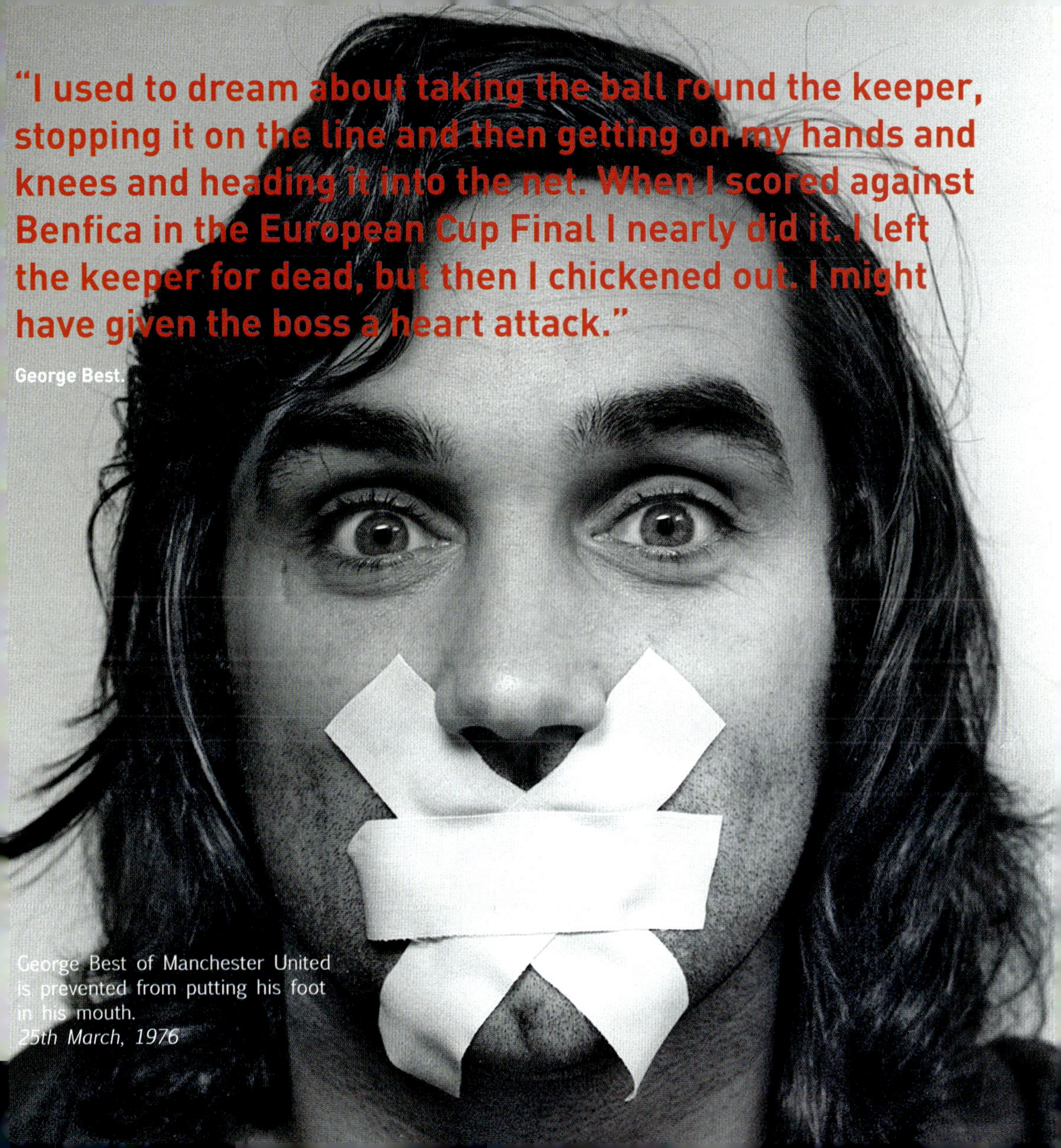

George Best of Manchester United is prevented from putting his foot in his mouth.
25th March, 1976

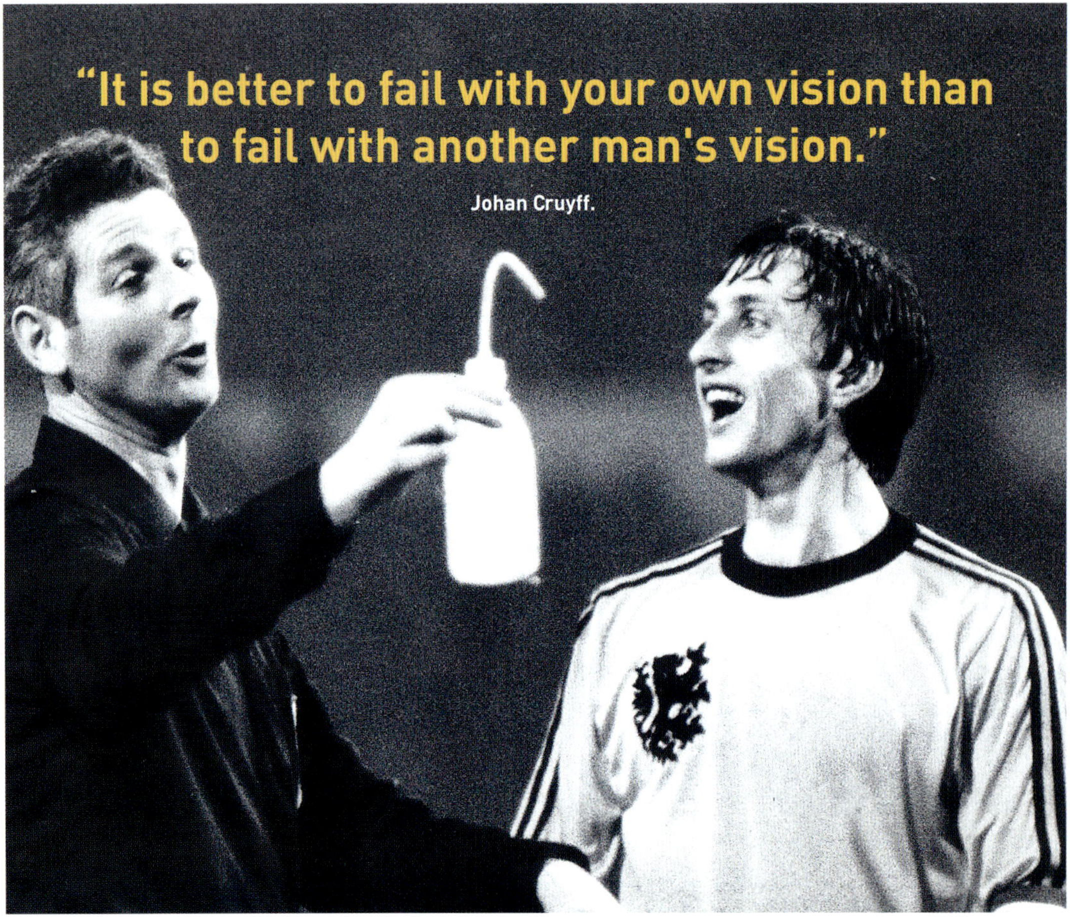

The final straw. Dutch footballer Johan Cruyff (R) shares a joke with the referee during an England v Holland international match at Wembley.
February, 1977

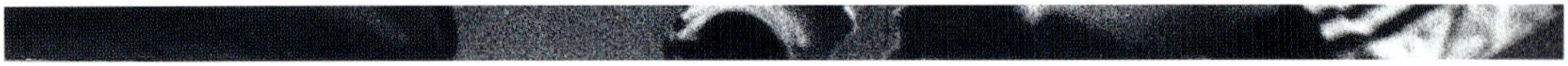

"I know what is around the corner – I just don't know where the corner is. But the onus is on us to perform and we must control the bandwagon."

Kevin Keegan.

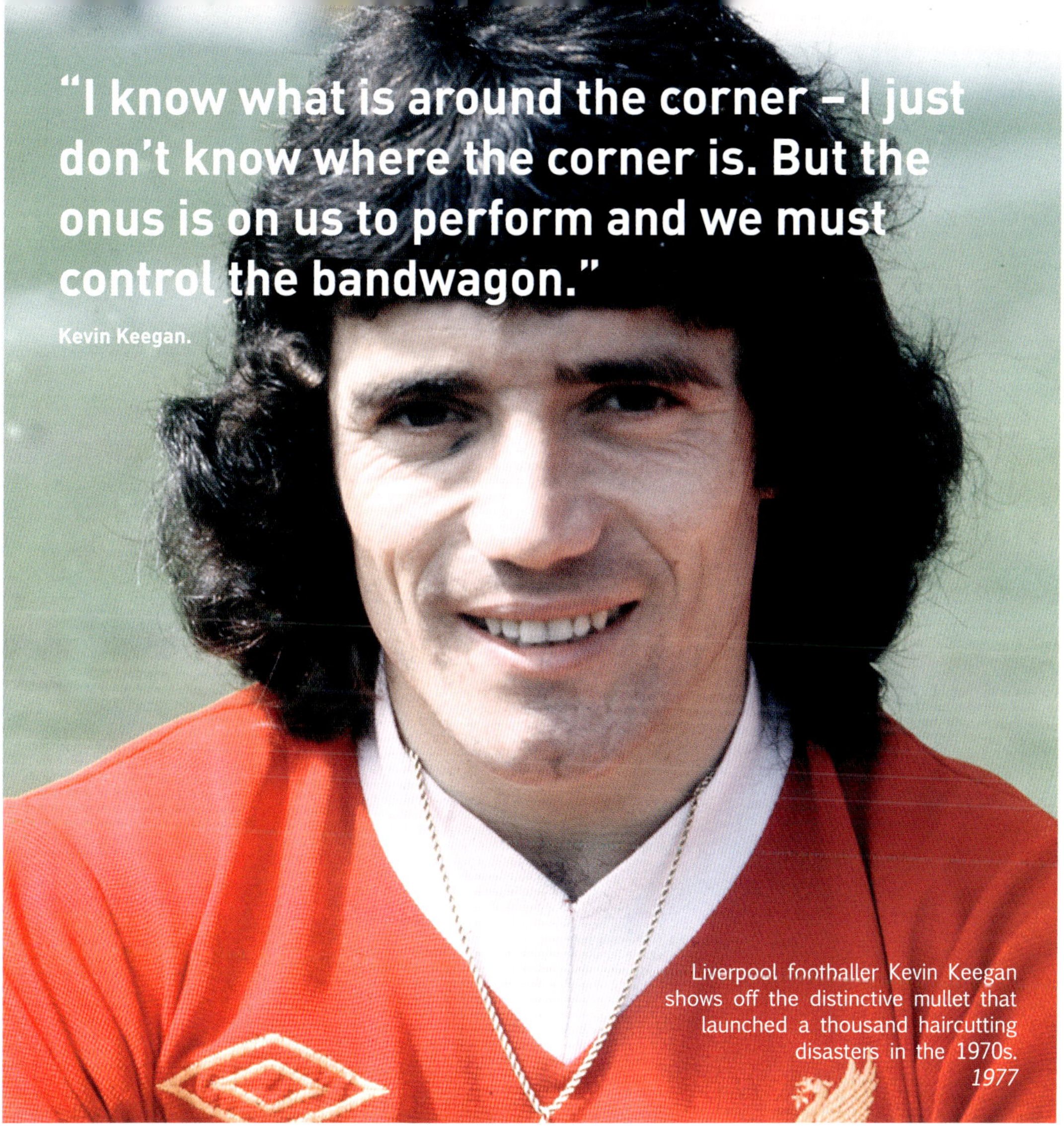

Liverpool footballer Kevin Keegan shows off the distinctive mullet that launched a thousand haircutting disasters in the 1970s. *1977*

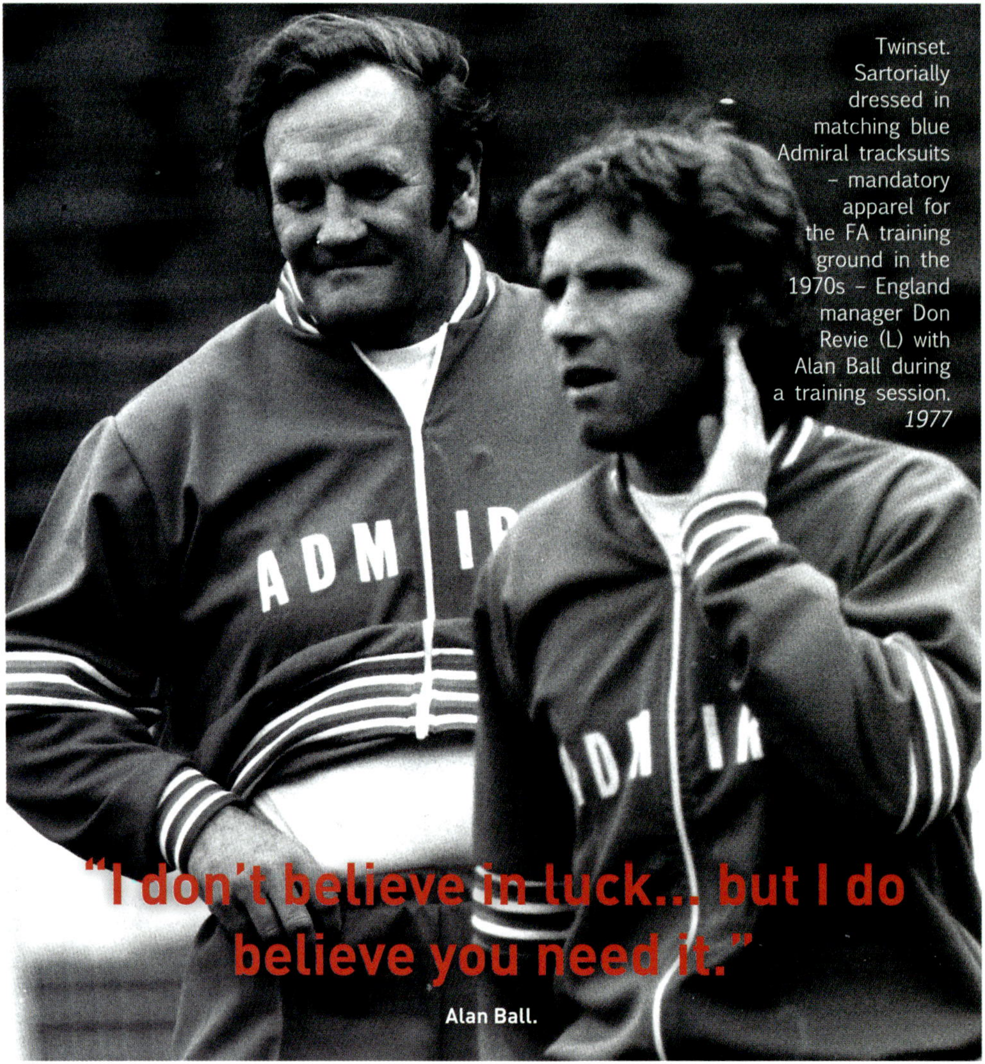

Twinset. Sartorially dressed in matching blue Admiral tracksuits – mandatory apparel for the FA training ground in the 1970s – England manager Don Revie (L) with Alan Ball during a training session. *1977*

"I don't believe in luck... but I do believe you need it."

Alan Ball.

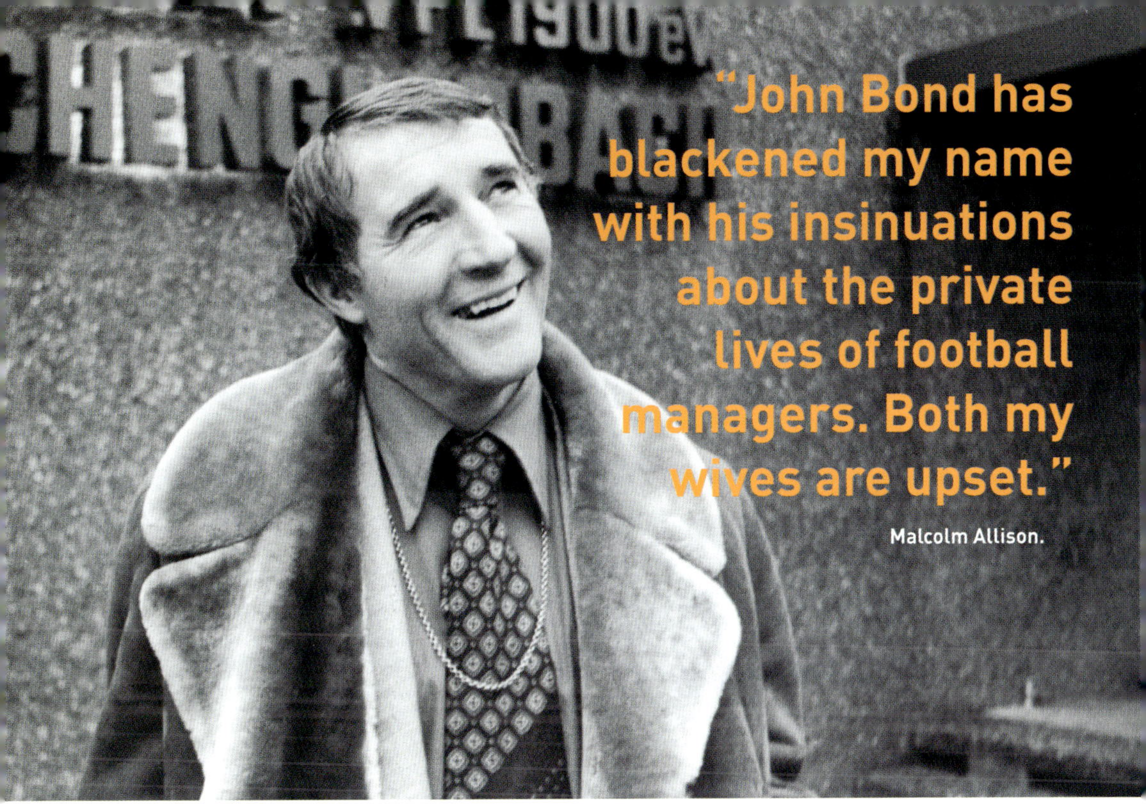

"John Bond has blackened my name with his insinuations about the private lives of football managers. Both my wives are upset."

Malcolm Allison.

Malcom Allison accepted an offer by chairman Peter Swales to return as manager of a lacklustre Manchester City. Despite some controversial transfers, Allison left again a year later, in 1980, with City still struggling in the league, against the backdrop of a verbal scrap with his successor and fellow maverick manager, John Bond.

3rd March, 1979

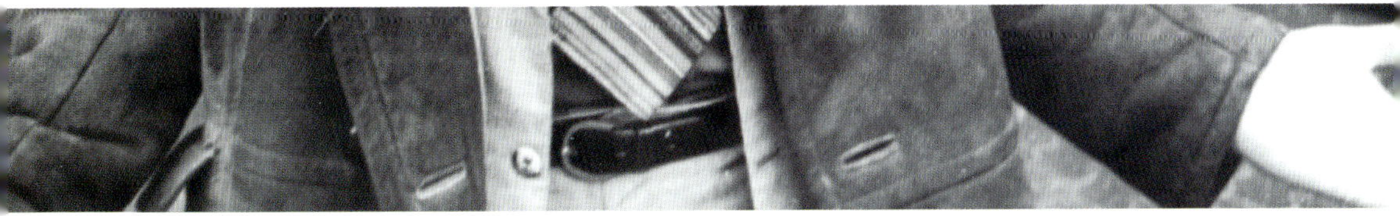

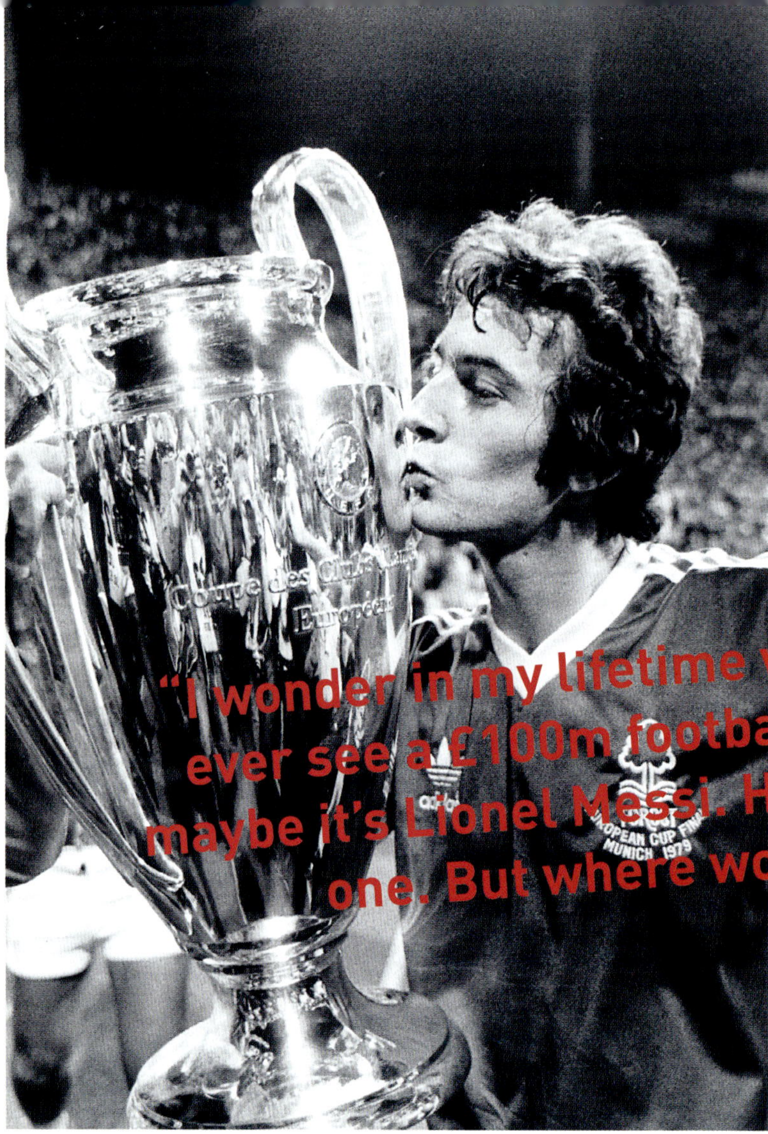

Nottingham Forest striker Trevor Francis kisses the European Cup after his winning goal against the Swedish club, Malmö, in Munich, Germany, won the trophy for Forest for the first time.
30th May, 1979

"I wonder in my lifetime whether I'll ever see a £100m footballer. If I do, maybe it's Lionel Messi. He's the only one. But where would he go?"

Trevor Francis, Britain's first million-pound footballer.

"Don't sit on the fence Terry. What chance do you think Germany has got of getting through?"

Jimmy Hill.

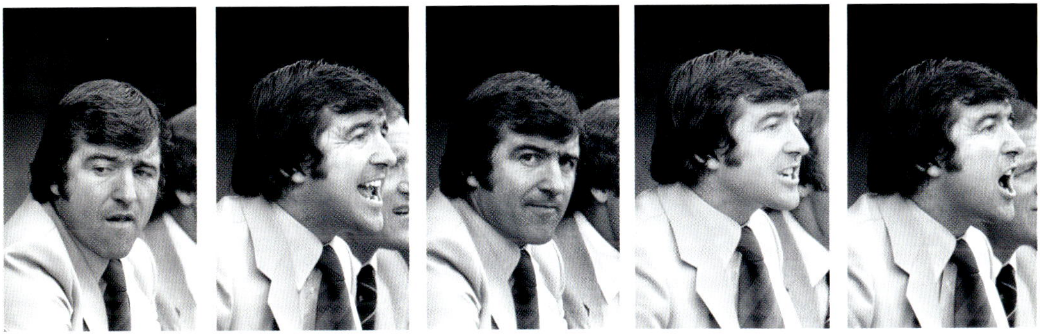

"I think it's fifty-fifty."

Terry Venables.

Terry Venables, Crystal Palace manager, considers tactics during the English League Division 1 match against Aston Villa, who won 1–0.
27th September, 1980

"Working with people on a field turns me on."

Graeme Souness, Scottish former footballer, captain of Liverpool FC in the early 1980s. After retiring as a player, he became a manager and later a media pundit.

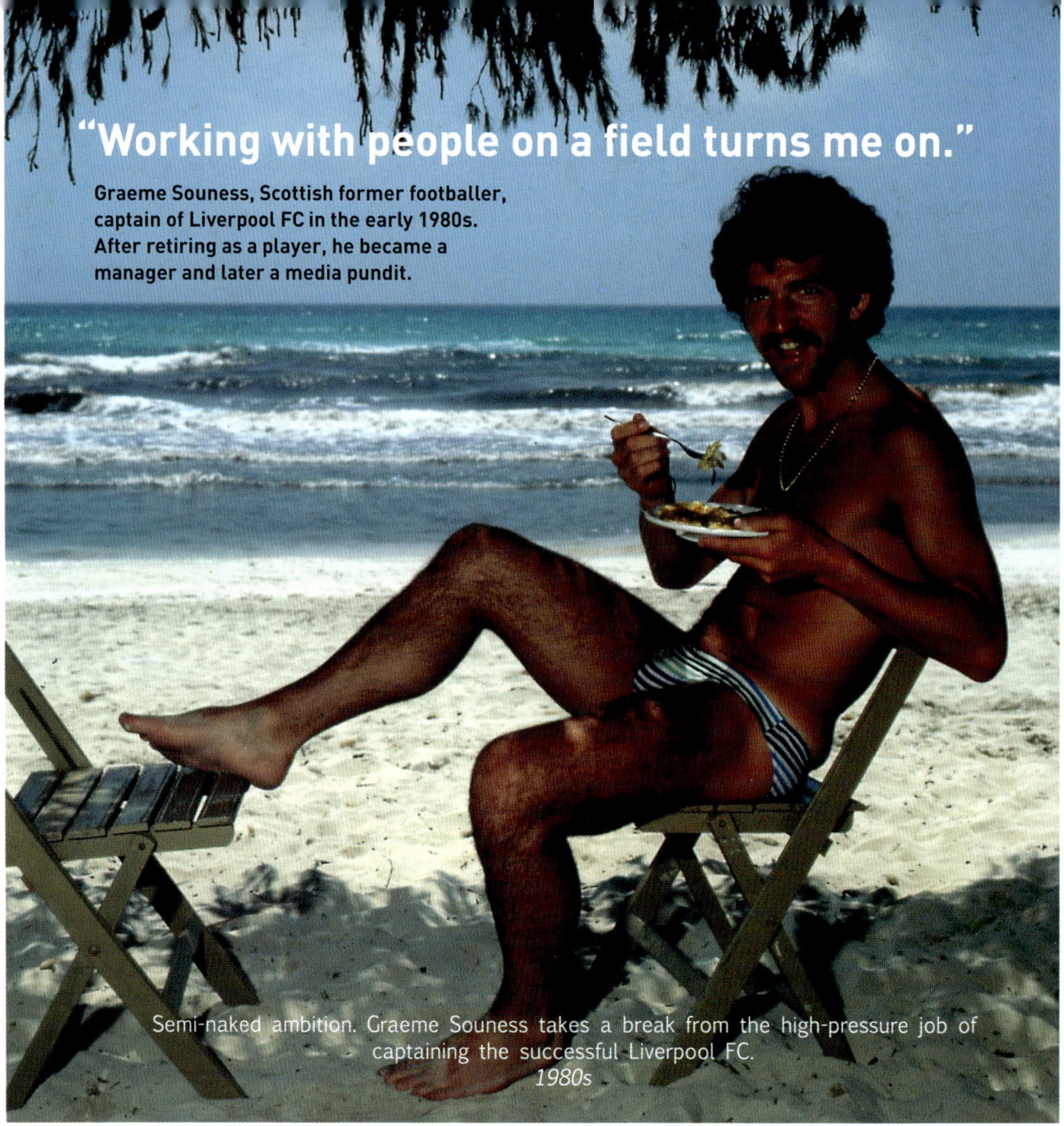

Semi-naked ambition. Graeme Souness takes a break from the high-pressure job of captaining the successful Liverpool FC.
1980s

"I've come to accept that the life of a front-runner is a hard one, that he will suffer more injuries than most men and that many of these injuries will not be accidental."

Pelé, Brazilian footballer, one of the greatest players of all time.

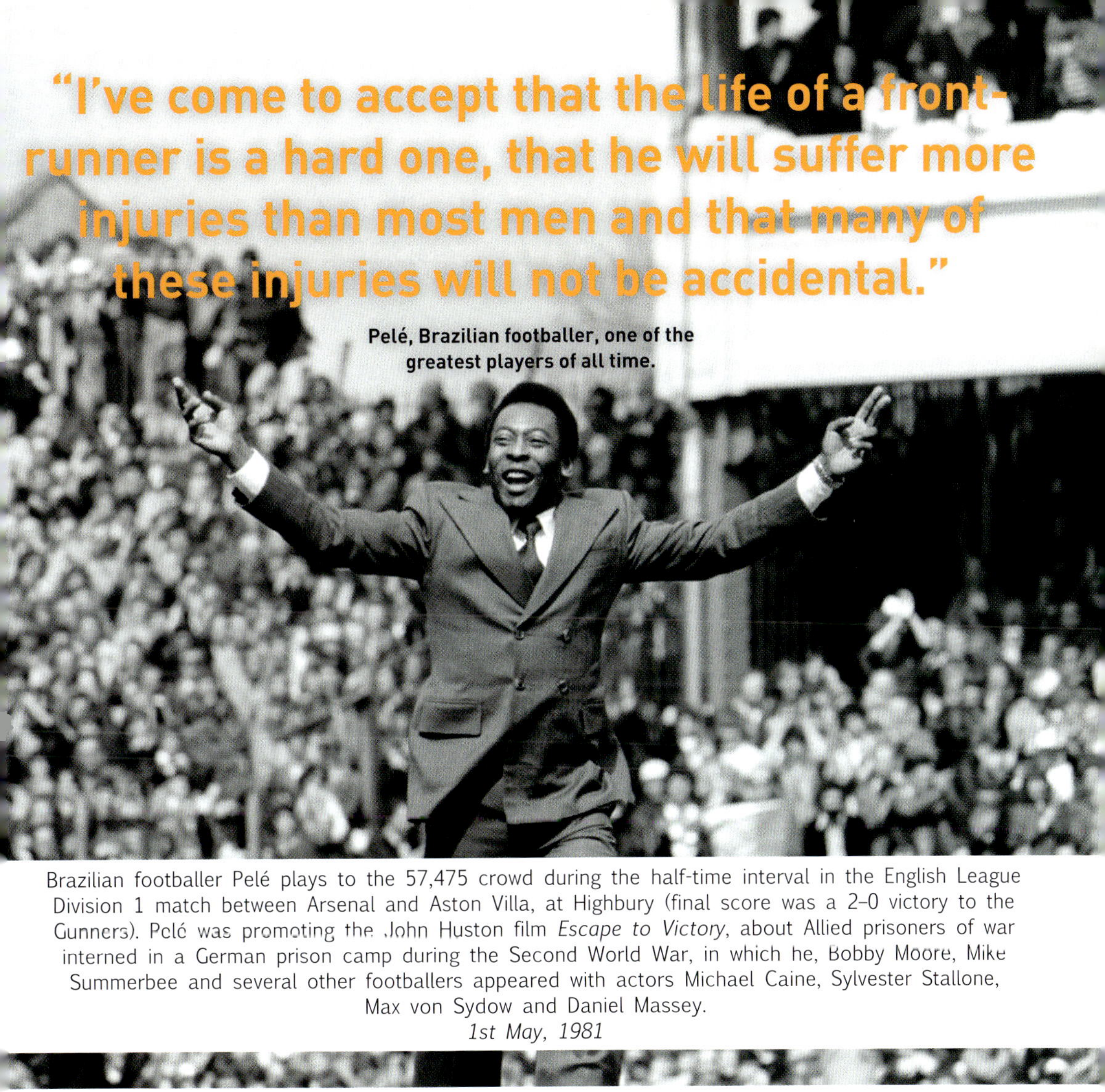

Brazilian footballer Pelé plays to the 57,475 crowd during the half-time interval in the English League Division 1 match between Arsenal and Aston Villa, at Highbury (final score was a 2–0 victory to the Gunners). Pelé was promoting the John Huston film *Escape to Victory*, about Allied prisoners of war interned in a German prison camp during the Second World War, in which he, Bobby Moore, Mike Summerbee and several other footballers appeared with actors Michael Caine, Sylvester Stallone, Max von Sydow and Daniel Massey.

1st May, 1981

“Well, Clive, it's all about the two M's – movement and positioning.”

Ron Atkinson.

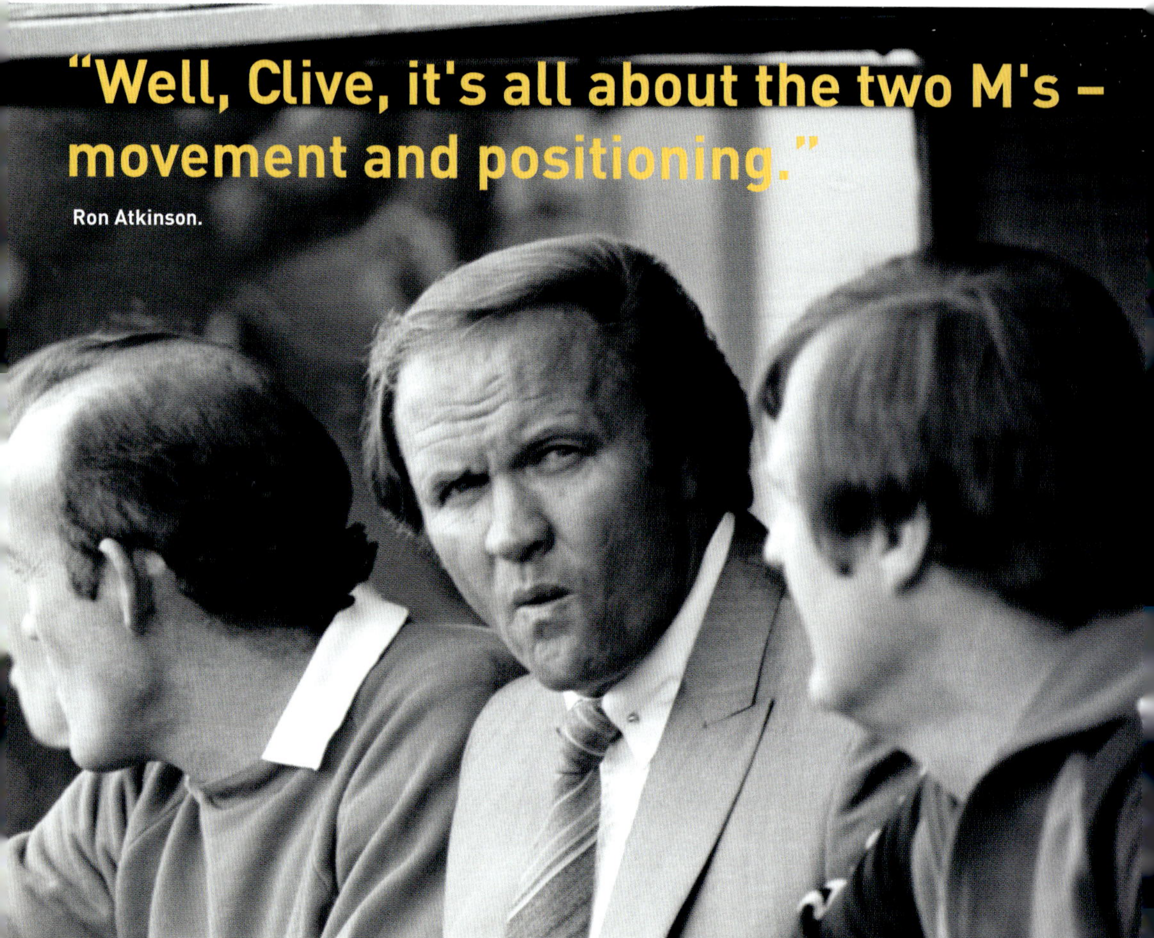

Manchester United manager Ron Atkinson looks pensive during the English League Division 1 match between his team and West Bromich Albion, at The Hawthorns. Albion triumphed 3–1.
4th September, 1982

"It was a very simple team talk. All I used to say was: 'Whenever possible, give the ball to George.'"

Matt Busby on George Best.

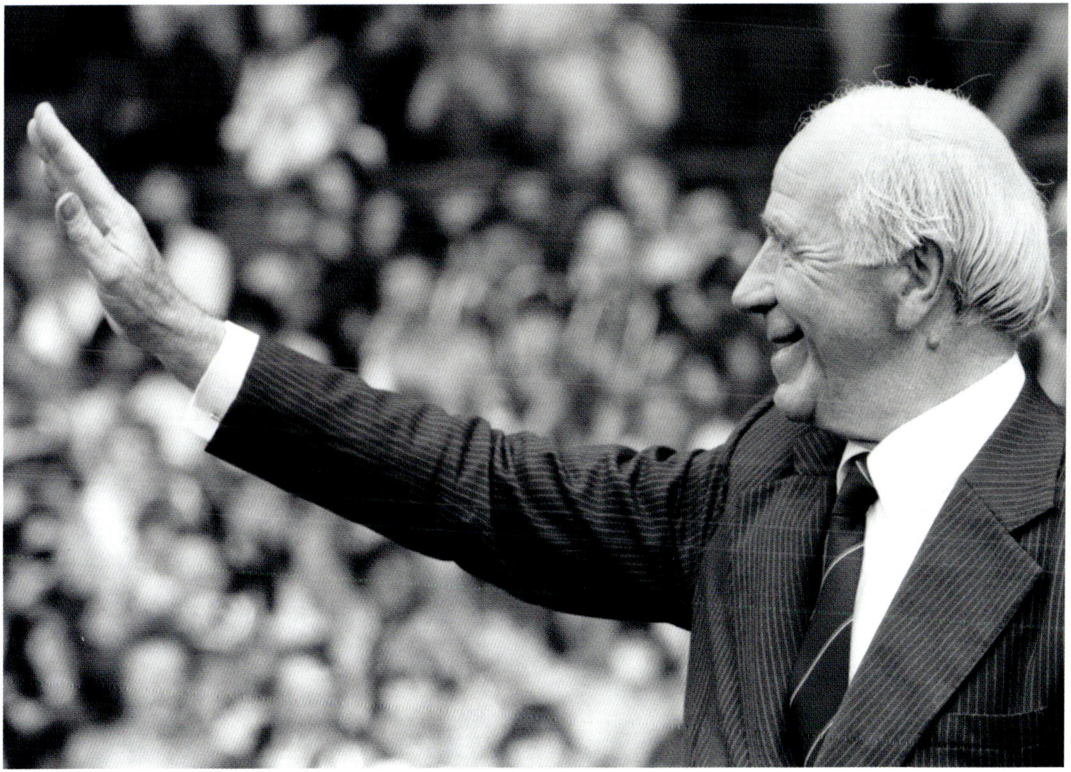

Sir Matt Busby waves to fans after his team, Manchester United, beat Stoke City 2–0 in a Division 1 match. Busby, ex-footballer and respected manager, had later been director of The Red Devils, and in 1982 was made president.
15th May, 1982

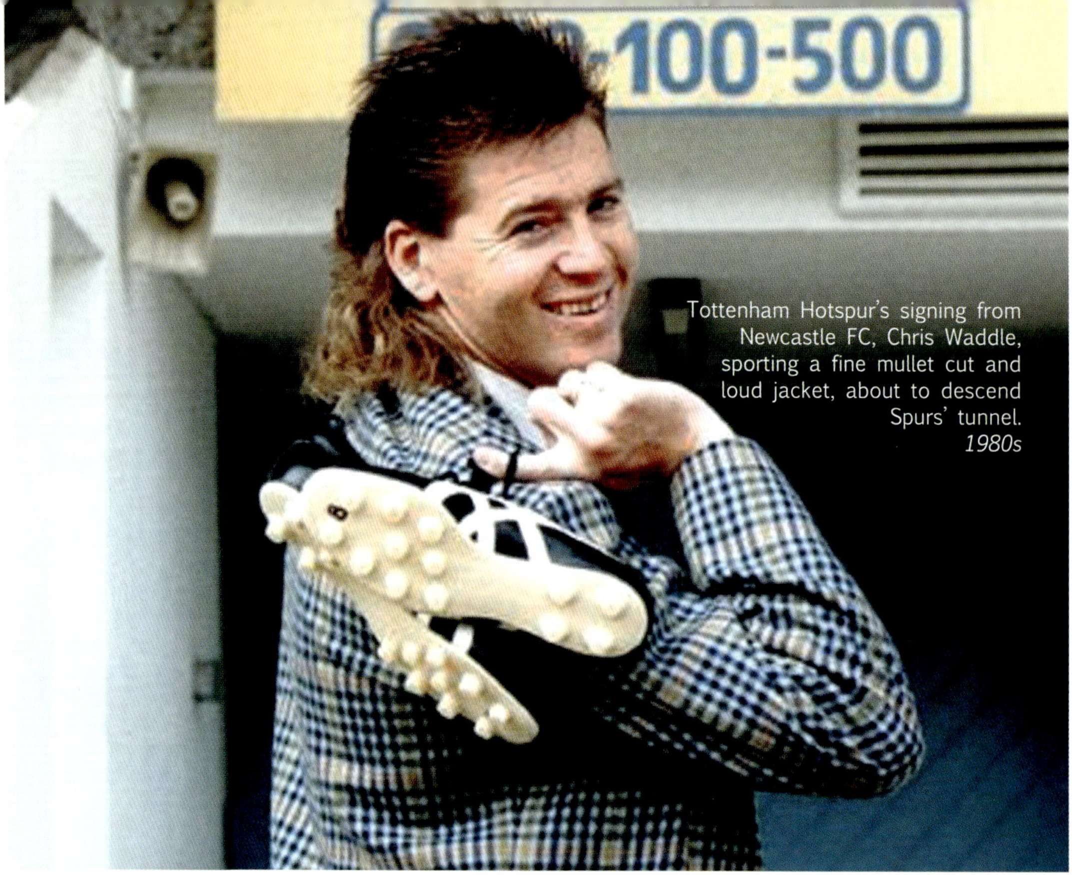

Tottenham Hotspur's signing from Newcastle FC, Chris Waddle, sporting a fine mullet cut and loud jacket, about to descend Spurs' tunnel.
1980s

"My legs sort of disappeared from nowhere."

Chris Waddle, English footballer and commentator, who made 62 appearances for England.

"I don't think he was ever born to be a rock 'n' roll star. He was probably born to be chairman of Watford Football Club, and now he's beginning to look like the chairman of Watford Football Club as well."

Rod Stewart on Elton John, 1977.

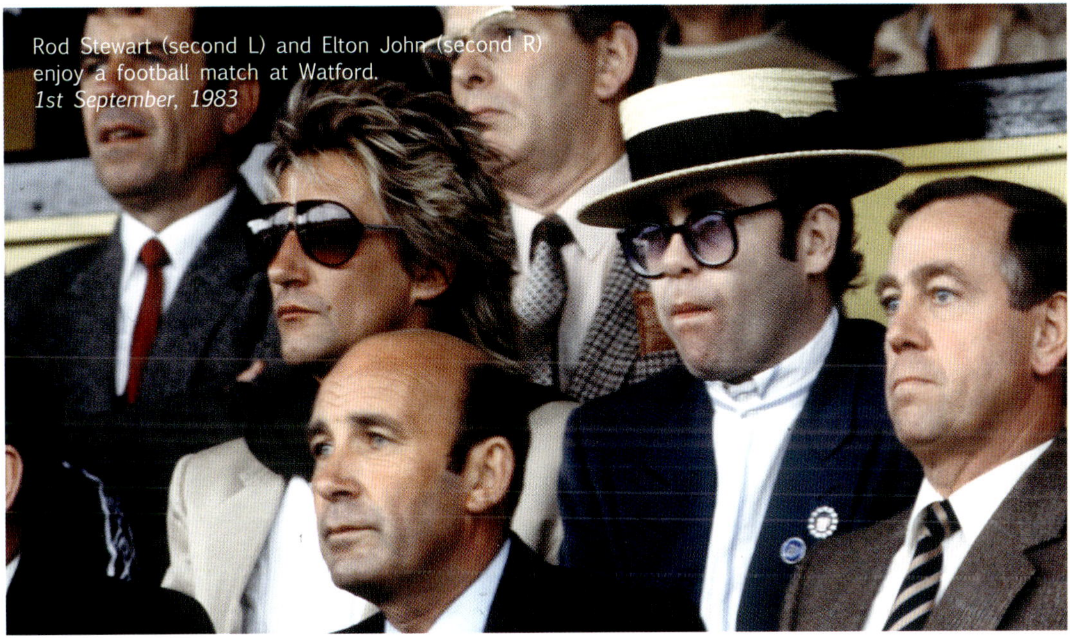

Rod Stewart (second L) and Elton John (second R) enjoy a football match at Watford.
1st September, 1983

"I am capable of being a rock 'n' roll star and the chairman of the Watford Football Club, and I sell more records throughout the world than Rod Stewart. Anyway, he should stick to grave-digging, 'cos that's where he belongs, six feet under."

Elton John's reply to Rod Stewart, 1977.

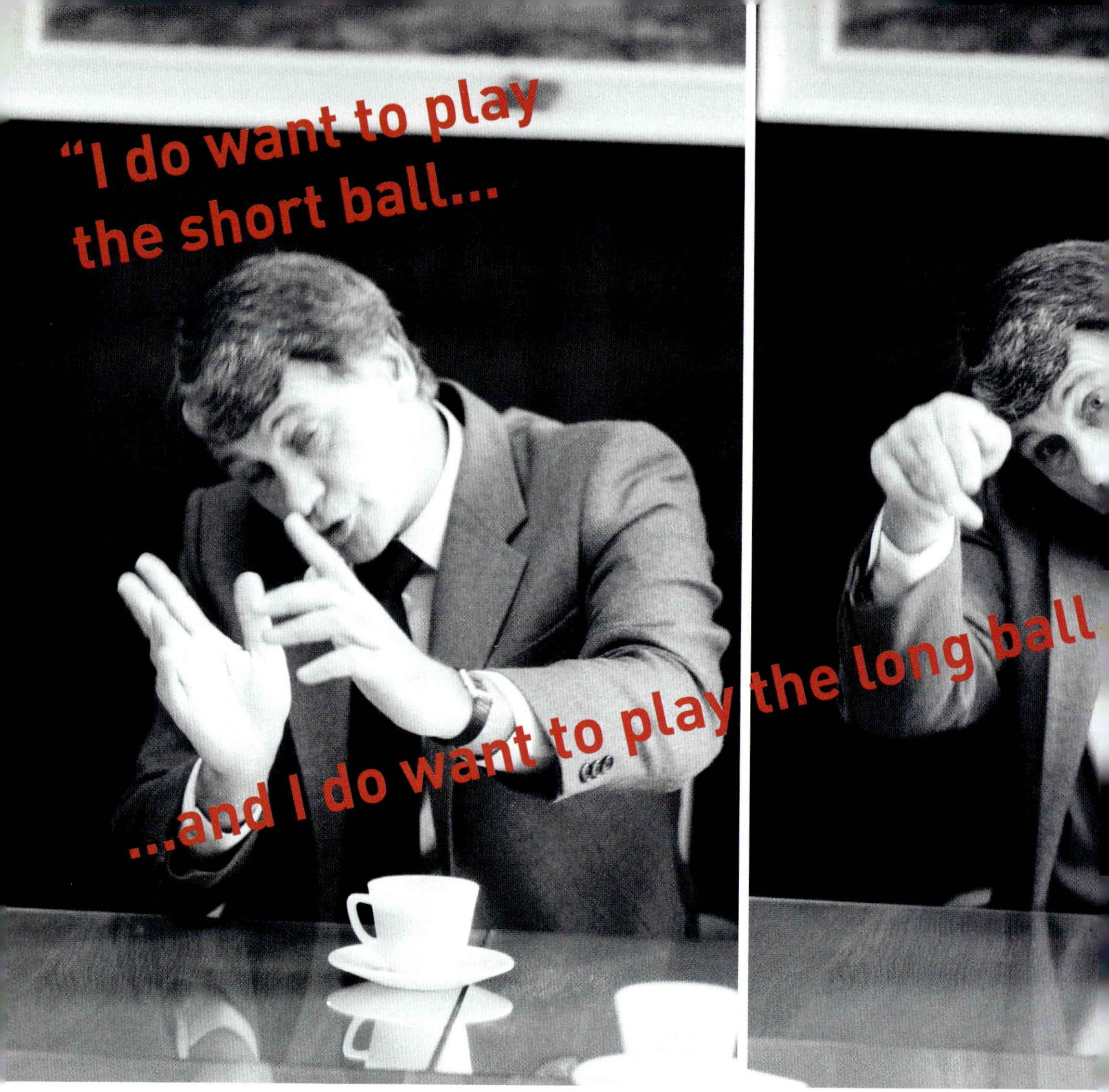
"I do want to play
the short ball...
...and I do want to play the long ball

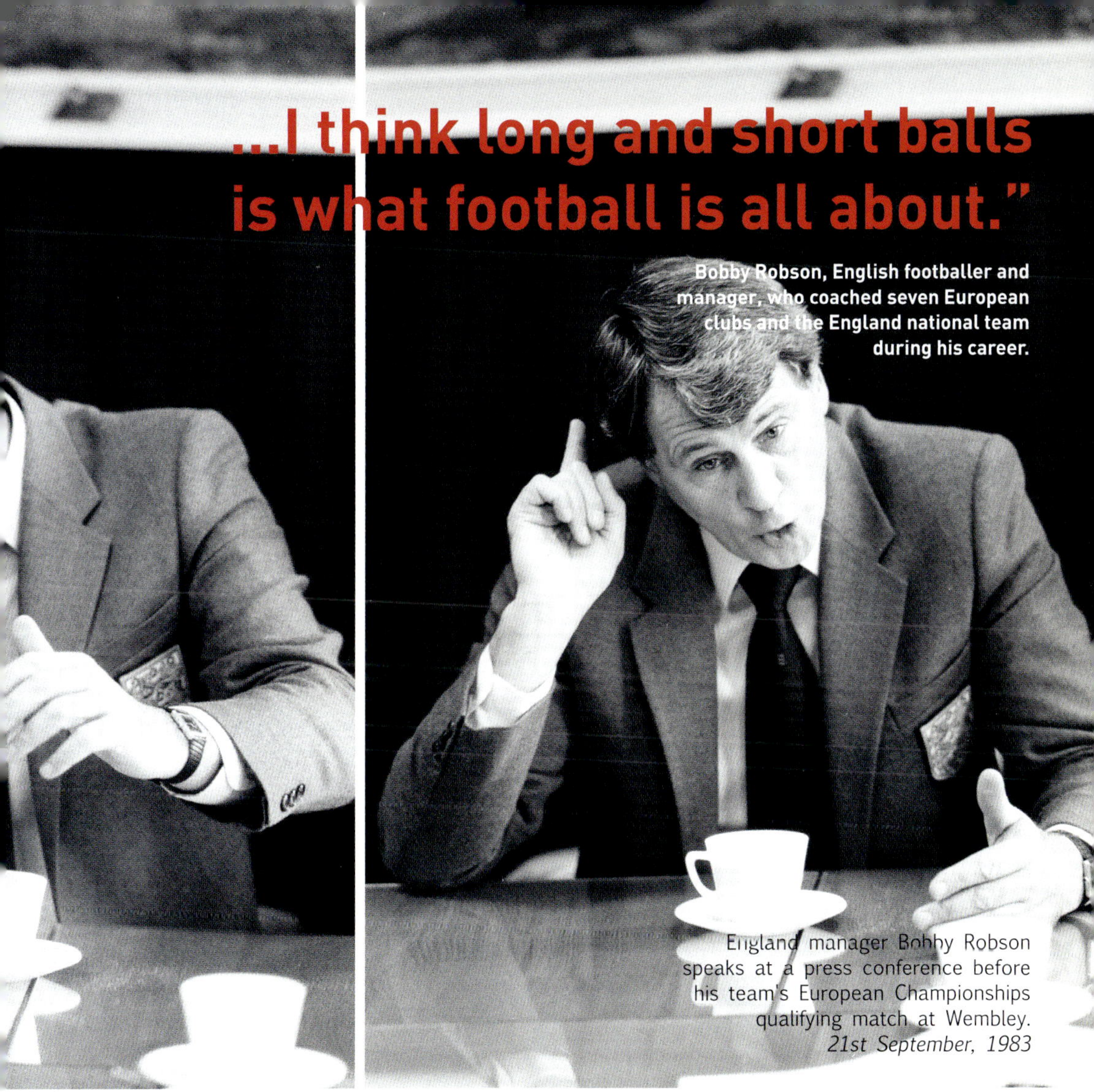

…I think long and short balls is what football is all about.”

Bobby Robson, English footballer and manager, who coached seven European clubs and the England national team during his career.

England manager Bobby Robson speaks at a press conference before his team's European Championships qualifying match at Wembley.
21st September, 1983

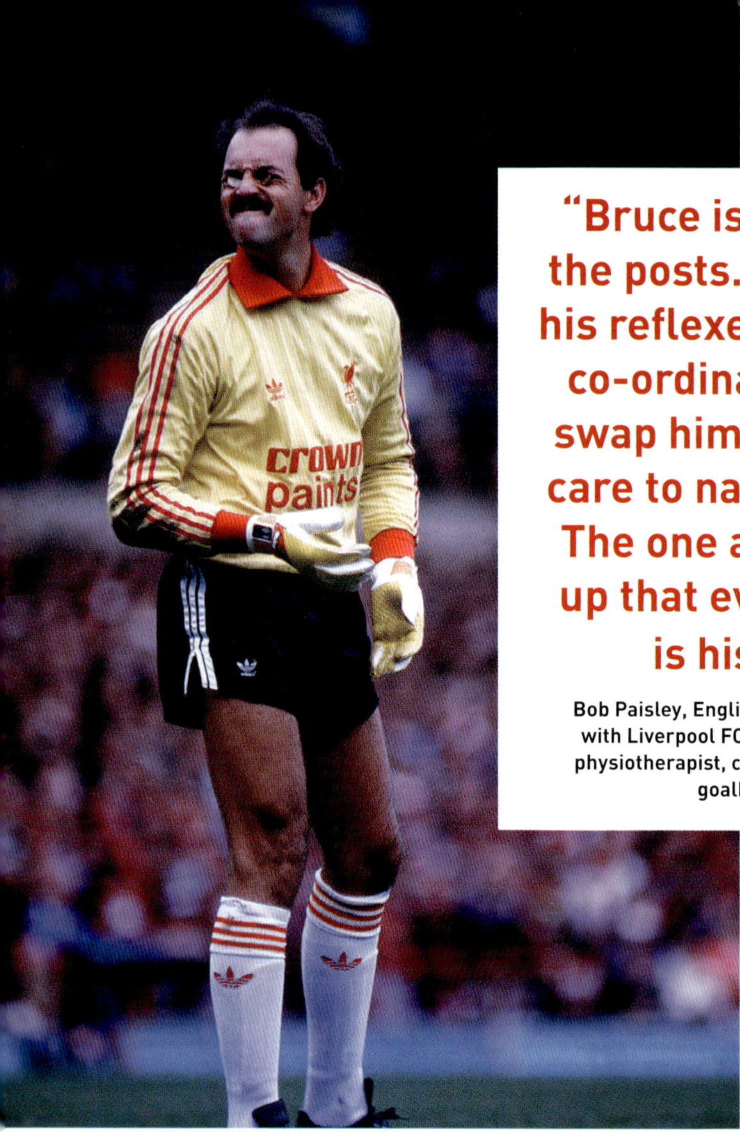

"Bruce is a natural between the posts. When you consider his reflexes, his agility and his co-ordination, you wouldn't swap him for any keeper you care to name past or present. The one aspect of his make-up that everybody questions is his personality."

Bob Paisley, English half-back turned manager, who was with Liverpool FC for almost half a century, as a player, physiotherapist, coach and finally manager, on Liverpool goalkeeper Bruce Grobbelaar.

Bruce Grobbelaar, South African goalkeeper with Liverpool FC, in characteristically eccentric style, fools around during an uninspiring Milk Cup Final between Liverpool and Everton. The final score was 0–0, and the match replayed three days later, with the score 1–0 to Liverpool.
25th March, 1984

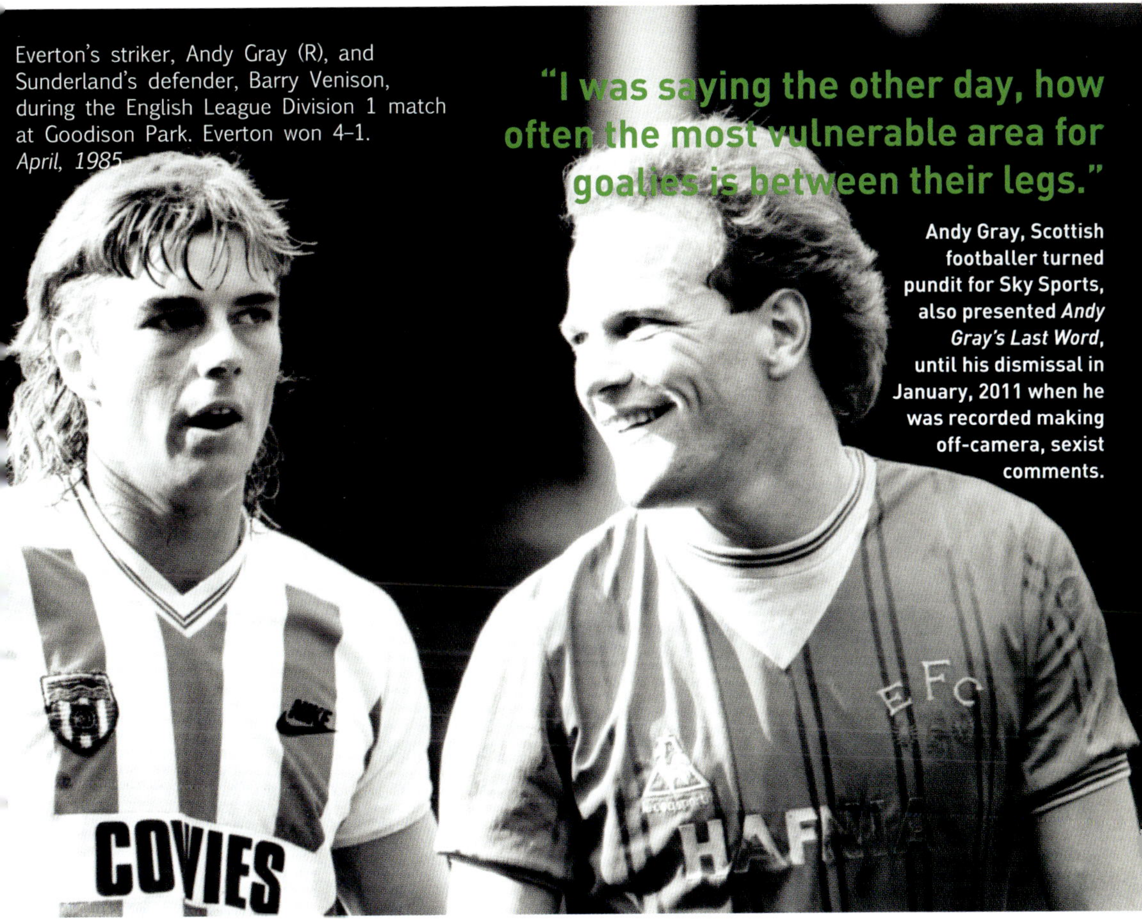

Everton's striker, Andy Gray (R), and Sunderland's defender, Barry Venison, during the English League Division 1 match at Goodison Park. Everton won 4–1. *April, 1985*

"I was saying the other day, how often the most vulnerable area for goalies is between their legs."

Andy Gray, Scottish footballer turned pundit for Sky Sports, also presented *Andy Gray's Last Word*, until his dismissal in January, 2011 when he was recorded making off-camera, sexist comments.

"I always used to put my right boot on first, and then obviously my right sock."

Barry Venison, English footballer from 1981 to 1997, later a TV pundit, on footballers' superstitions.

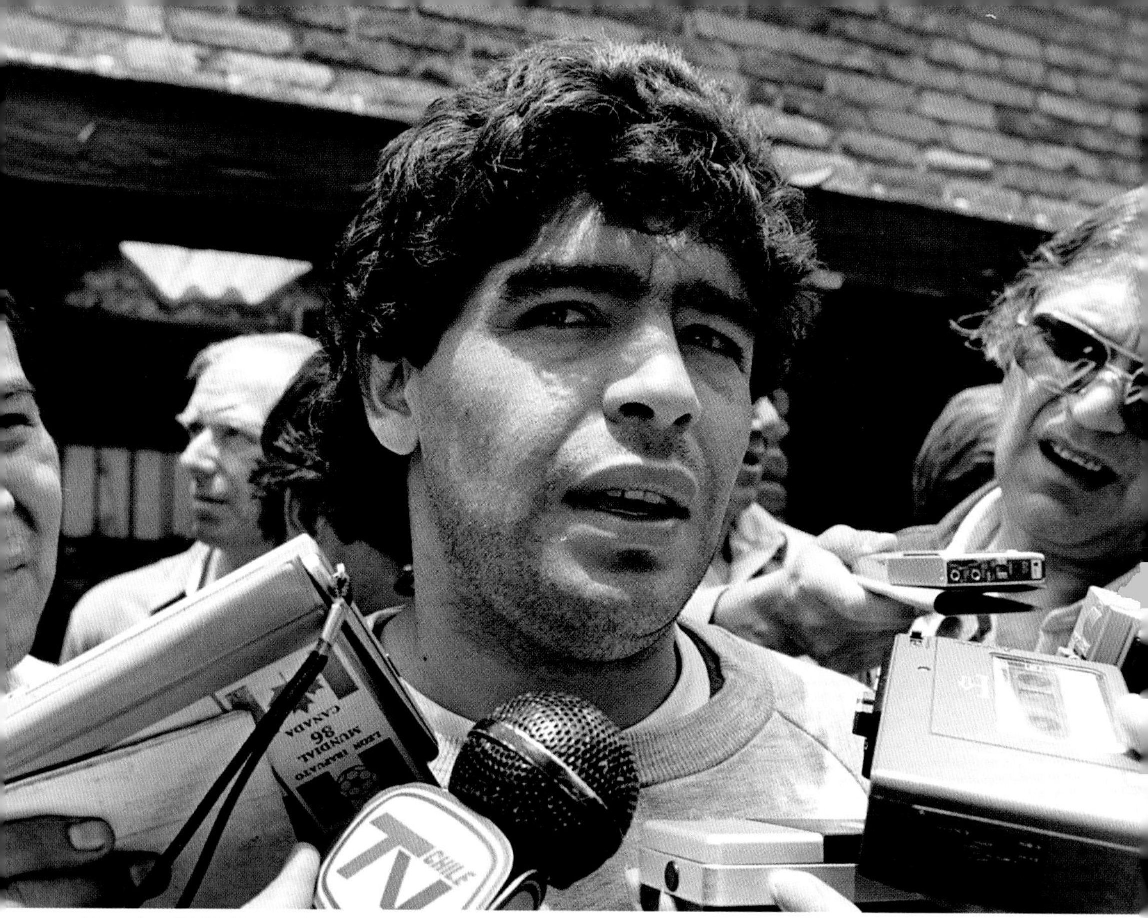

After the 1986 World Cup match between Argentina and England, Argentinian footballer Diego Maradona talks to the press about the controversial goal, scored after 51 minutes. The diminutive Maradona had beaten 6ft 1in-tall England goalkeeper Peter Shilton to the ball, sending it into the goal with the outside of his left fist – an unpenalised handball that became known as the 'Hand of God'. After video footage later confirmed the infringement, England manager Bobby Robson commented that the goal had been scored by "the hand of a rascal."

"The goal was scored a little by the head of Maradona,

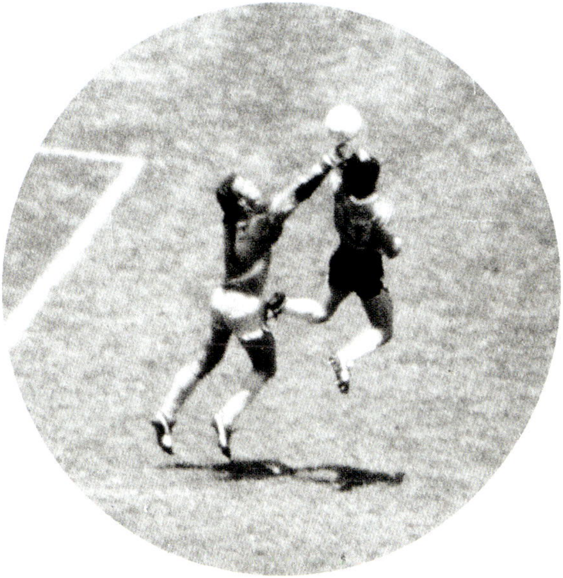

and a little by the hand of God."

Diego Maradona.

Fifty-one minutes into the already controversial match, Maradona skilfully dribbled the ball past six England players – Beardsley, Reid, Butcher, Fenwick, Butcher (again) and finally goalkeeper Peter Shilton – resulting in a second and winning goal for Argentina, who went on to win the World Cup with a victory over West Germany in the final.

"An inch or two either side of the post and that would have been a goal."

Dave Bassett, English manager and former football player, who managed eight teams between 1981 and 2008.

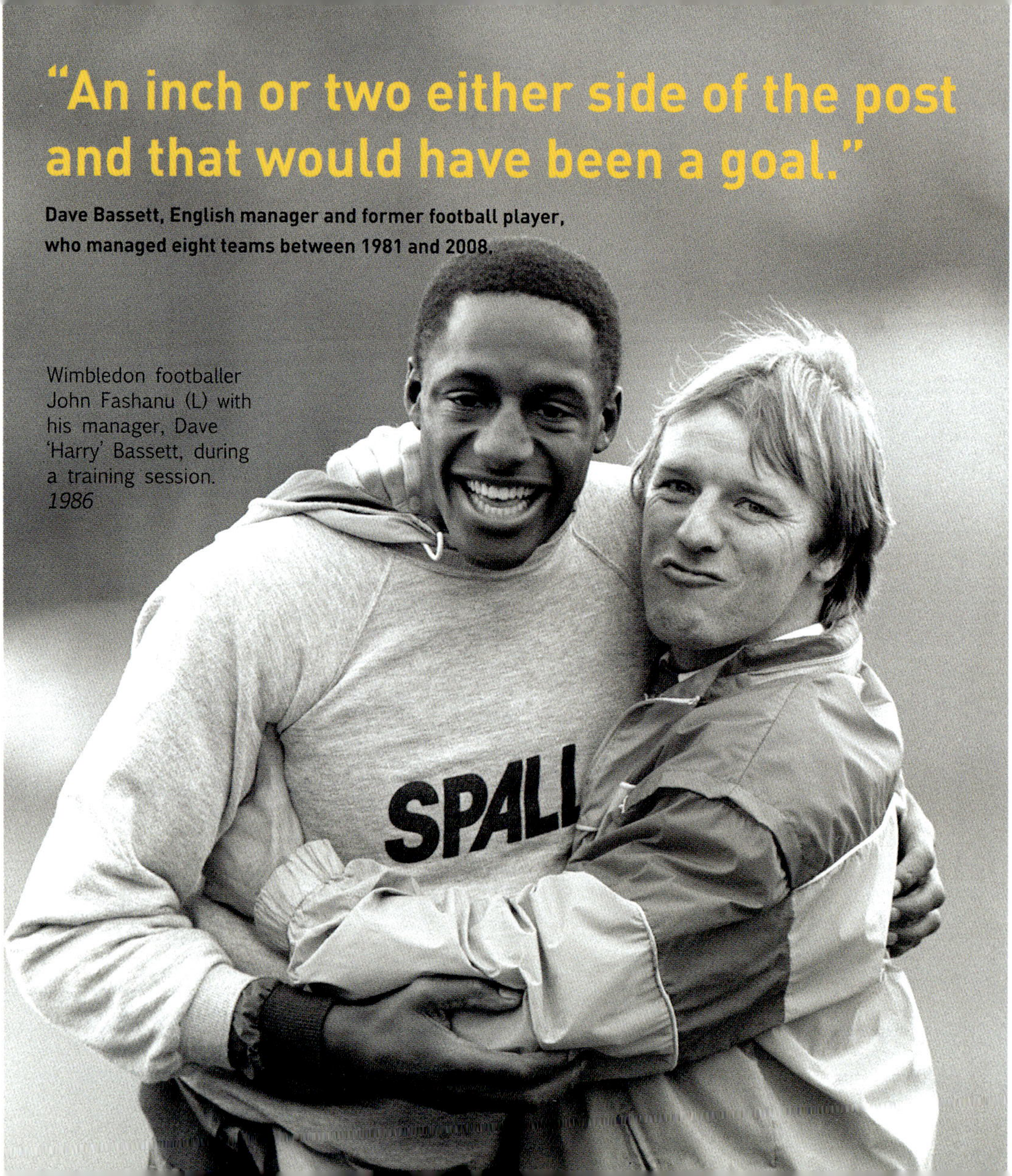

Wimbledon footballer John Fashanu (L) with his manager, Dave 'Harry' Bassett, during a training session.
1986

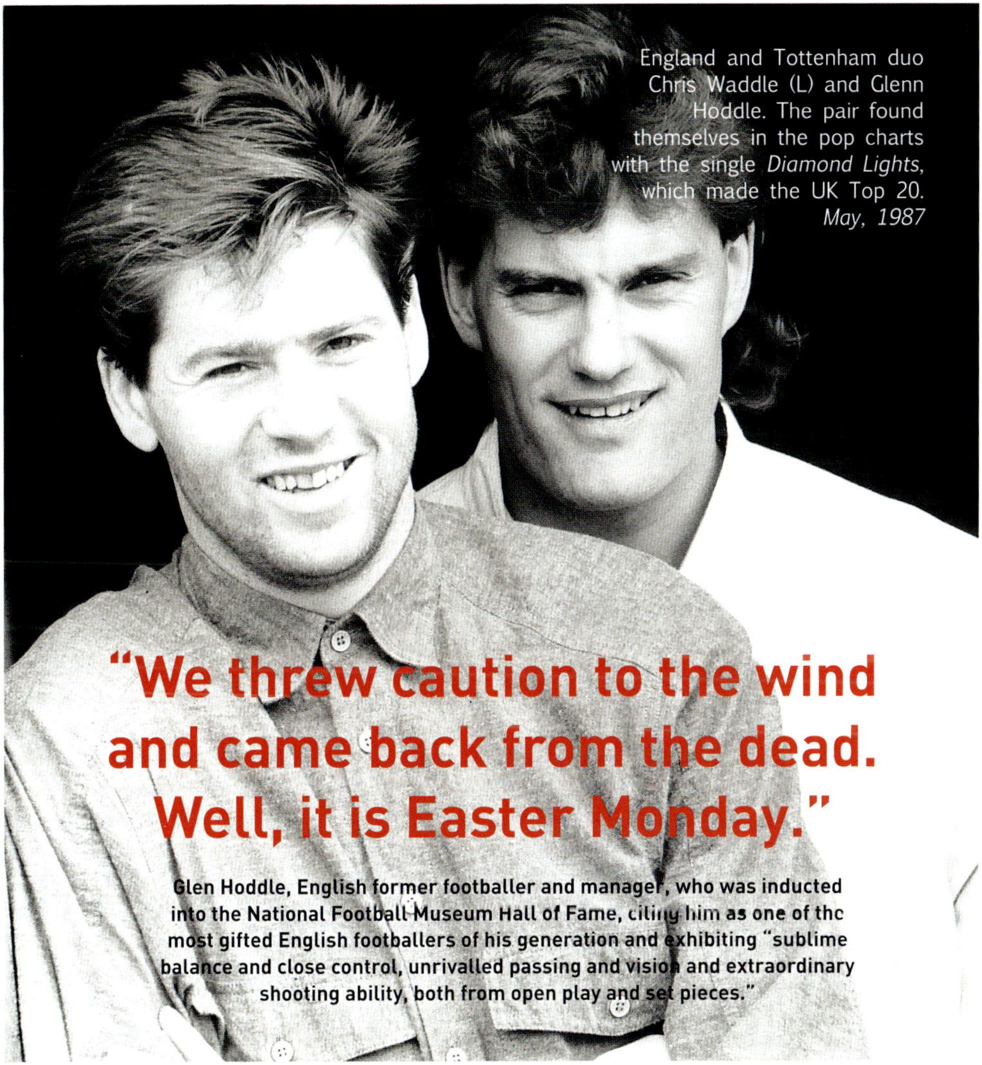

England and Tottenham duo Chris Waddle (L) and Glenn Hoddle. The pair found themselves in the pop charts with the single *Diamond Lights*, which made the UK Top 20. *May, 1987*

"We threw caution to the wind and came back from the dead. Well, it is Easter Monday."

Glen Hoddle, English former footballer and manager, who was inducted into the National Football Museum Hall of Fame, citing him as one of the most gifted English footballers of his generation and exhibiting "sublime balance and close control, unrivalled passing and vision and extraordinary shooting ability, both from open play and set pieces."

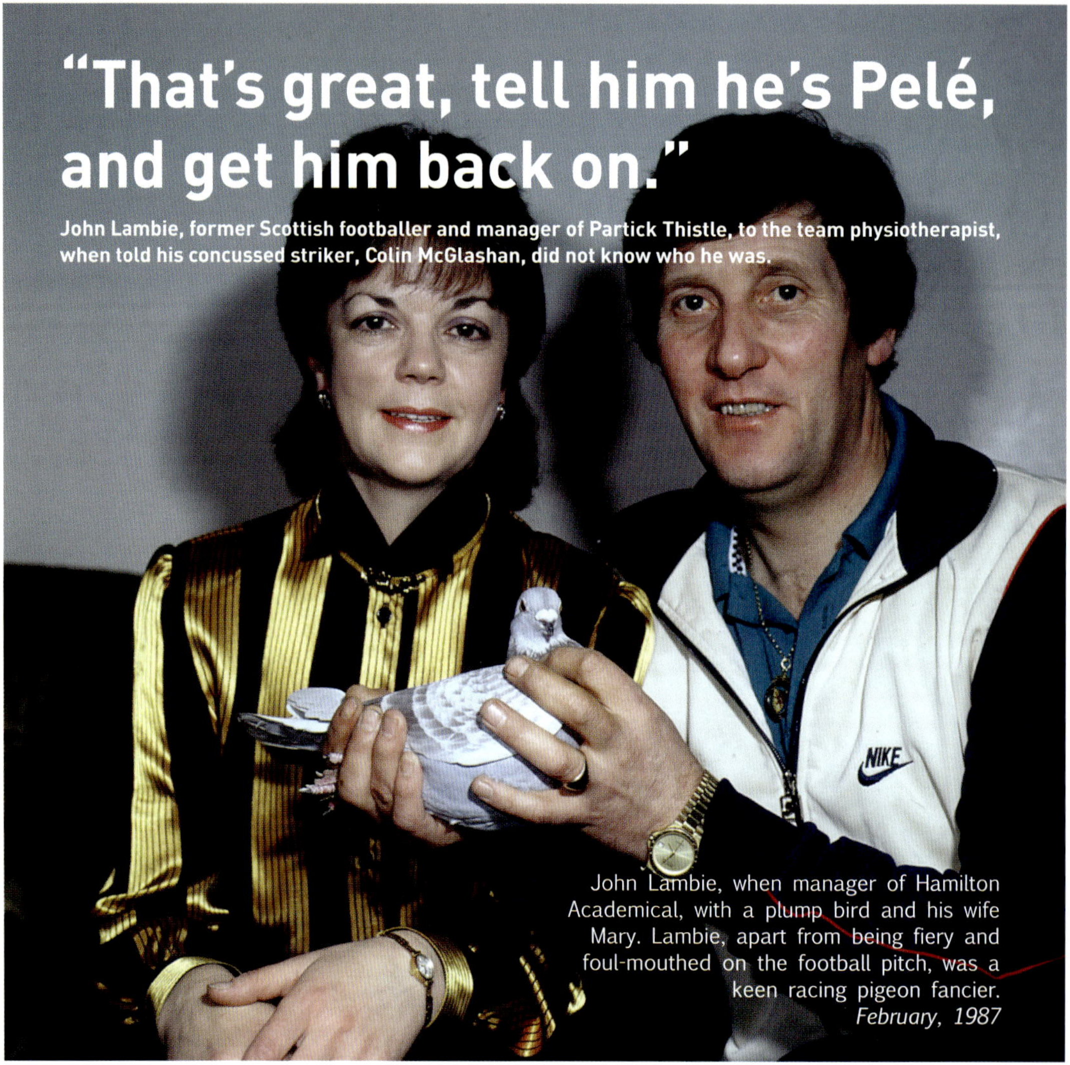

"That's great, tell him he's Pelé, and get him back on."

John Lambie, former Scottish footballer and manager of Partick Thistle, to the team physiotherapist, when told his concussed striker, Colin McGlashan, did not know who he was.

John Lambie, when manager of Hamilton Academical, with a plump bird and his wife Mary. Lambie, apart from being fiery and foul-mouthed on the football pitch, was a keen racing pigeon fancier.
February, 1987

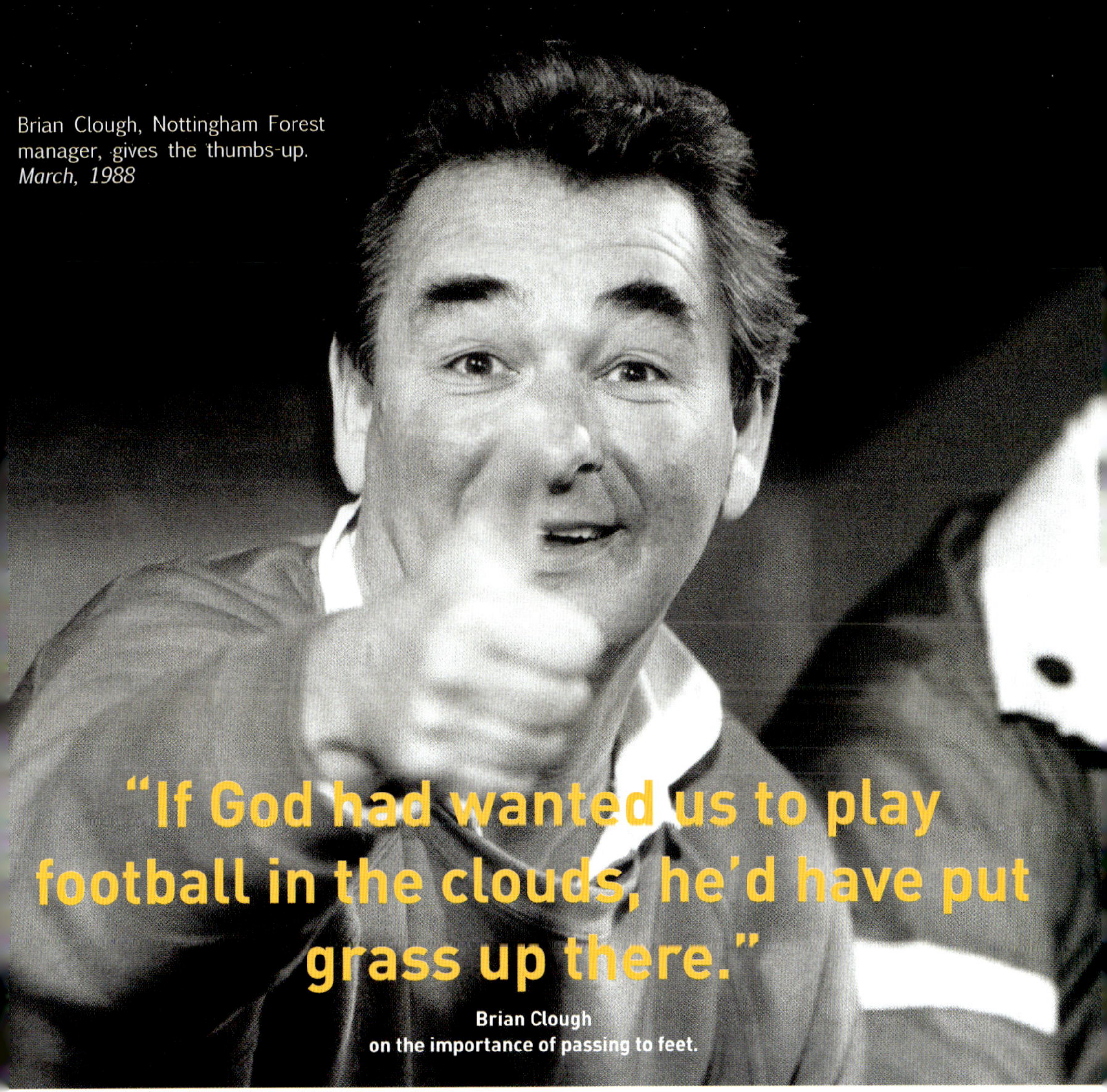

Brian Clough, Nottingham Forest manager, gives the thumbs-up. *March, 1988*

"If God had wanted us to play football in the clouds, he'd have put grass up there."

Brian Clough
on the importance of passing to feet.

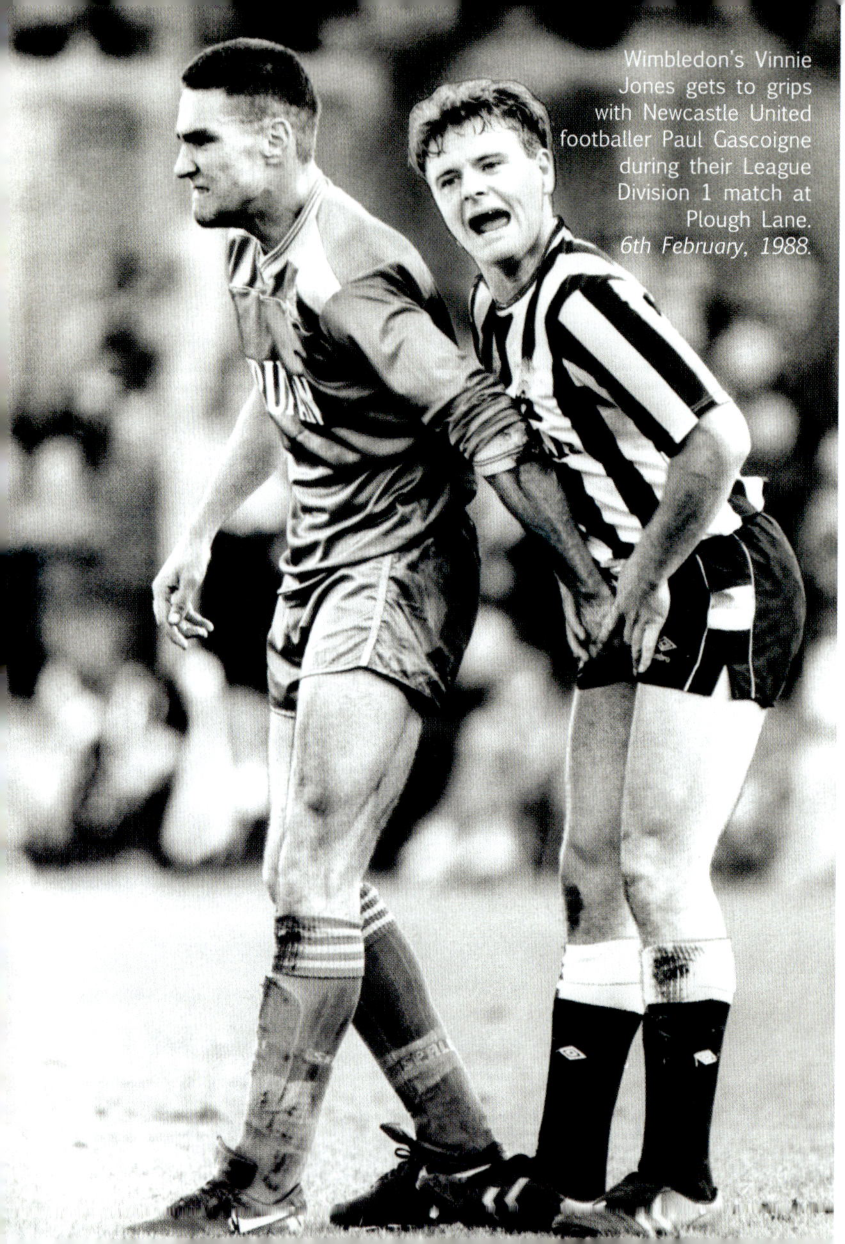

Wimbledon's Vinnie Jones gets to grips with Newcastle United footballer Paul Gascoigne during their League Division 1 match at Plough Lane. *6th February, 1988.*

"The FA have given me a pat on the back. I've taken violence off the terracing and on to the pitch."

Vinnie Jones, English actor and former Welsh footballer, renowned for his tough-guy image, intimidating demeanour and aggressive style, after a 1992 suspension and fine for bringing the game into disrepute through his participation in the video *Soccer's Hard Men*.

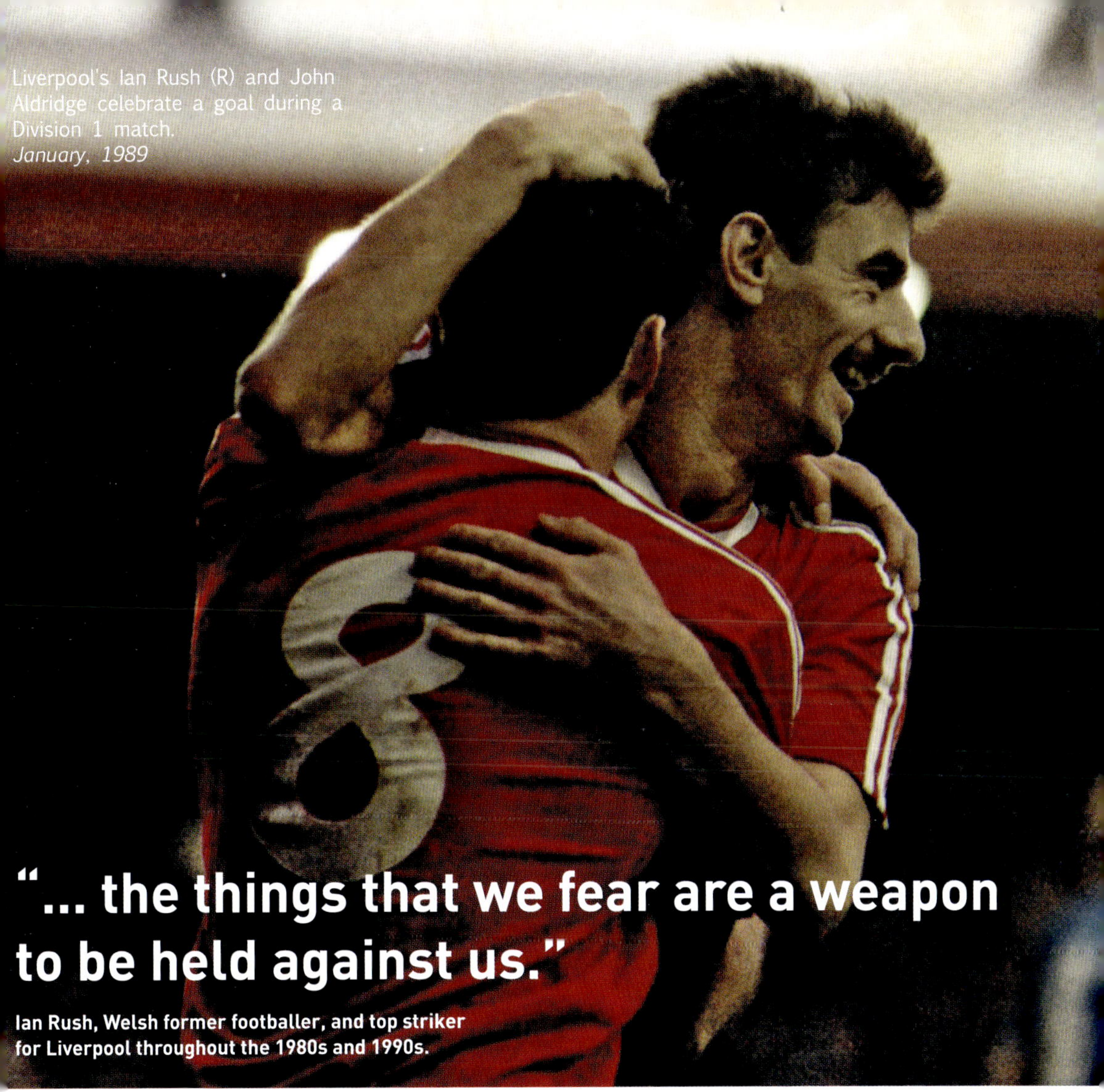

Liverpool's Ian Rush (R) and John Aldridge celebrate a goal during a Division 1 match.
January, 1989

"... the things that we fear are a weapon to be held against us."

Ian Rush, Welsh former footballer, and top striker for Liverpool throughout the 1980s and 1990s.

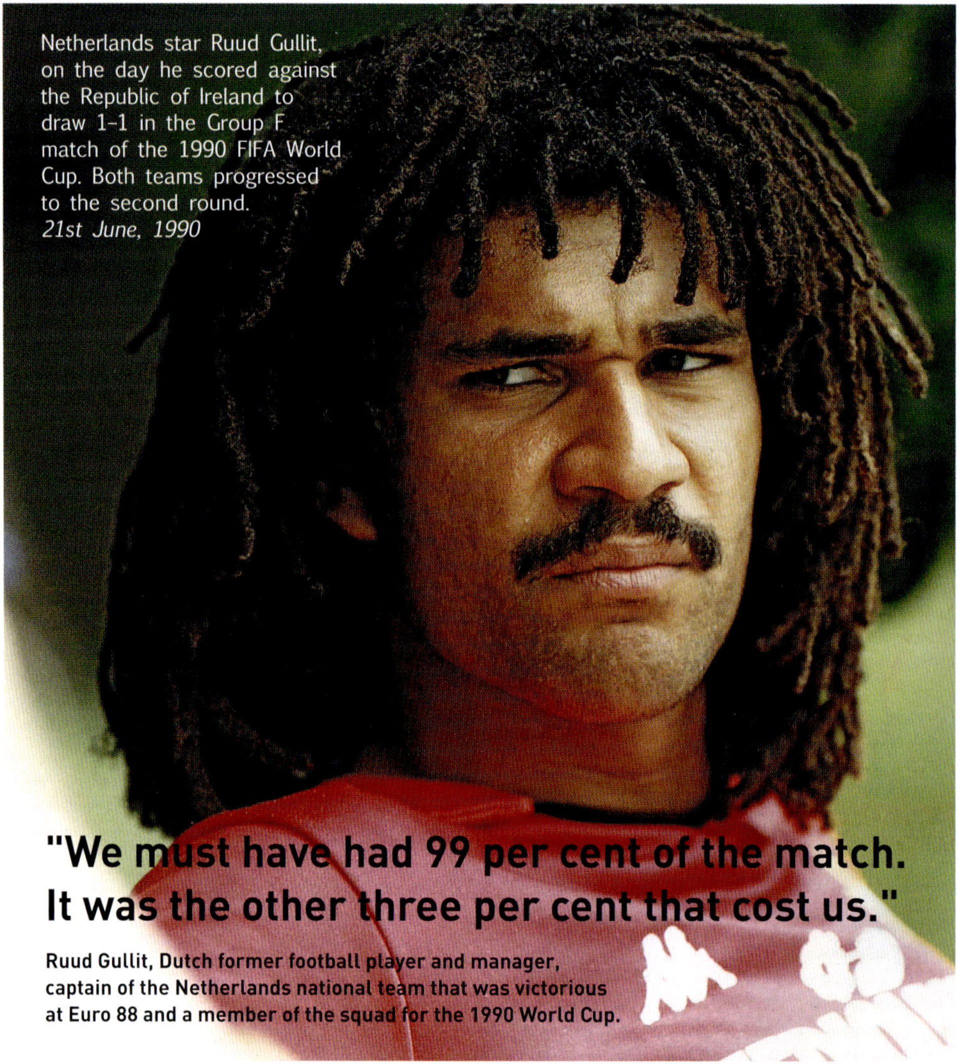

Netherlands star Ruud Gullit, on the day he scored against the Republic of Ireland to draw 1-1 in the Group F match of the 1990 FIFA World Cup. Both teams progressed to the second round.
21st June, 1990

"We must have had 99 per cent of the match. It was the other three per cent that cost us."

Ruud Gullit, Dutch former football player and manager, captain of the Netherlands national team that was victorious at Euro 88 and a member of the squad for the 1990 World Cup.

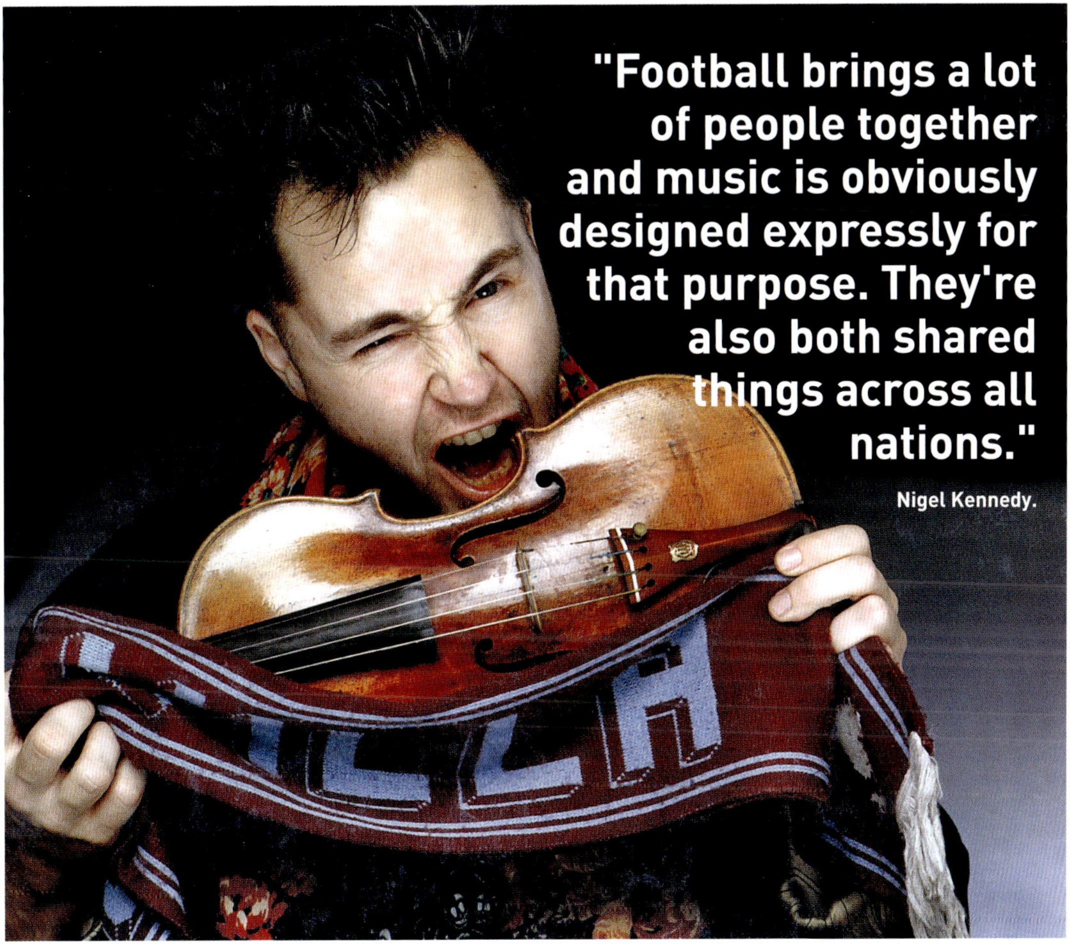

Violinist Nigel Kennedy, child prodigy and former pupil at the Yehudi Menuhin School of Music, famed for his virtuoso interpretations of classical music, who includes jazz, klezmer and rock in his repertoire, is also a devoted fan of football, supporting Aston Villa FC.

13th December, 1989

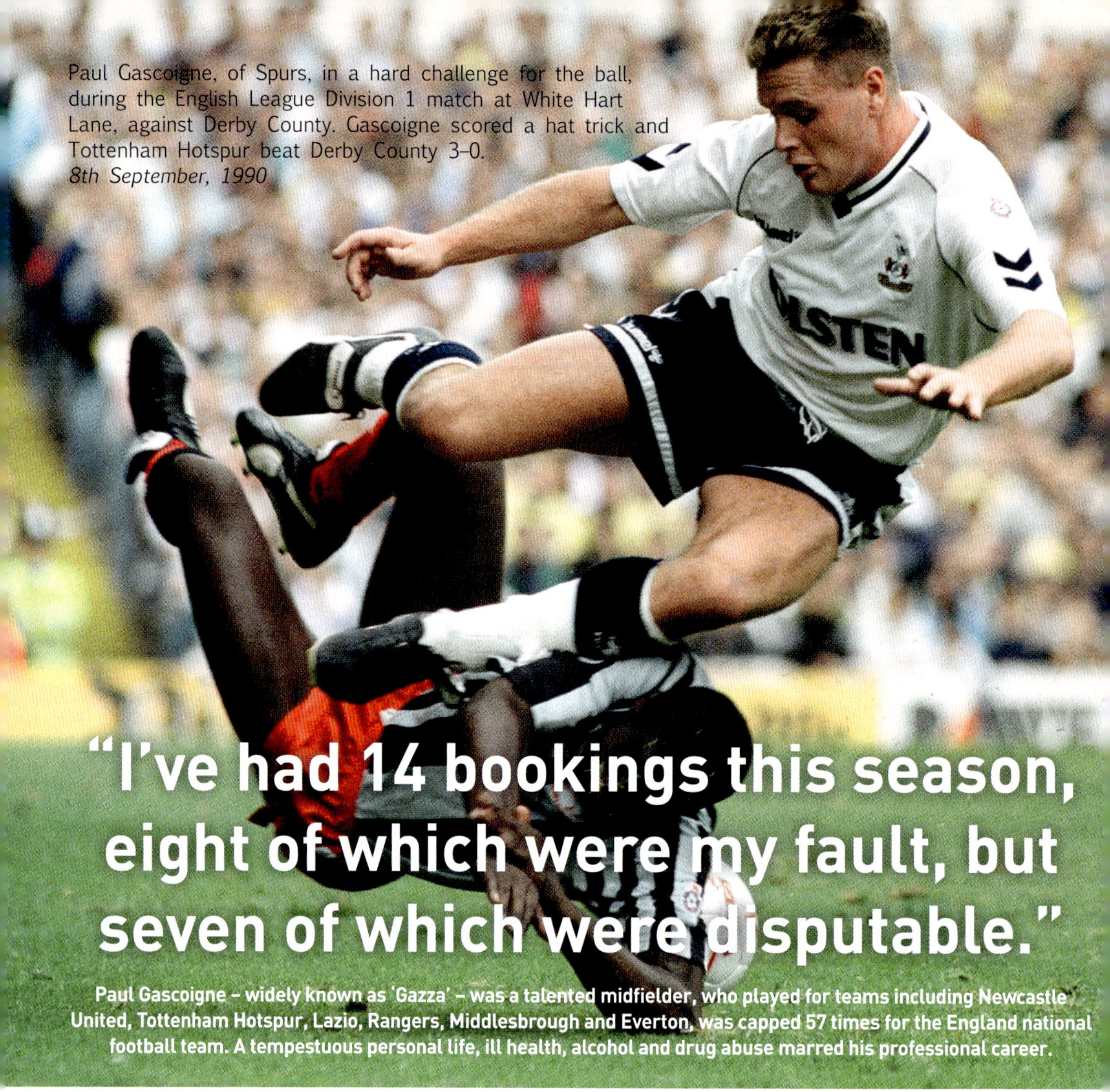

Paul Gascoigne, of Spurs, in a hard challenge for the ball, during the English League Division 1 match at White Hart Lane, against Derby County. Gascoigne scored a hat trick and Tottenham Hotspur beat Derby County 3–0.
8th September, 1990

"I've had 14 bookings this season, eight of which were my fault, but seven of which were disputable."

Paul Gascoigne – widely known as 'Gazza' – was a talented midfielder, who played for teams including Newcastle United, Tottenham Hotspur, Lazio, Rangers, Middlesbrough and Everton, was capped 57 times for the England national football team. A tempestuous personal life, ill health, alcohol and drug abuse marred his professional career.

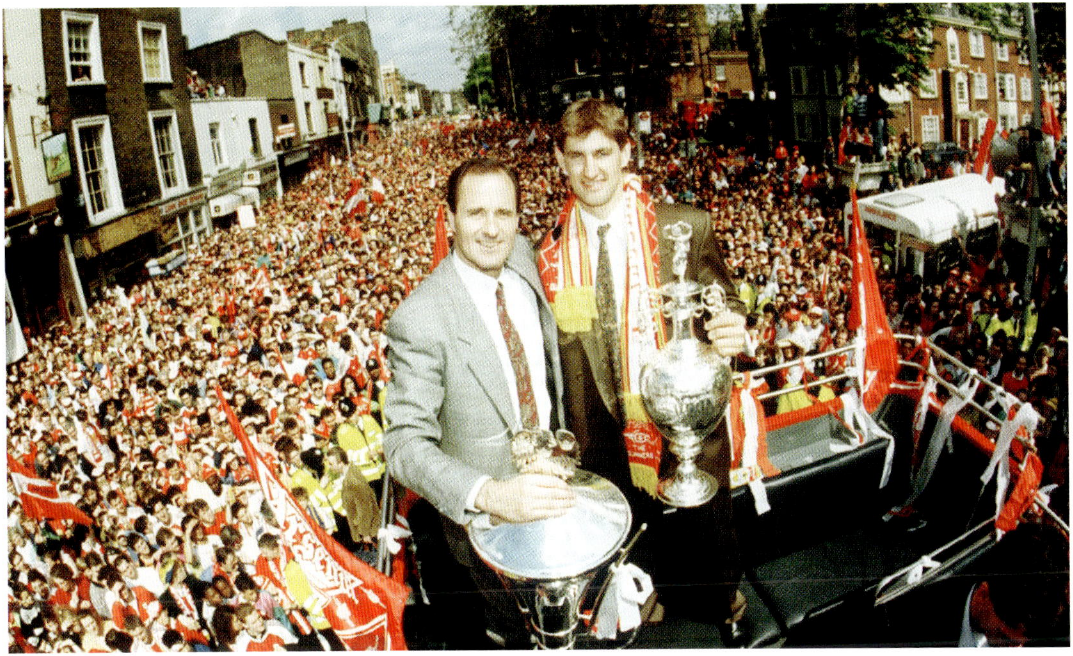

Arsenal manager George Graham (L) and captain Tony Adams show off the League Championship trophy to thousands of fans gathered in the streets of North London for the team's open-top bus parade. 'Graham's Gunners' clinched the league title on 6th May, 1991 without kicking a ball, after Liverpool were defeated by Nottingham Forest at lunchtime. Arsenal's evening match against Manchester United was academic, although the Gunners won by a respectable 3–1, with Alan Smith taking the Golden Boot.
13th May, 1991

"The goalkeeper is the jewel in the crown and getting at him should be almost impossible. It's the biggest sin in football to make him do any work."

George Graham, Scottish former footballer and manager of Arsenal 1986–1995.

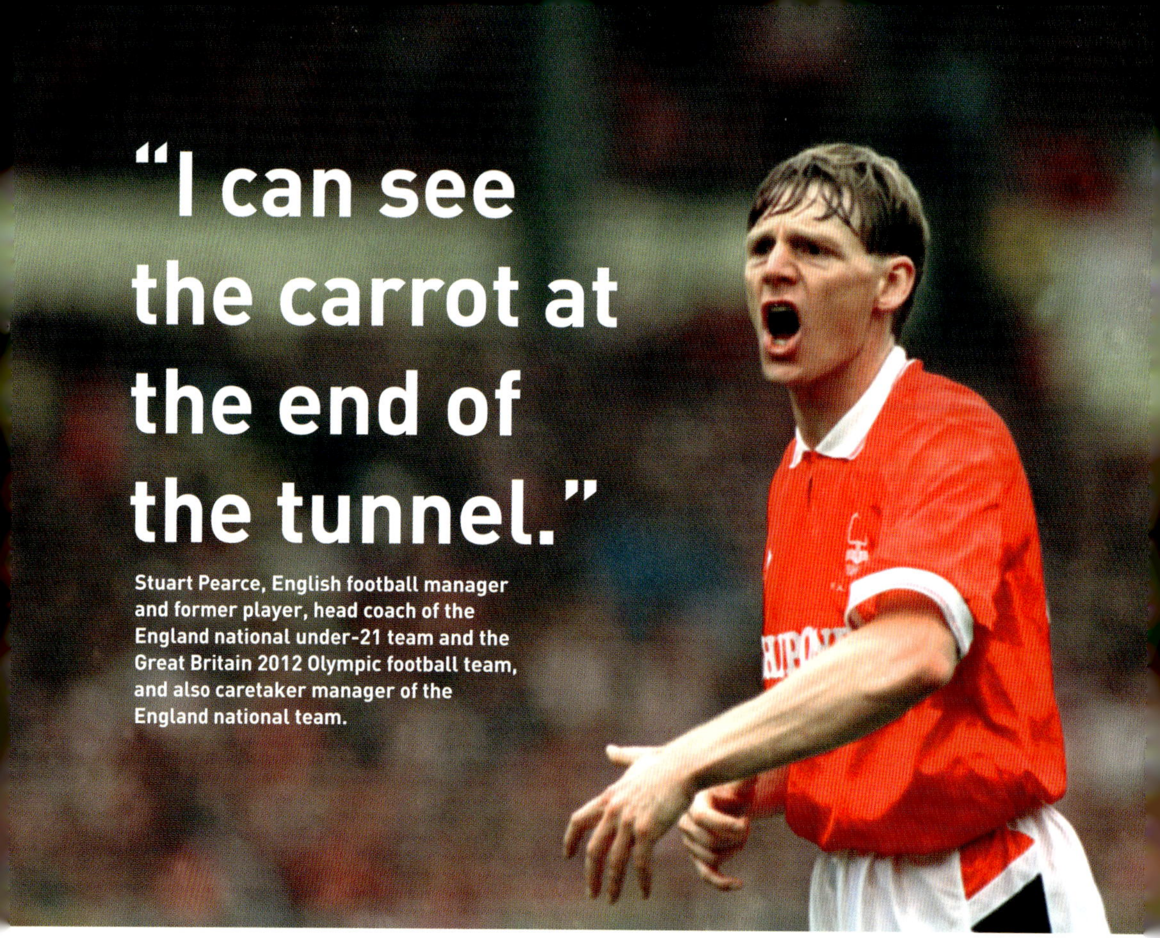

"I can see the carrot at the end of the tunnel."

Stuart Pearce, English football manager and former player, head coach of the England national under-21 team and the Great Britain 2012 Olympic football team, and also caretaker manager of the England national team.

Stuart Pearce, Nottingham Forest player captain, shouts instructions to team-mates during the FA Cup Final against Tottenham Hotspur, at Wembley Stadium. Despite his efforts, Spurs won this 110th Cup Final for a then-record eighth time, by beating Forest 2–1.
18th May, 1991

"Geoff Hurst had a hammer in his left boot and good left feet are like bricks of gold."

Jimmy Greaves.

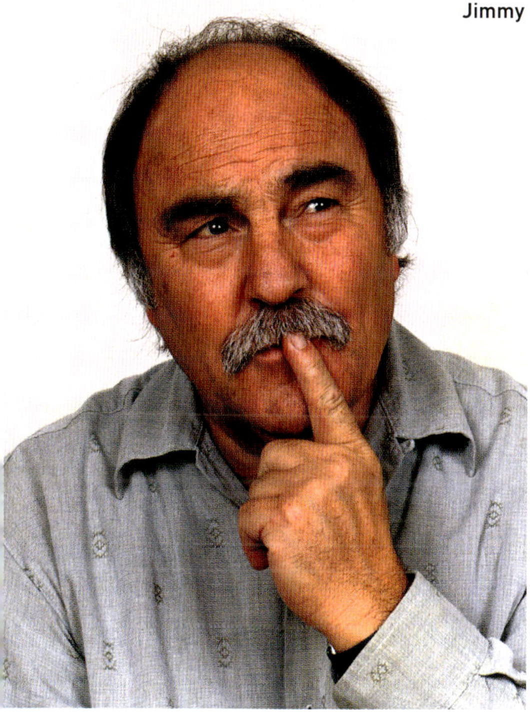

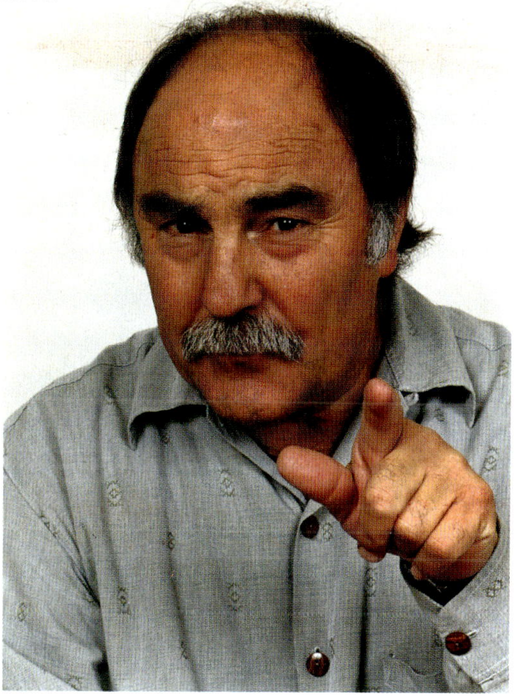

No laughing matter. Jimmy Greaves, former striker, represented England 57 times, scoring 44 goals; scored 124 goals in 157 appearances for Chelsea; 220 goals in 321 appearances for Tottenham Hotspur; remains the highest goal scorer in the history of English top-flight football, is now known as a TV pundit, famous for his catchphrase "It's a funny old game."

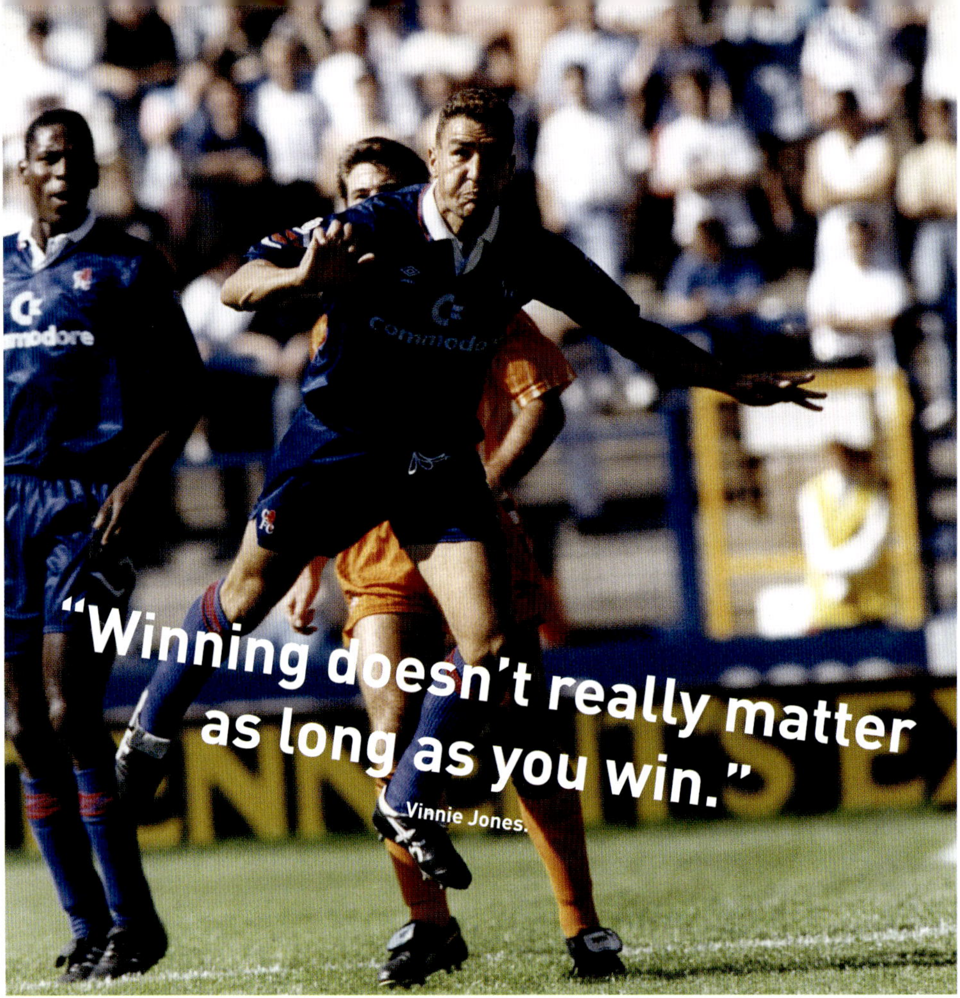

Full of hot air? Airborne Vinnie Jones plays for Chelsea against Luton Town in a League Division 1 match, which saw his team triumph 4–1.
31st August, 1991

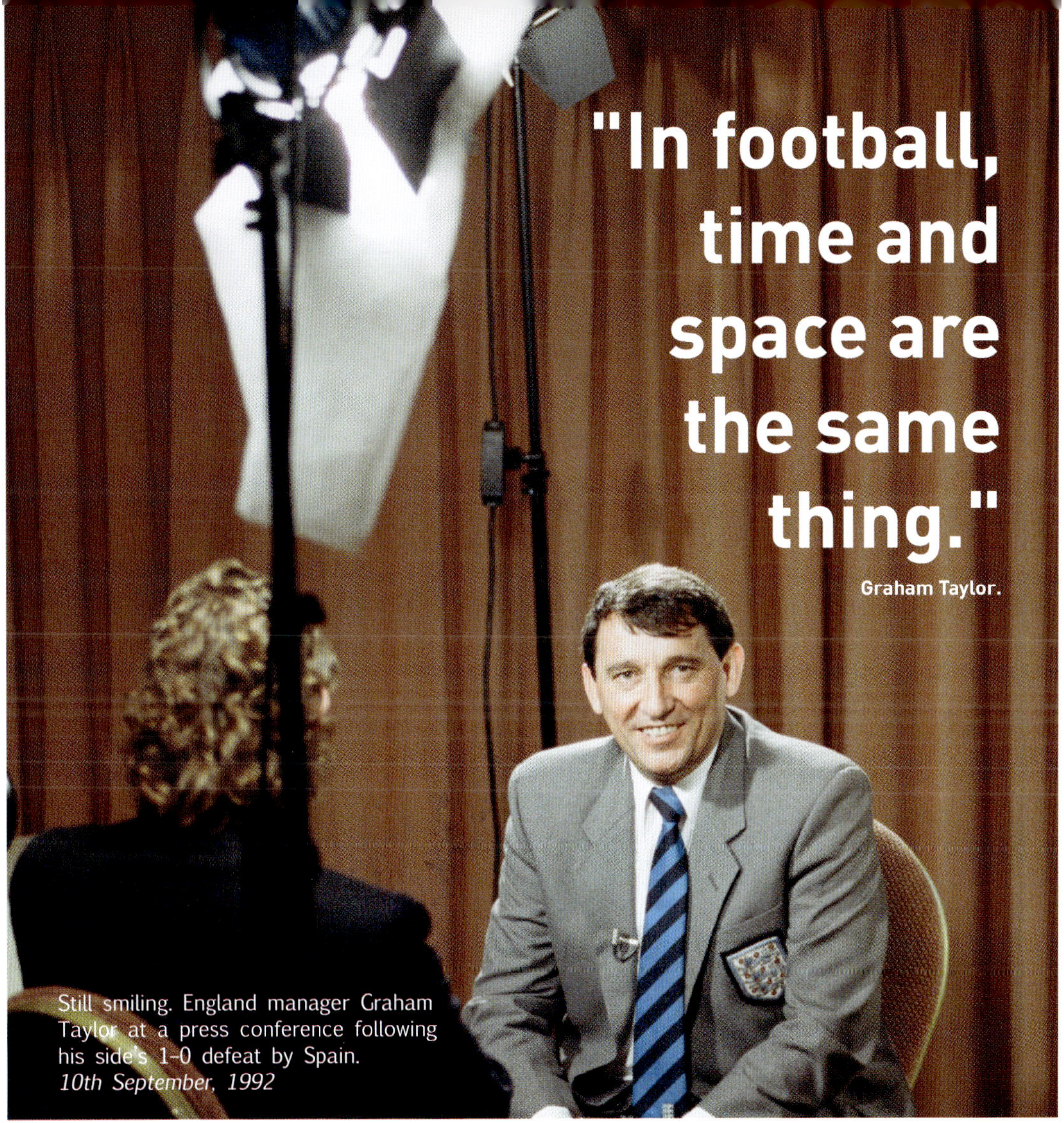

"In football, time and space are the same thing."

Graham Taylor.

Still smiling. England manager Graham Taylor at a press conference following his side's 1-0 defeat by Spain.
10th September, 1992

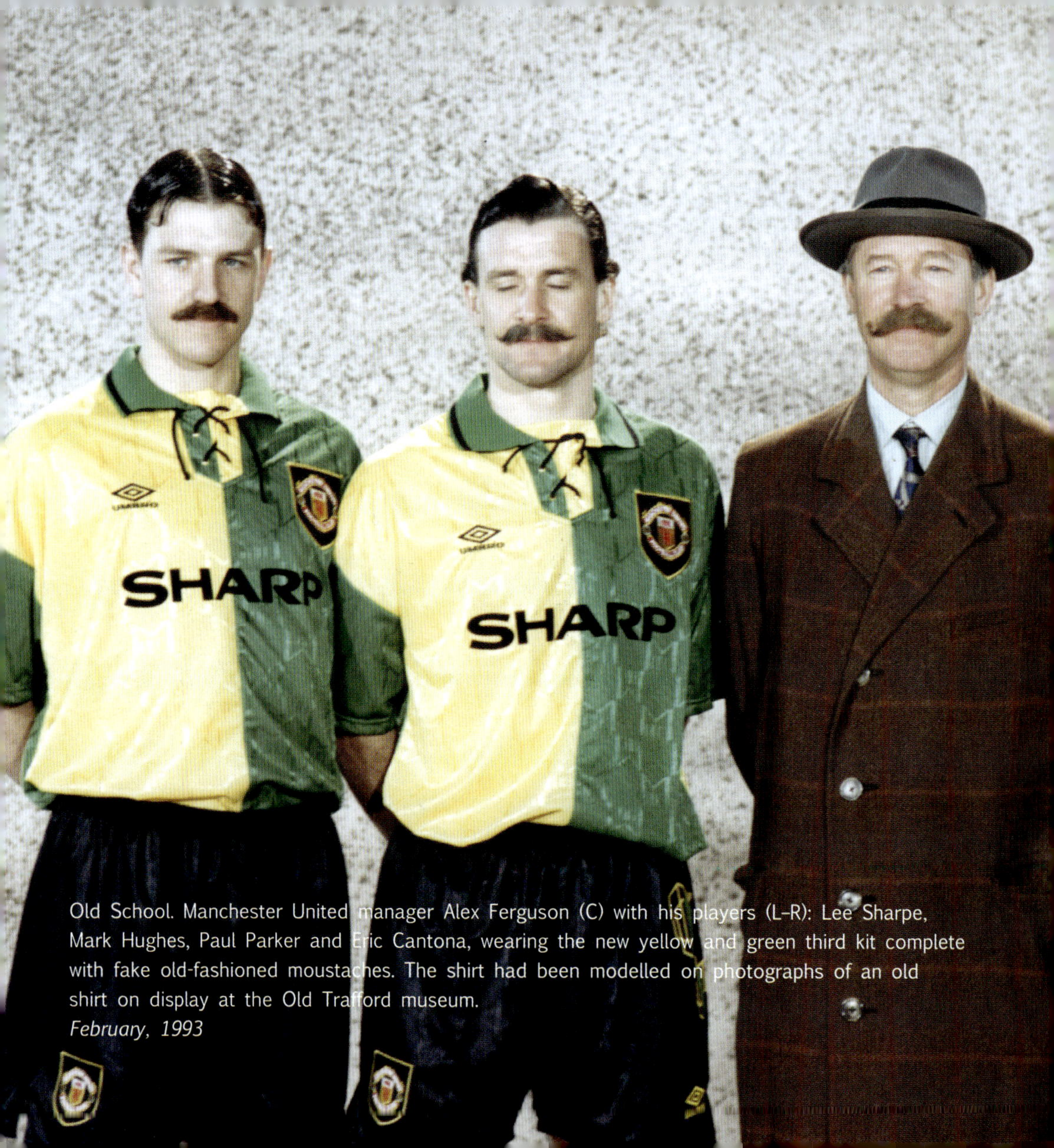

Old School. Manchester United manager Alex Ferguson (C) with his players (L–R): Lee Sharpe, Mark Hughes, Paul Parker and Eric Cantona, wearing the new yellow and green third kit complete with fake old-fashioned moustaches. The shirt had been modelled on photographs of an old shirt on display at the Old Trafford museum.
February, 1993

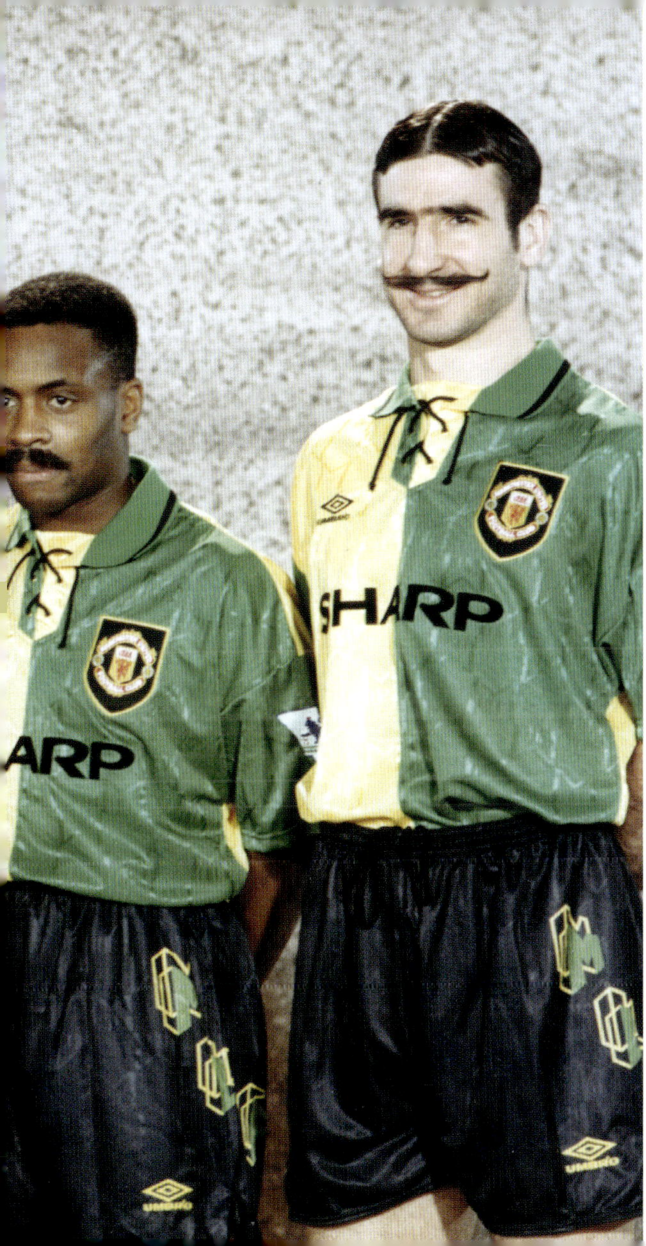

To say that these men paid their shillings to watch twenty-two hirelings kick a ball is merely to say that a violin is wood and catgut, that Hamlet is so much paper and ink.

J.B. Priestley, English novelist, playwright and broadcaster, in *The Good Companions.*

“Bobby Charlton had gifts to die for. He was basically a quiet man whose talking came from the magic of his boots. Wherever you went in the world the foreign football fans knew everything about Bobby Charlton. He was our Pelé.”

Alan Ball.

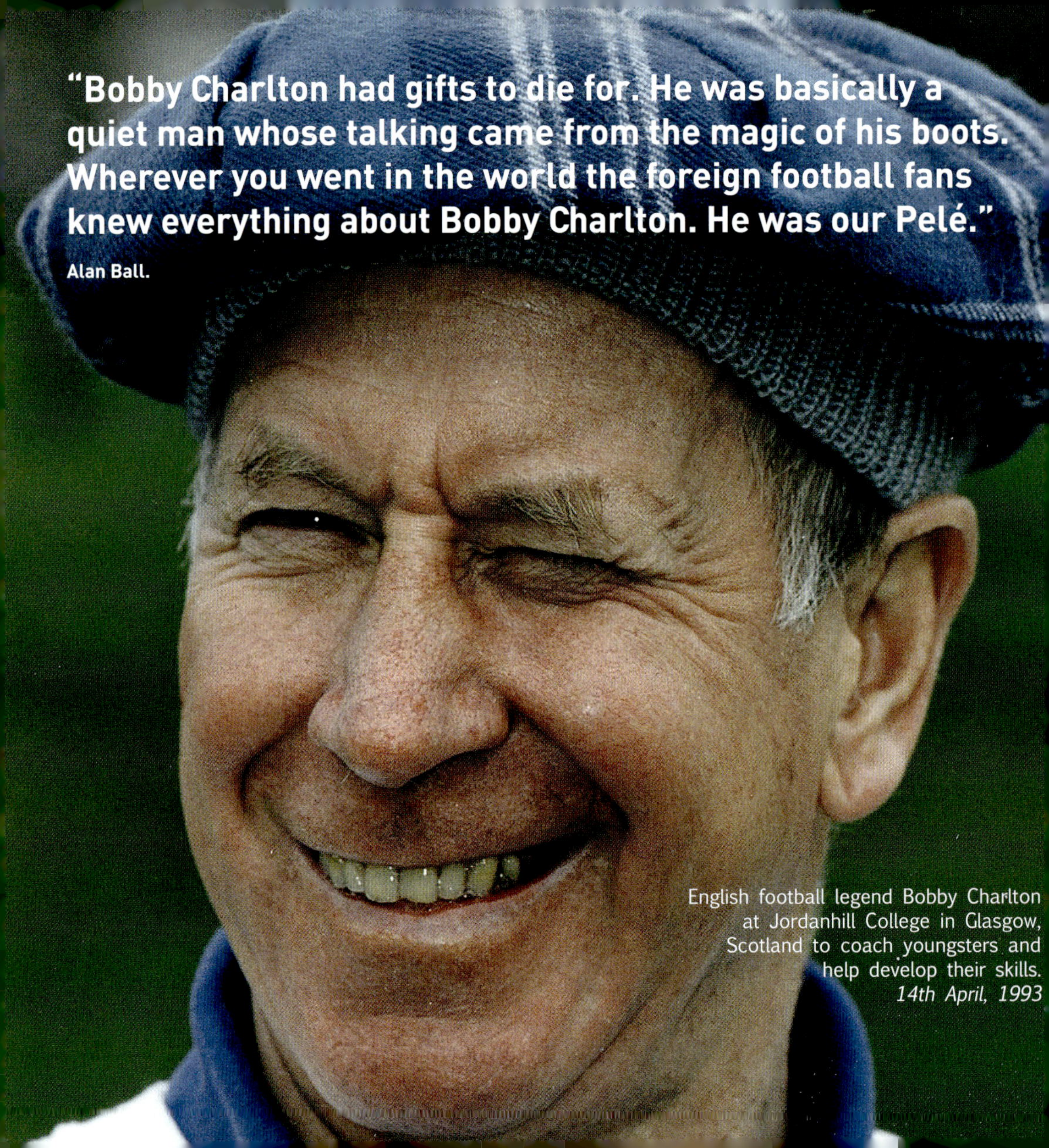

English football legend Bobby Charlton at Jordanhill College in Glasgow, Scotland to coach youngsters and help develop their skills.
14th April, 1993

"You've got to take the rough with the smooth. It's like love and hate, war and peace, all that bollocks."

Ian Wright, English footballer and TV personality, who made 93 appearances for England, played 581 league games and scored 387 goals.

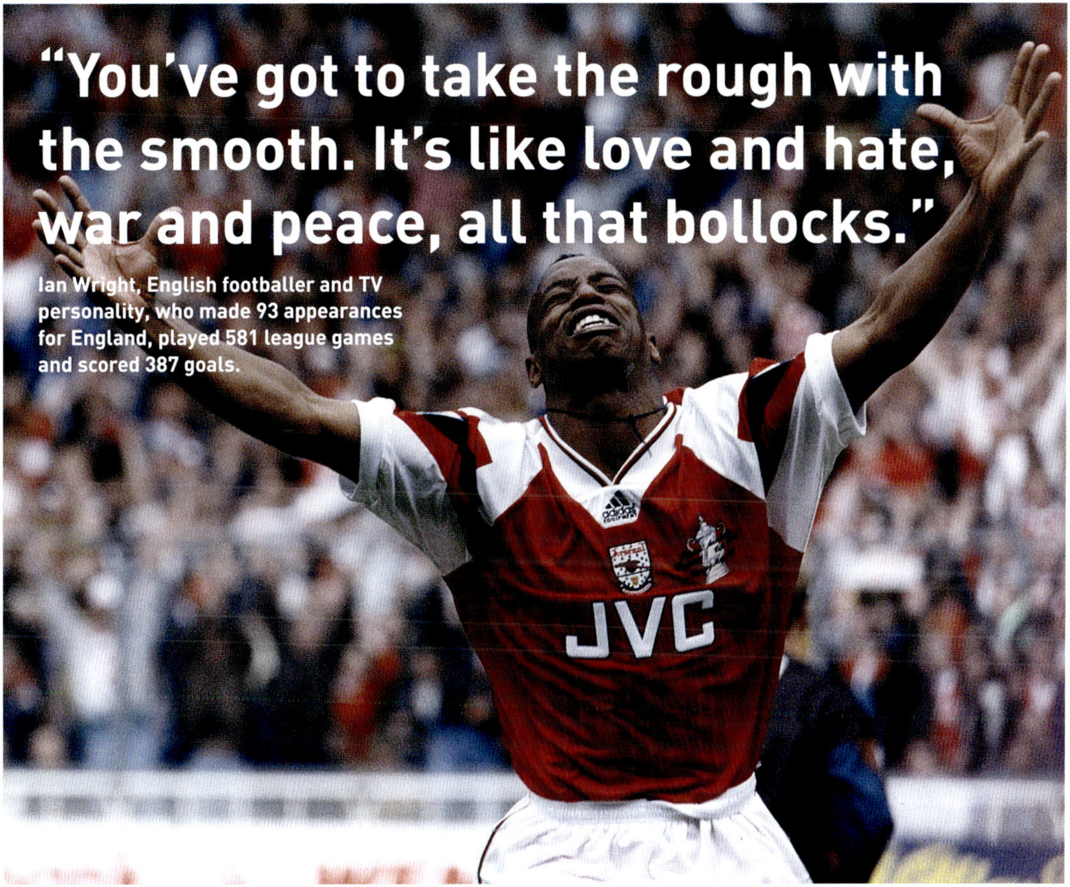

Arsenal's Ian Wright celebrates after scoring a goal in the FA Cup Final Replay at Wembley Stadium.
The final score was Arsenal 2 Sheffield Wednesday 1.
20th May, 1993

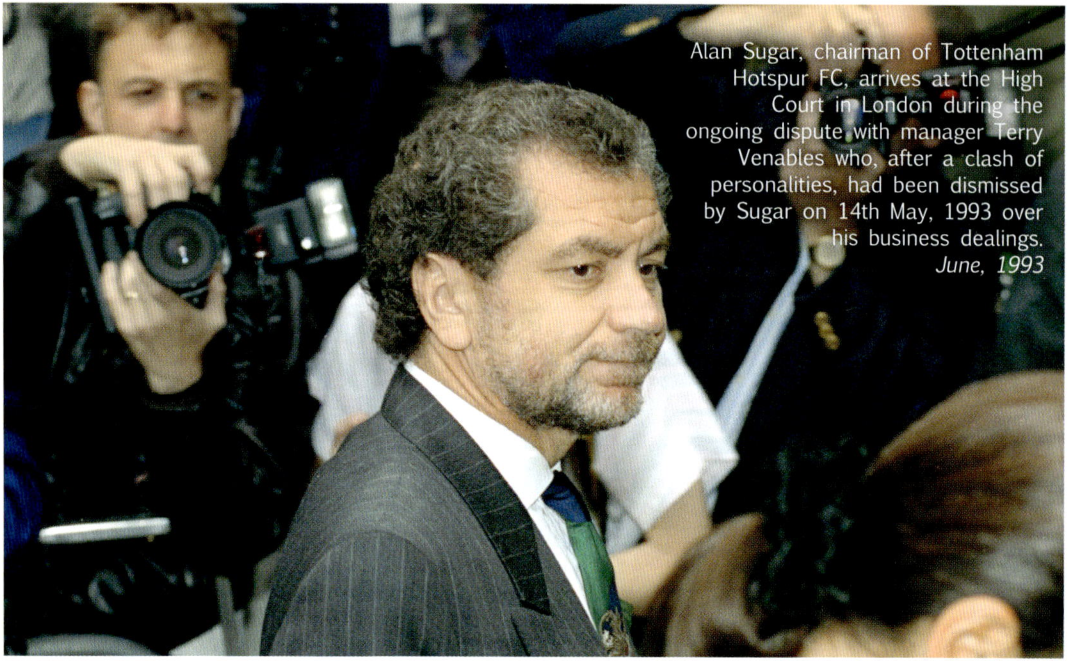

Alan Sugar, chairman of Tottenham Hotspur FC, arrives at the High Court in London during the ongoing dispute with manager Terry Venables who, after a clash of personalities, had been dismissed by Sugar on 14th May, 1993 over his business dealings. *June, 1993*

"Football is about the only business in the world where it's embarrassing to make money. Sorry. What can I say, but I touch things and people say they turn to gold. Sorry. It's a natural instinct. Sorry. I had to apologise that the club actually started to make a profit. Sorry. We should have been doing our bollocks like everyone else. Sorry."

Alan Sugar, responding to fans of Tottenham Hotspur FC, which he took over as chairman, who wanted him to invest in more players, even if it meant putting the club into debt. They saw him as a money man trying to bring 'buy-low, sell-high' to football.

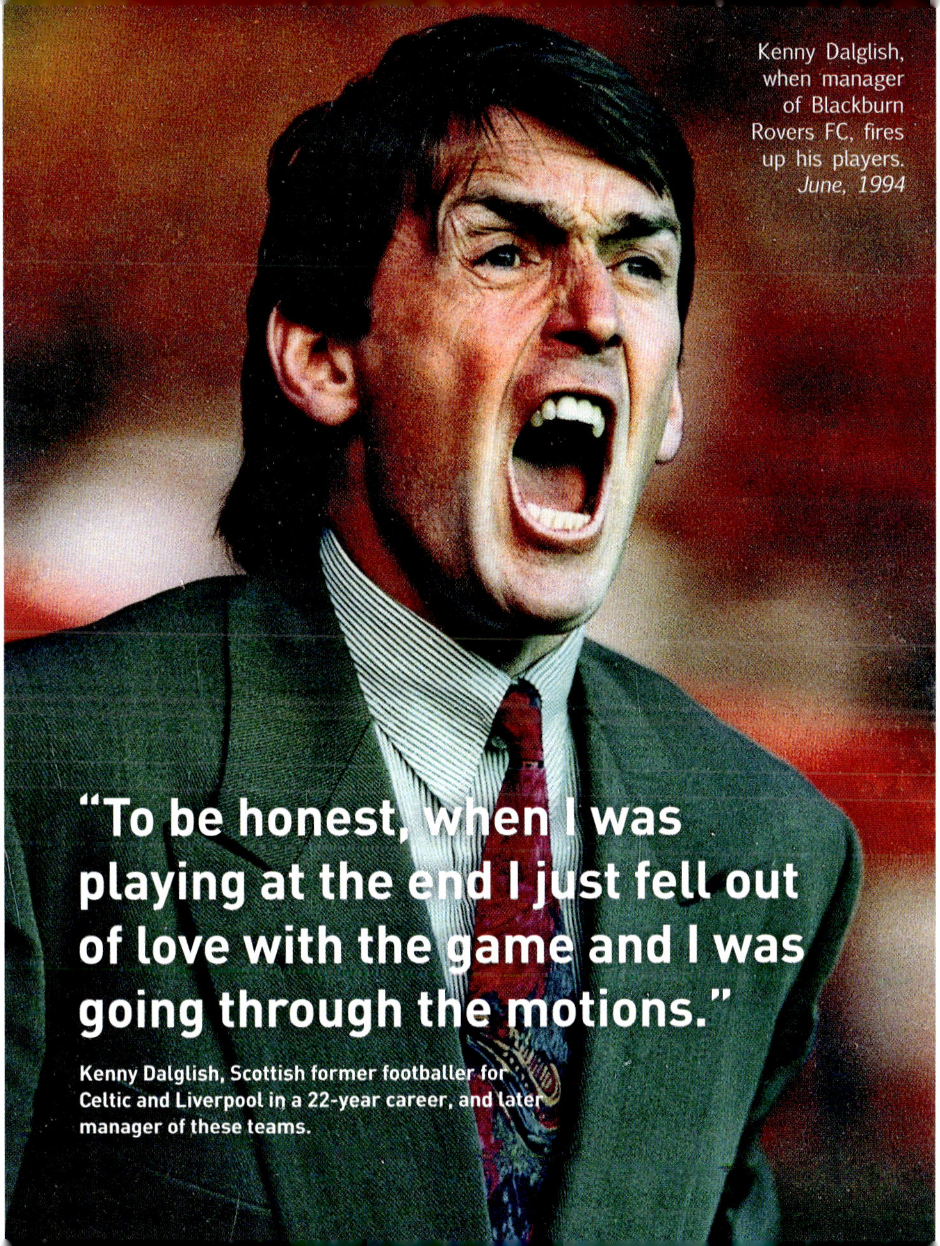

Kenny Dalglish, when manager of Blackburn Rovers FC, fires up his players. *June, 1994*

“To be honest, when I was playing at the end I just fell out of love with the game and I was going through the motions.”

Kenny Dalglish, Scottish former footballer for Celtic and Liverpool in a 22-year career, and later manager of these teams.

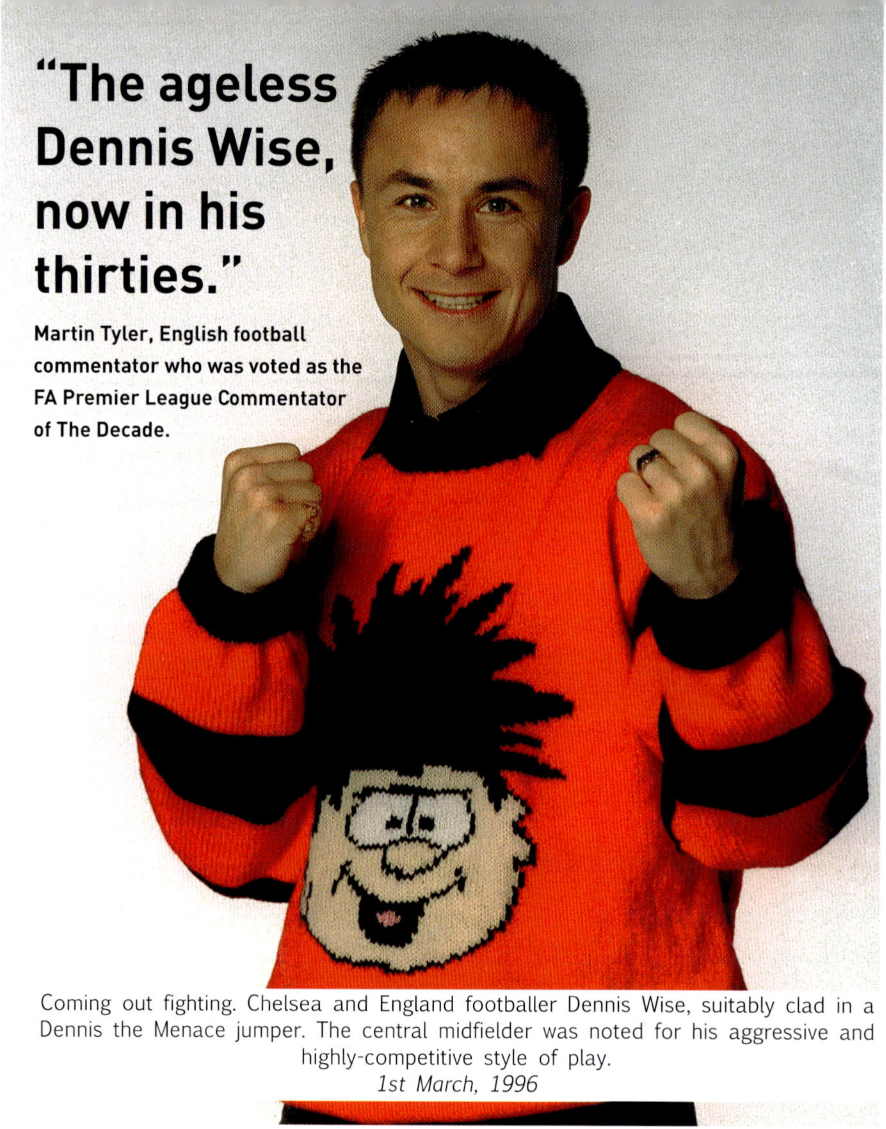

"The ageless Dennis Wise, now in his thirties."

Martin Tyler, English football commentator who was voted as the FA Premier League Commentator of The Decade.

Coming out fighting. Chelsea and England footballer Dennis Wise, suitably clad in a Dennis the Menace jumper. The central midfielder was noted for his aggressive and highly-competitive style of play.
1st March, 1996

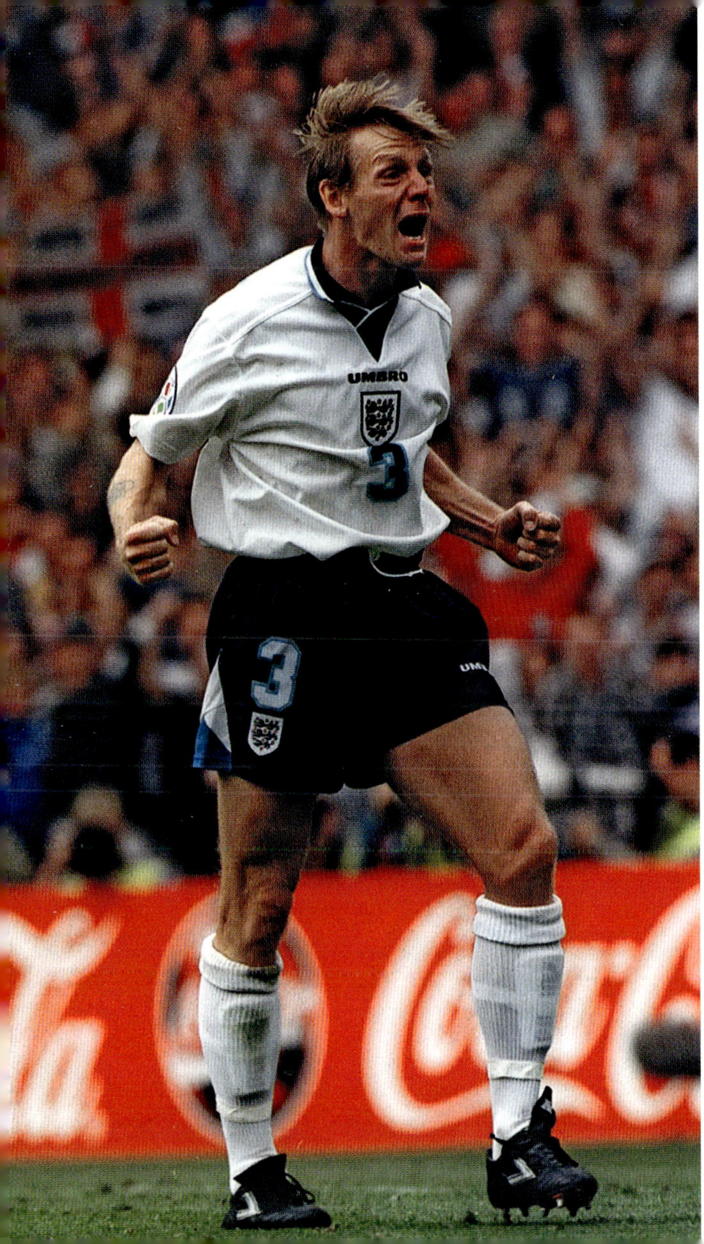

"I will do whatever it takes to win a football match."

Stuart Pearce.

Stuart Pearce, ecstatic after scoring from his penalty kick in the England v Spain European Championships Quarter-Final match at Wembley Stadium. The final score was a 0–0, but England won 4–2 on penalties.
22nd June, 1996

"I know I can't go on forever – how can I forget it when my so-called team-mates keep asking me which king was on the throne when I started and what was football like in the Dark Ages?"

Les Ferdinand, former English footballer, the first to score for six different Premier League clubs and joint fifth highest scorer of all time in the Premier League, with 149 goals.

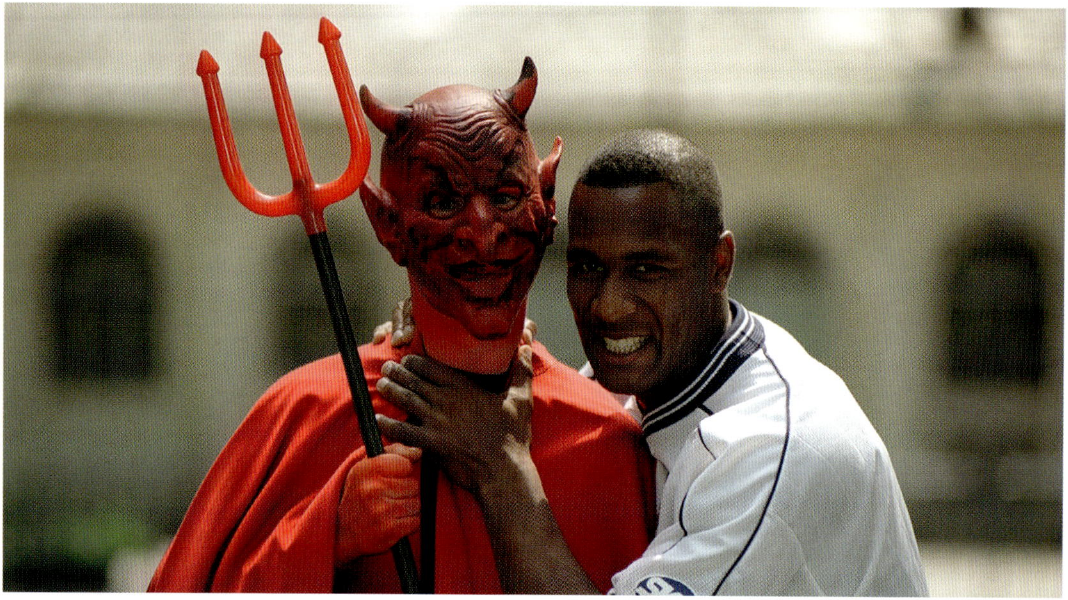

Tottenham Hotspur striker Les Ferdinand poses with Manchester United's Red Devil mascot, prior to a Premier League match, which Spurs would win 2–0. The prolific goal scorer was a recent acquisition from Newcastle United, for £6m.
7th August, 1997

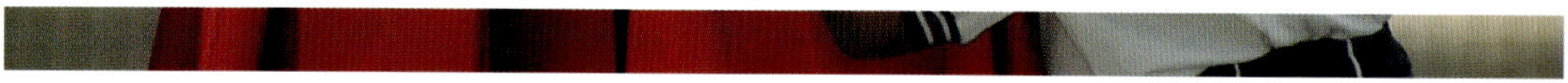

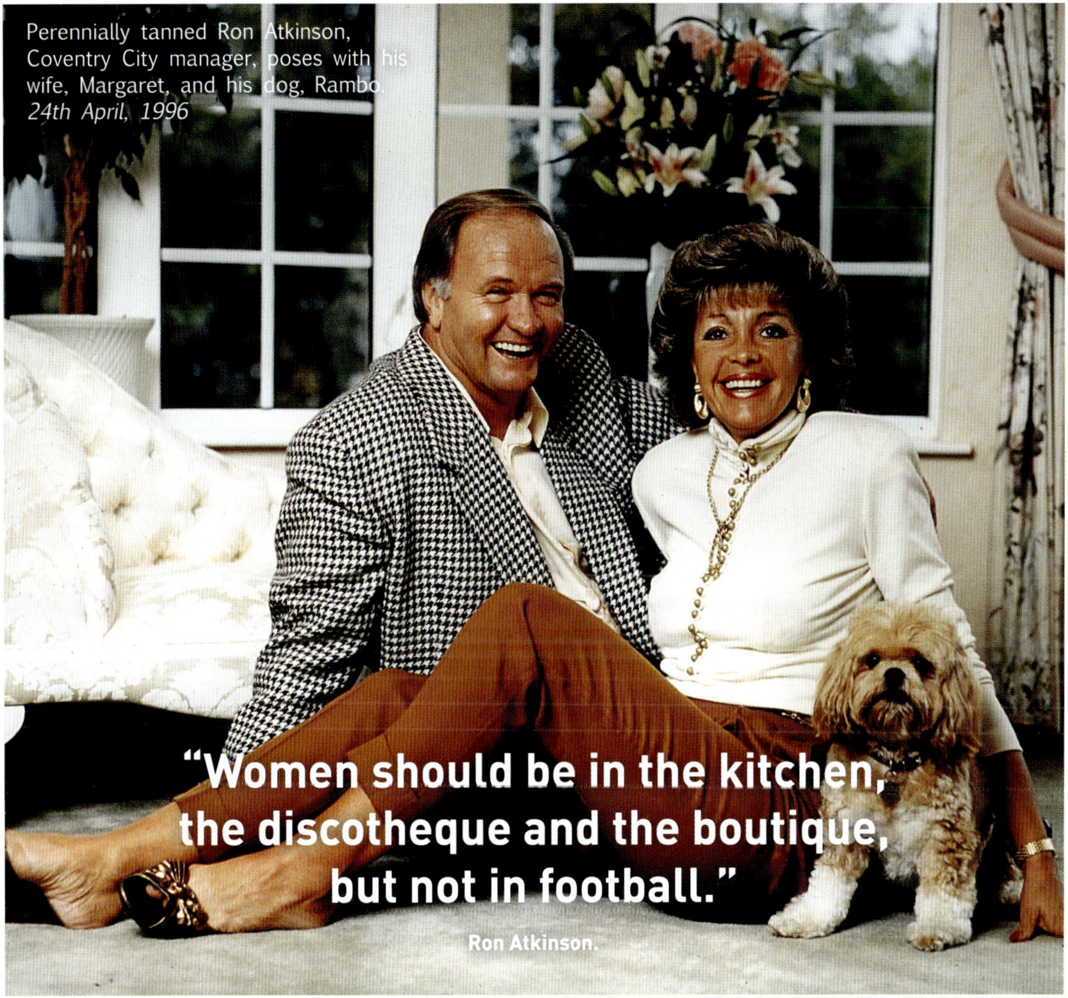

Perennially tanned Ron Atkinson, Coventry City manager, poses with his wife, Margaret, and his dog, Rambo.
24th April, 1996

"Women should be in the kitchen, the discotheque and the boutique, but not in football."

Ron Atkinson.

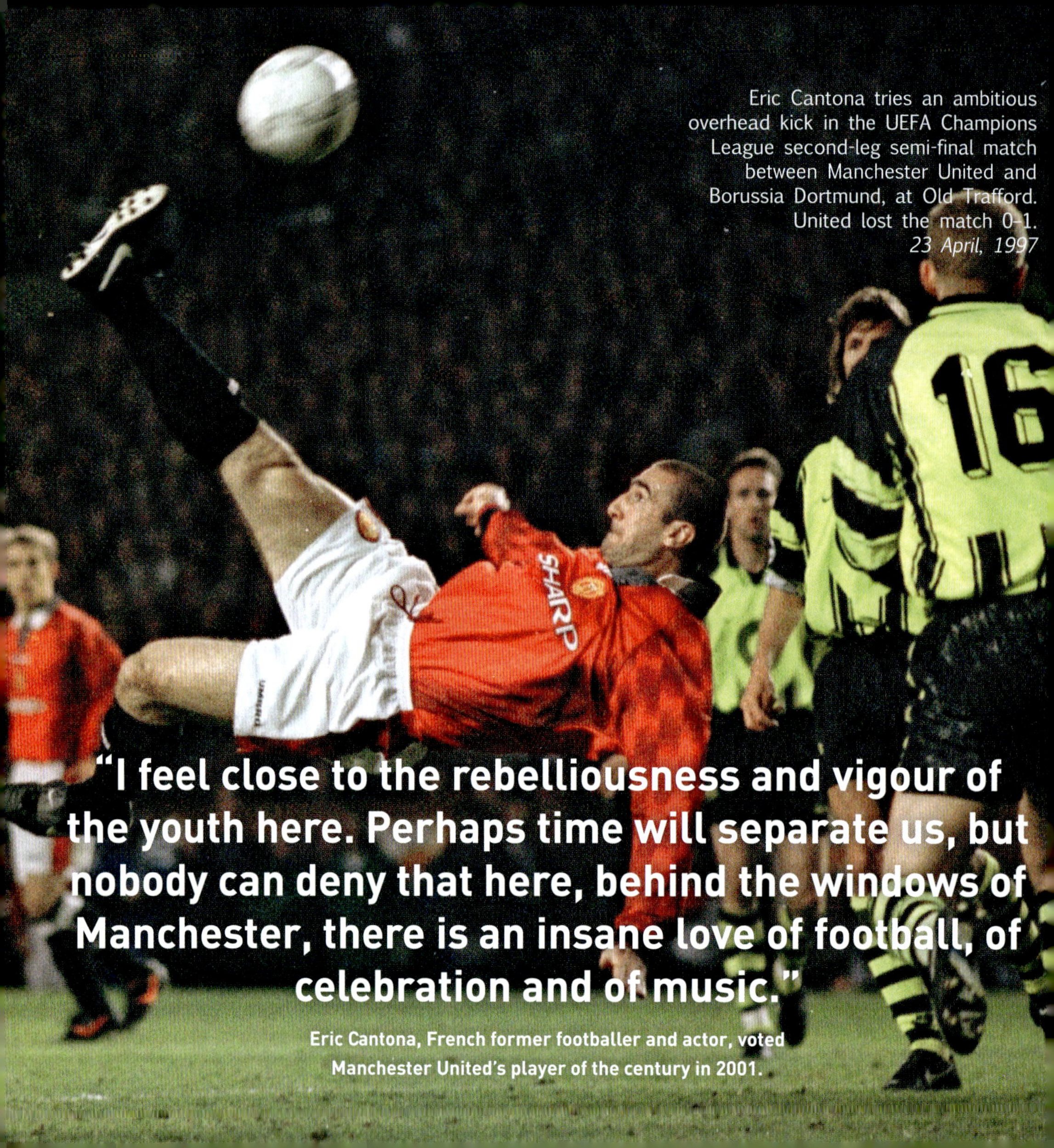

Eric Cantona tries an ambitious overhead kick in the UEFA Champions League second-leg semi-final match between Manchester United and Borussia Dortmund, at Old Trafford. United lost the match 0–1. *23 April, 1997*

"I feel close to the rebelliousness and vigour of the youth here. Perhaps time will separate us, but nobody can deny that here, behind the windows of Manchester, there is an insane love of football, of celebration and of music."

Eric Cantona, French former footballer and actor, voted Manchester United's player of the century in 2001.

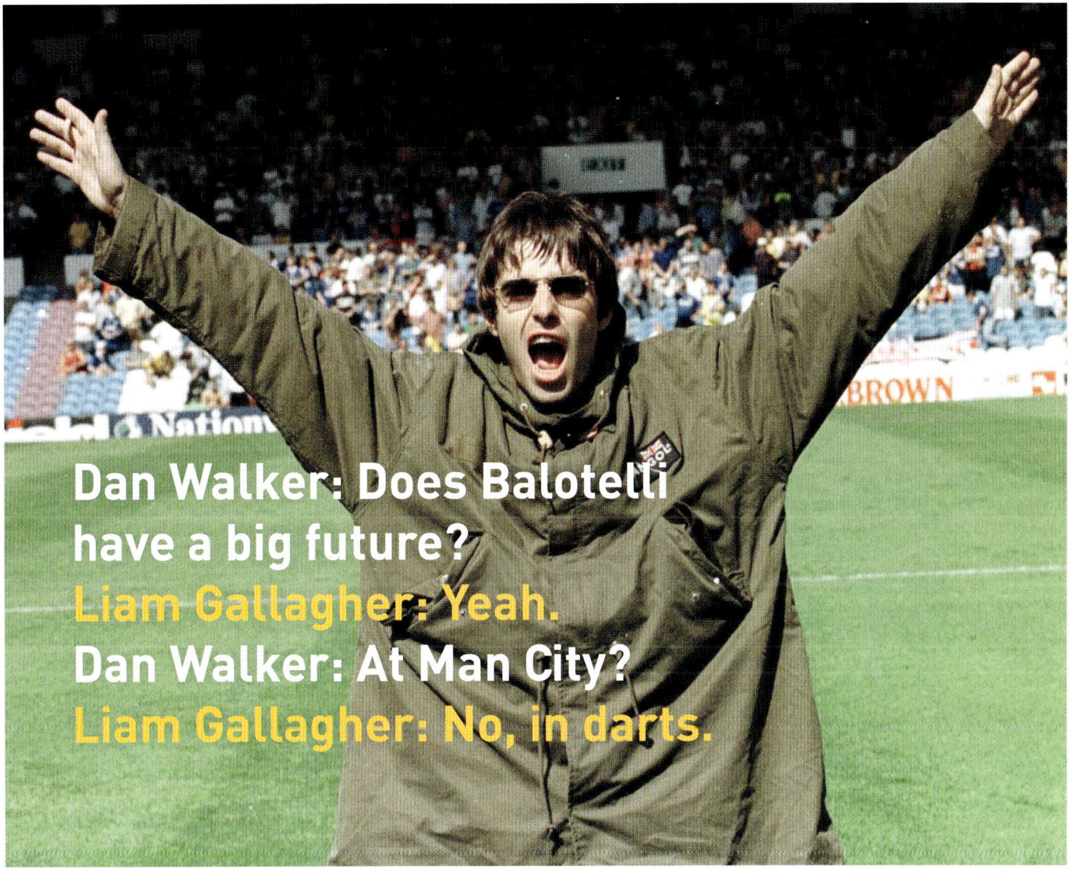

Dan Walker: Does Balotelli have a big future?
Liam Gallagher: Yeah.
Dan Walker: At Man City?
Liam Gallagher: No, in darts.

Liam Gallagher of rock band Oasis at the Maine Road football ground to watch his team, Manchester City, play Portsmouth Town in a League Division 1 match. The teams drew 2–2.
9th August, 1997

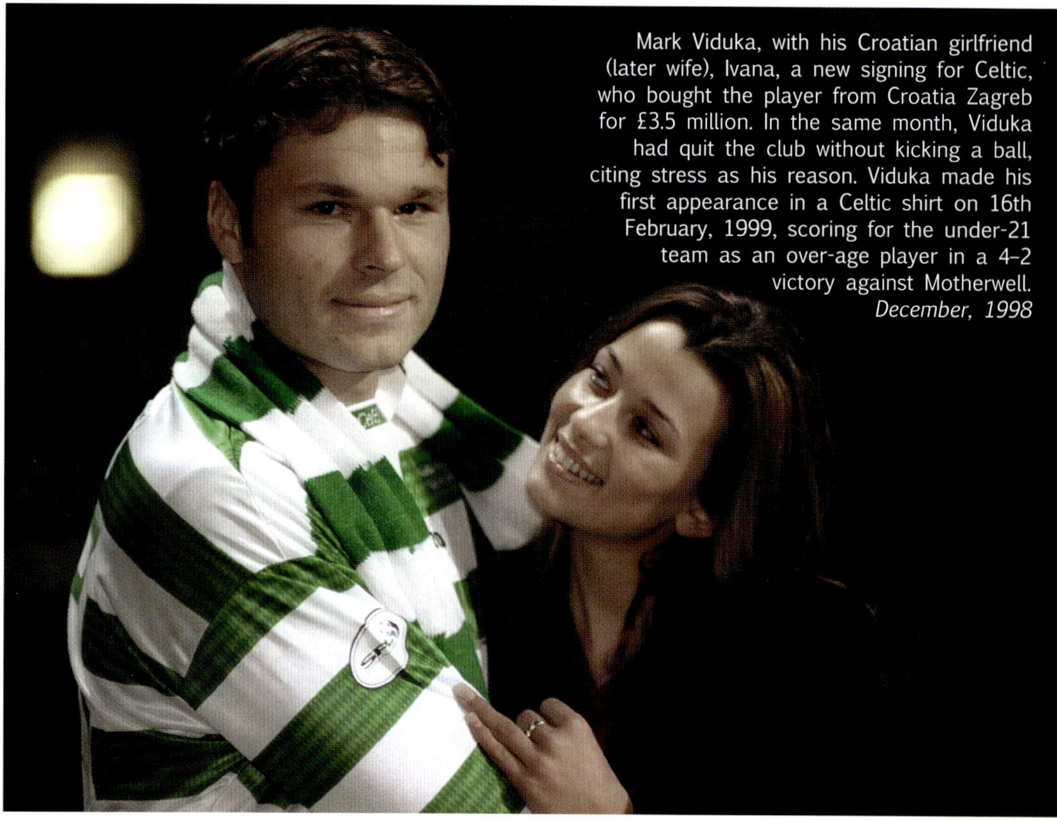

Mark Viduka, with his Croatian girlfriend (later wife), Ivana, a new signing for Celtic, who bought the player from Croatia Zagreb for £3.5 million. In the same month, Viduka had quit the club without kicking a ball, citing stress as his reason. Viduka made his first appearance in a Celtic shirt on 16th February, 1999, scoring for the under-21 team as an over-age player in a 4–2 victory against Motherwell.
December, 1998

"I would not be bothered if we lost every game as long as we won the League."

Mark Viduka, former Australian centre forward, who captained the Australian national team at the 2006 FIFA World Cup in Germany, to the last 16. He holds the record of most goals scored by an Australian in the UEFA Champions League competition.

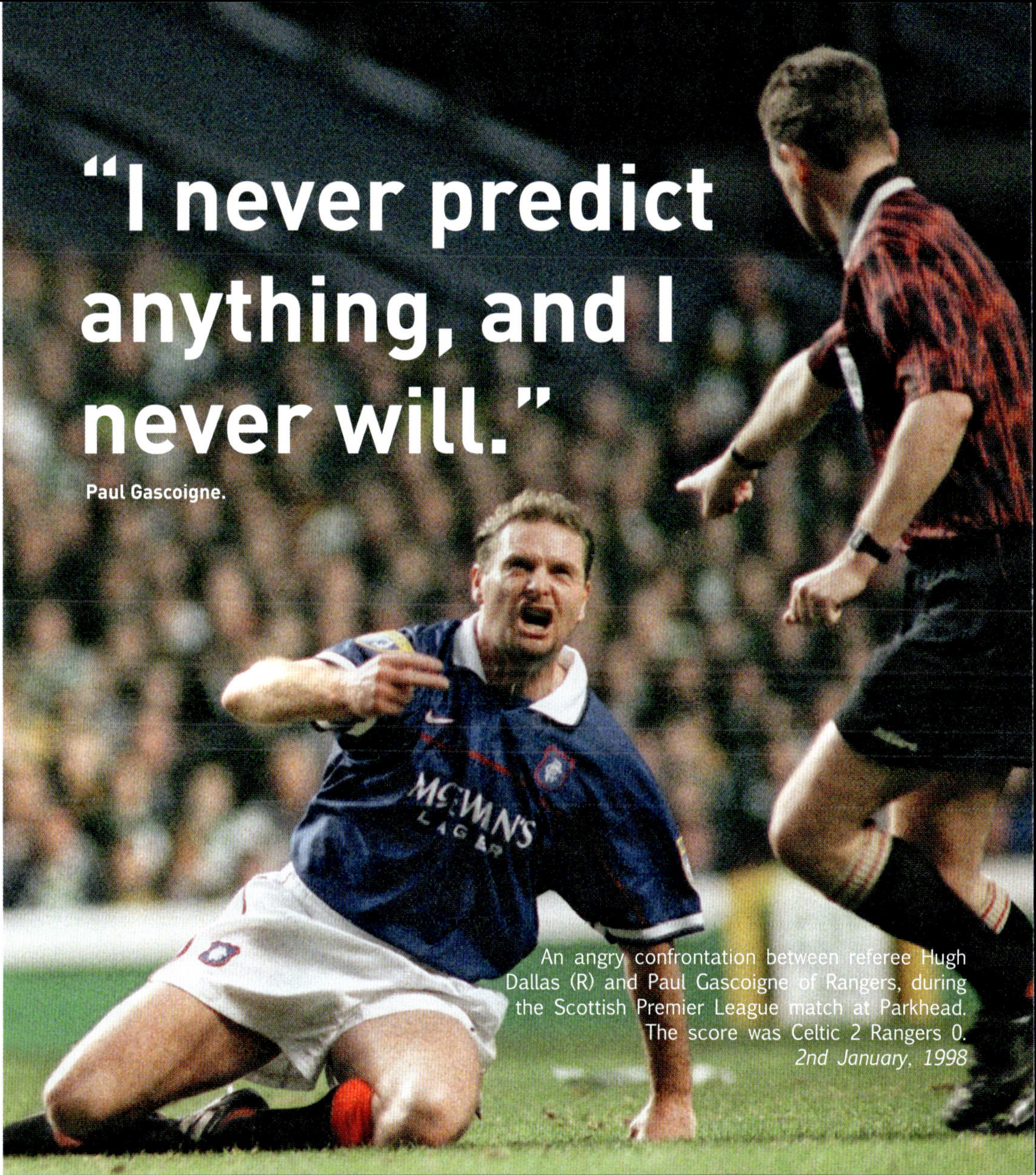

"I never predict anything, and I never will."

Paul Gascoigne.

An angry confrontation between referee Hugh Dallas (R) and Paul Gascoigne of Rangers, during the Scottish Premier League match at Parkhead. The score was Celtic 2 Rangers 0.
2nd January, 1998

"People go on about my foul on Simeone and the red card, but I'd obviously rather people talk about me scoring the penalty four years later."

David Beckham, English footballer, holder of the all-time appearance record (115) with the national team, captain of England between 2000 and 2006.

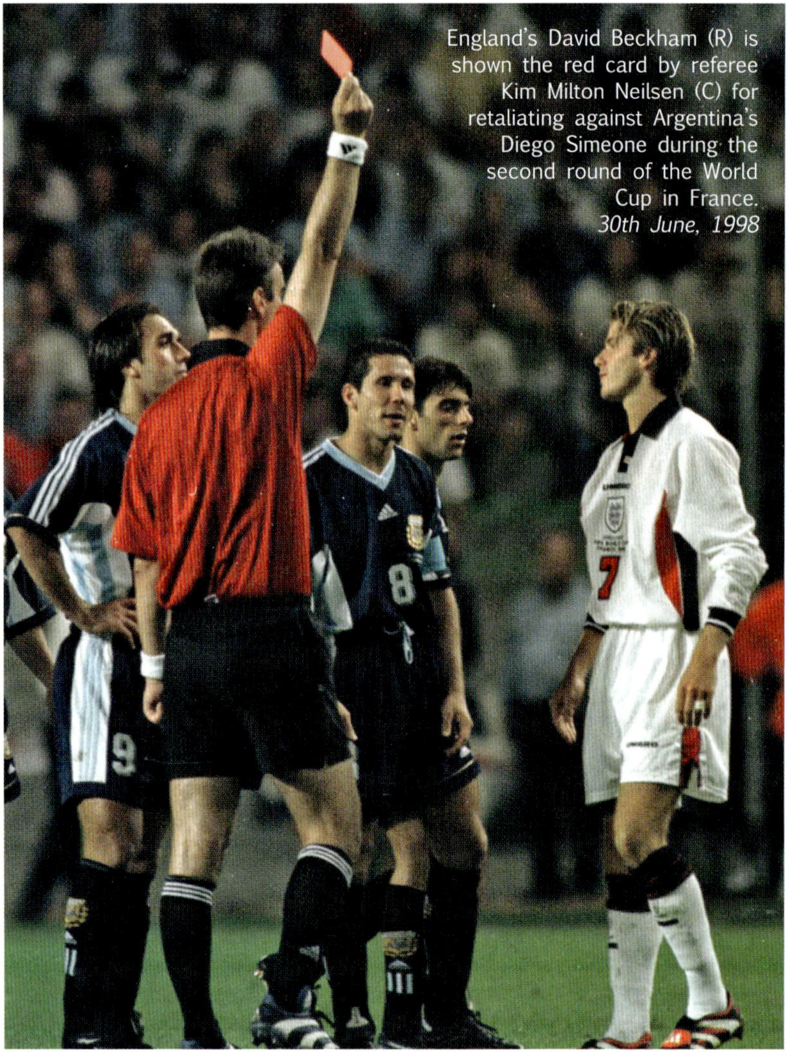

England's David Beckham (R) is shown the red card by referee Kim Milton Neilsen (C) for retaliating against Argentina's Diego Simeone during the second round of the World Cup in France. *30th June, 1998*

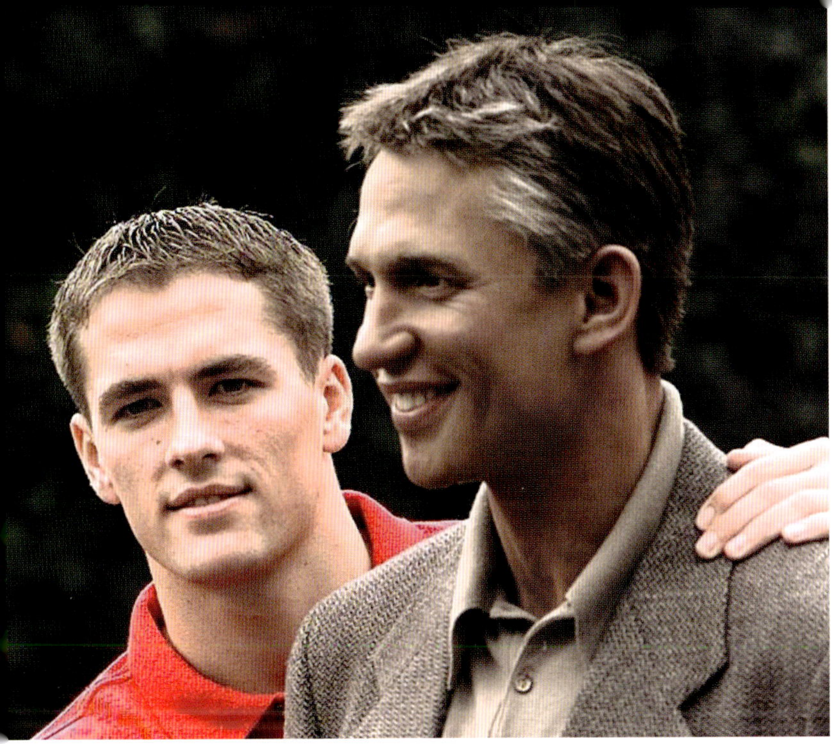

Liverpool footballer Michael Owen (L) with former footballer turned TV presenter Gary Lineker. The pair were to promote Walkers Crisps in a series of witty television adverts. *October, 1998*

"I don't believe in superstitions. I just do certain things because I'm scared in case something will happen if I don't do them."

Michael Owen.

"What makes this game so delightful is that when both teams get the ball, they are attacking their opponents' goal."

Jimmy Hill.

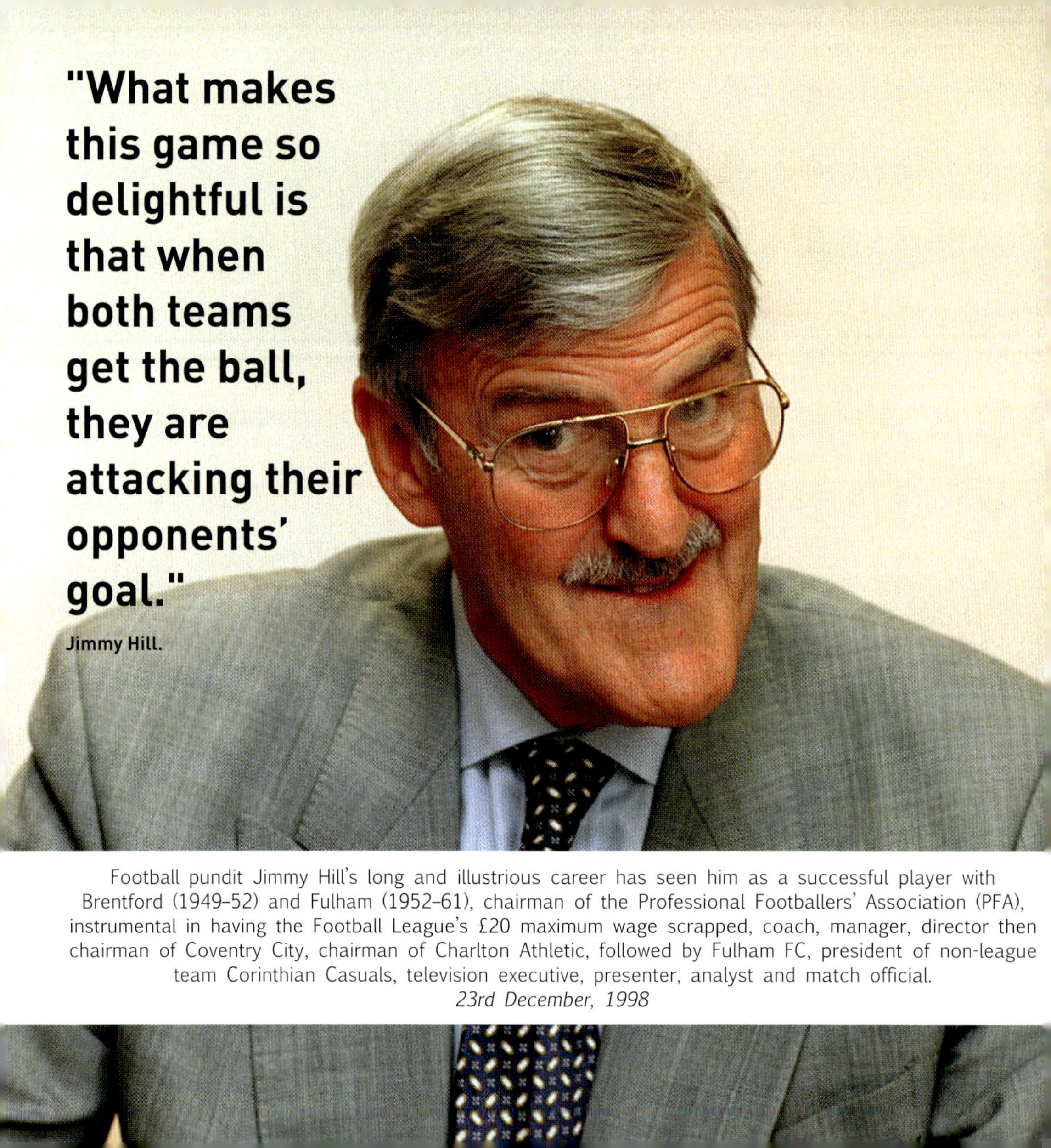

Football pundit Jimmy Hill's long and illustrious career has seen him as a successful player with Brentford (1949–52) and Fulham (1952–61), chairman of the Professional Footballers' Association (PFA), instrumental in having the Football League's £20 maximum wage scrapped, coach, manager, director then chairman of Coventry City, chairman of Charlton Athletic, followed by Fulham FC, president of non-league team Corinthian Casuals, television executive, presenter, analyst and match official.

23rd December, 1998

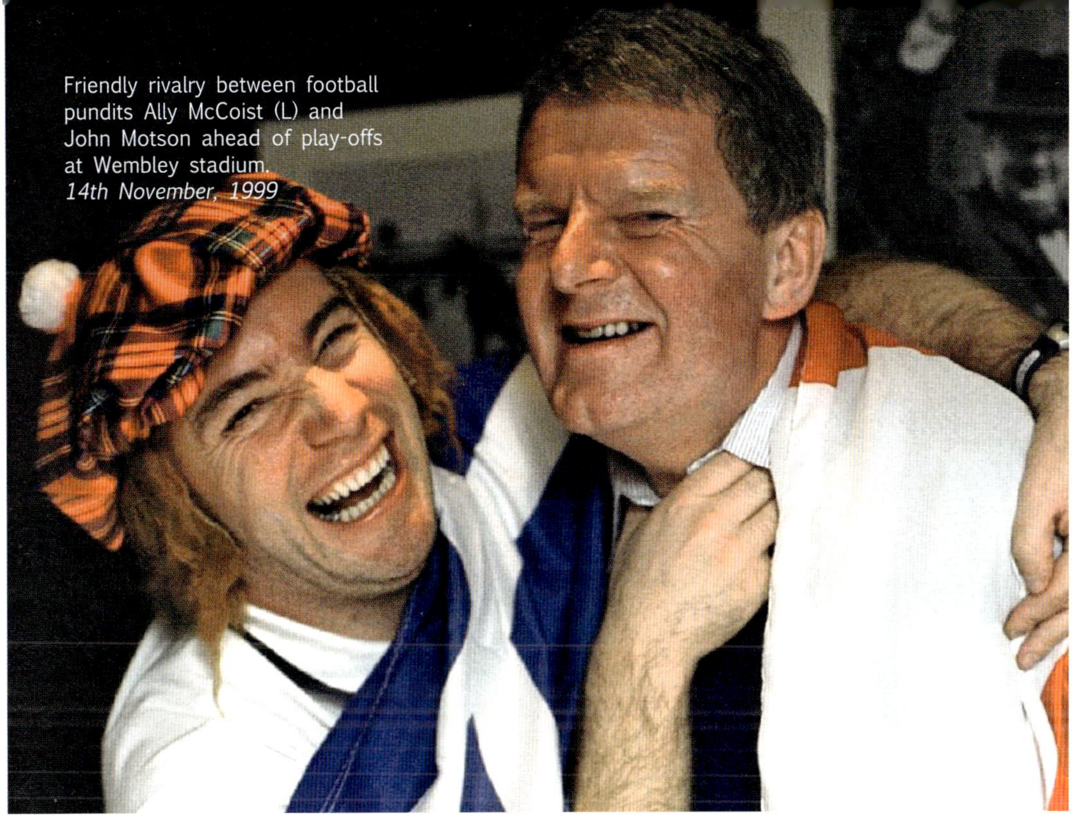

Friendly rivalry between football pundits Ally McCoist (L) and John Motson ahead of play-offs at Wembley stadium.
14th November, 1999

"Brazil – they're so good it's like they are running round the pitch playing with themselves."

John Motson, also known as 'Motty', English football commentator on television and radio.

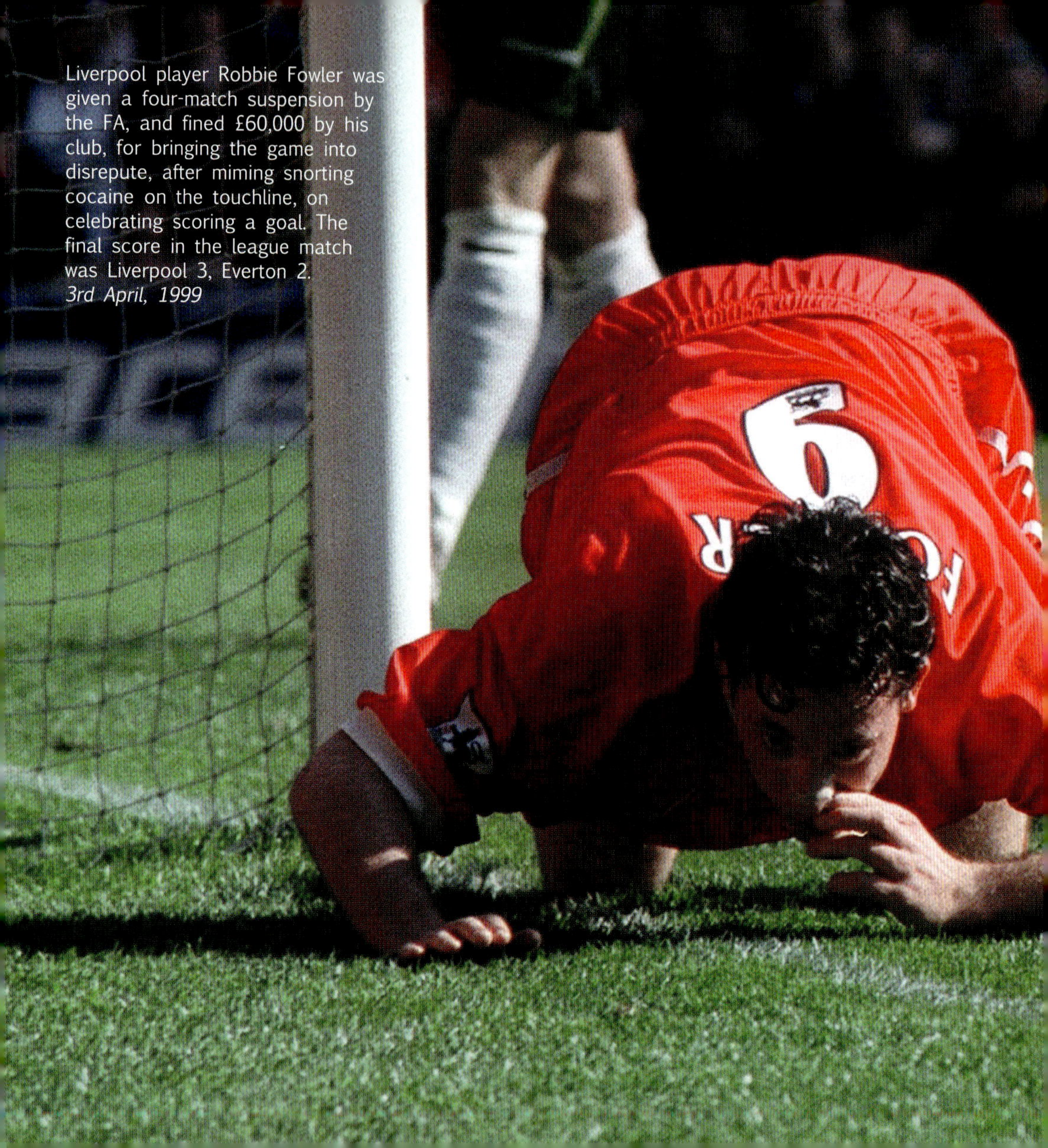

Liverpool player Robbie Fowler was given a four-match suspension by the FA, and fined £60,000 by his club, for bringing the game into disrepute, after miming snorting cocaine on the touchline, on celebrating scoring a goal. The final score in the league match was Liverpool 3, Everton 2.
3rd April, 1999

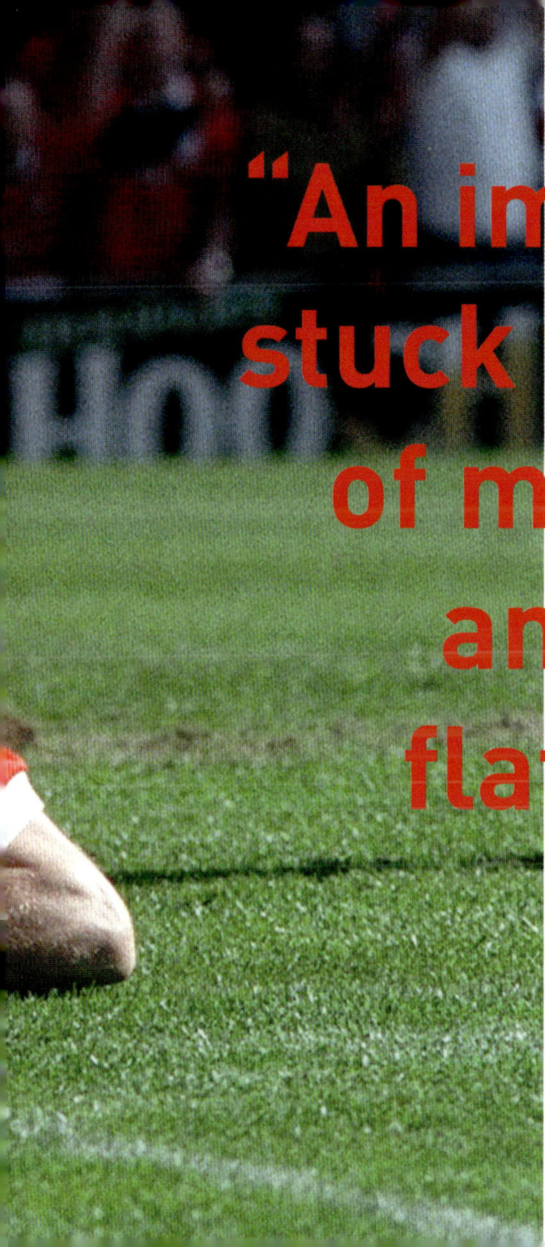

"An image has stuck for most of my career and it isn't flattering."

Robbie Fowler, English footballer notable for his days at Liverpool FC, and the fourth-highest goal scorer in the history of the Premier League.

"Every one of our players respects every one of their players and their team as a whole. But once we cross that white line most of the respect will be out the window and we will be fighting to win the game."

David Beckham.

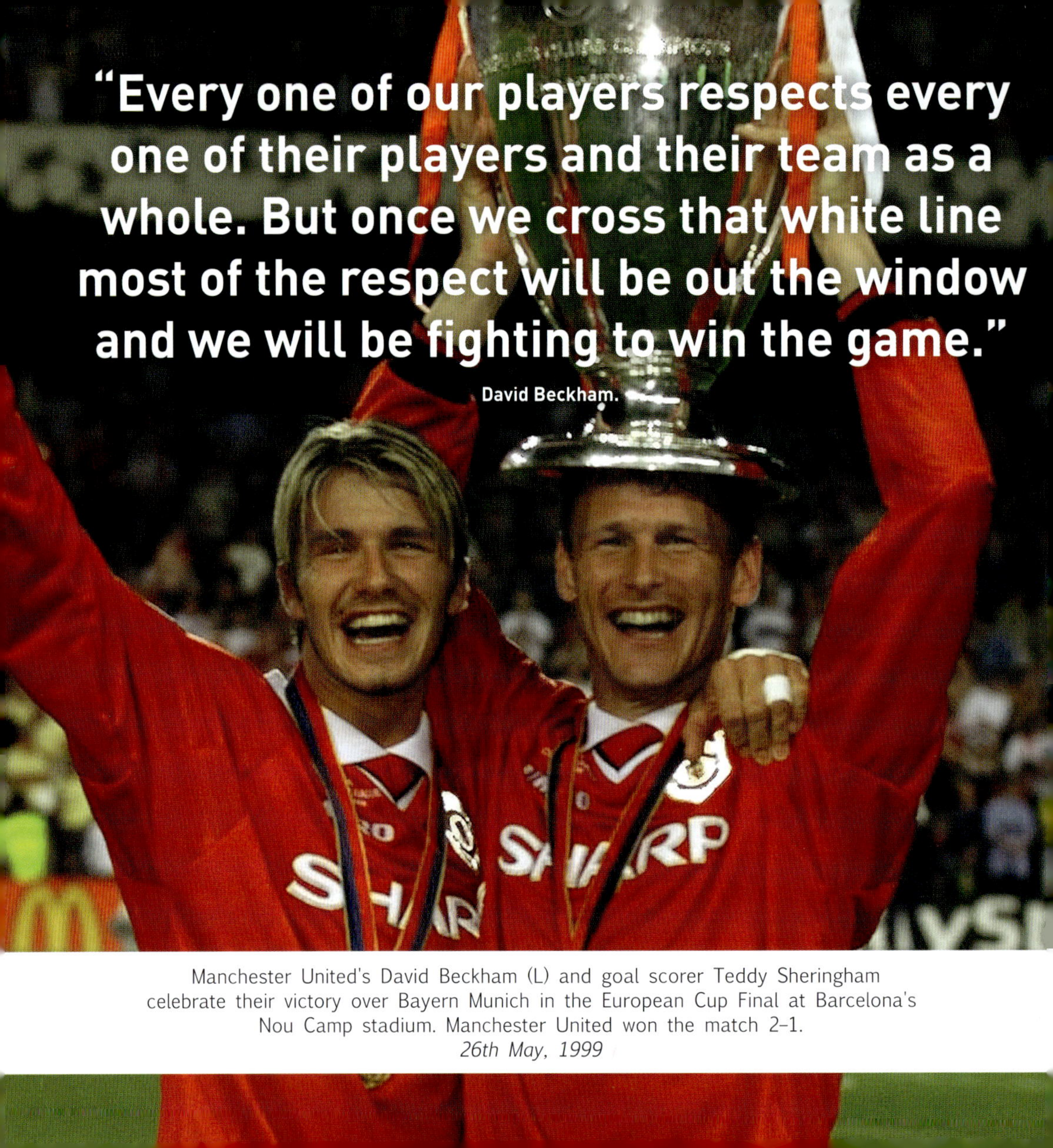

Manchester United's David Beckham (L) and goal scorer Teddy Sheringham celebrate their victory over Bayern Munich in the European Cup Final at Barcelona's Nou Camp stadium. Manchester United won the match 2–1.

26th May, 1999

"...Right now the Liverpool midfield man is starring in his own real-life soap drama – the remaking of England's likely lad."

David Emery, sports editor, on the contractual saga surrounding Steve McManaman in the 1990s, in which his transfer became a controversial Bosman ruling-related issue. McManaman was the highest paid British player in history between 1999 and 2001.

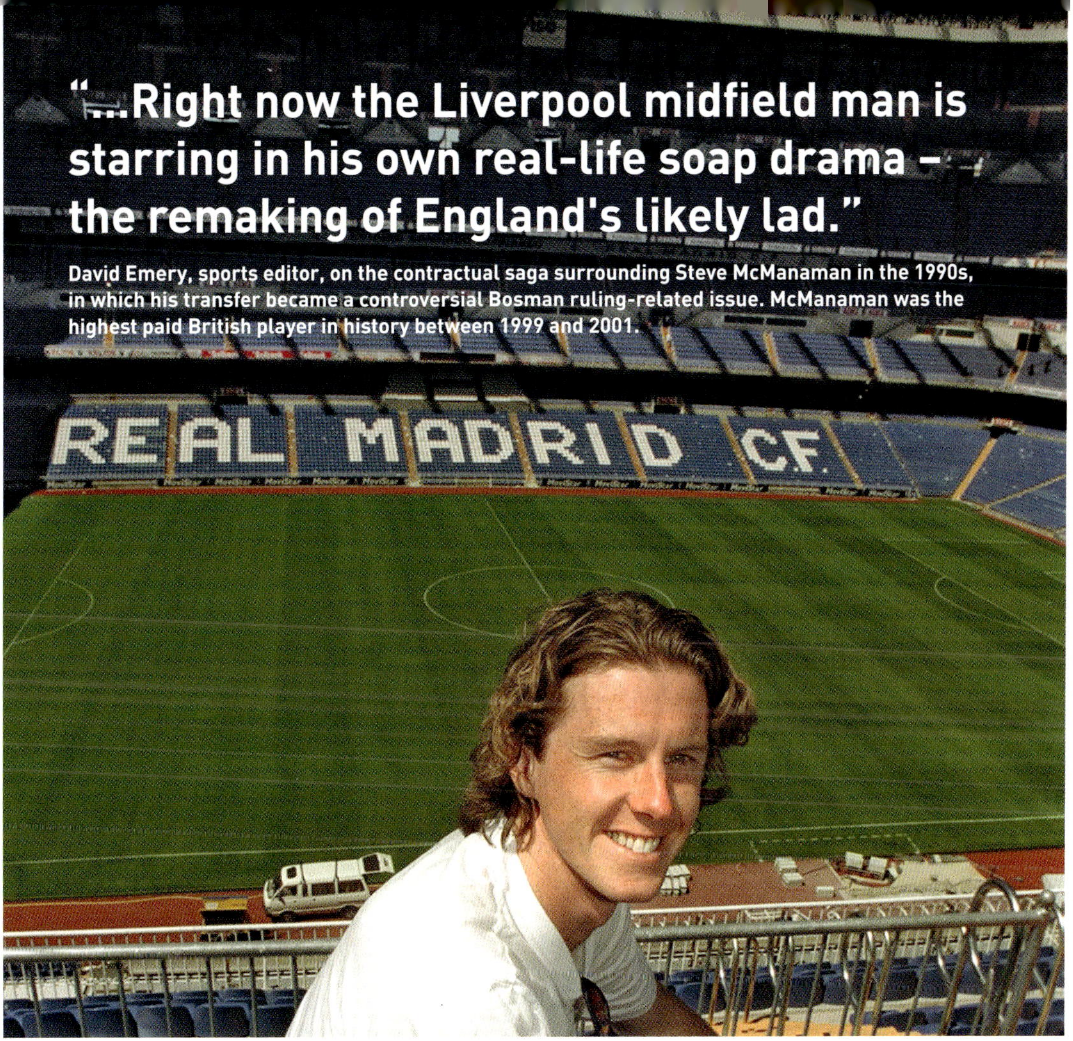

Real Madrid's new winger Steve McManaman at the Santiago Bernabeu Stadium. The midfielder, winger and playmaker played for two of Europe's most successful clubs, Liverpool and Real Madrid. He is the most decorated English footballer to have played at any foreign club in terms of trophies won overseas.
26th August, 1999

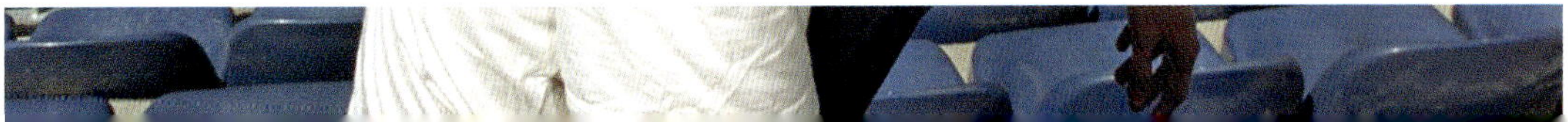

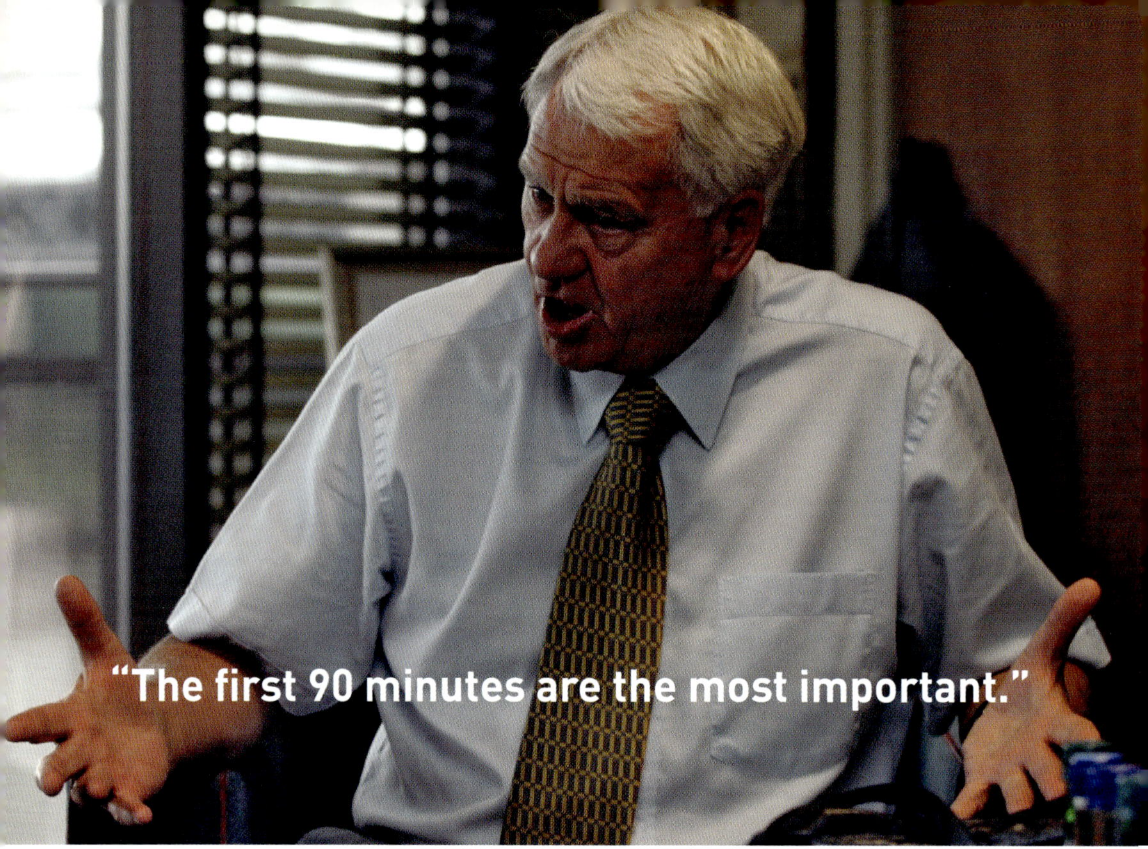

Sir Bobby Robson, Newcastle United manager (1999–2004), whose playing career spanned the 1950s and 1960s, with Fulham, West Bromwich Albion and Vancouver, Canada, with 20 appearances for England. After retiring from playing, he managed the English clubs Fulham and Ipswich Town, the Netherlands club PSV Eindhoven, Portugal's Sporting SVP and FC Porto, and Spain's FC Barcelona. He also led England to the semi-final of the 1990 World Cup. Robson was knighted in 2002, inducted into the English Football Hall of Fame in 2003 and became the honorary president of Ipswich Town FC.

January, 2000

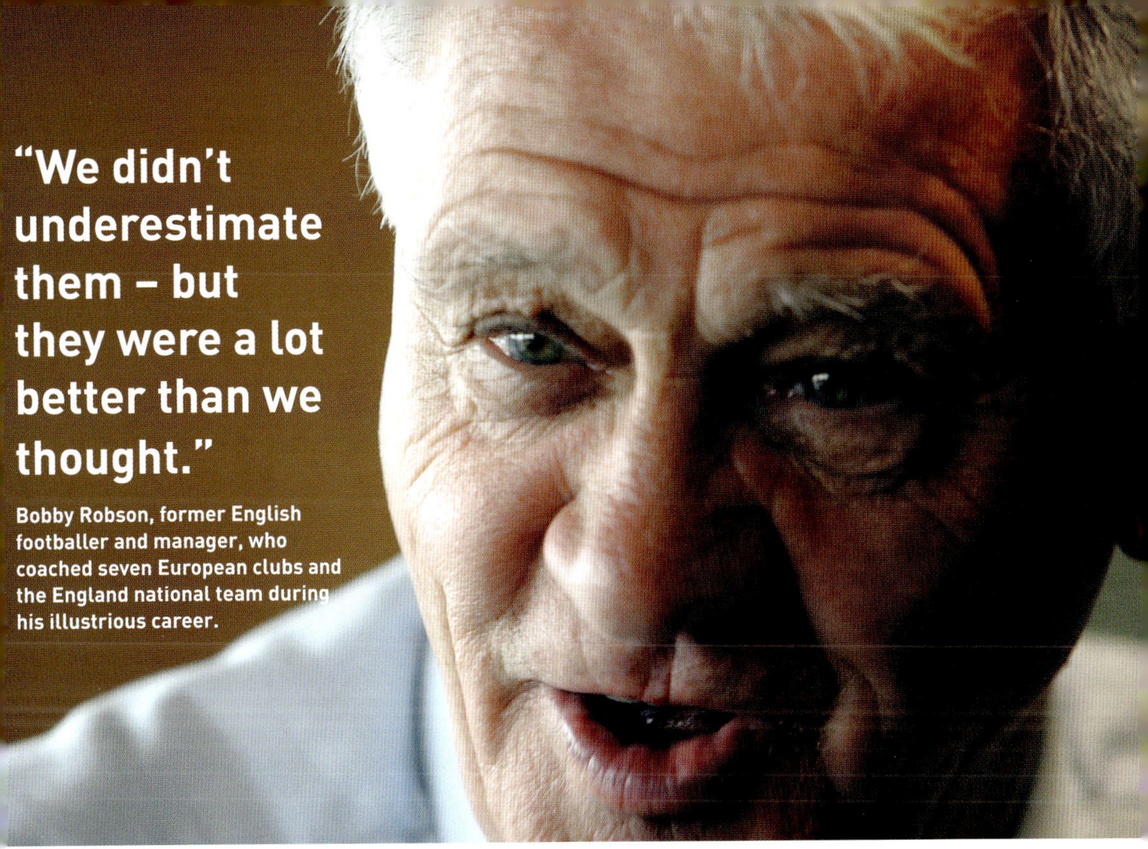

"We didn't underestimate them – but they were a lot better than we thought."

Bobby Robson, former English footballer and manager, who coached seven European clubs and the England national team during his illustrious career.

The popular figure had suffered from cancer since 1991 and, in March 2008, lent his name to The Sir Bobby Robson Foundation, a charity that focuses on early detection and treatment of the disease. In August, 2008, he confirmed that his lung cancer was terminal: "I am going to die sooner rather than later. But then everyone has to go sometime and I have enjoyed every minute". He passed away on 31st July, 2009 at the age of 76.

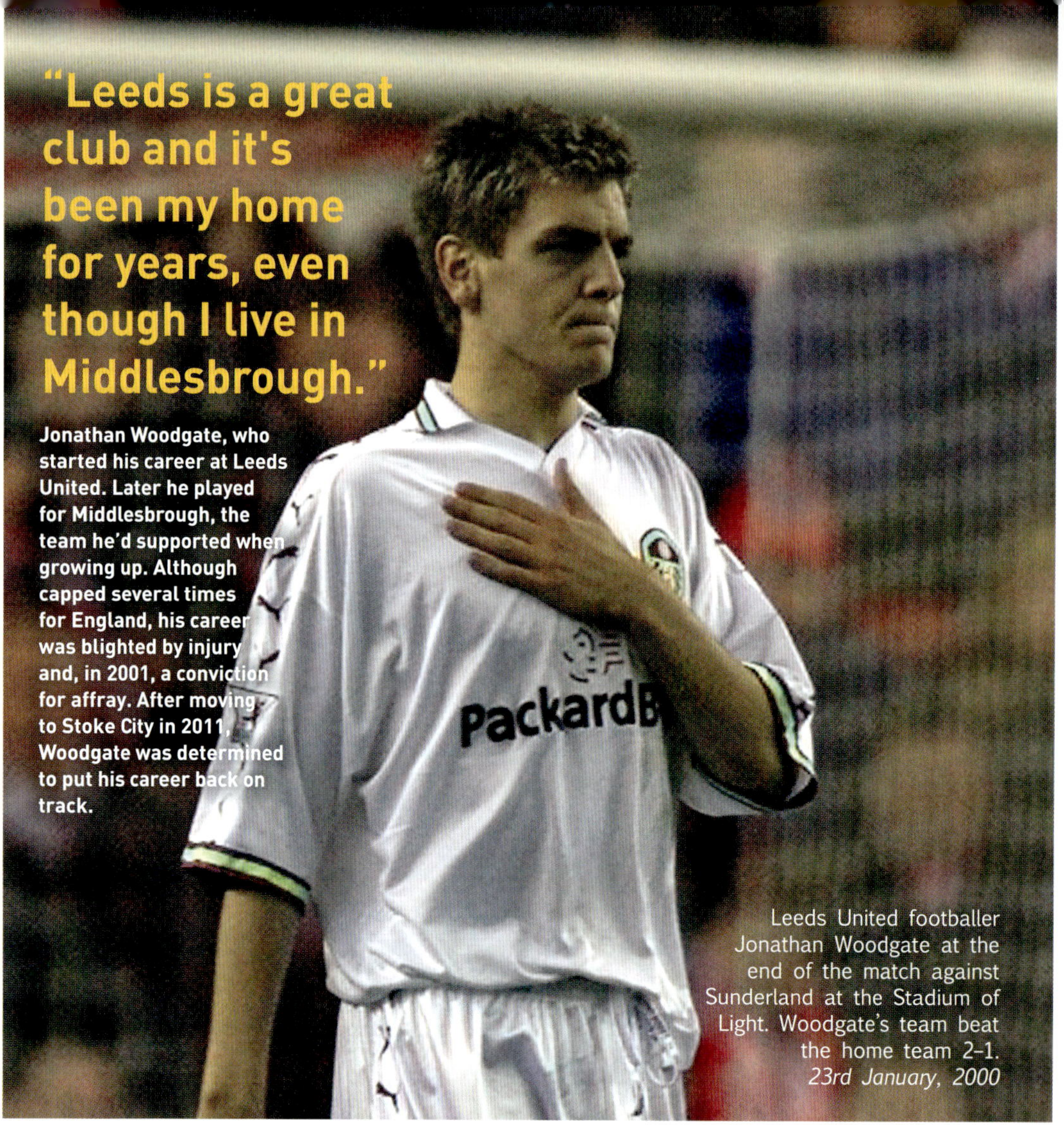

"Leeds is a great club and it's been my home for years, even though I live in Middlesbrough."

Jonathan Woodgate, who started his career at Leeds United. Later he played for Middlesbrough, the team he'd supported when growing up. Although capped several times for England, his career was blighted by injury and, in 2001, a conviction for affray. After moving to Stoke City in 2011, Woodgate was determined to put his career back on track.

Leeds United footballer Jonathan Woodgate at the end of the match against Sunderland at the Stadium of Light. Woodgate's team beat the home team 2–1. *23rd January, 2000*

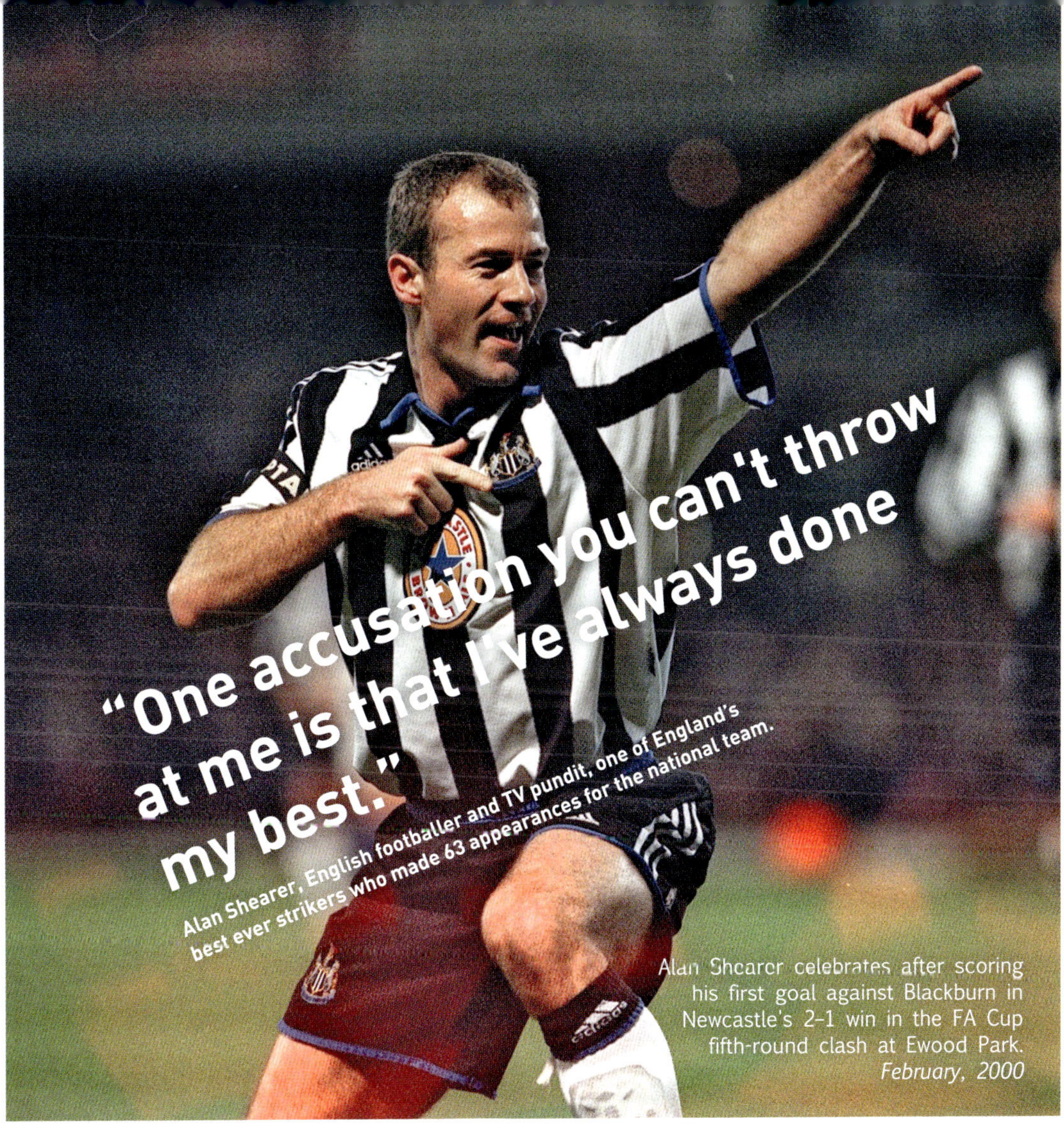

"One accusation you can't throw at me is that I've always done my best."

Alan Shearer, English footballer and TV pundit, one of England's best ever strikers who made 63 appearances for the national team.

Alan Shearer celebrates after scoring his first goal against Blackburn in Newcastle's 2-1 win in the FA Cup fifth-round clash at Ewood Park.
February, 2000

“I faxed a transfer request to the club at the beginning of the week, but let me state that I don't want to leave Leicester.”

Stan Collymore, former English footballer, a talented player whose turbulent private life and bouts of depression marred his promising career. He re-emerged as a successful pundit on television and radio.

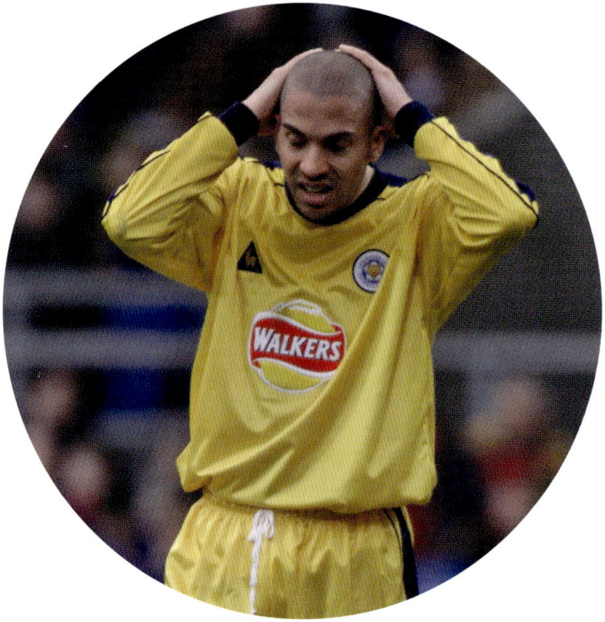

Leicester City footballer Stan Collymore, a free transfer from Aston Villa the previous month, looks dejected during the Premier League match against Wimbledon, although his team won 2–1. Collymore's time at Leicester City was brief, after the striker was involved in a disturbance at a hotel during a training break in Spain. He transferred to Bradford City in October, 2000, but retired as a player in 2001.
11th March, 2000

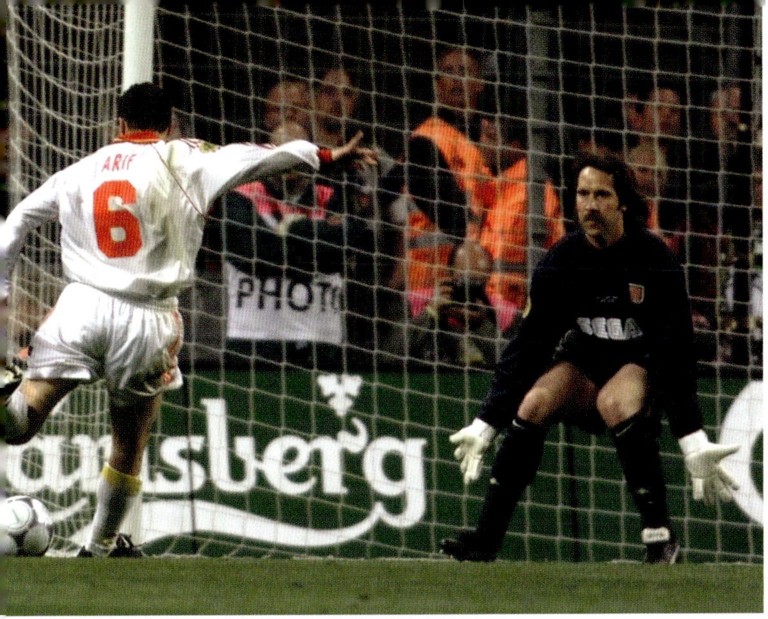

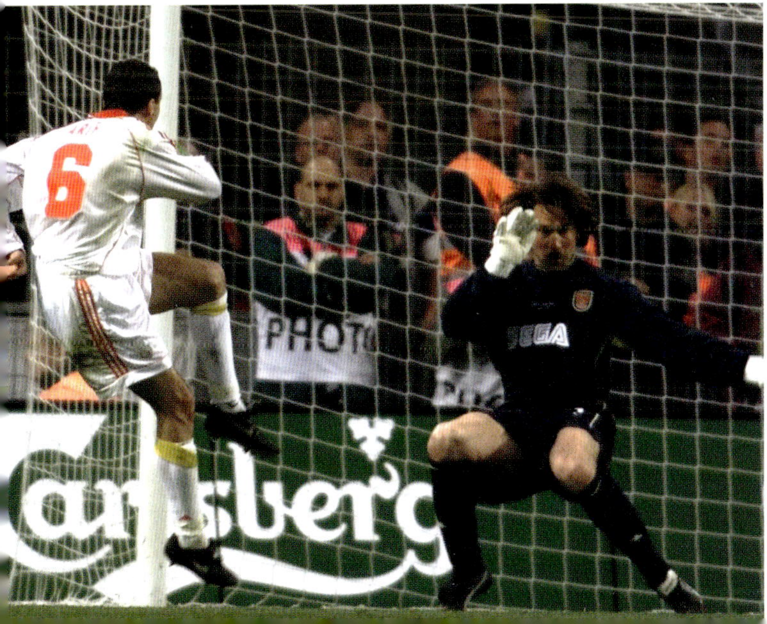

"That Seaman is a handsome young man, but he spends too much time looking in his mirror, rather than at the ball. You can't keep goal with hair like that."

Brian Clough.

Galatasaray's Erdim Arif shoots past Arsenal's goalkeeper David Seaman, although the ball is wide, in the UEFA Cup Final in Copenhagen, Denmark. The Turkish club won the match 4–1 on penalties. *May, 2000*

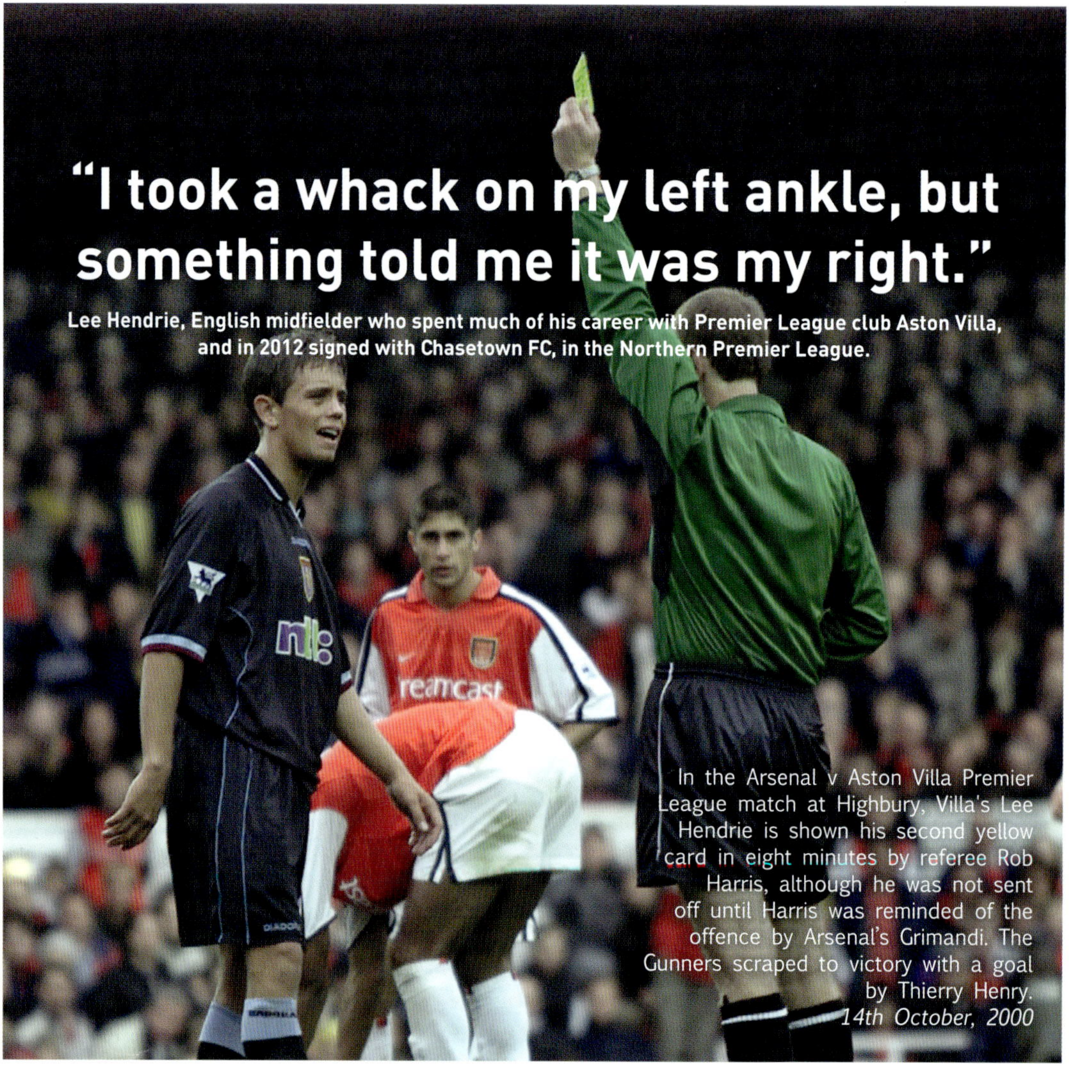

"I took a whack on my left ankle, but something told me it was my right."

Lee Hendrie, English midfielder who spent much of his career with Premier League club Aston Villa, and in 2012 signed with Chasetown FC, in the Northern Premier League.

In the Arsenal v Aston Villa Premier League match at Highbury, Villa's Lee Hendrie is shown his second yellow card in eight minutes by referee Rob Harris, although he was not sent off until Harris was reminded of the offence by Arsenal's Grimandi. The Gunners scraped to victory with a goal by Thierry Henry.
14th October, 2000

"It was like the ref had a brand-new yellow card and wanted to see if it worked."

Richard Rufus, English footballer, who spent his entire career with Charlton Athletic, making 288 appearances and scoring 12 goals.

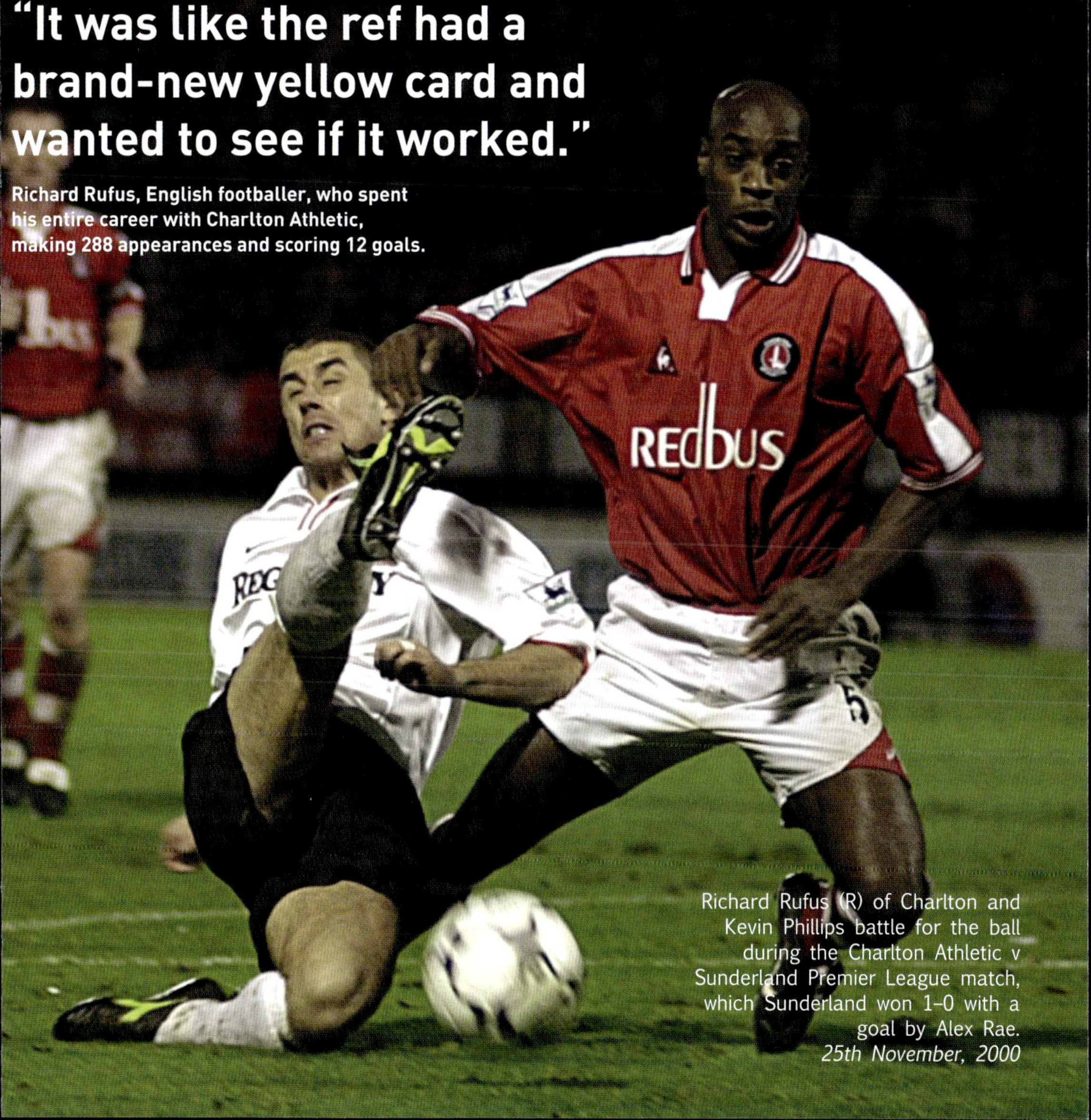

Richard Rufus (R) of Charlton and Kevin Phillips battle for the ball during the Charlton Athletic v Sunderland Premier League match, which Sunderland won 1-0 with a goal by Alex Rae.
25th November, 2000

FIFA President Sepp Blatter attending the match at the West Lothian Courier Stadium between Livingston and Peterhead in the Scottish Cup Quarter-Final.
6th March, 2001

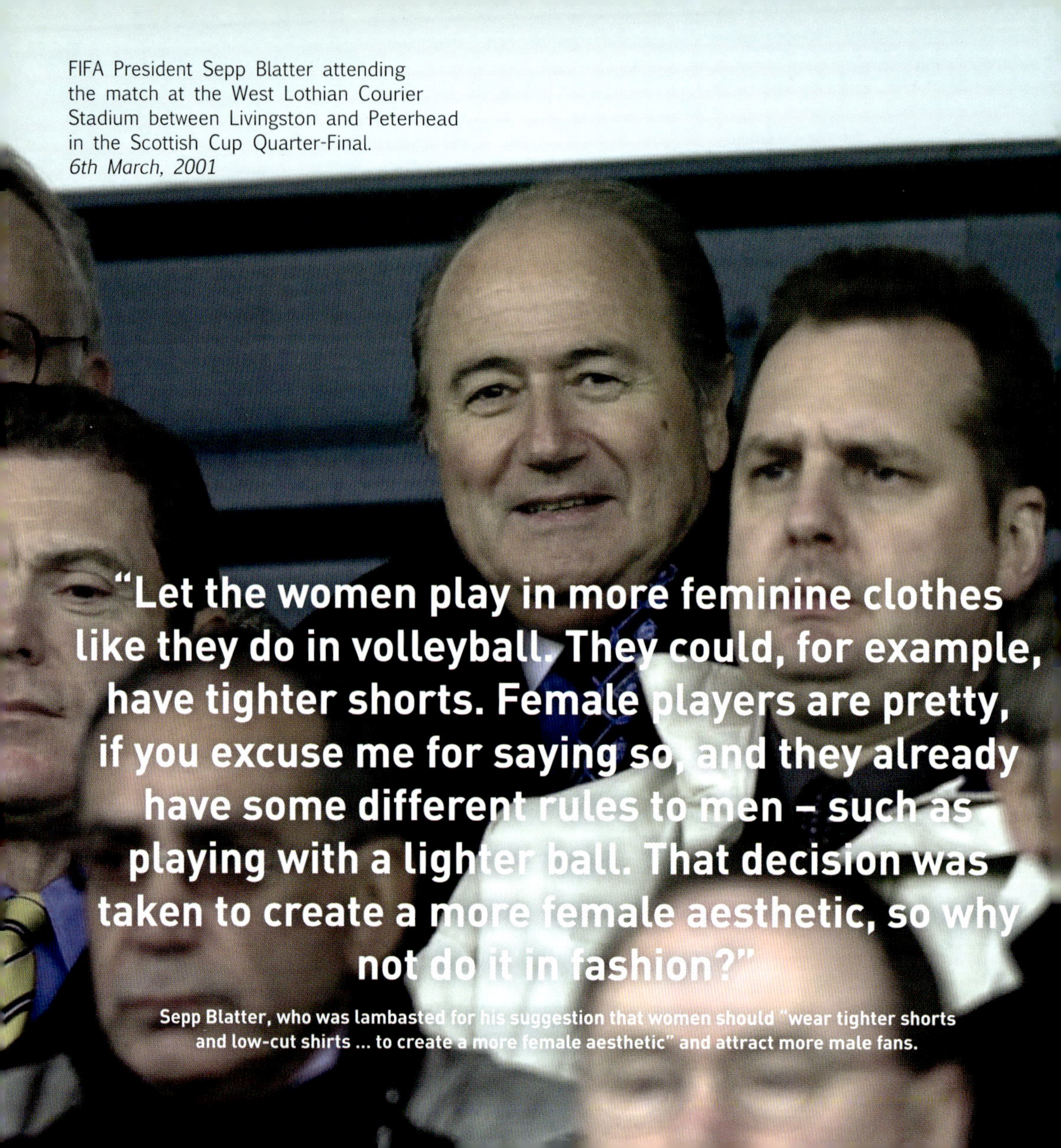

"Let the women play in more feminine clothes like they do in volleyball. They could, for example, have tighter shorts. Female players are pretty, if you excuse me for saying so, and they already have some different rules to men – such as playing with a lighter ball. That decision was taken to create a more female aesthetic, so why not do it in fashion?"

Sepp Blatter, who was lambasted for his suggestion that women should "wear tighter shorts and low-cut shirts ... to create a more female aesthetic" and attract more male fans.

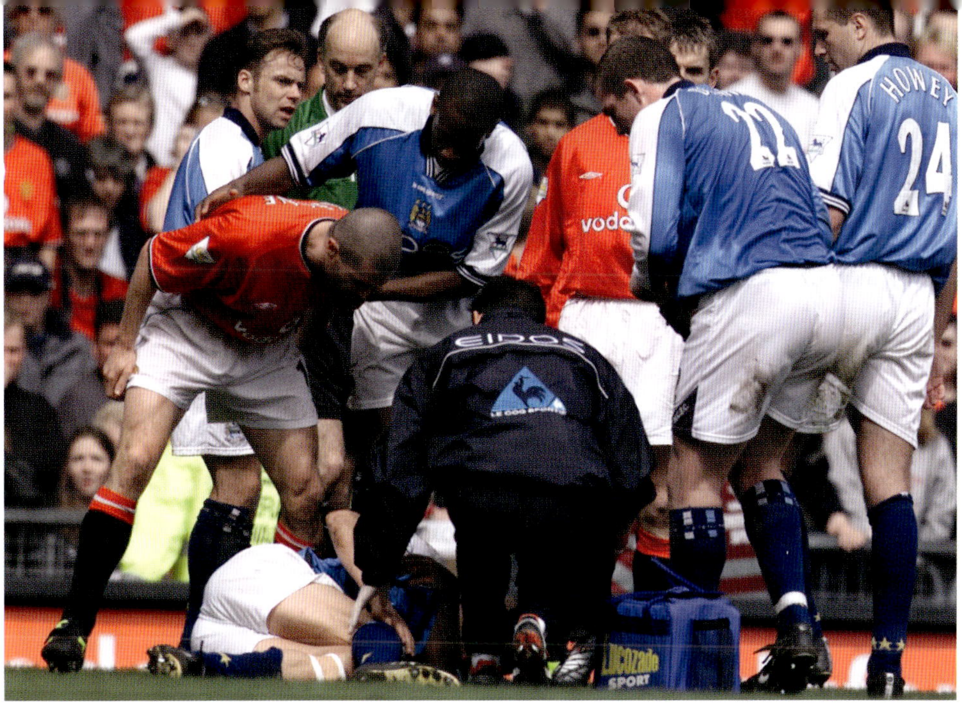

"I'd waited long enough. I f***ing hit him hard. The ball was there (I think). Take that you c**t. And don't ever stand over me sneering about fake injuries."

Roy Keane, Irish former footballer and manager, in his biography, on the dispute with Alf-Inge Haaland.

Manchester United's captain, Roy Keane (L), taunts Manchester City's Alf-Inge Haaland (on ground) after being sent off for a blatant knee-high foul on the Norwegian. In Keane's autobiography, he stated that the foul was revenge for a cruciate ligament injury he'd sustained in 1997, during an attempt to tackle the then Leeds player in a Premier League game. As Keane lay on the ground, Haaland accused him of feigning injury to escape punishment for the foul. Haaland never played a full game of football again. *21st April, 2001*

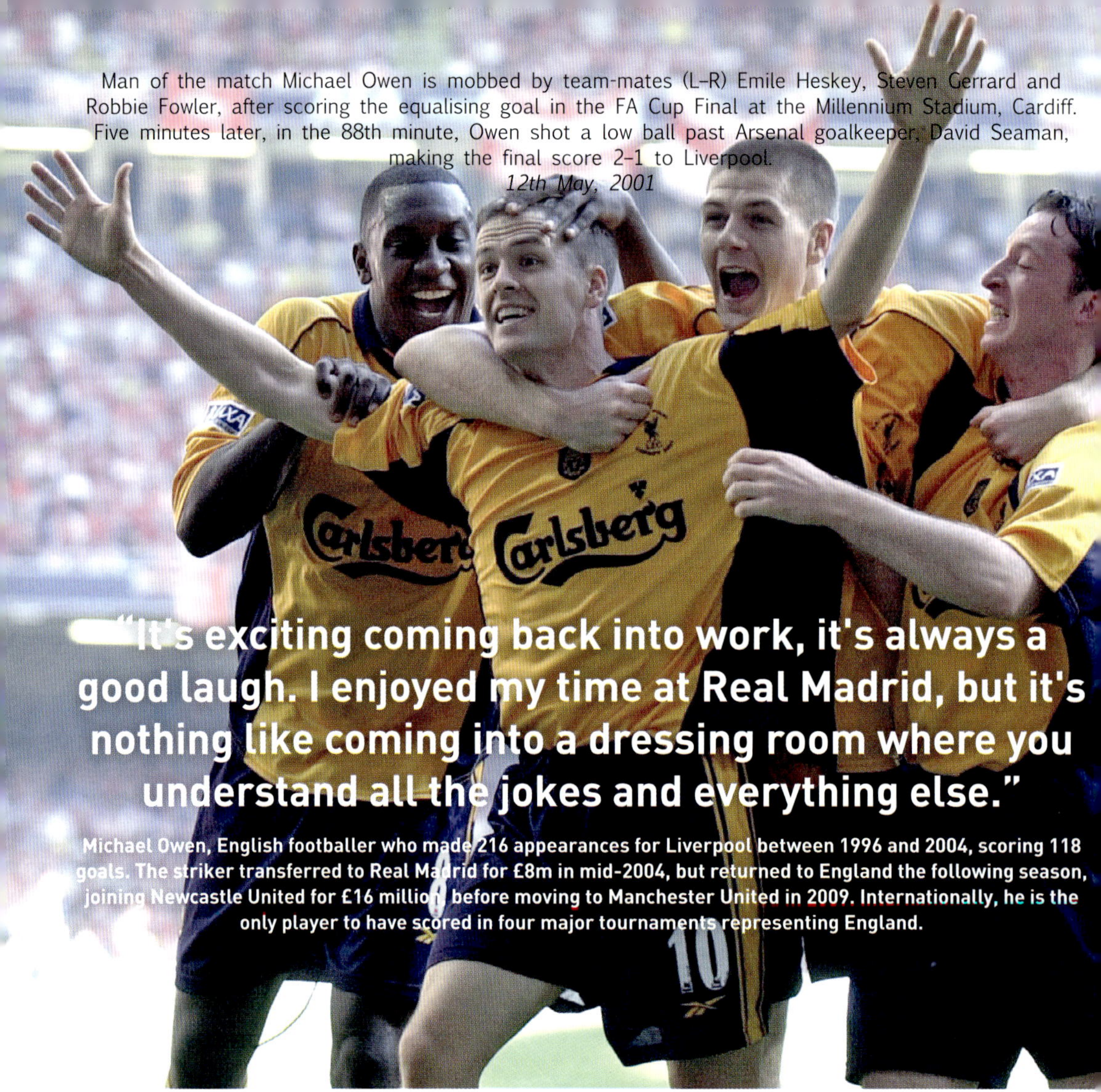

Man of the match Michael Owen is mobbed by team-mates (L–R) Emile Heskey, Steven Gerrard and Robbie Fowler, after scoring the equalising goal in the FA Cup Final at the Millennium Stadium, Cardiff. Five minutes later, in the 88th minute, Owen shot a low ball past Arsenal goalkeeper, David Seaman, making the final score 2–1 to Liverpool.
12th May, 2001

"It's exciting coming back into work, it's always a good laugh. I enjoyed my time at Real Madrid, but it's nothing like coming into a dressing room where you understand all the jokes and everything else."

Michael Owen, English footballer who made 216 appearances for Liverpool between 1996 and 2004, scoring 118 goals. The striker transferred to Real Madrid for £8m in mid-2004, but returned to England the following season, joining Newcastle United for £16 million, before moving to Manchester United in 2009. Internationally, he is the only player to have scored in four major tournaments representing England.

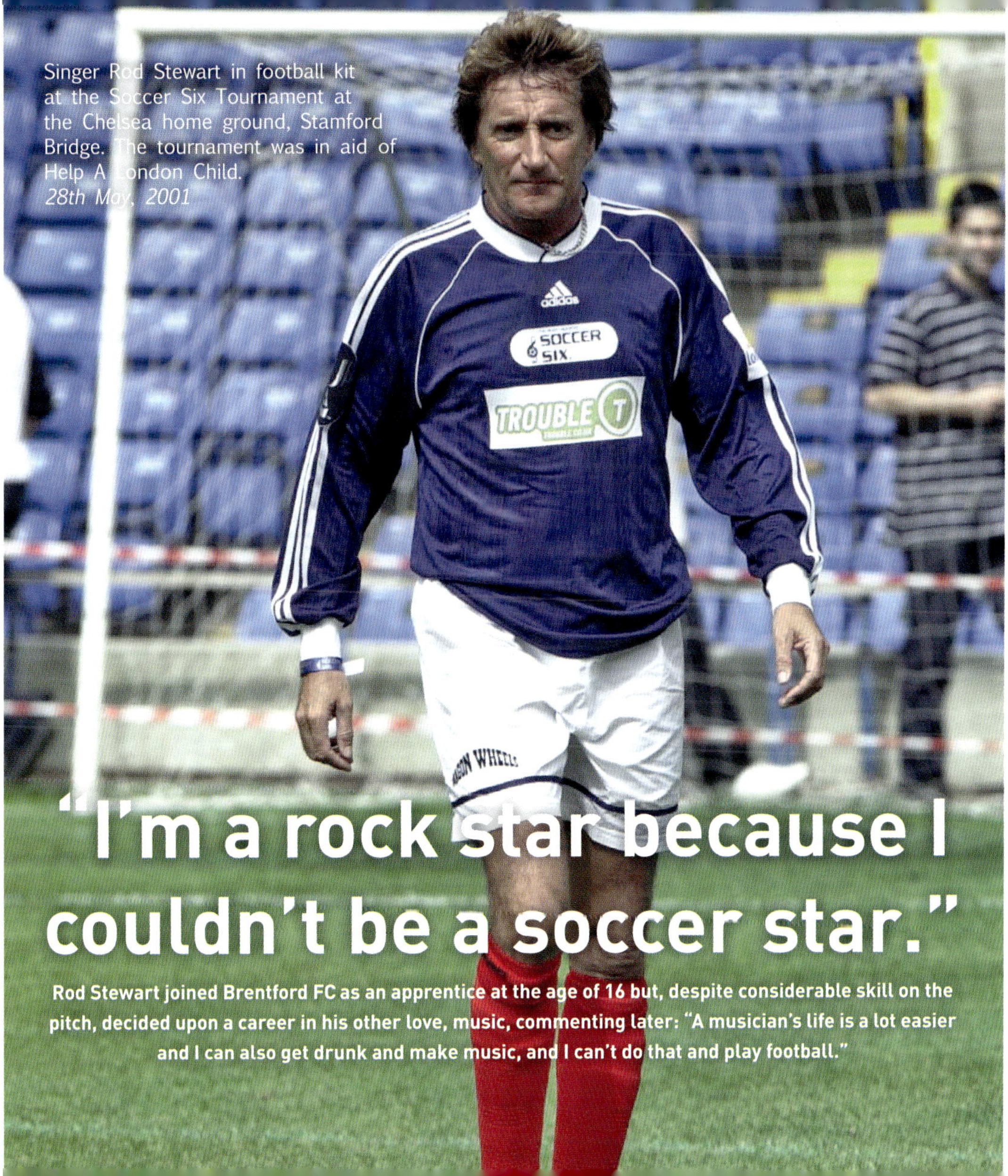

Singer Rod Stewart in football kit at the Soccer Six Tournament at the Chelsea home ground, Stamford Bridge. The tournament was in aid of Help A London Child.
28th May, 2001

"I'm a rock star because I couldn't be a soccer star."

Rod Stewart joined Brentford FC as an apprentice at the age of 16 but, despite considerable skill on the pitch, decided upon a career in his other love, music, commenting later: "A musician's life is a lot easier and I can also get drunk and make music, and I can't do that and play football."

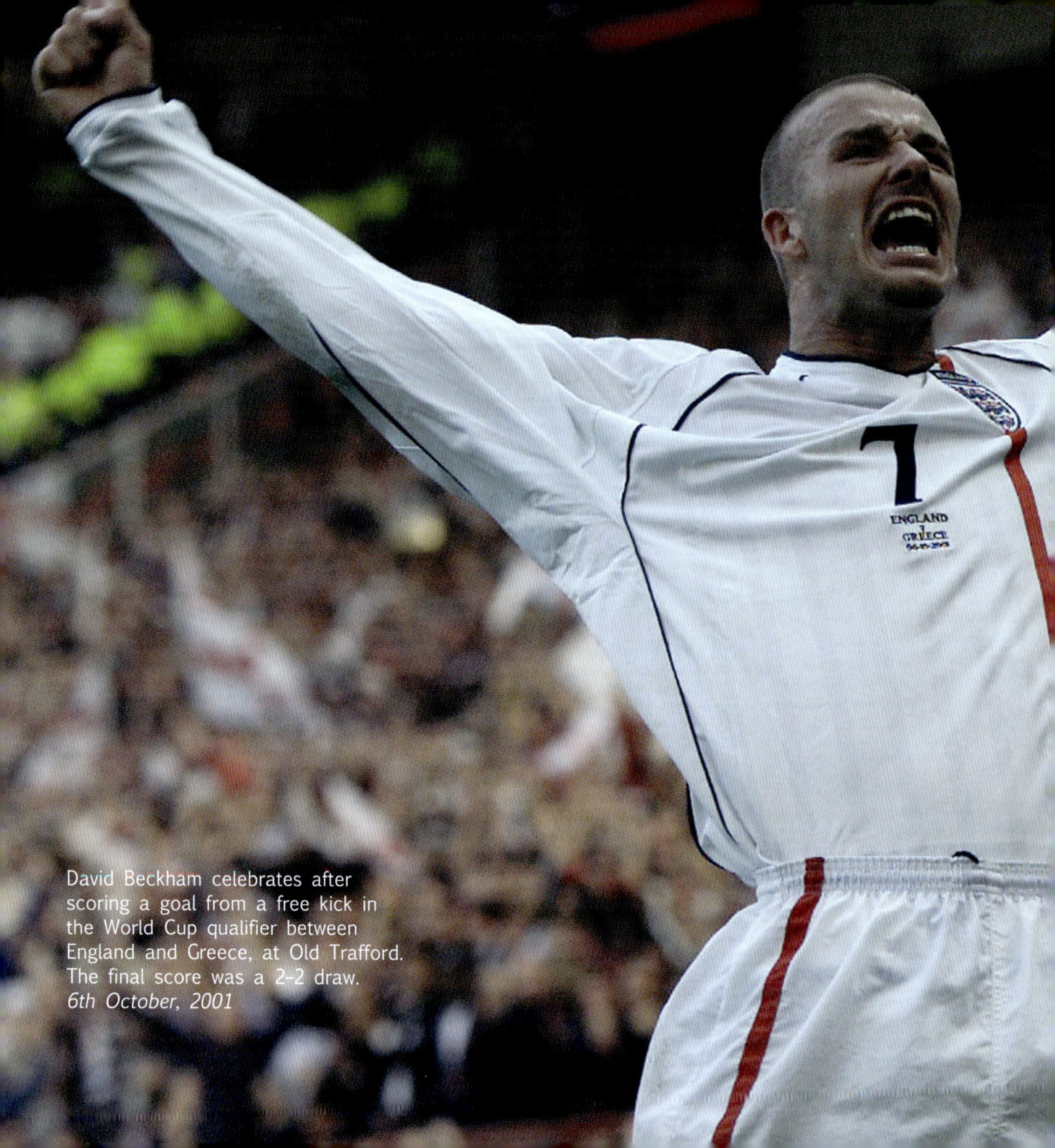

David Beckham celebrates after scoring a goal from a free kick in the World Cup qualifier between England and Greece, at Old Trafford. The final score was a 2-2 draw.
6th October, 2001

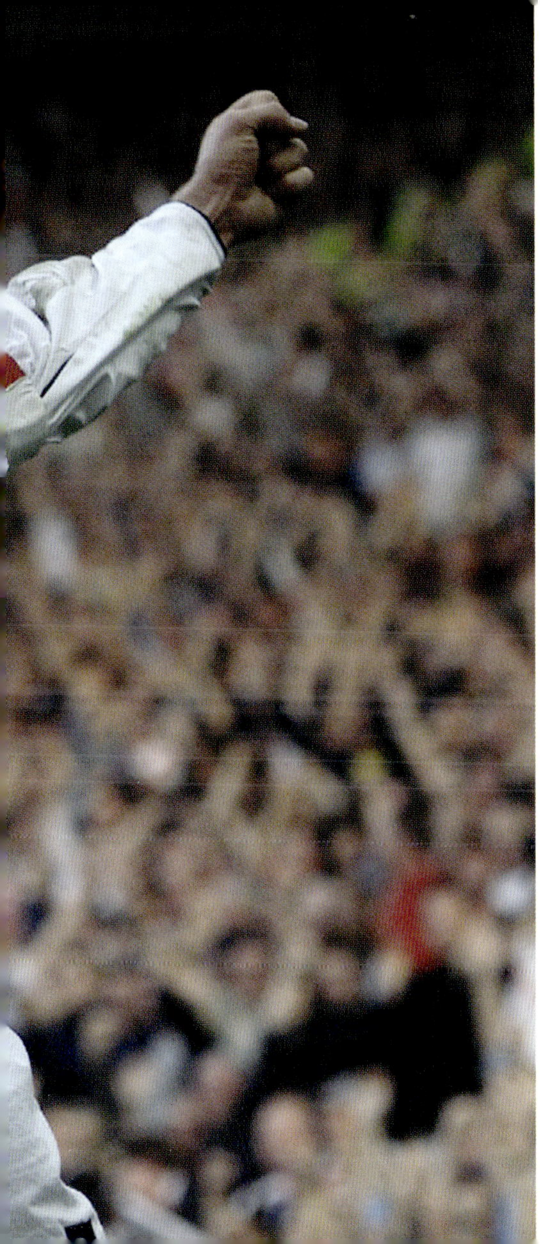

"My parents have been there for me, ever since I was about seven."

David Beckham.

"It had nothing to do with women and booze, car crashes or court cases. It was purely football. Losing wasn't in my vocabulary. When the wonderful players I had been brought up with – Charlton, Law, Crerand, Stiles – went into decline, United made no real attempt to buy the best replacements. I was left struggling among fellas who should not have been allowed through the door. It sickened me that we ended up being just about the worst team in the First Division."

George Best, on the disenchantment that led him to retire from football in 1984.

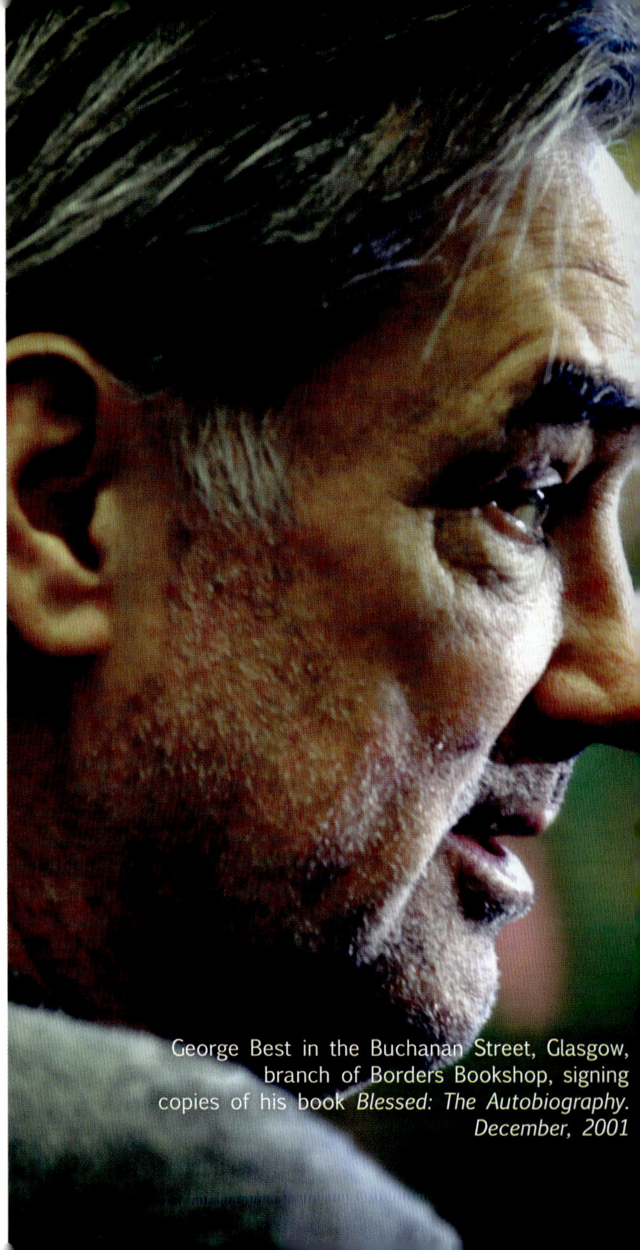

George Best in the Buchanan Street, Glasgow, branch of Borders Bookshop, signing copies of his book *Blessed: The Autobiography.* *December, 2001*

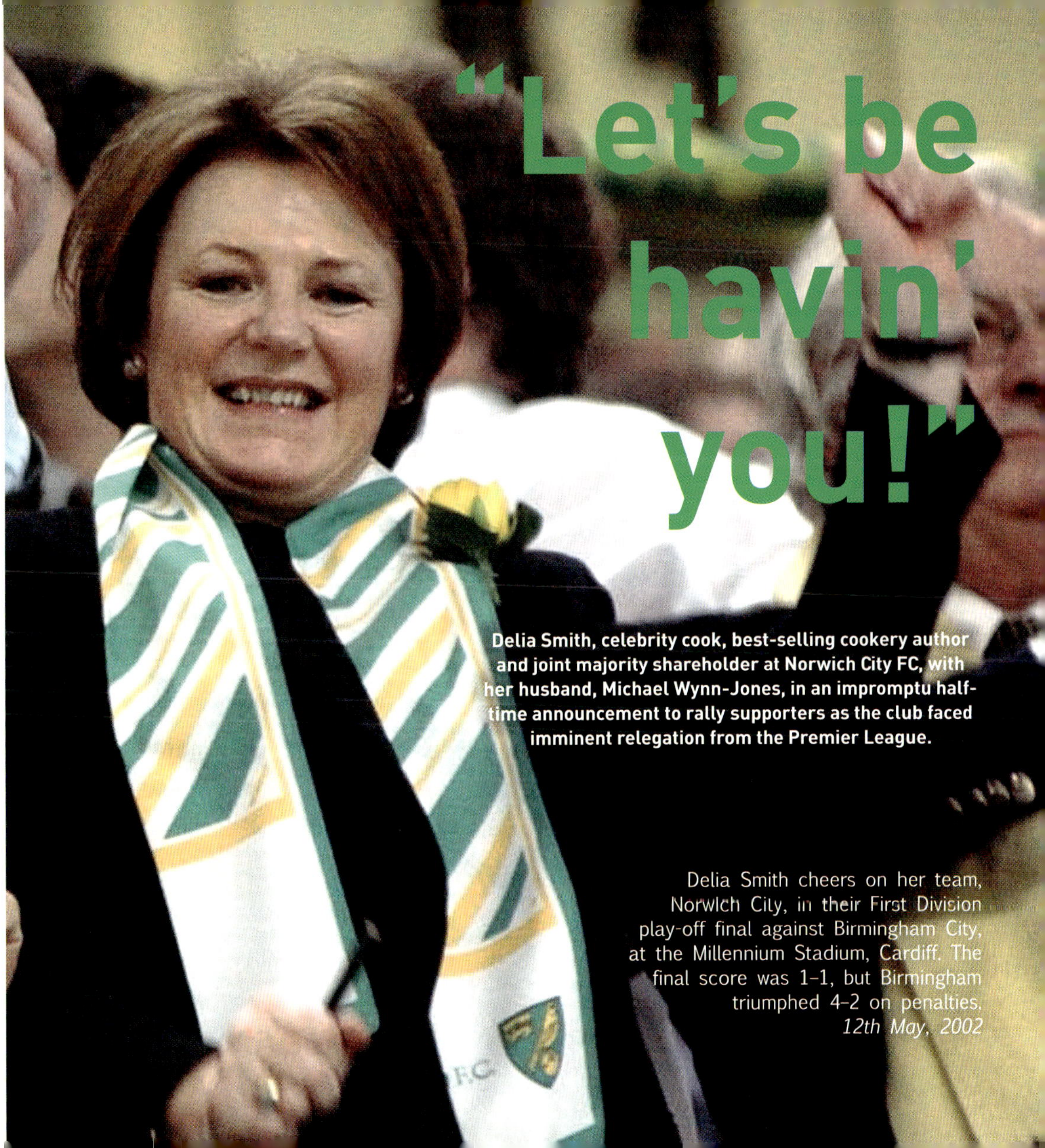

"Let's be havin' you!"

Delia Smith, celebrity cook, best-selling cookery author and joint majority shareholder at Norwich City FC, with her husband, Michael Wynn-Jones, in an impromptu half-time announcement to rally supporters as the club faced imminent relegation from the Premier League.

Delia Smith cheers on her team, Norwich City, in their First Division play-off final against Birmingham City, at the Millennium Stadium, Cardiff. The final score was 1–1, but Birmingham triumphed 4–2 on penalties. *12th May, 2002*

"Well, I can play in the centre, on the right and occasionally on the left side."

David Beckham, in response to an interviewer's question: "Would it be fair to describe you as a volatile player?"

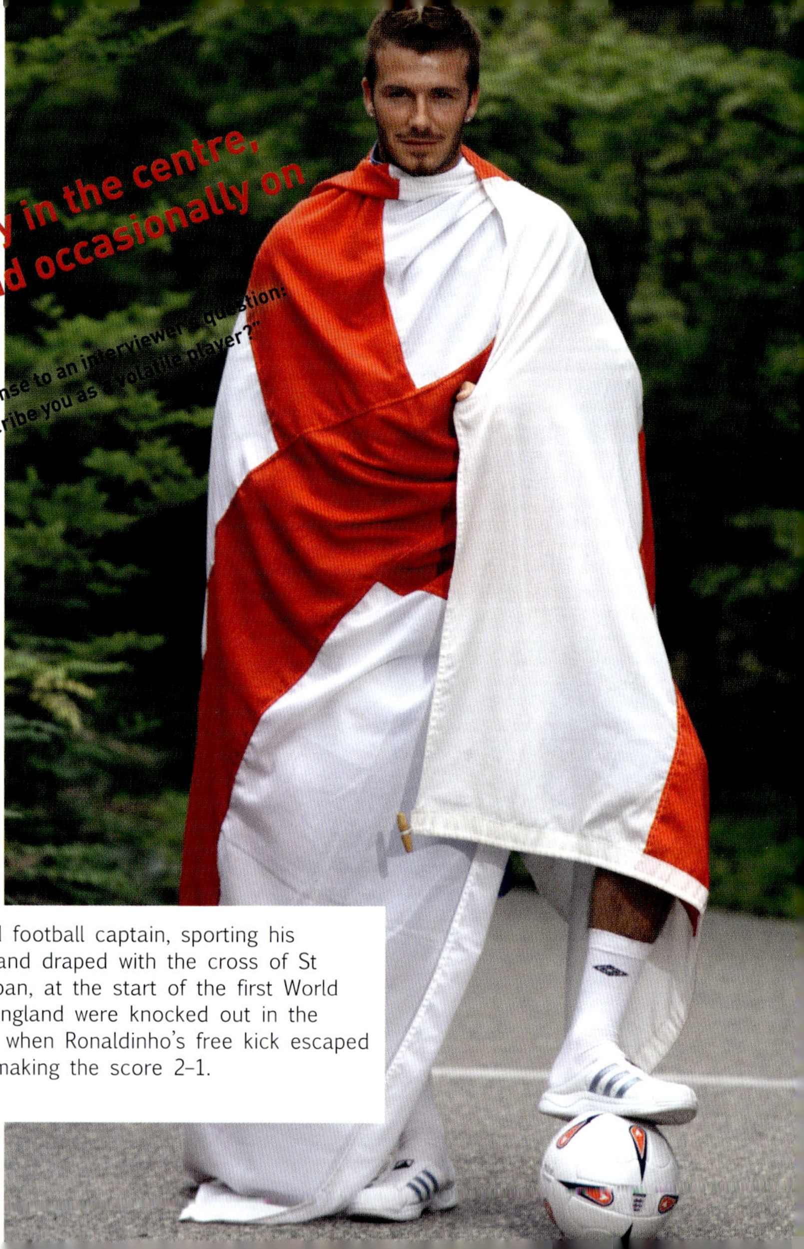

David Beckham, the England football captain, sporting his distinctive mohican hairdo, and draped with the cross of St George, on Awaji Island, Japan, at the start of the first World Cup to be staged in Asia. England were knocked out in the quarter-finals against Brazil, when Ronaldinho's free kick escaped goalkeeper David Seaman, making the score 2–1.
31st May, 2002

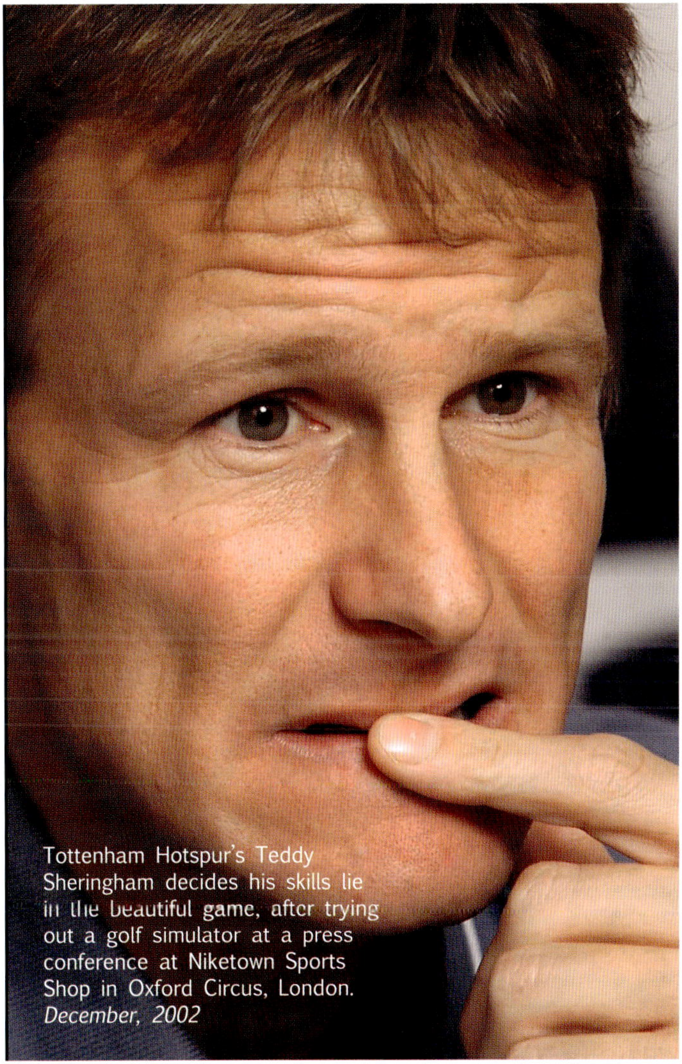

Tottenham Hotspur's Teddy Sheringham decides his skills lie in the beautiful game, after trying out a golf simulator at a press conference at Niketown Sports Shop in Oxford Circus, London. *December, 2002*

"I love going into the centre of London because people don't give a monkey's about you or who you are. You can be in a restaurant and no one notices you or if they do they won't show it."

Teddy Sheringham, retired English striker, with an illustrious career at club level over 25 years and 51 appearances for England, reflecting on the fickle nature of fame.

"Football is a simple game. Twenty-two men chase a ball for 90 minutes and at the end, the Germans always win."

Gary Lineker, English former footballer and sports broadcaster, who appeared 80 times for England, becoming the national side's top goal scorer in the World Cup Final.

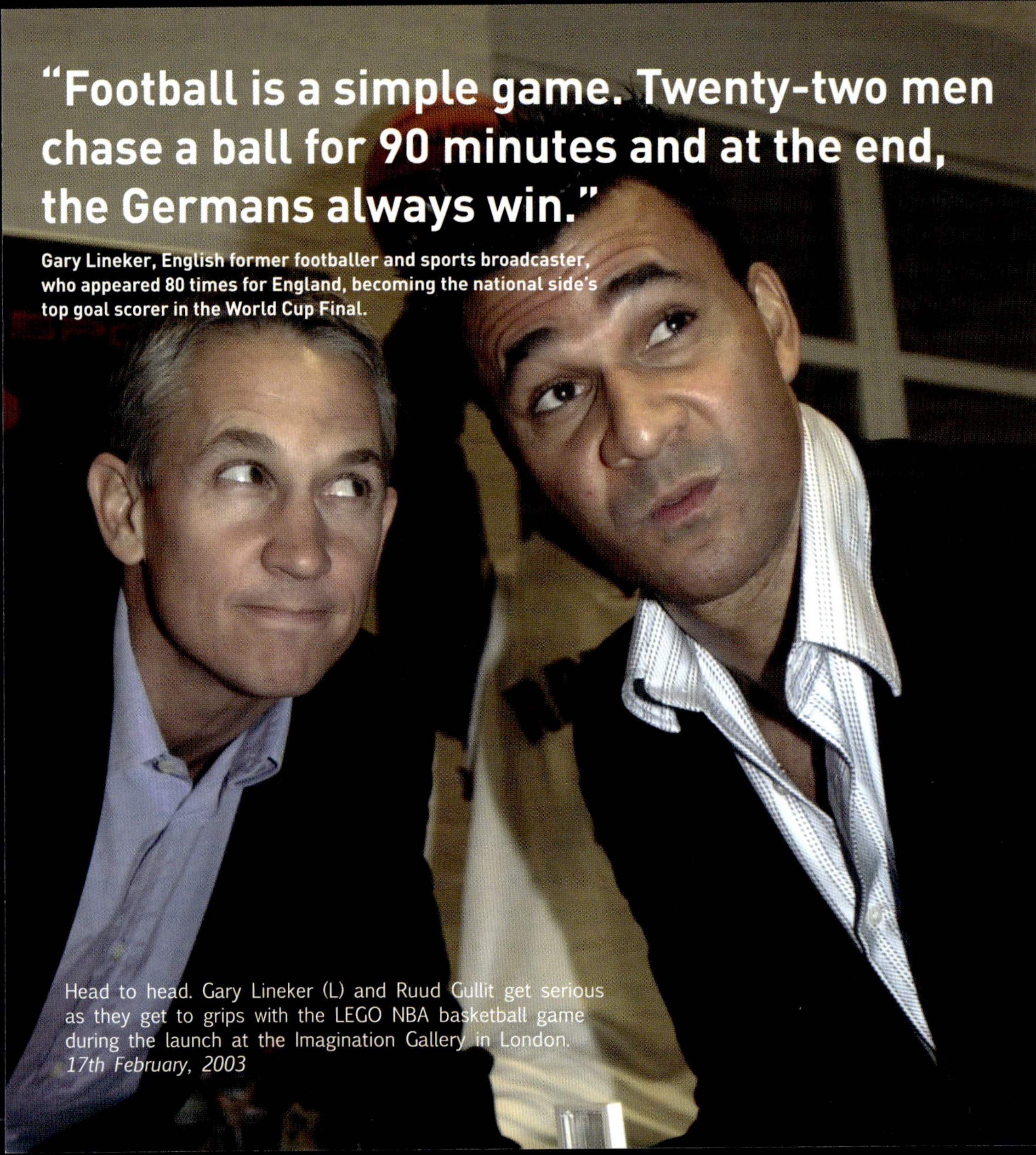

Head to head. Gary Lineker (L) and Ruud Gullit get serious as they get to grips with the LEGO NBA basketball game during the launch at the Imagination Gallery in London. *17th February, 2003*

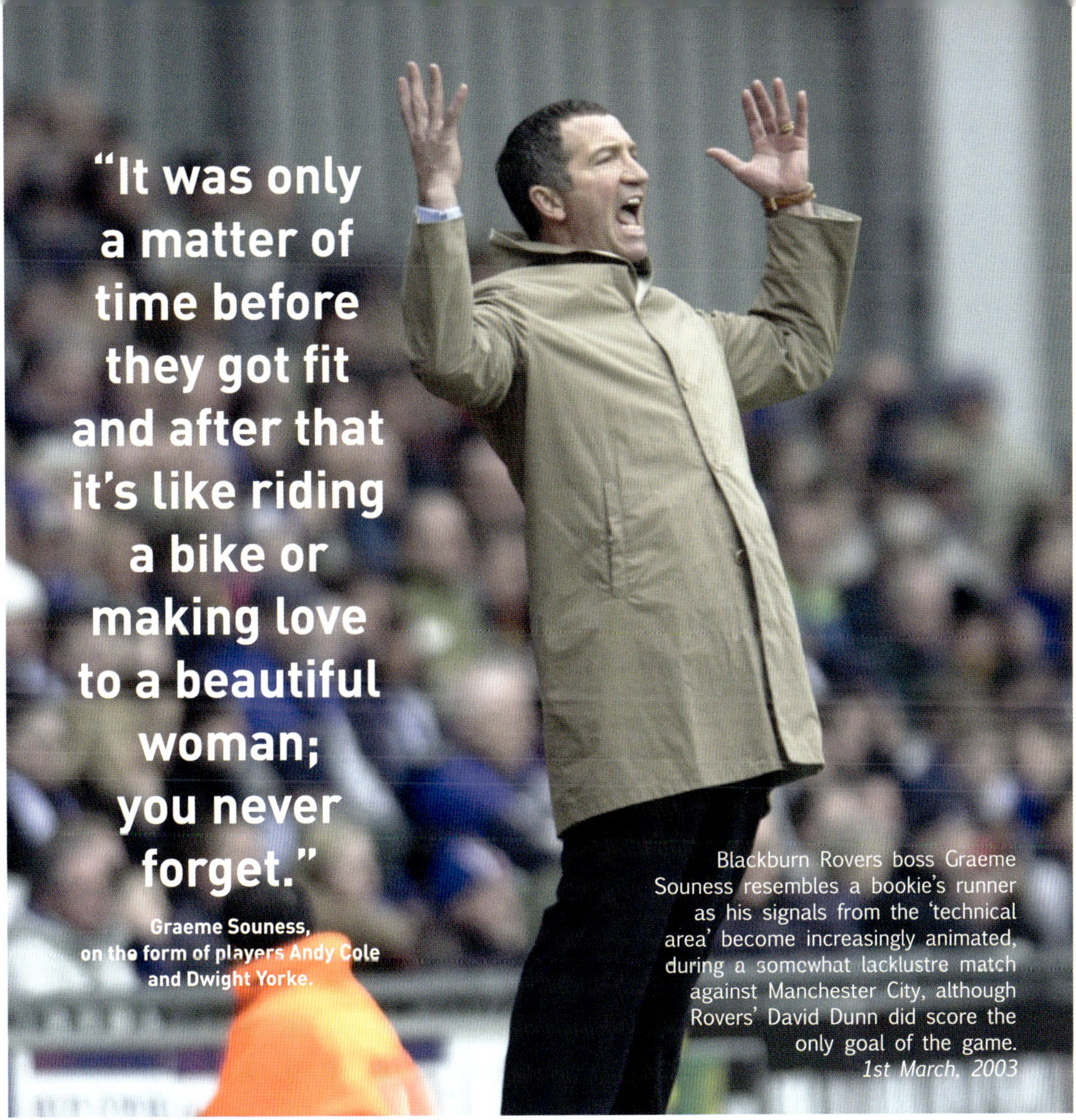

"It was only a matter of time before they got fit and after that it's like riding a bike or making love to a beautiful woman; you never forget."

Graeme Souness, on the form of players Andy Cole and Dwight Yorke.

Blackburn Rovers boss Graeme Souness resembles a bookie's runner as his signals from the 'technical area' become increasingly animated, during a somewhat lacklustre match against Manchester City, although Rovers' David Dunn did score the only goal of the game.
1st March, 2003

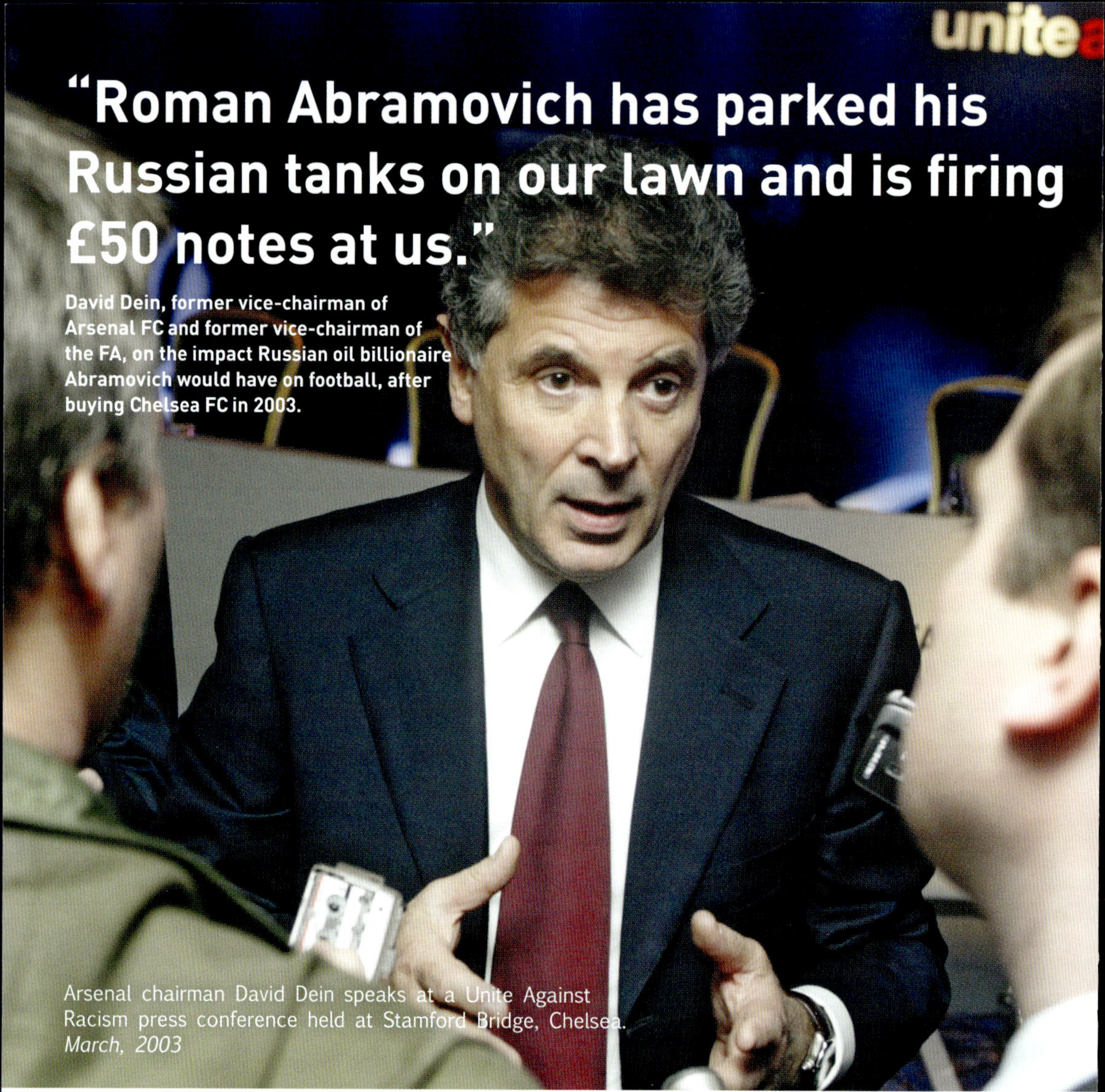

"Roman Abramovich has parked his Russian tanks on our lawn and is firing £50 notes at us."

David Dein, former vice-chairman of Arsenal FC and former vice-chairman of the FA, on the impact Russian oil billionaire Abramovich would have on football, after buying Chelsea FC in 2003.

Arsenal chairman David Dein speaks at a Unite Against Racism press conference held at Stamford Bridge, Chelsea. *March, 2003*

"Germany are a very difficult team to play... they had 11 internationals out there today."

Steve Lomas, former Northern Ireland midfield player, who made 111 appearances for Manchester City, 187 for West Ham United, and subsequently played for three other English clubs before turning to management in 2009.

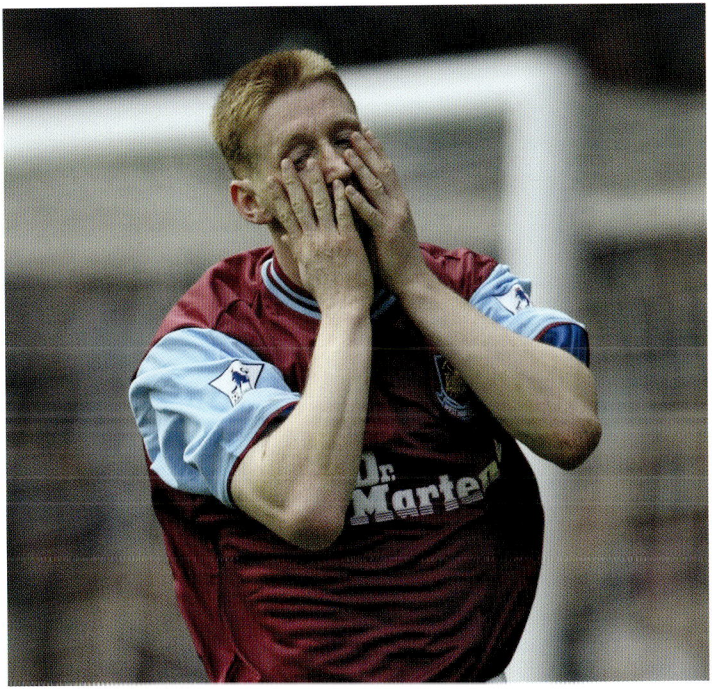

A downhearted Steve Lomas of West Ham United during the Premier League match against Aston Villa. The game ended in a 2–2 draw.
12th April, 2003

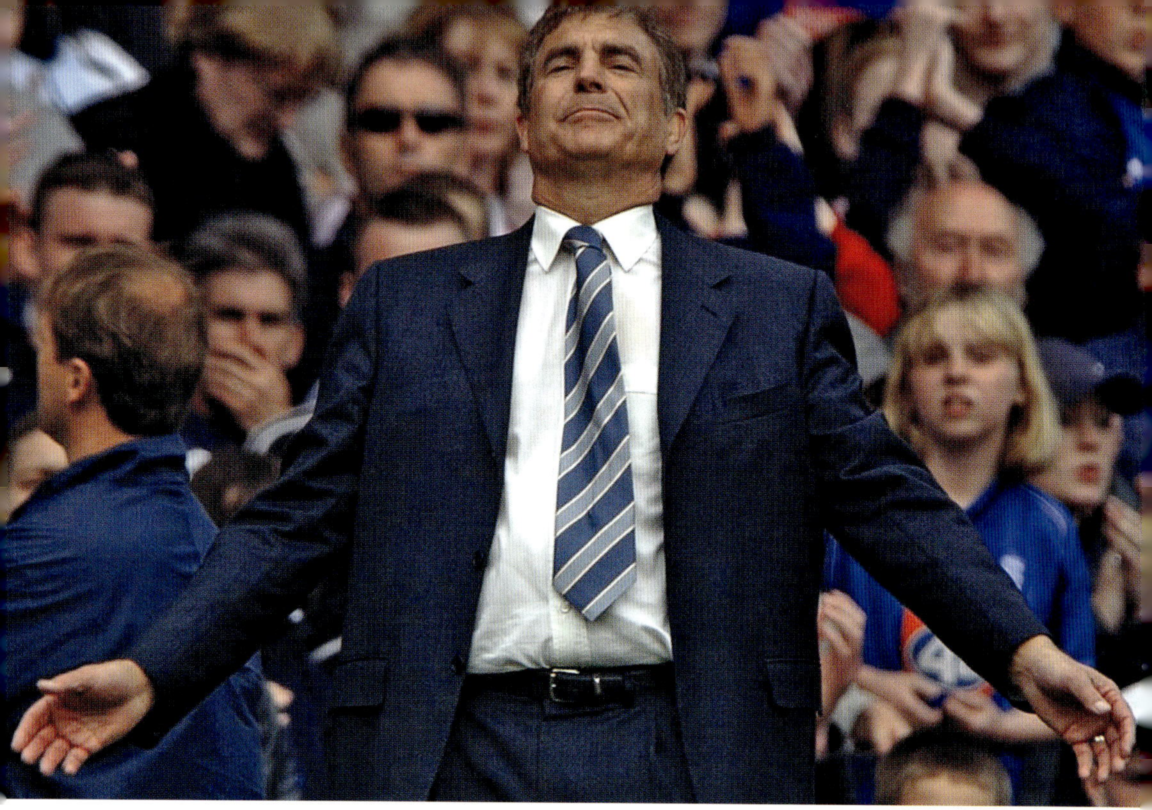

"Unfortunately, we don't get a second chance. We've already played them twice."

West Ham caretaker manager Trevor Brooking summons up positive energy during the league match against Birmingham City at St Andrews – but the next minute, it all goes horribly wrong. West Ham were on the brink of relegation, and although Birmingham only managed a 2–2 draw, thanks to goals from Horsfield and John, it was enough to send the Hammers down.
11th May, 2003

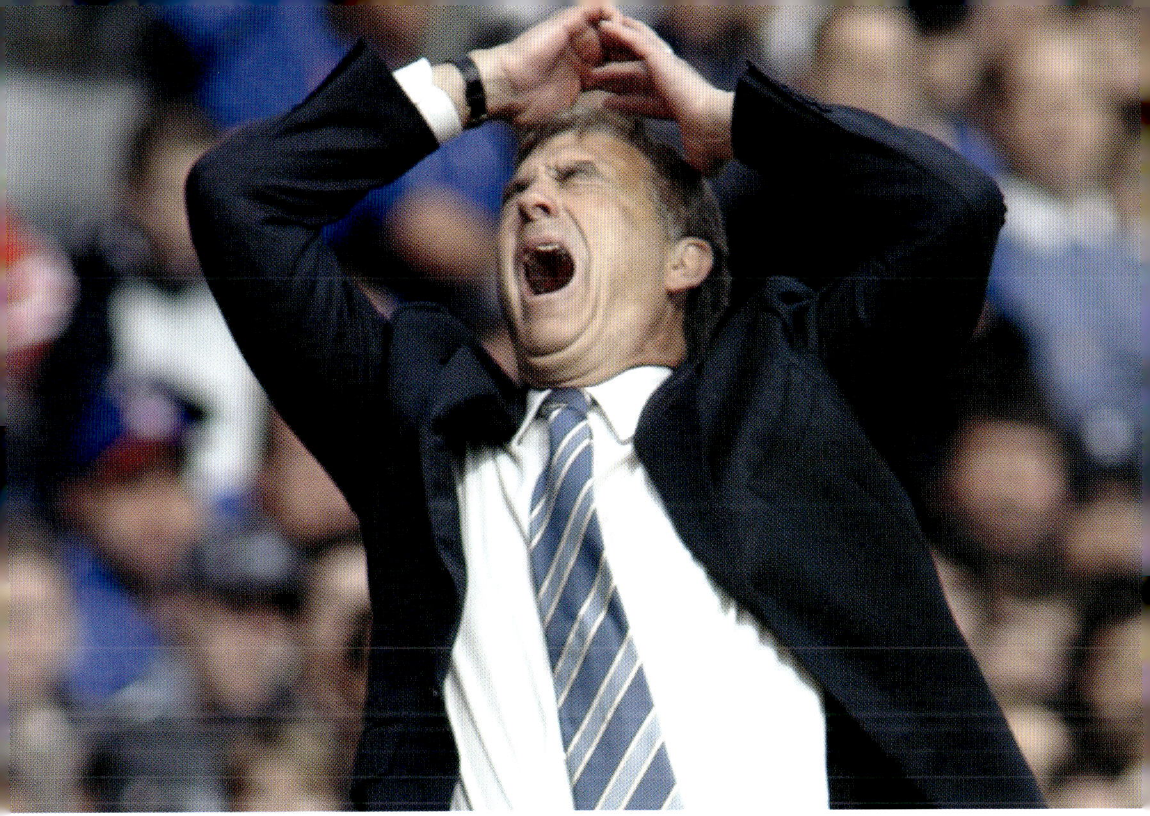

"If you're going to score one goal or less, you're not going to get your victories."

Trevor Brooking, former footballer turned manager, broadcast analyst and administrator, chiefly associated with West Ham United. A popular caretaker manager for two periods during 2003, Brooking is known as 'the best manager West Ham never had'.

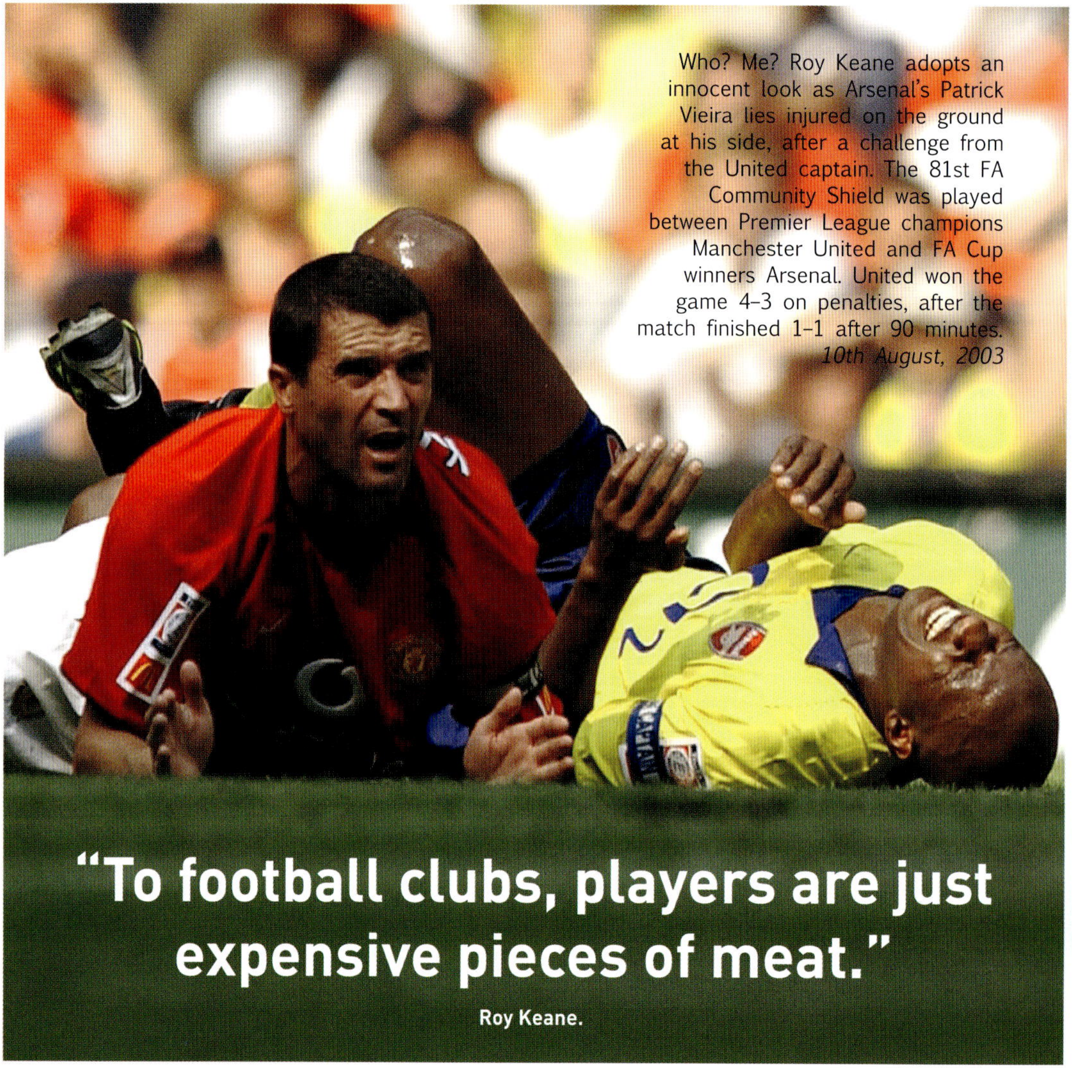

Who? Me? Roy Keane adopts an innocent look as Arsenal's Patrick Vieira lies injured on the ground at his side, after a challenge from the United captain. The 81st FA Community Shield was played between Premier League champions Manchester United and FA Cup winners Arsenal. United won the game 4–3 on penalties, after the match finished 1–1 after 90 minutes.
10th August, 2003

"To football clubs, players are just expensive pieces of meat."

Roy Keane.

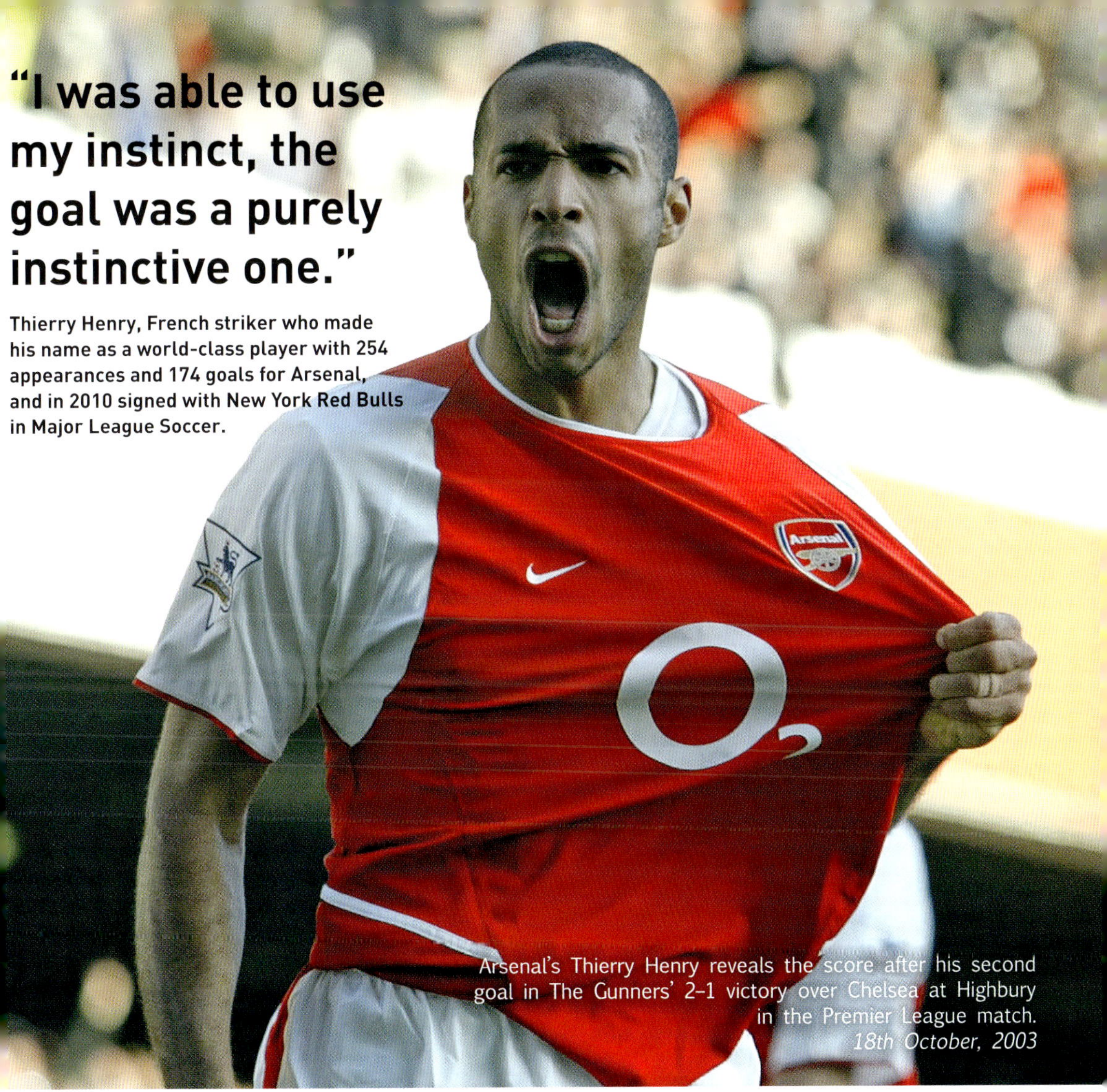

"I was able to use my instinct, the goal was a purely instinctive one."

Thierry Henry, French striker who made his name as a world-class player with 254 appearances and 174 goals for Arsenal, and in 2010 signed with New York Red Bulls in Major League Soccer.

Arsenal's Thierry Henry reveals the score after his second goal in The Gunners' 2–1 victory over Chelsea at Highbury in the Premier League match.
18th October, 2003

“Because I love football and I love the footballers.”

Sepp Blatter.

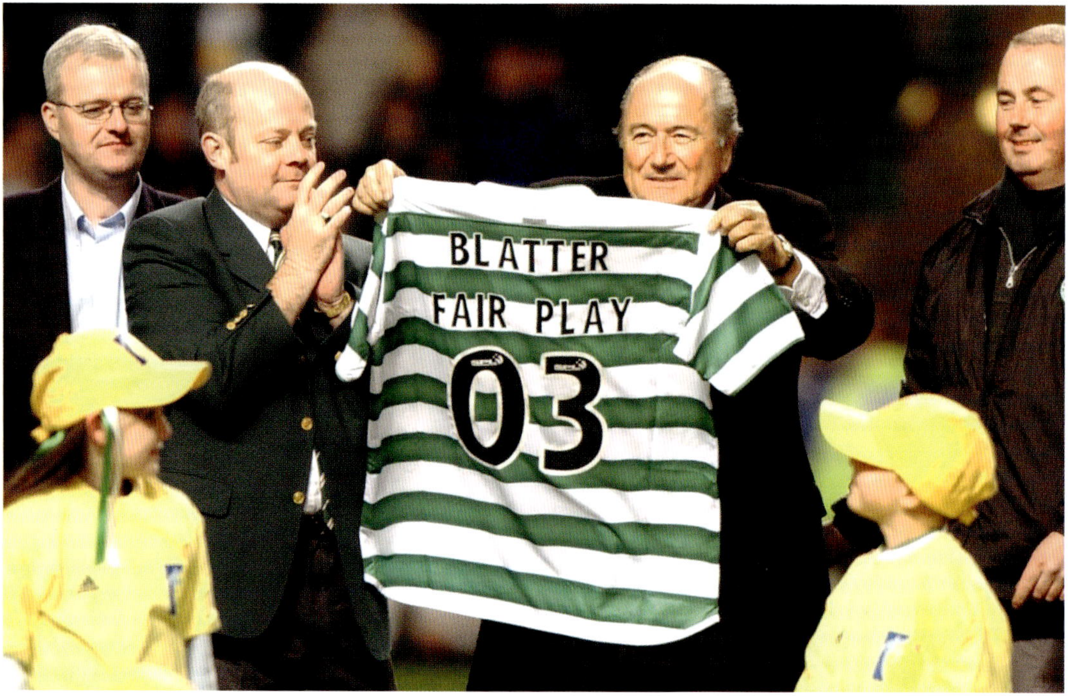

FIFA President Sepp Blatter (second R) with the FIFA Fair Play Award, presented to Celtic supporters for their exemplary behaviour in the days surrounding the 2003 UEFA Cup Final, in Spain, in which the Scottish team played. The score of the UEFA Cup Final match at Celtic Park was Celtic 3 FK Teplice 0.
26th February, 2004

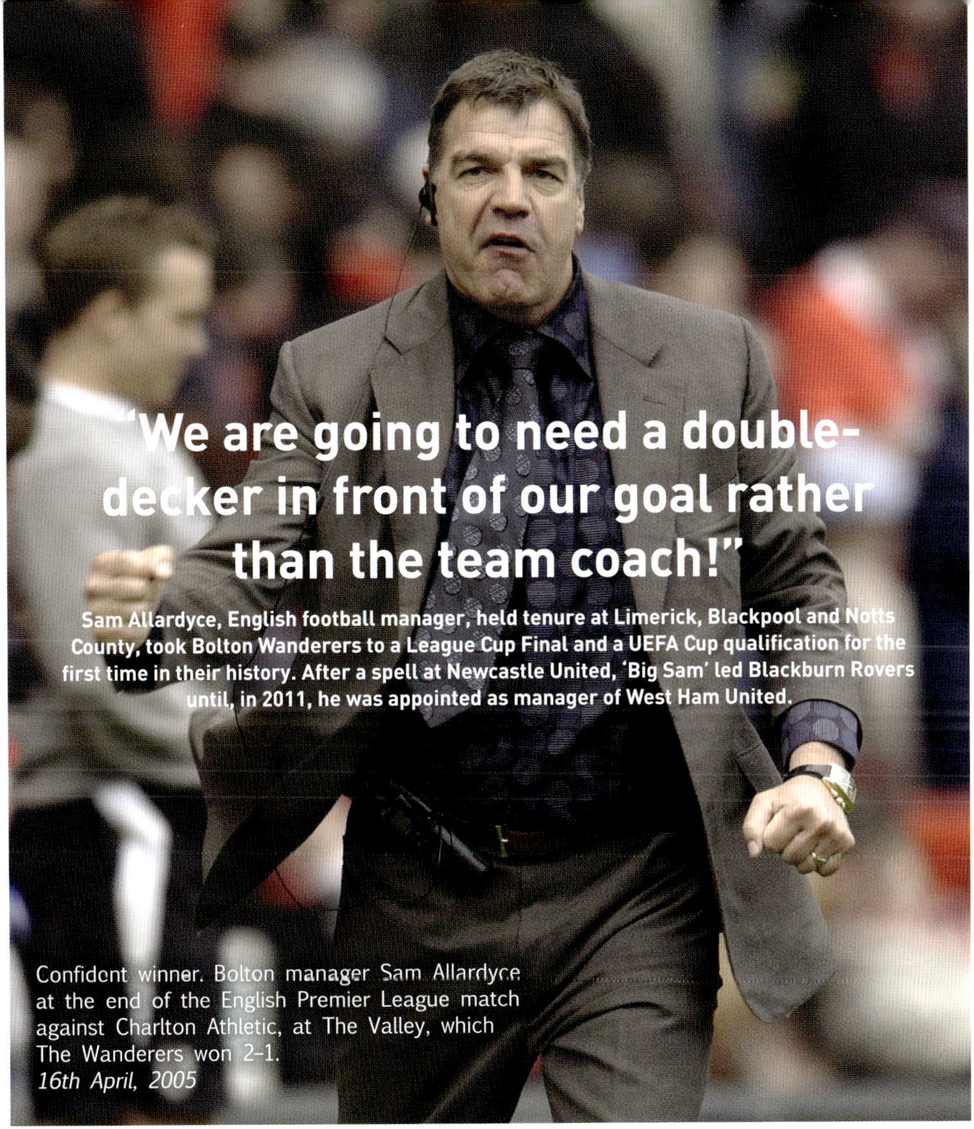

"We are going to need a double-decker in front of our goal rather than the team coach!"

Sam Allardyce, English football manager, held tenure at Limerick, Blackpool and Notts County, took Bolton Wanderers to a League Cup Final and a UEFA Cup qualification for the first time in their history. After a spell at Newcastle United, 'Big Sam' led Blackburn Rovers until, in 2011, he was appointed as manager of West Ham United.

Confident winner. Bolton manager Sam Allardyce at the end of the English Premier League match against Charlton Athletic, at The Valley, which The Wanderers won 2–1.
16th April, 2005

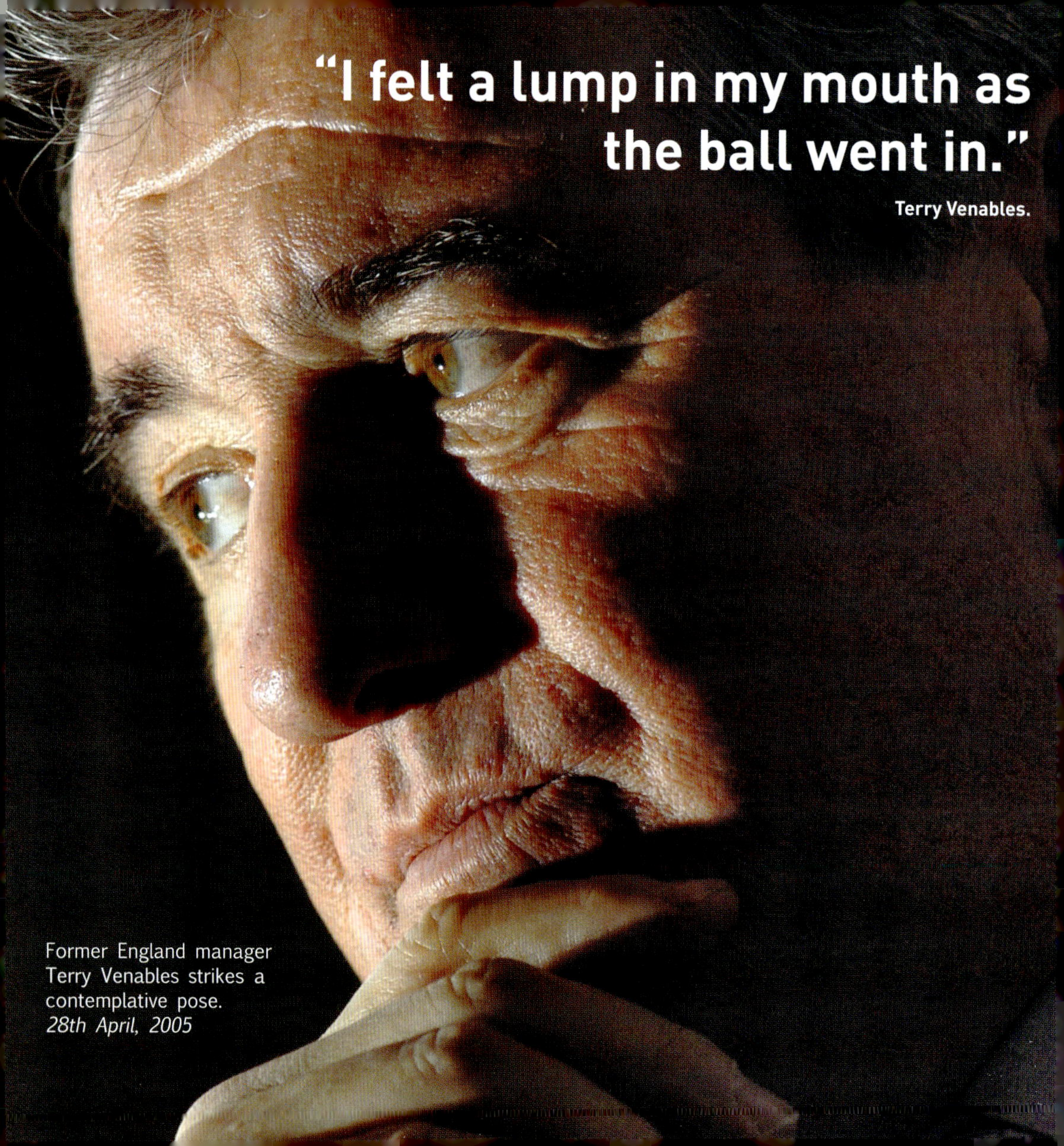

Former England manager Terry Venables strikes a contemplative pose.
28th April, 2005

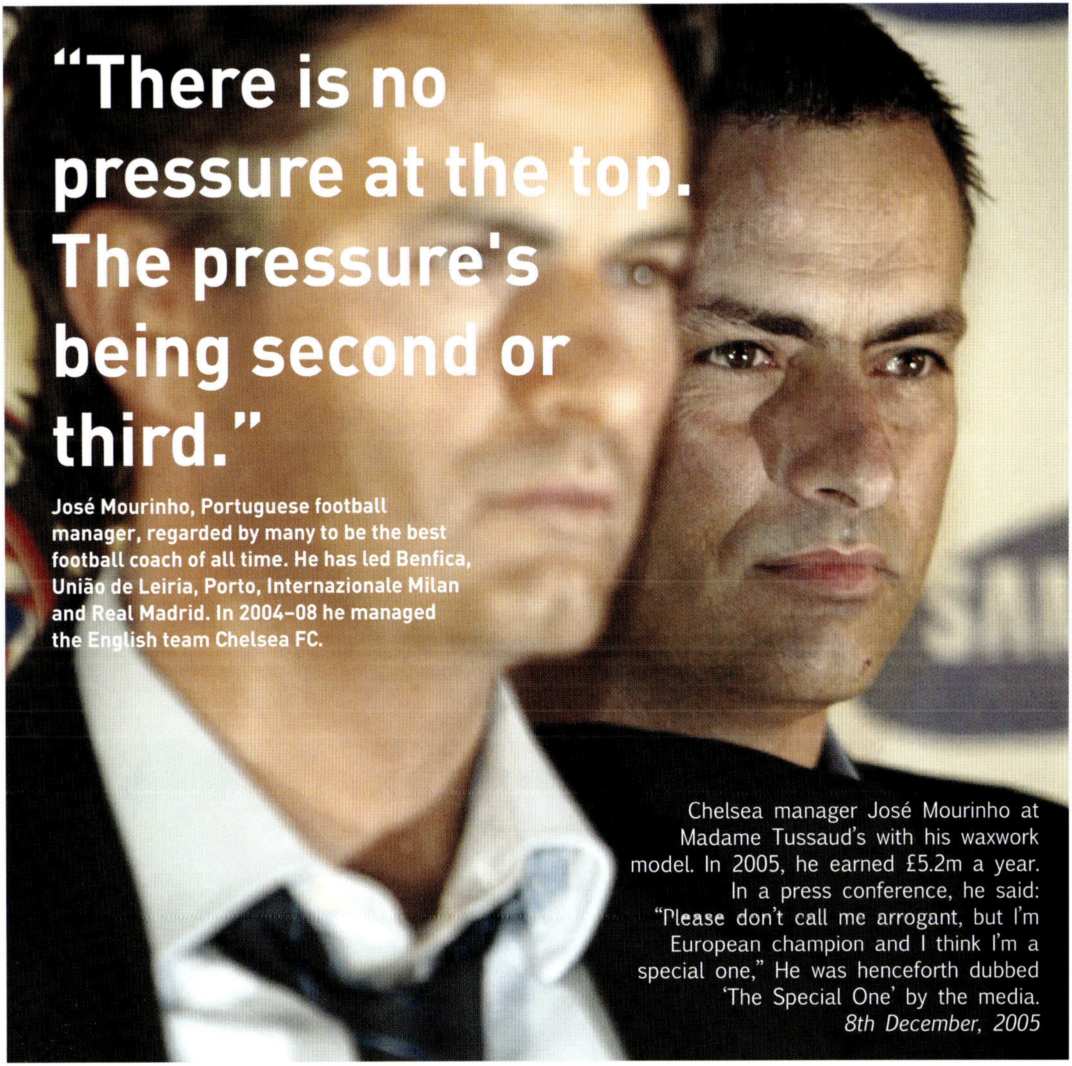

"There is no pressure at the top. The pressure's being second or third."

José Mourinho, Portuguese football manager, regarded by many to be the best football coach of all time. He has led Benfica, União de Leiria, Porto, Internazionale Milan and Real Madrid. In 2004–08 he managed the English team Chelsea FC.

Chelsea manager José Mourinho at Madame Tussaud's with his waxwork model. In 2005, he earned £5.2m a year. In a press conference, he said: "Please don't call me arrogant, but I'm European champion and I think I'm a special one," He was henceforth dubbed 'The Special One' by the media. *8th December, 2005*

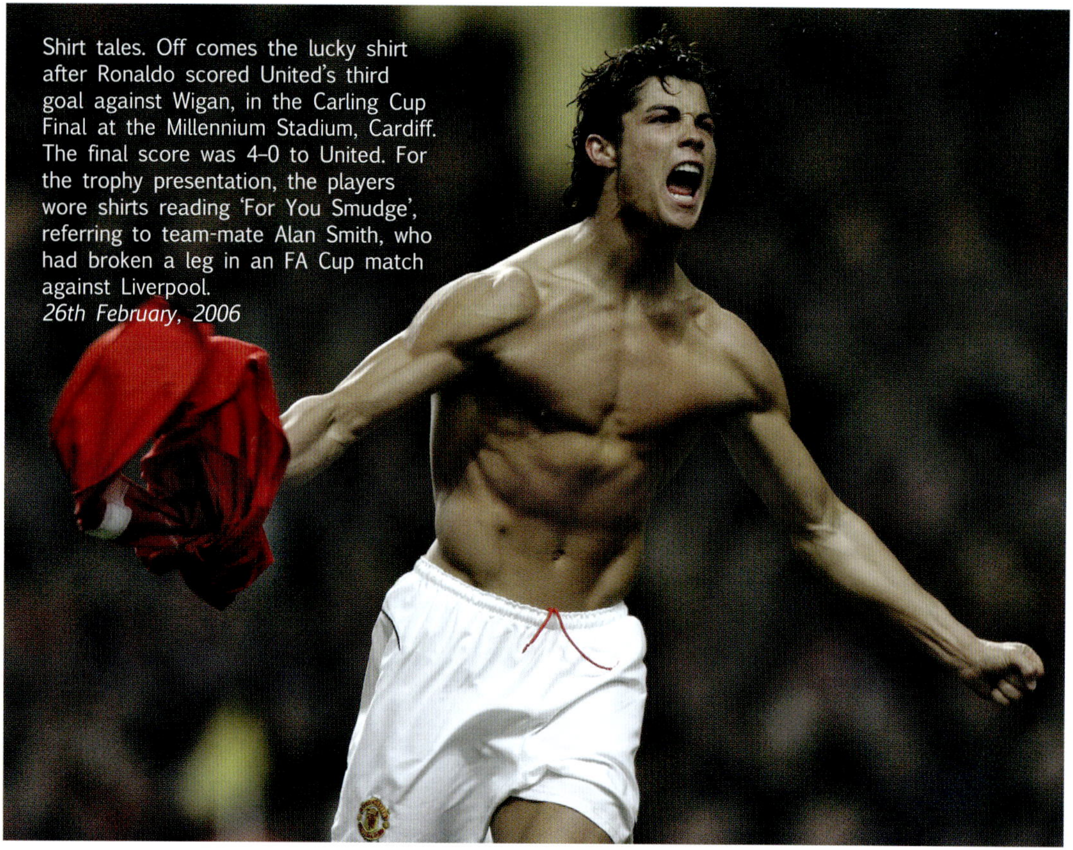

Shirt tales. Off comes the lucky shirt after Ronaldo scored United's third goal against Wigan, in the Carling Cup Final at the Millennium Stadium, Cardiff. The final score was 4–0 to United. For the trophy presentation, the players wore shirts reading 'For You Smudge', referring to team-mate Alan Smith, who had broken a leg in an FA Cup match against Liverpool.
26th February, 2006

"The No 7 shirt is an honor and a responsibility. I hope it brings me a lot of luck."

Cristiano Ronaldo, Portuguese footballer, who signed for Manchester United in 2003, on being asked to wear the shirt previously worn by George Best, Eric Cantona and David Beckham. He became the most expensive player in football history after moving from United to Real Madrid in 2009, in a transfer deal worth £80m.

"Peter Schmeichel says that the present Man United team would beat the 1968 European Cup winners. He's got a point, because we're over 50 now."

Nobby Stiles, on a comment by the retired 6ft 4in-tall Danish goalkeeper, a former captain of Manchester United in the 1990s.

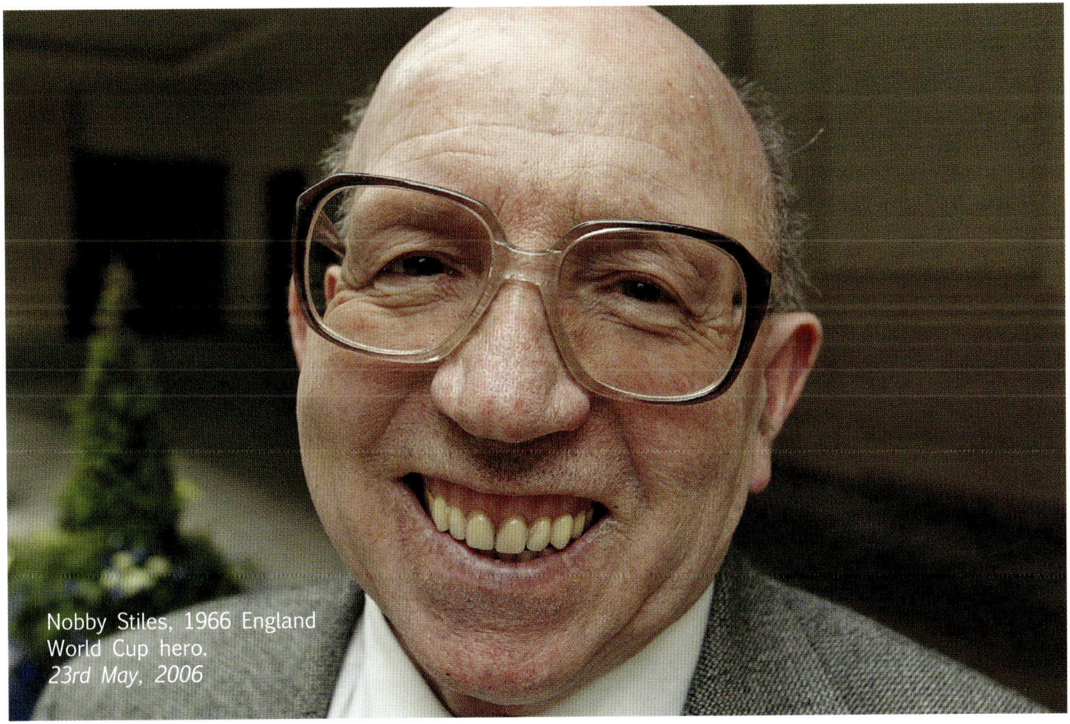

Nobby Stiles, 1966 England World Cup hero.
23rd May, 2006

"Please do not insist on the technology. The day that the referee takes two captains aside to study monitors and see if something is inside the box or outside is the day the spectators will say, no, we are not coming to the game."

Sepp Blatter, on the controversial issue of goal-line technology and video replays in football matches.

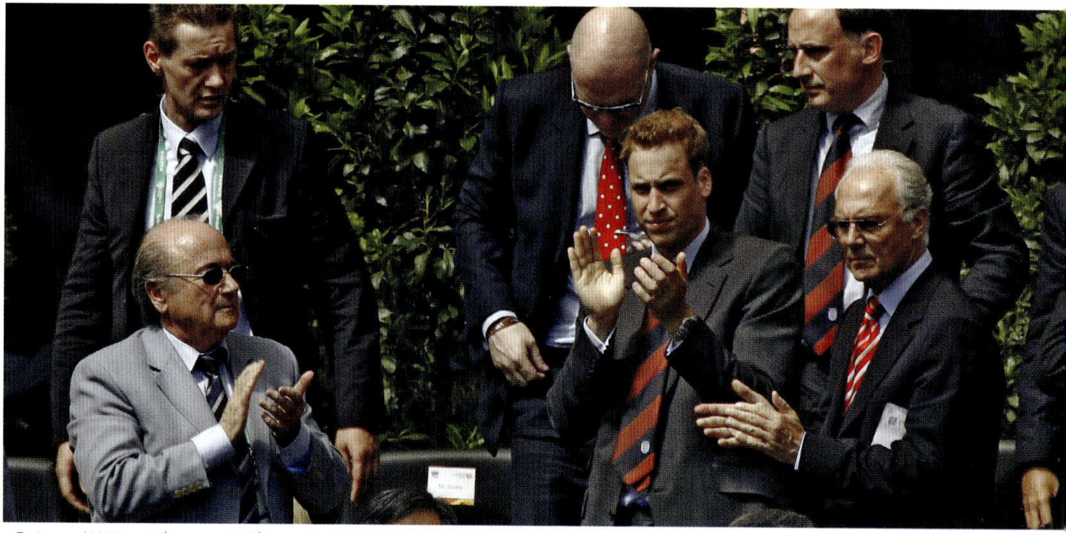

Prince William (second R) applauds England at the end of their 1-0 win over Paraguay during the 2006 World Cup tournament, in Frankfurt, Germany. Also pictured is FIFA president Sepp Blatter (L) and Franz Beckenbauer (R), a German football coach, manager and former player.
10th June, 2006

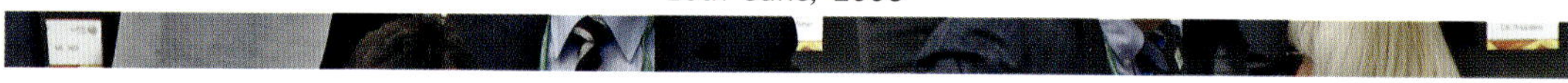

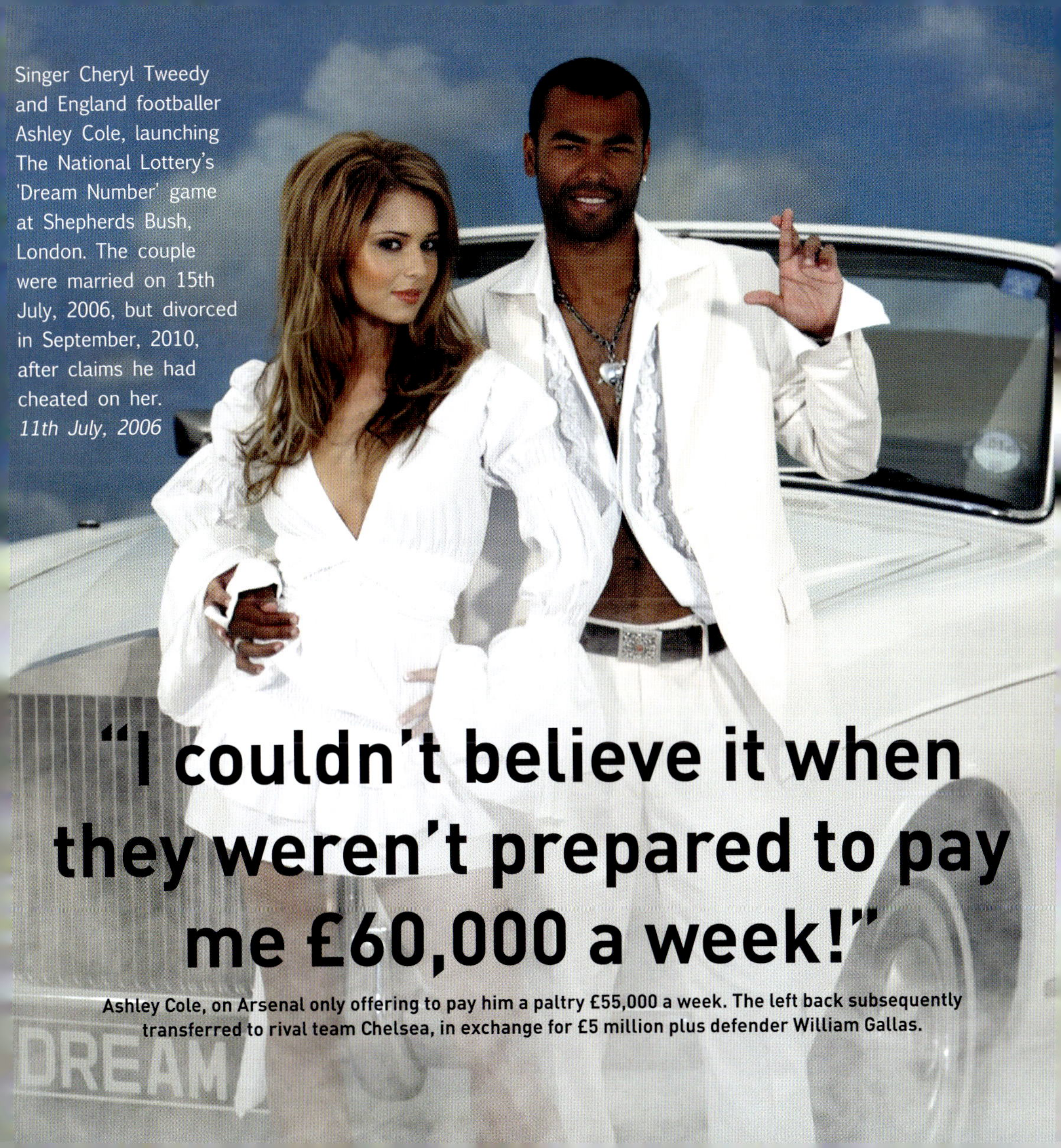

Singer Cheryl Tweedy and England footballer Ashley Cole, launching The National Lottery's 'Dream Number' game at Shepherds Bush, London. The couple were married on 15th July, 2006, but divorced in September, 2010, after claims he had cheated on her.
11th July, 2006

"I couldn't believe it when they weren't prepared to pay me £60,000 a week!"

Ashley Cole, on Arsenal only offering to pay him a paltry £55,000 a week. The left back subsequently transferred to rival team Chelsea, in exchange for £5 million plus defender William Gallas.

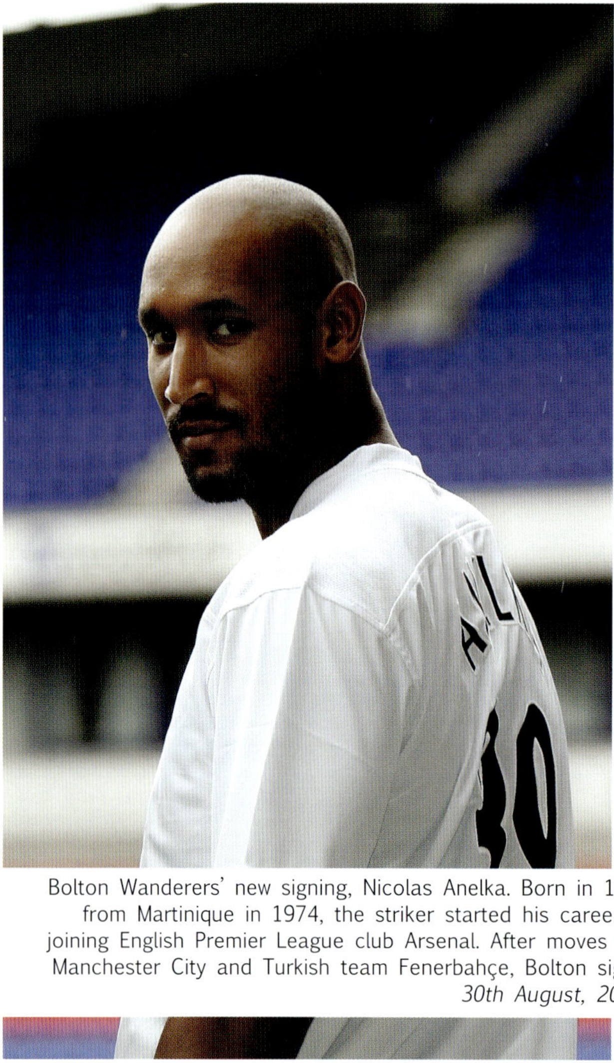

"Players need to change how they play in their thirties and even more so in England because it is so physical and quick with a lot of contact. You are not like you were when you were younger so you need to adapt your game – and this is exactly what I want to do."

Nicolas Anelka, who made 125 appearances for Chelsea and signed with Chinese Super League team Shanghai Shenhua in 2012 for a reported £175,000 per week.

Bolton Wanderers' new signing, Nicolas Anelka. Born in 1979 in France, to parents who had migrated from Martinique in 1974, the striker started his career at Paris Saint-Germain, aged 16, before joining English Premier League club Arsenal. After moves to Real Madrid, back to Paris Saint-Germain, Manchester City and Turkish team Fenerbahçe, Bolton signed Anelka for a club record of £8 million. *30th August, 2006*

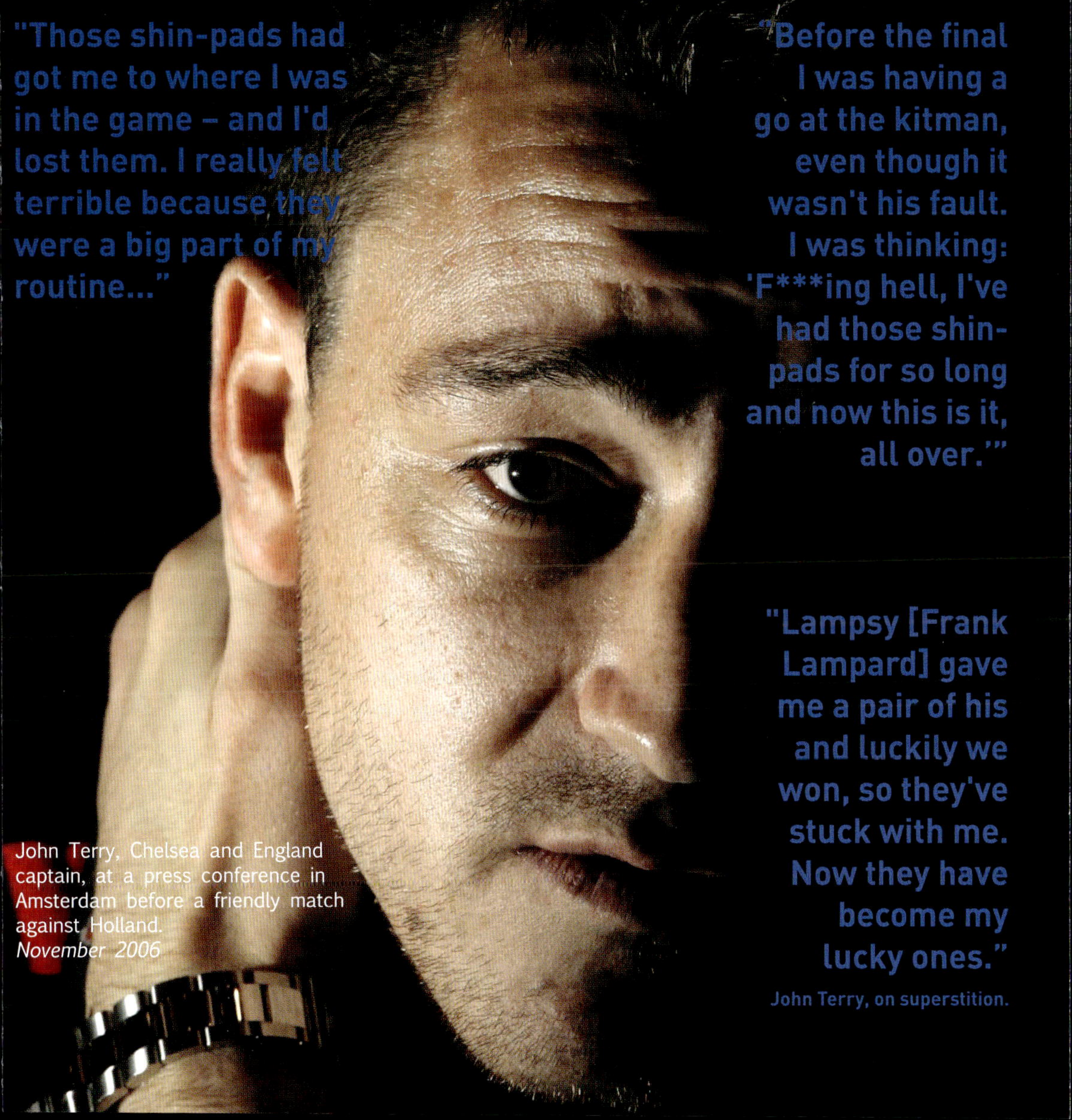

"Those shin-pads had got me to where I was in the game – and I'd lost them. I really felt terrible because they were a big part of my routine..."

"Before the final I was having a go at the kitman, even though it wasn't his fault. I was thinking: 'F***ing hell, I've had those shin-pads for so long and now this is it, all over.'"

"Lampsy [Frank Lampard] gave me a pair of his and luckily we won, so they've stuck with me. Now they have become my lucky ones."

John Terry, on superstition.

John Terry, Chelsea and England captain, at a press conference in Amsterdam before a friendly match against Holland.
November 2006

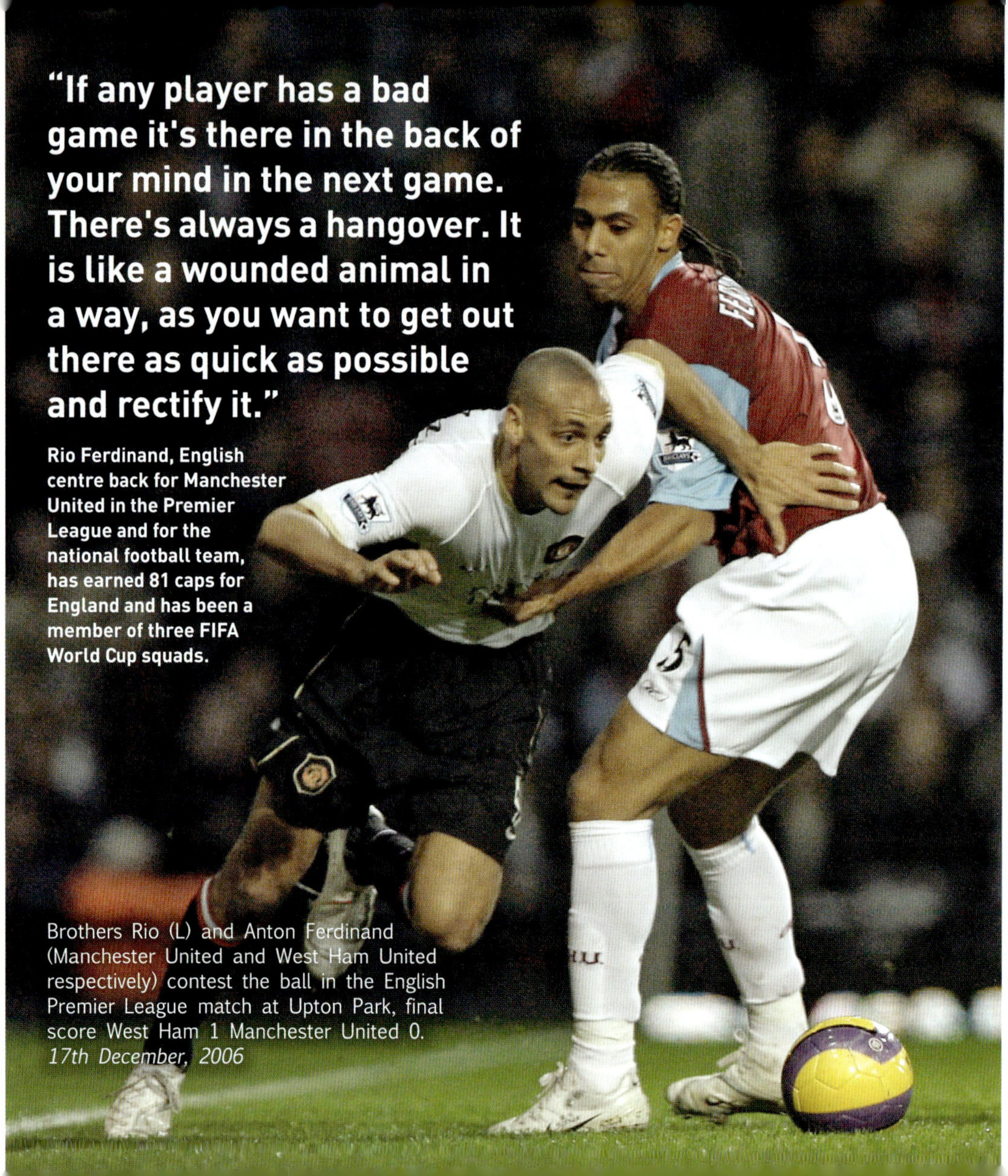

"If any player has a bad game it's there in the back of your mind in the next game. There's always a hangover. It is like a wounded animal in a way, as you want to get out there as quick as possible and rectify it."

Rio Ferdinand, English centre back for Manchester United in the Premier League and for the national football team, has earned 81 caps for England and has been a member of three FIFA World Cup squads.

Brothers Rio (L) and Anton Ferdinand (Manchester United and West Ham United respectively) contest the ball in the English Premier League match at Upton Park, final score West Ham 1 Manchester United 0. *17th December, 2006*

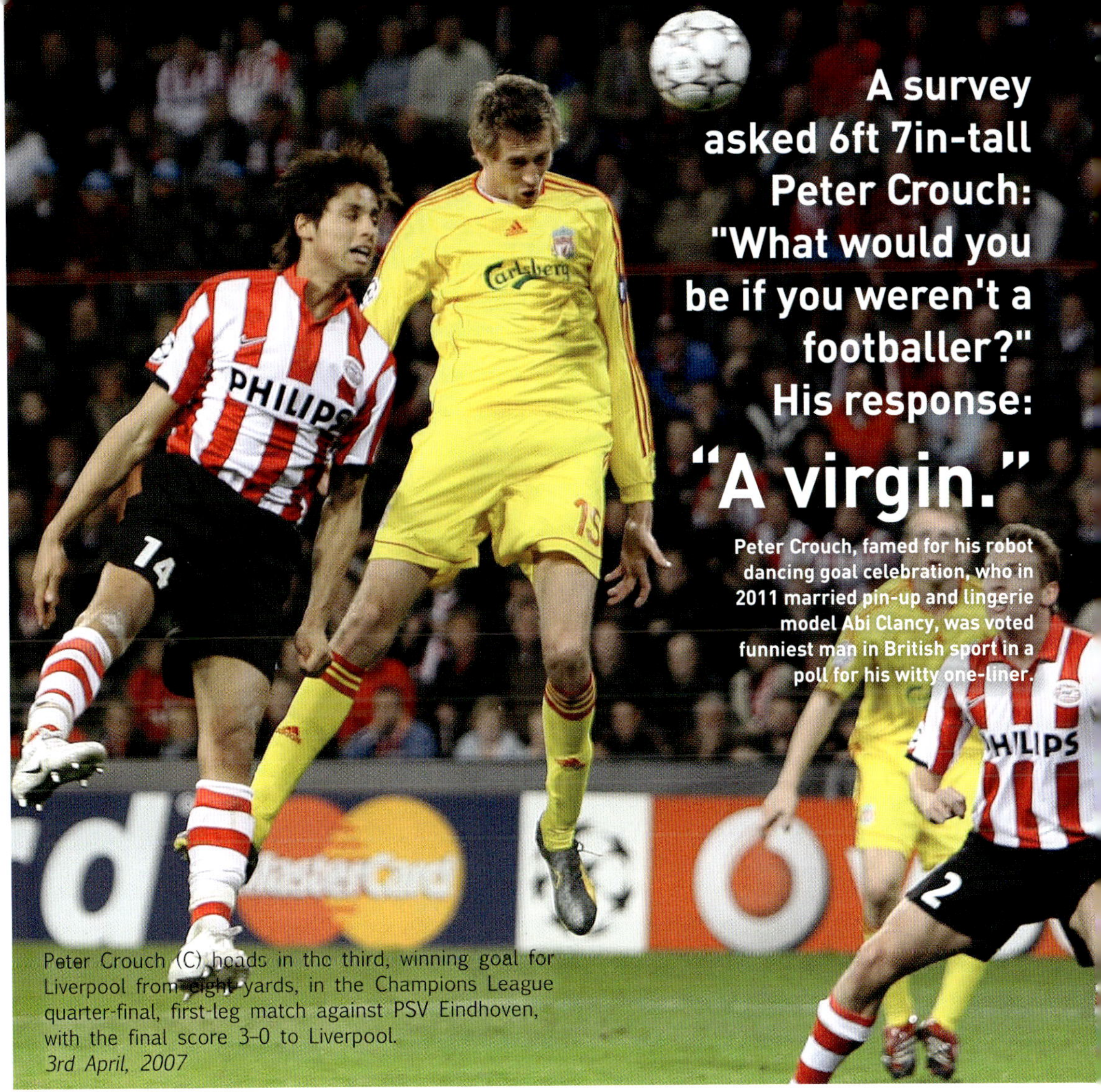

A survey asked 6ft 7in-tall Peter Crouch: "What would you be if you weren't a footballer?" His response:

"A virgin."

Peter Crouch, famed for his robot dancing goal celebration, who in 2011 married pin-up and lingerie model Abi Clancy, was voted funniest man in British sport in a poll for his witty one-liner.

Peter Crouch (C) heads in the third, winning goal for Liverpool from eight yards, in the Champions League quarter-final, first-leg match against PSV Eindhoven, with the final score 3-0 to Liverpool.
3rd April, 2007

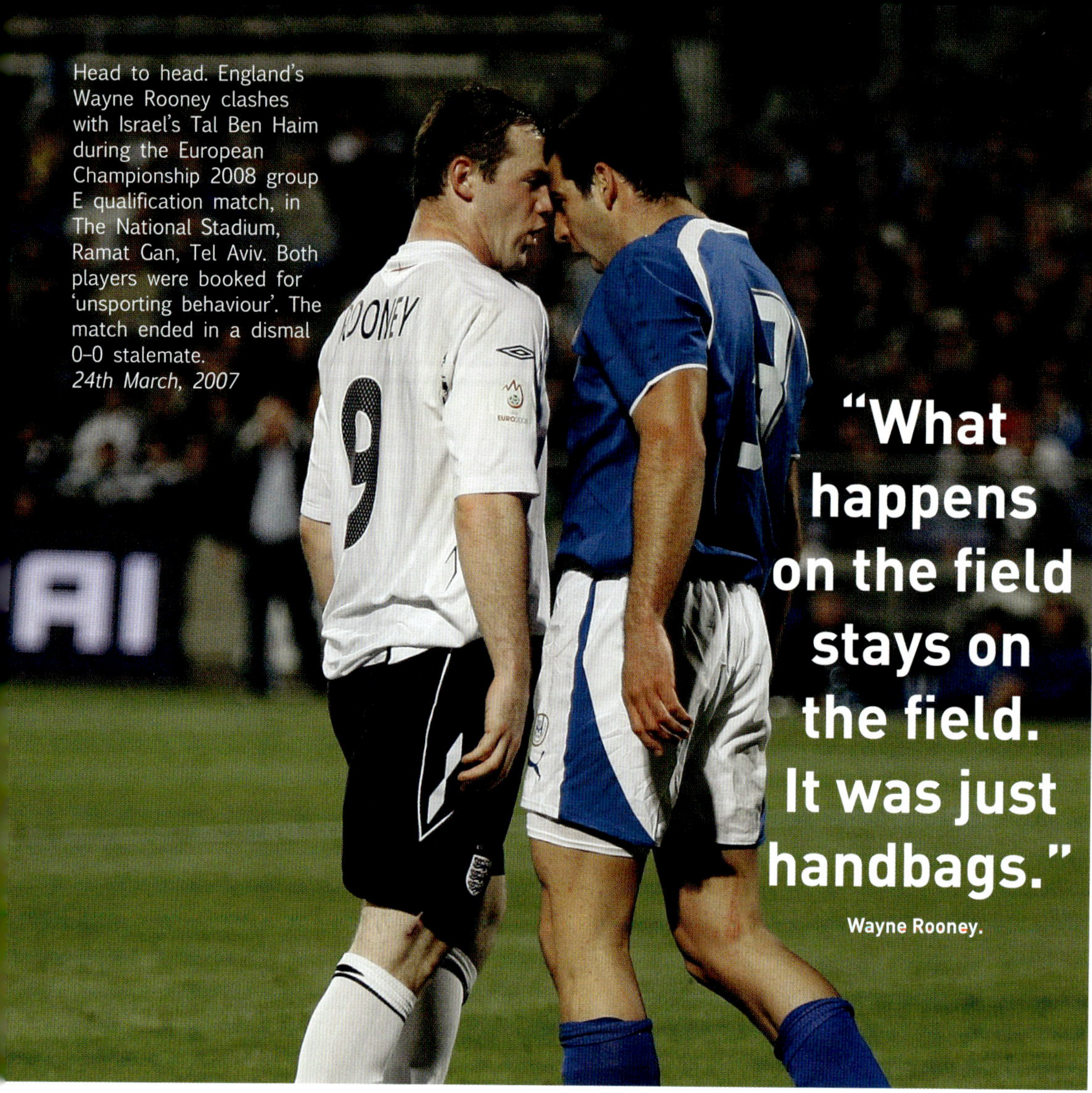

Head to head. England's Wayne Rooney clashes with Israel's Tal Ben Haim during the European Championship 2008 group E qualification match, in The National Stadium, Ramat Gan, Tel Aviv. Both players were booked for 'unsporting behaviour'. The match ended in a dismal 0–0 stalemate.
24th March, 2007

"What happens on the field stays on the field. It was just handbags."

Wayne Rooney.

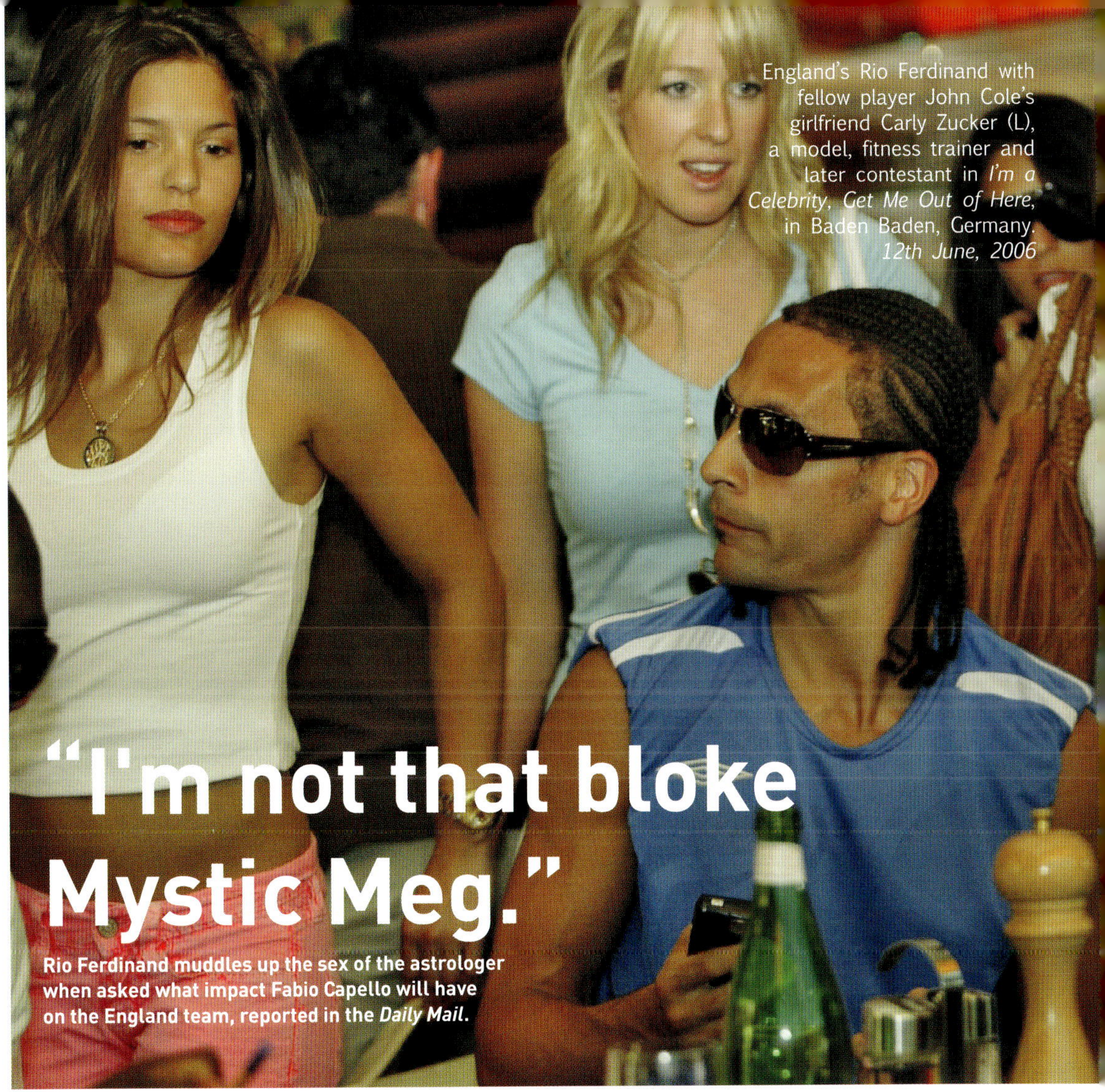

England's Rio Ferdinand with fellow player John Cole's girlfriend Carly Zucker (L), a model, fitness trainer and later contestant in *I'm a Celebrity, Get Me Out of Here*, in Baden Baden, Germany. *12th June, 2006*

"I'm not that bloke Mystic Meg."

Rio Ferdinand muddles up the sex of the astrologer when asked what impact Fabio Capello will have on the England team, reported in the *Daily Mail*.

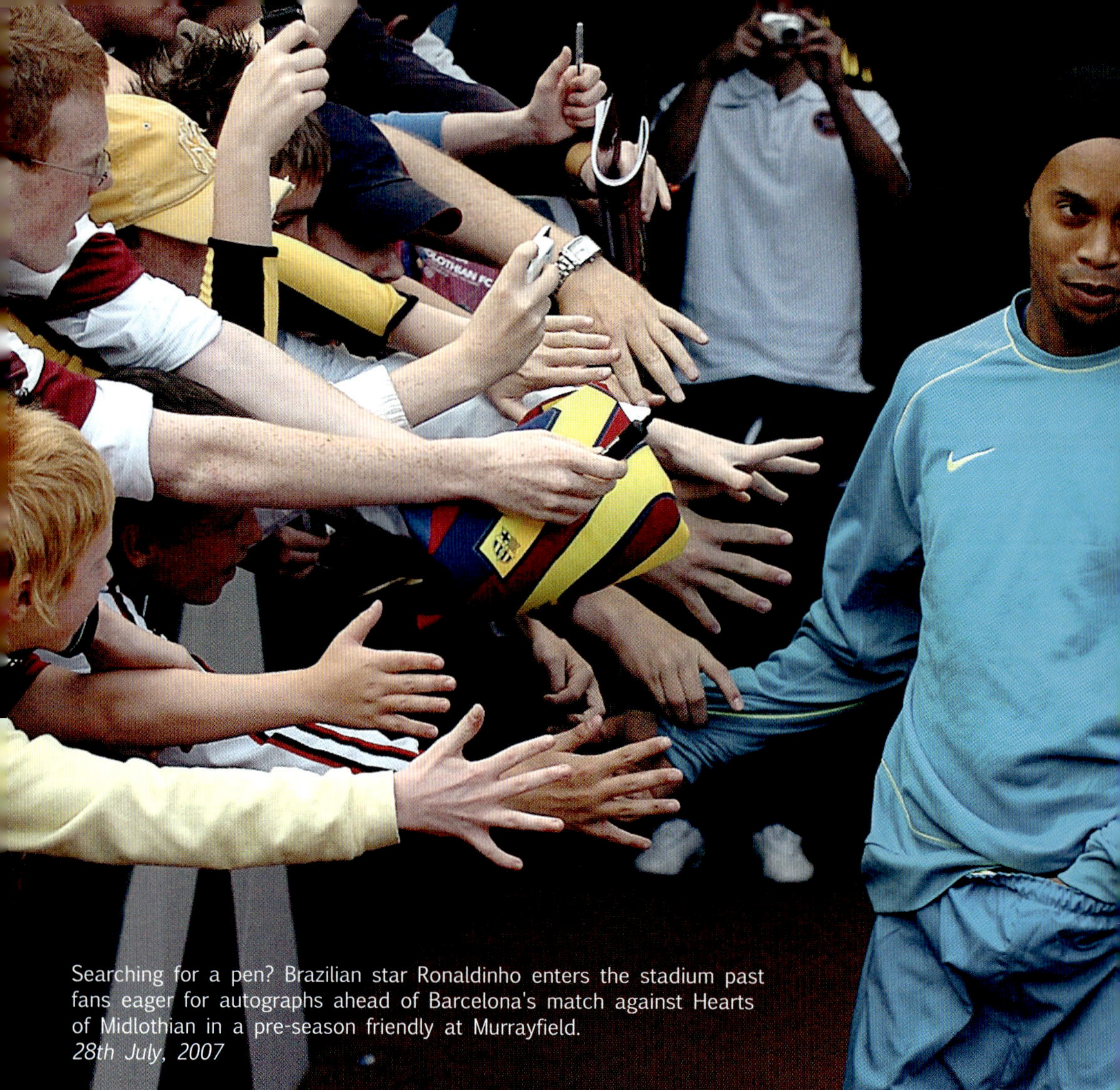

Searching for a pen? Brazilian star Ronaldinho enters the stadium past fans eager for autographs ahead of Barcelona's match against Hearts of Midlothian in a pre-season friendly at Murrayfield.
28th July, 2007

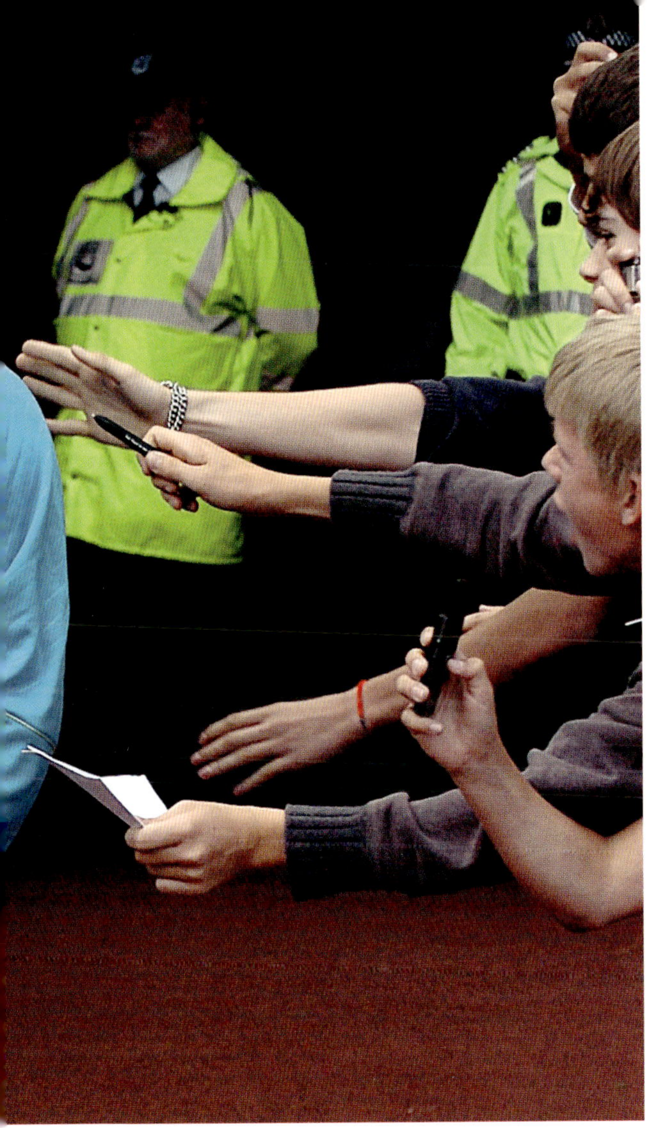

"There are criticisms that achieve nothing and others that can be useful, motivating, constructive and from which you can learn. These are the types of criticism that I use."

Ronaldinho, a Brazilian footballer who plays for Flamengo and the Brazilian national team as an attacking midfielder or forward, two-time winner of the FIFA World Player of the Year in 2004 and 2005.

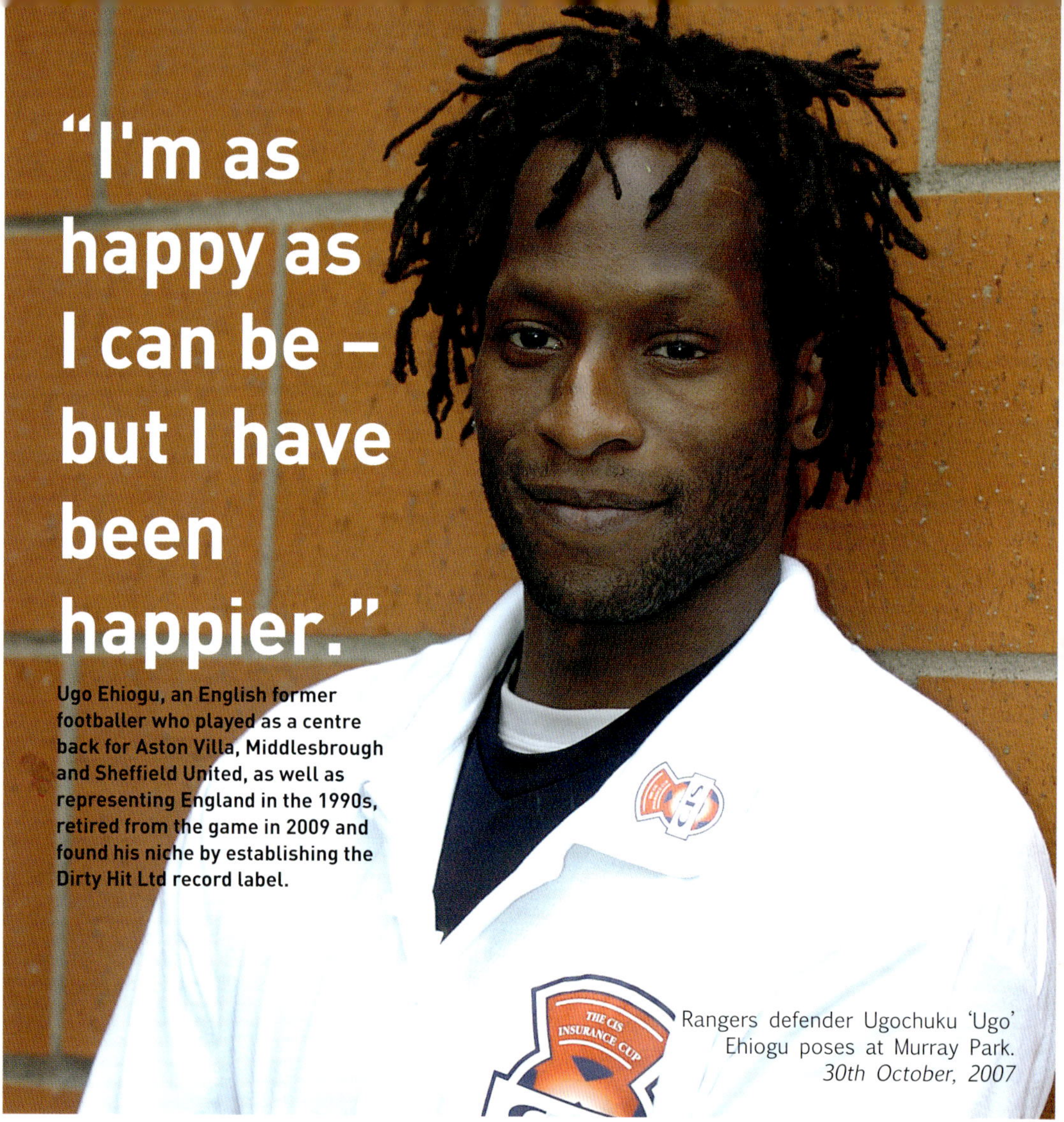

"I'm as happy as I can be – but I have been happier."

Ugo Ehiogu, an English former footballer who played as a centre back for Aston Villa, Middlesbrough and Sheffield United, as well as representing England in the 1990s, retired from the game in 2009 and found his niche by establishing the Dirty Hit Ltd record label.

Rangers defender Ugochuku 'Ugo' Ehiogu poses at Murray Park.
30th October, 2007

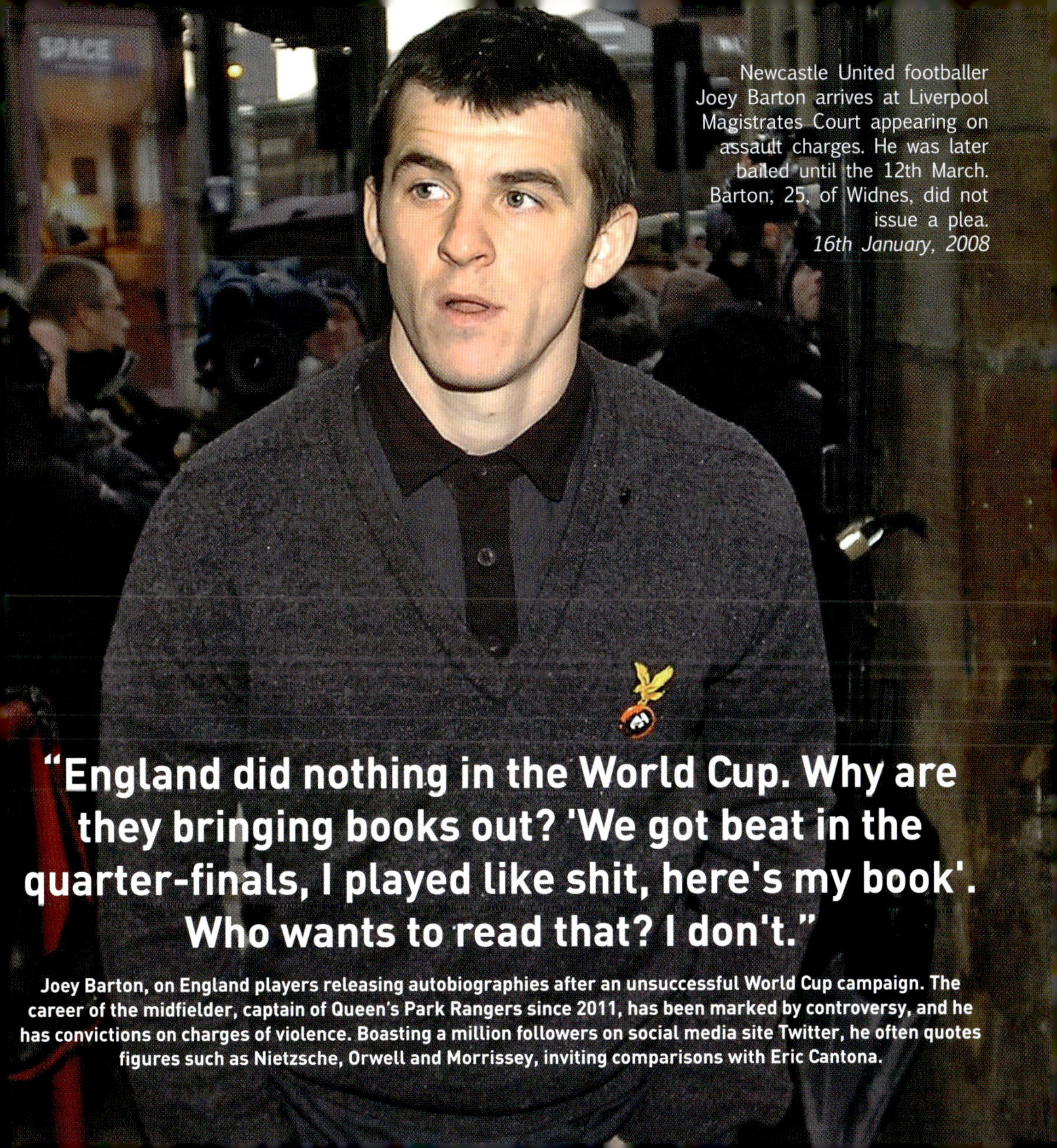

Newcastle United footballer Joey Barton arrives at Liverpool Magistrates Court appearing on assault charges. He was later bailed until the 12th March. Barton, 25, of Widnes, did not issue a plea.
16th January, 2008

"England did nothing in the World Cup. Why are they bringing books out? 'We got beat in the quarter-finals, I played like shit, here's my book'. Who wants to read that? I don't."

Joey Barton, on England players releasing autobiographies after an unsuccessful World Cup campaign. The career of the midfielder, captain of Queen's Park Rangers since 2011, has been marked by controversy, and he has convictions on charges of violence. Boasting a million followers on social media site Twitter, he often quotes figures such as Nietzsche, Orwell and Morrissey, inviting comparisons with Eric Cantona.

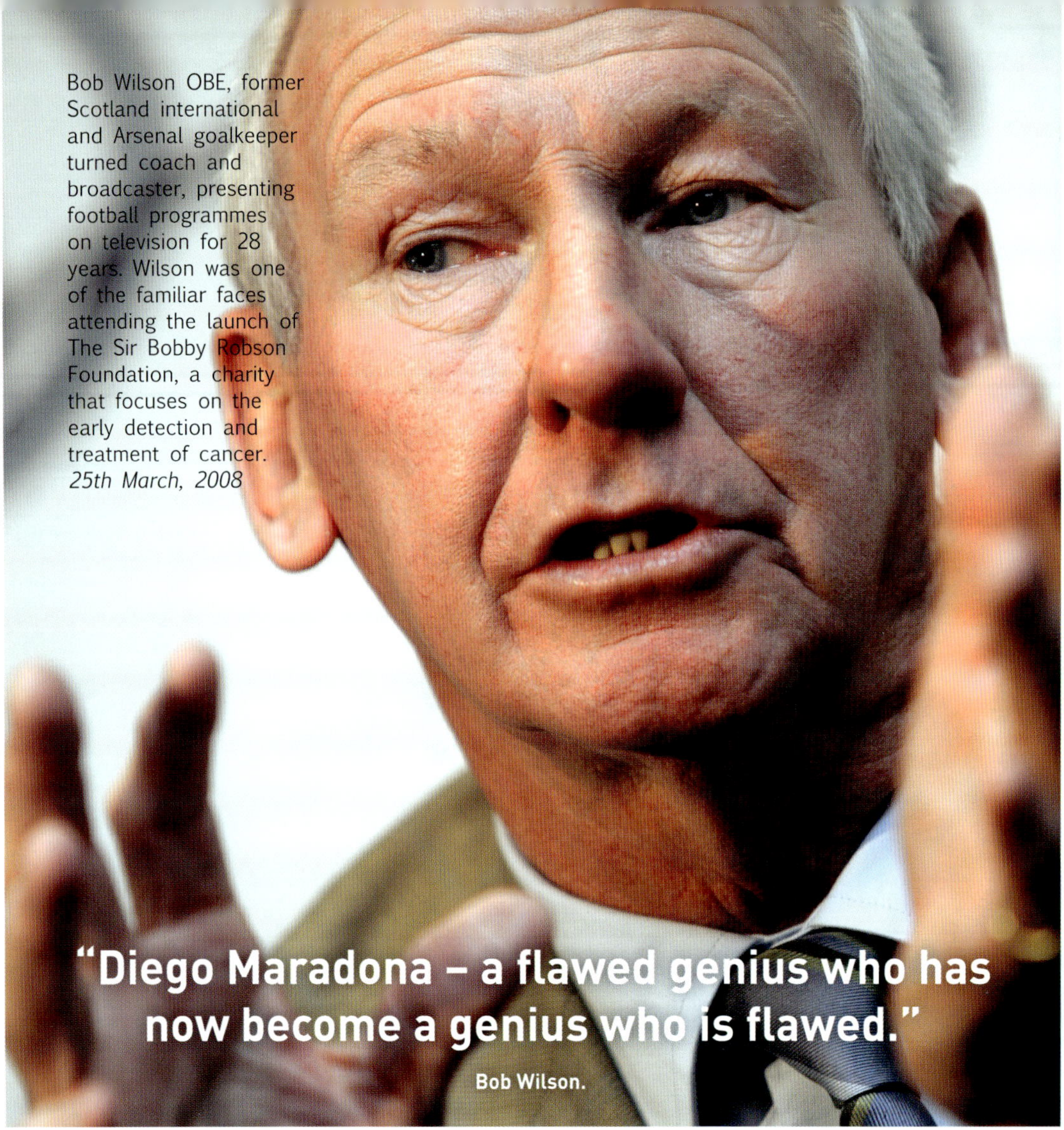

Bob Wilson OBE, former Scotland international and Arsenal goalkeeper turned coach and broadcaster, presenting football programmes on television for 28 years. Wilson was one of the familiar faces attending the launch of The Sir Bobby Robson Foundation, a charity that focuses on the early detection and treatment of cancer. *25th March, 2008*

"Diego Maradona – a flawed genius who has now become a genius who is flawed."

Bob Wilson.

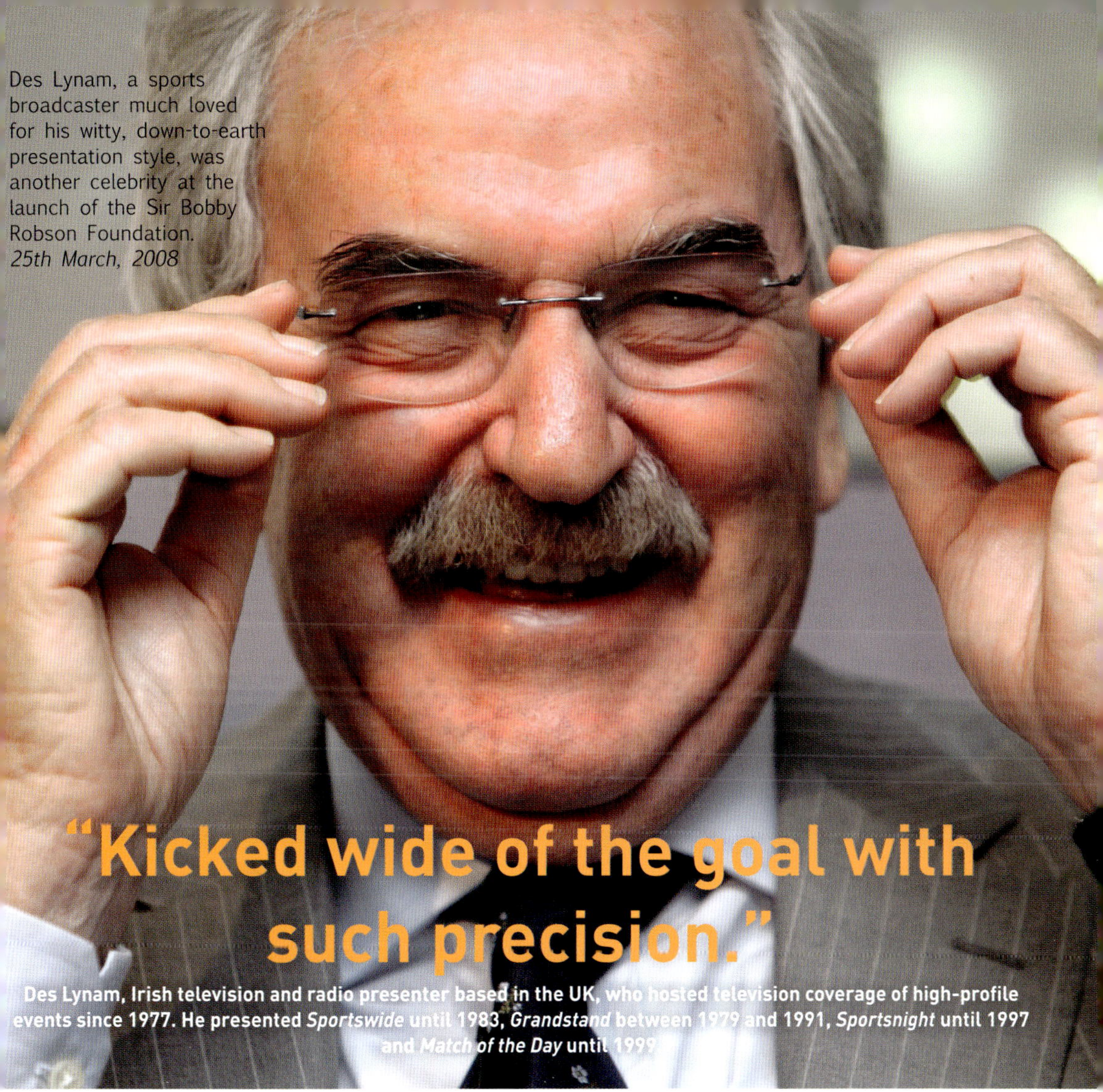

Des Lynam, a sports broadcaster much loved for his witty, down-to-earth presentation style, was another celebrity at the launch of the Sir Bobby Robson Foundation.
25th March, 2008

"Kicked wide of the goal with such precision."

Des Lynam, Irish television and radio presenter based in the UK, who hosted television coverage of high-profile events since 1977. He presented *Sportswide* until 1983, *Grandstand* between 1979 and 1991, *Sportsnight* until 1997 and *Match of the Day* until 1999.

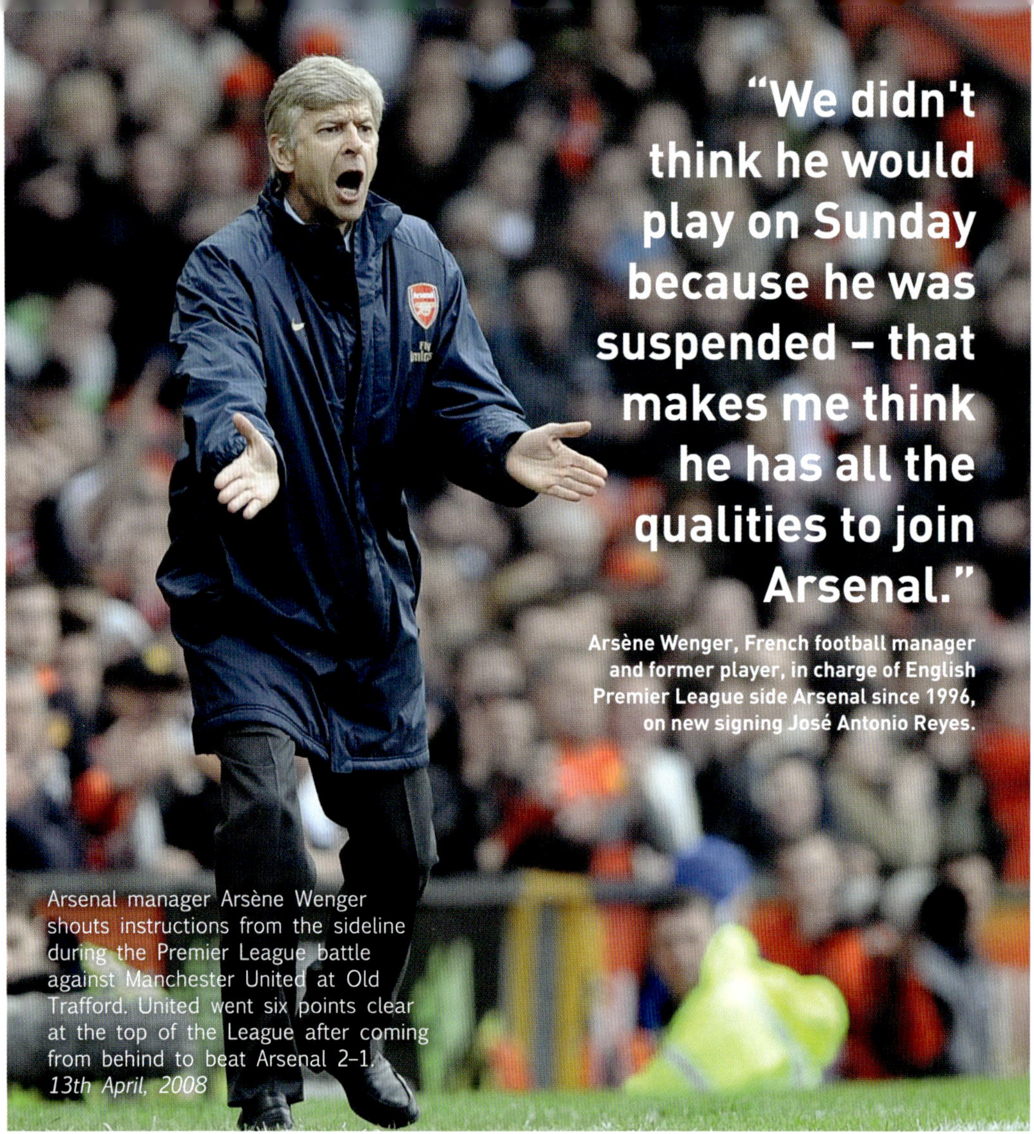

"We didn't think he would play on Sunday because he was suspended – that makes me think he has all the qualities to join Arsenal."

Arsène Wenger, French football manager and former player, in charge of English Premier League side Arsenal since 1996, on new signing José Antonio Reyes.

Arsenal manager Arsène Wenger shouts instructions from the sideline during the Premier League battle against Manchester United at Old Trafford. United went six points clear at the top of the League after coming from behind to beat Arsenal 2–1. *13th April, 2008*

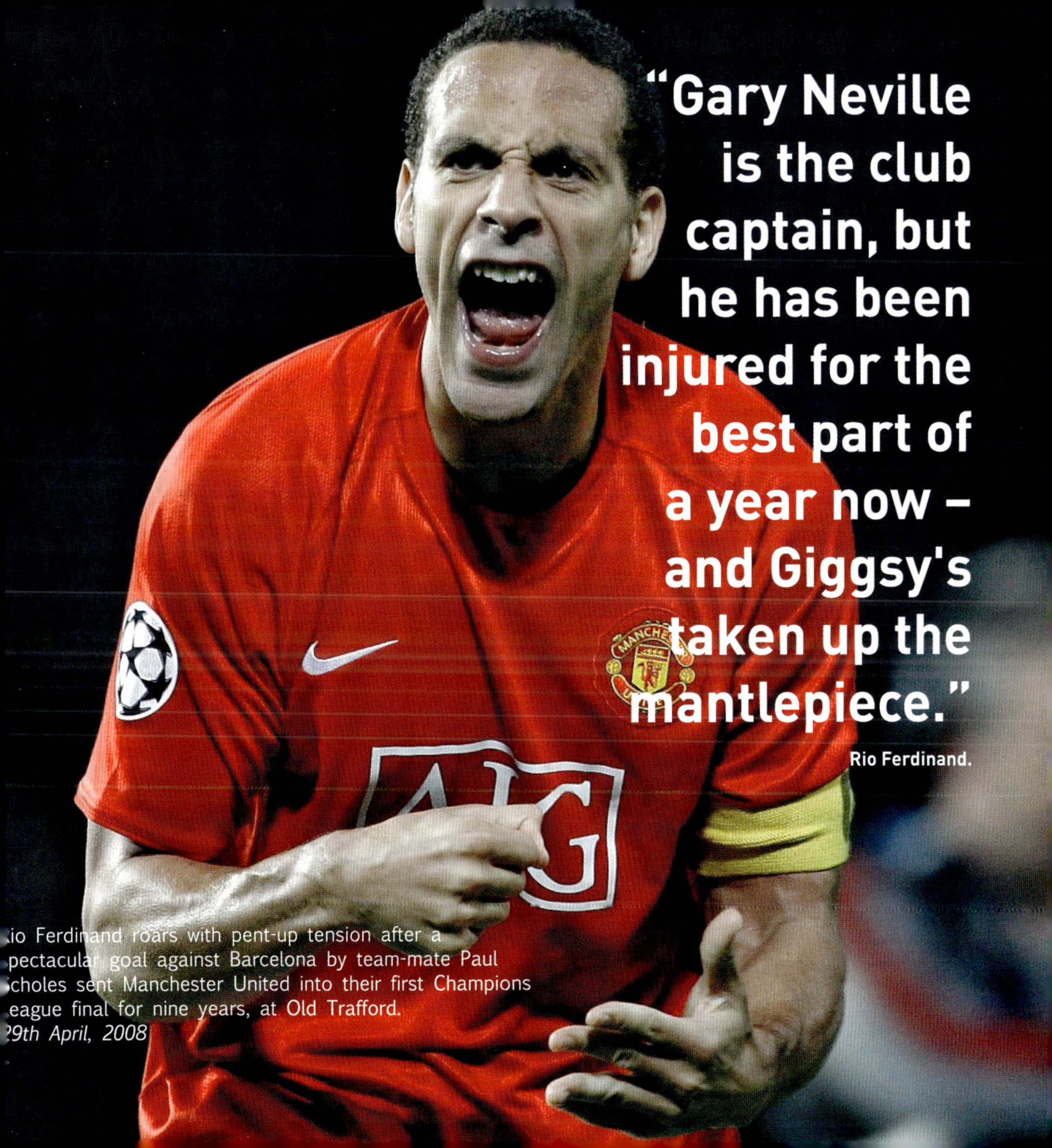

"Gary Neville is the club captain, but he has been injured for the best part of a year now – and Giggsy's taken up the mantlepiece."

Rio Ferdinand.

io Ferdinand roars with pent-up tension after a pectacular goal against Barcelona by team-mate Paul choles sent Manchester United into their first Champions eague final for nine years, at Old Trafford.
9th April, 2008

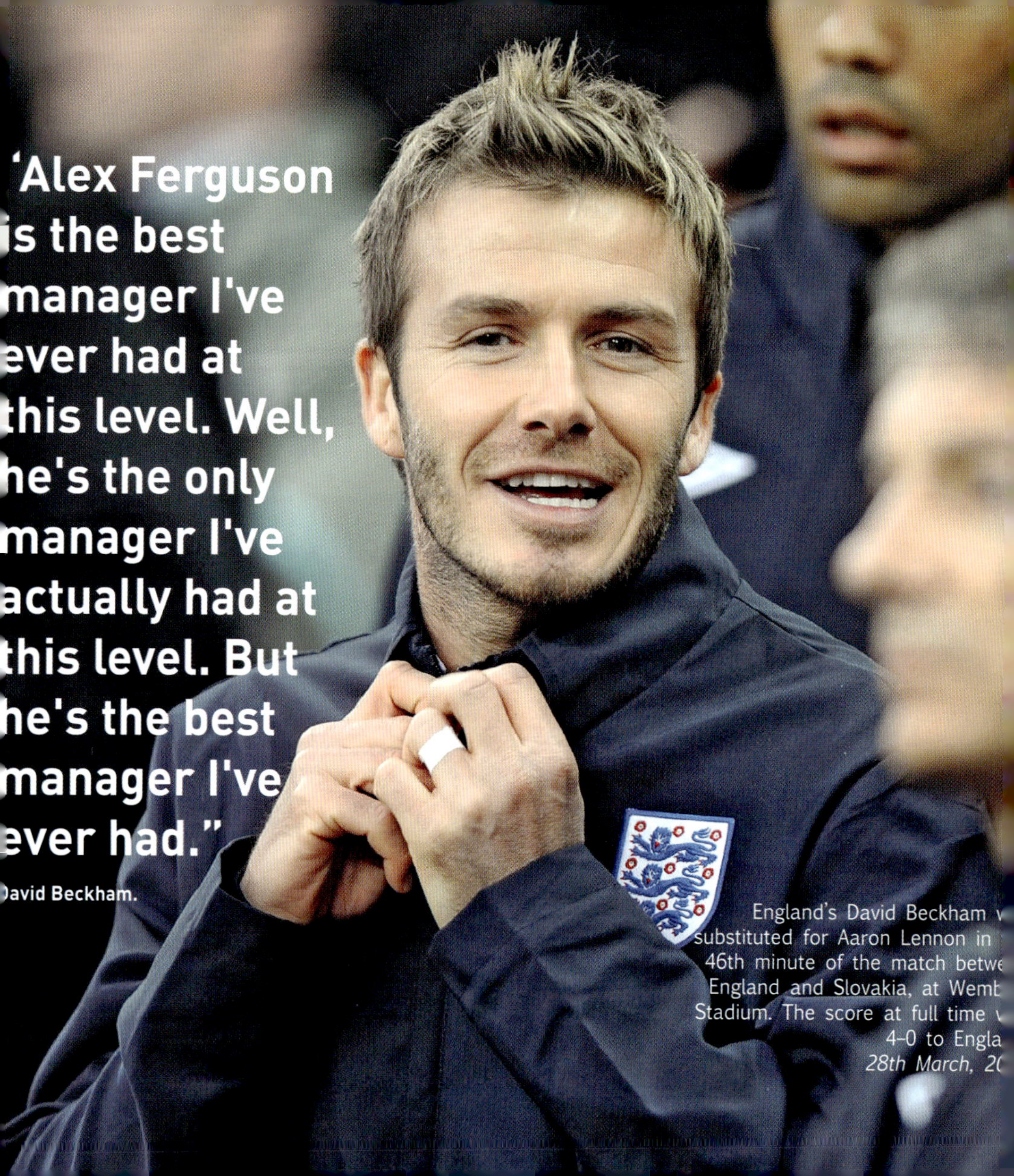

"Alex Ferguson is the best manager I've ever had at this level. Well, he's the only manager I've actually had at this level. But he's the best manager I've ever had."

David Beckham.

England's David Beckham w substituted for Aaron Lennon in 46th minute of the match betwe England and Slovakia, at Wemb Stadium. The score at full time w 4-0 to Engla
28th March, 2C

"I got my first-team games. I was with the first-team squad. I played three first-team games."

Gordon Ramsay, to Sue Lawley,
host of *Desert Island Discs*, 2002,
in which the foul-mouthed celebrity chef
revealed details of his 'football career'.

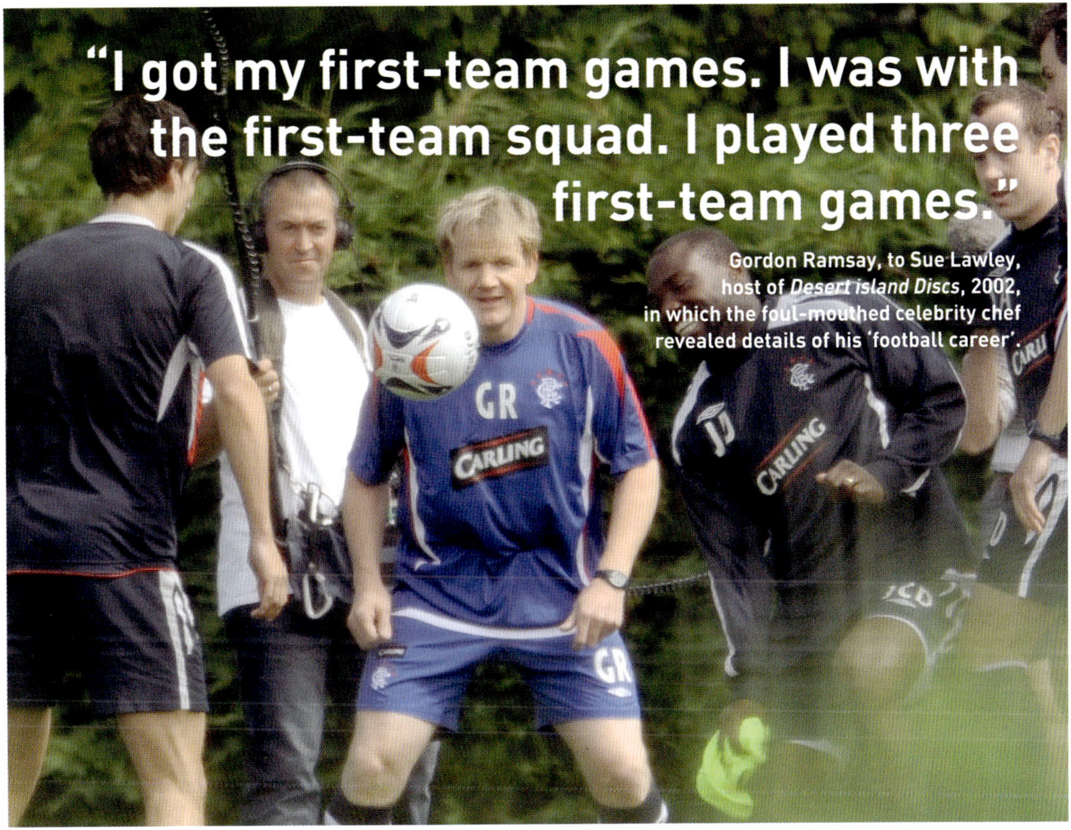

Filming *The F Word* cookery show, celebrity chef Gordon Ramsay (C) visited Glasgow Rangers FC at their Murray Park training base, where he enjoyed a kickabout with first-team stars. Ramsay had boasted of his link with Rangers in interviews during the launch of his first restaurant, Aubergine, in 1994, claiming to have spent three years with the club, until a knee injury, at the age of 18, forced him to give up football. A Rangers spokesman explained: "Ramsay was a triallist. He trained with us for a few months, but then got injured."
July, 2008

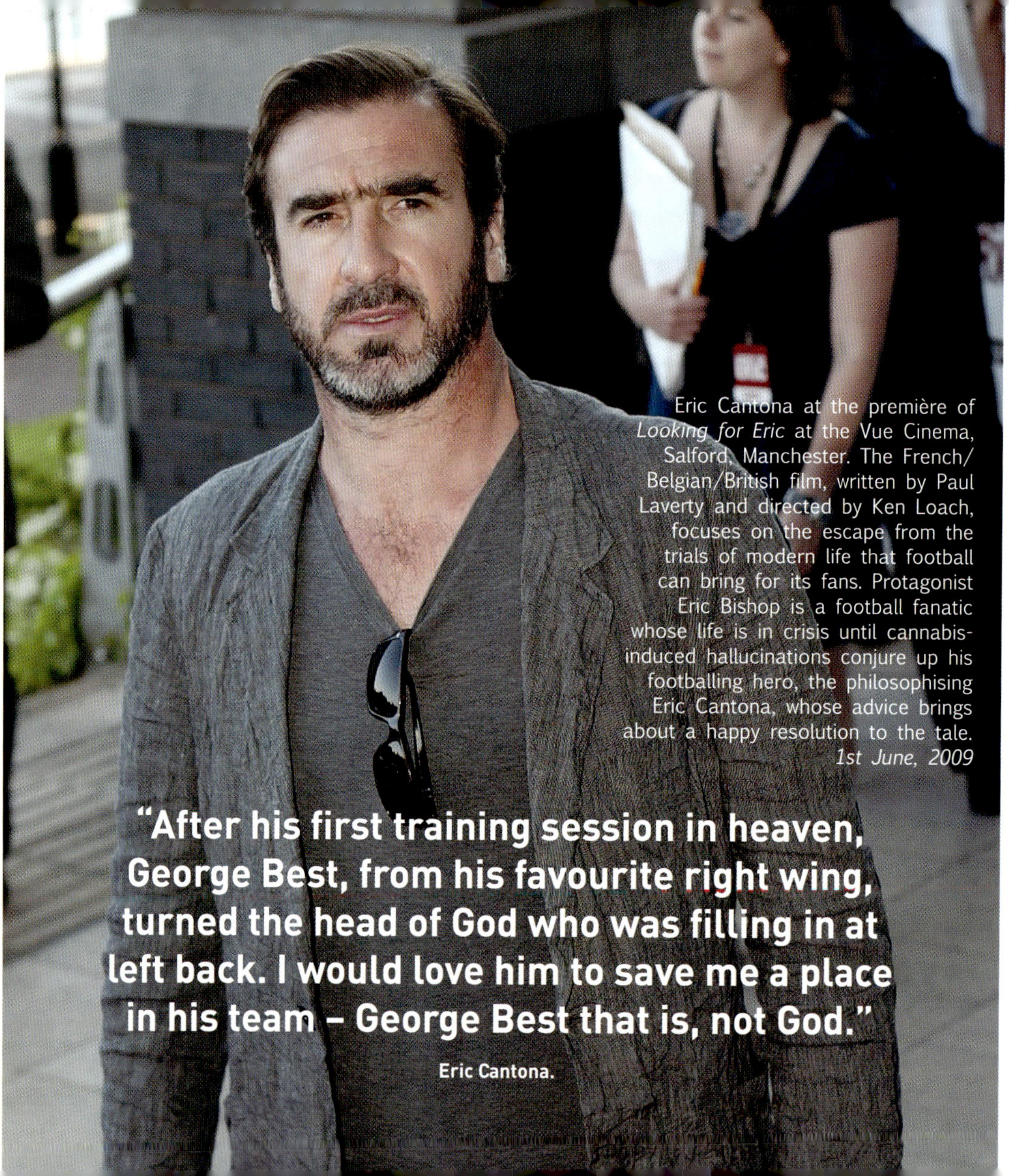

Eric Cantona at the première of *Looking for Eric* at the Vue Cinema, Salford, Manchester. The French/Belgian/British film, written by Paul Laverty and directed by Ken Loach, focuses on the escape from the trials of modern life that football can bring for its fans. Protagonist Eric Bishop is a football fanatic whose life is in crisis until cannabis-induced hallucinations conjure up his footballing hero, the philosophising Eric Cantona, whose advice brings about a happy resolution to the tale. *1st June, 2009*

"After his first training session in heaven, George Best, from his favourite right wing, turned the head of God who was filling in at left back. I would love him to save me a place in his team – George Best that is, not God."

Eric Cantona.

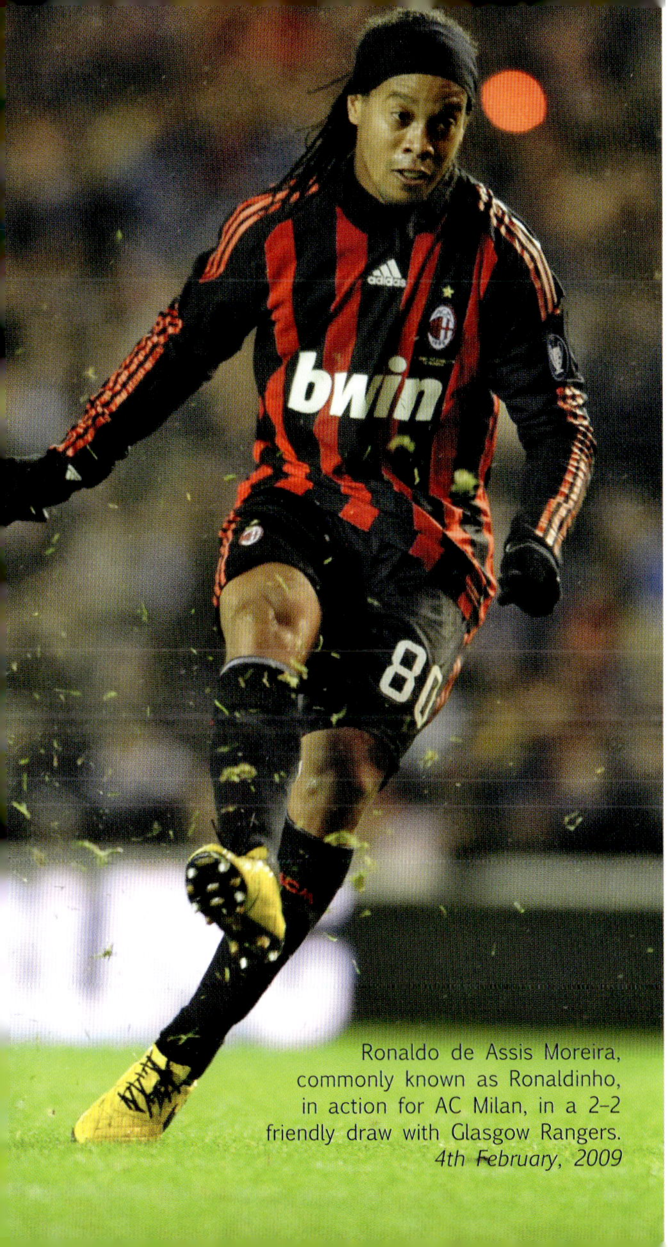

Ronaldo de Assis Moreira, commonly known as Ronaldinho, in action for AC Milan, in a 2-2 friendly draw with Glasgow Rangers. *4th February, 2009*

"Sometimes I think my fans are going to have a heart attack or like they're thinking I'm either drunk or dreaming. Some people even start shouting when they see me – it's funny."

Ronaldinho.

"I love playing football, but I think I am like everyone else, I hate losing and love winning. And if the time comes when I am not disappointed when things are definitely not going right, then that's when people should worry."

Wayne Rooney, English footballer, who has made 73 appearances for England, scoring 28 goals.

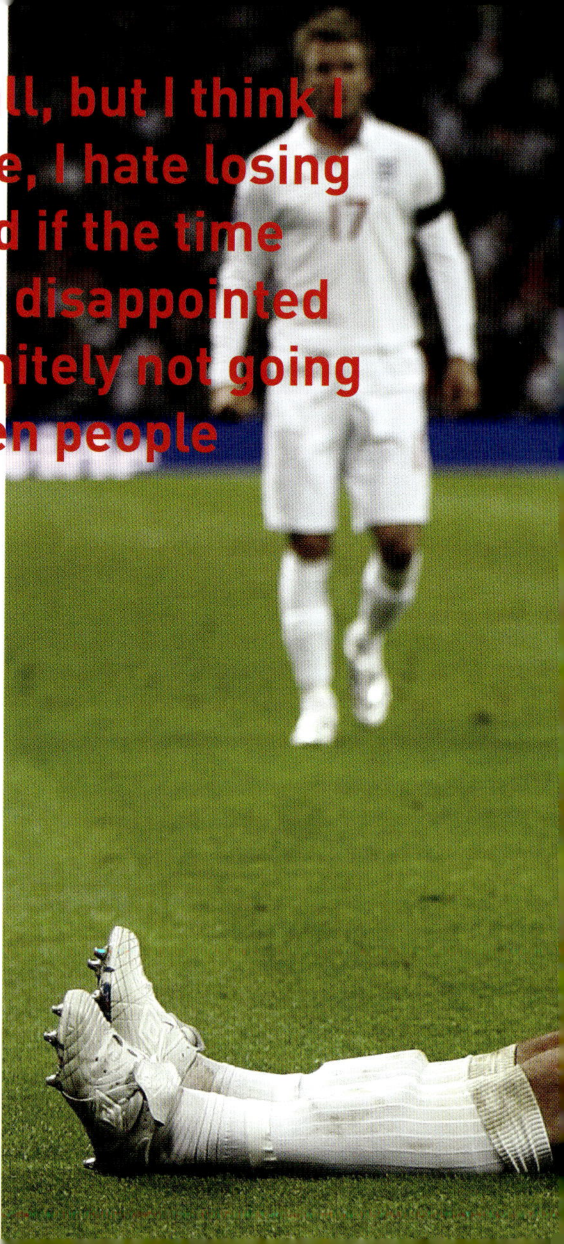

April fools? England's John Terry landed a winning goal in the 85th minute of the World Cup qualifier against Ukraine, at Wembley, making the score 2–1. In bizarre celebration, Rooney pretended to trim his skipper's barnet, having given him a real haircut earlier in the week: "I needed a haircut, but we weren't allowed to leave the hotel," said Terry. "I asked Wazza and he obliged by giving me a little trim."
1st April, 2009

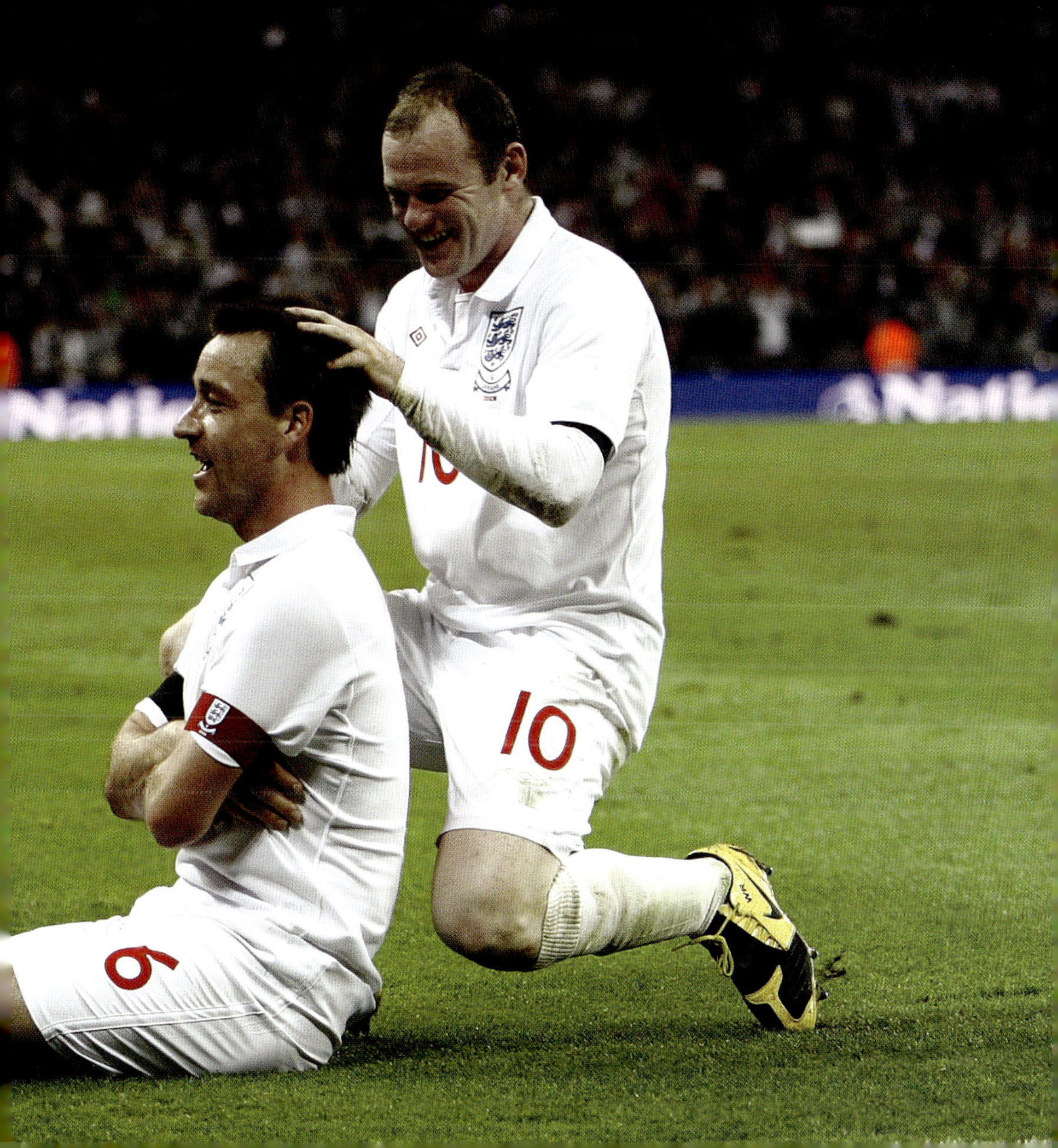
10
6

"Once a Blue, always a Blue."

Wayne Rooney, prior to leaving Everton for Manchester United.

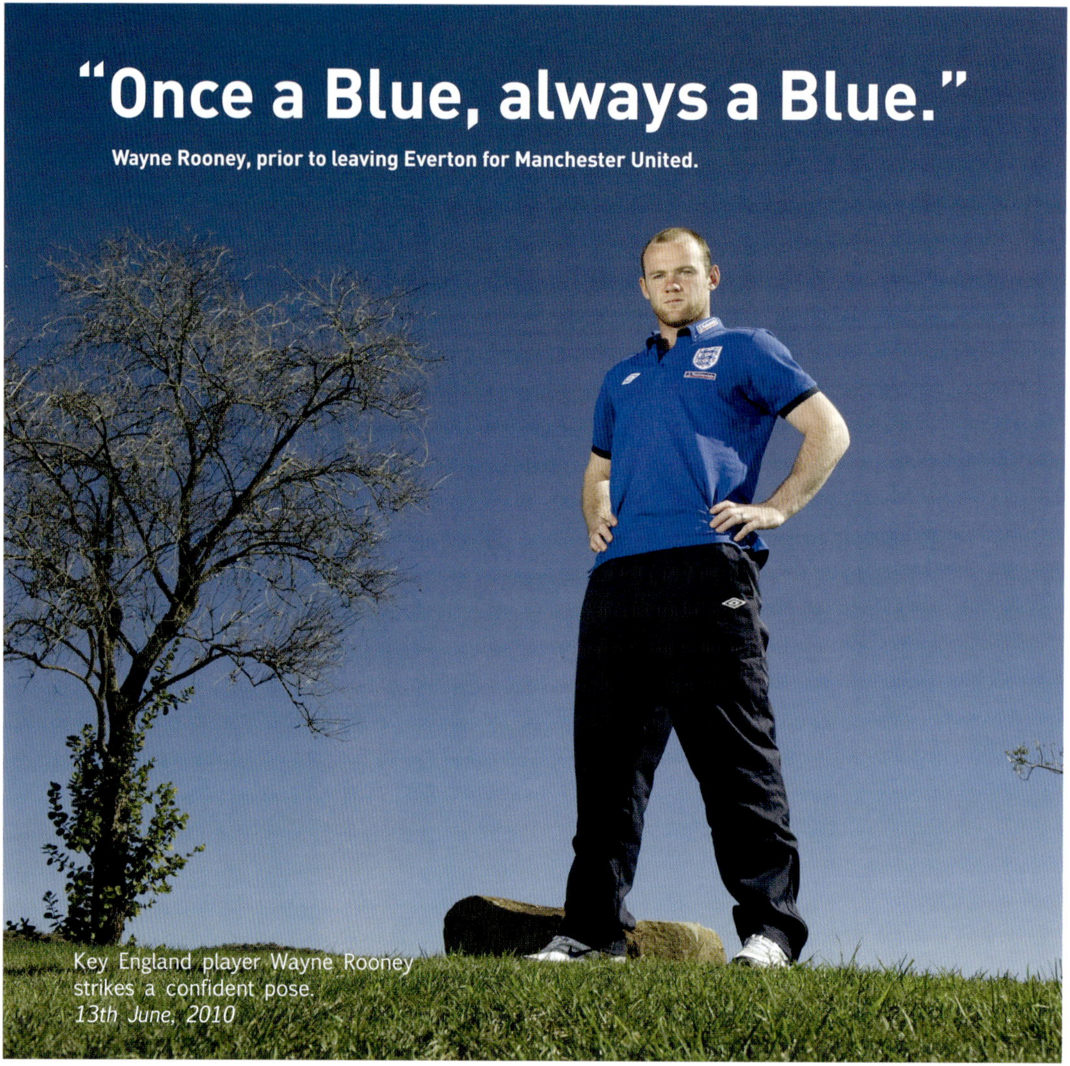

Key England player Wayne Rooney strikes a confident pose.
13th June, 2010

"Leadership is vital, you can't buy it. You need to have it to be successful. The players will follow a strong leader, you need to be able to convince the players of your methods and ideas at all times and you can only do this by being a good leader."

Fabio Capello, Italian football manager, who took over the reins of the England national team in 2008. In February, 2012, he quit after a dispute with the FA, after their decision to remove John Terry from the captaincy pending the outcome of a court case in July regarding allegations that he racially abused QPR's Anton Ferdinand.

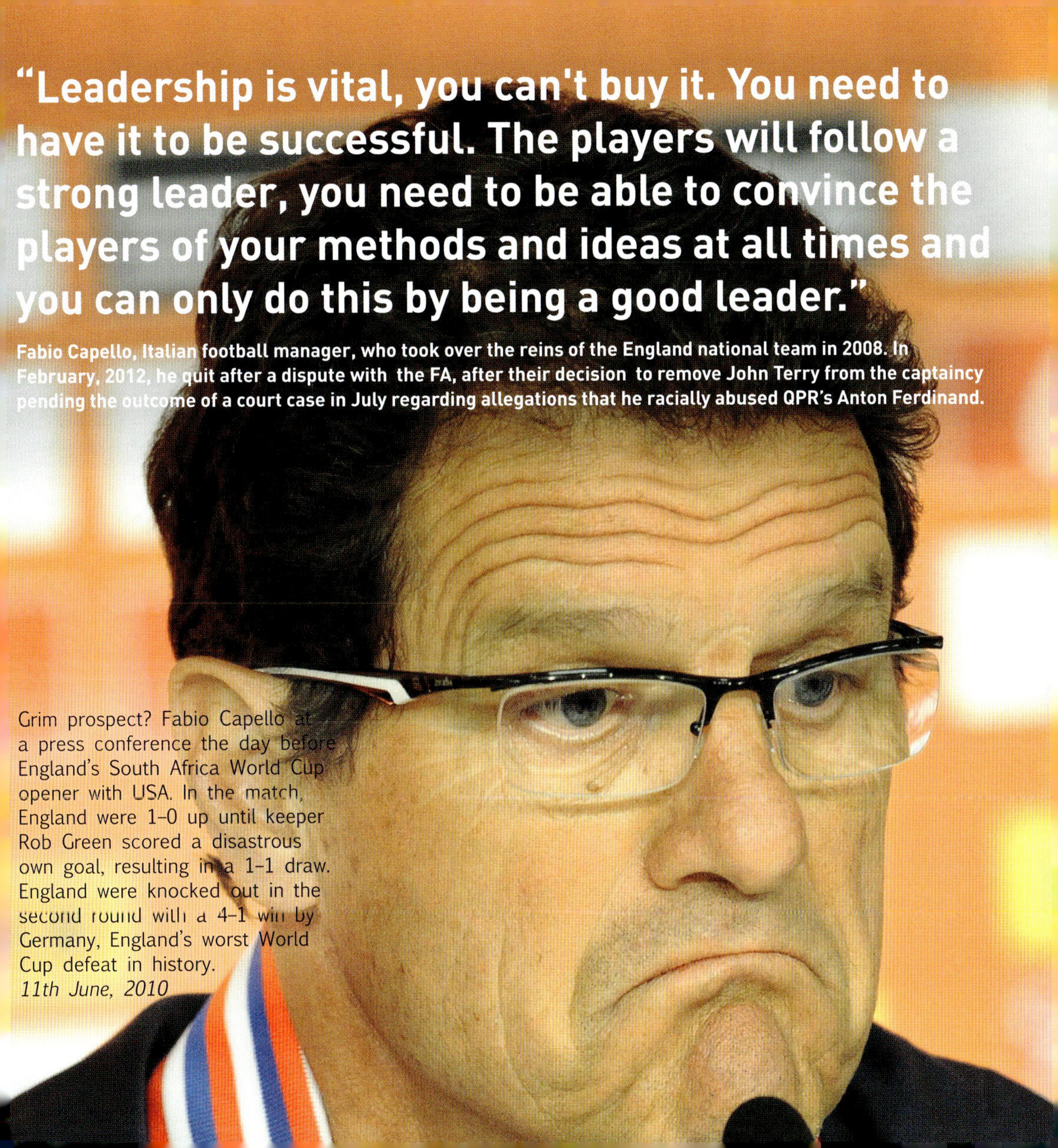

Grim prospect? Fabio Capello at a press conference the day before England's South Africa World Cup opener with USA. In the match, England were 1–0 up until keeper Rob Green scored a disastrous own goal, resulting in a 1–1 draw. England were knocked out in the second round with a 4–1 win by Germany, England's worst World Cup defeat in history.
11th June, 2010

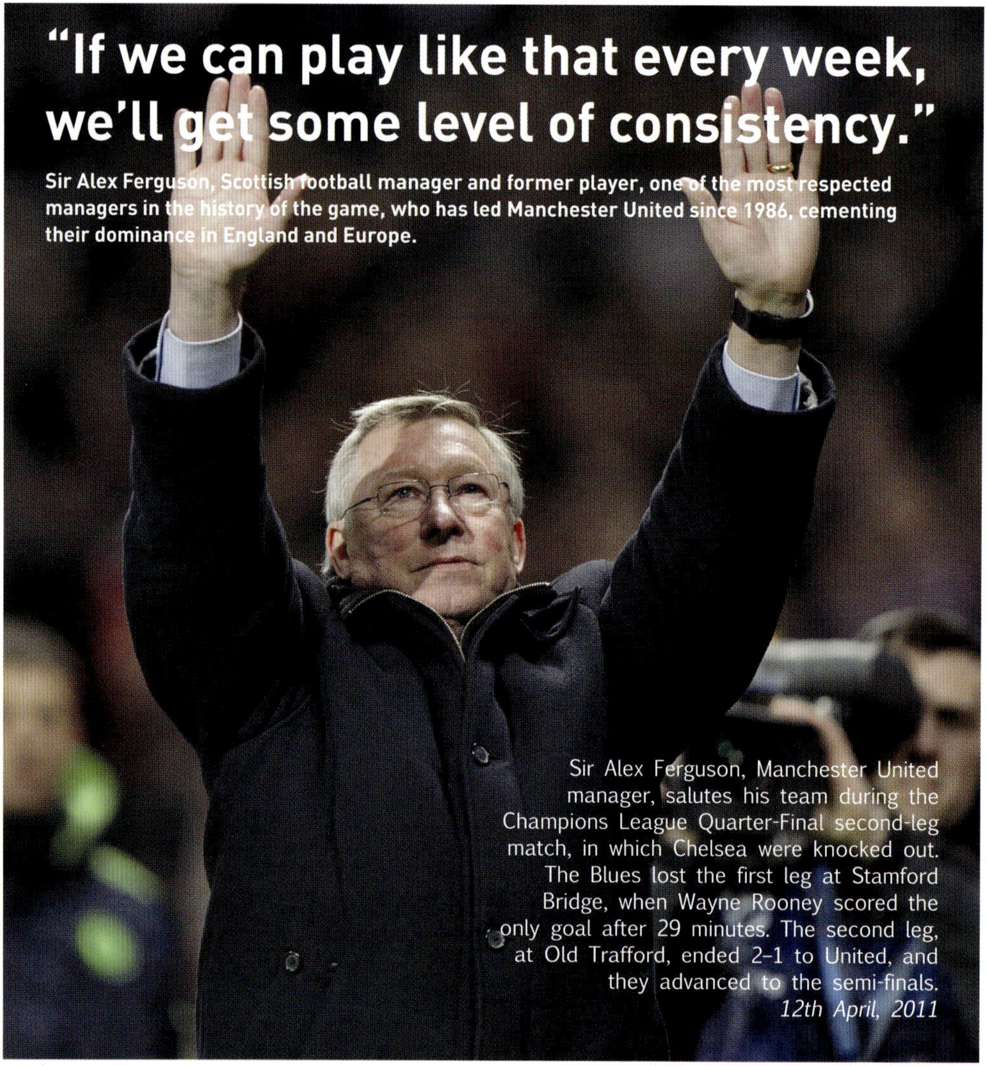

"If we can play like that every week, we'll get some level of consistency."

Sir Alex Ferguson, Scottish football manager and former player, one of the most respected managers in the history of the game, who has led Manchester United since 1986, cementing their dominance in England and Europe.

Sir Alex Ferguson, Manchester United manager, salutes his team during the Champions League Quarter-Final second-leg match, in which Chelsea were knocked out. The Blues lost the first leg at Stamford Bridge, when Wayne Rooney scored the only goal after 29 minutes. The second leg, at Old Trafford, ended 2–1 to United, and they advanced to the semi-finals.
12th April, 2011

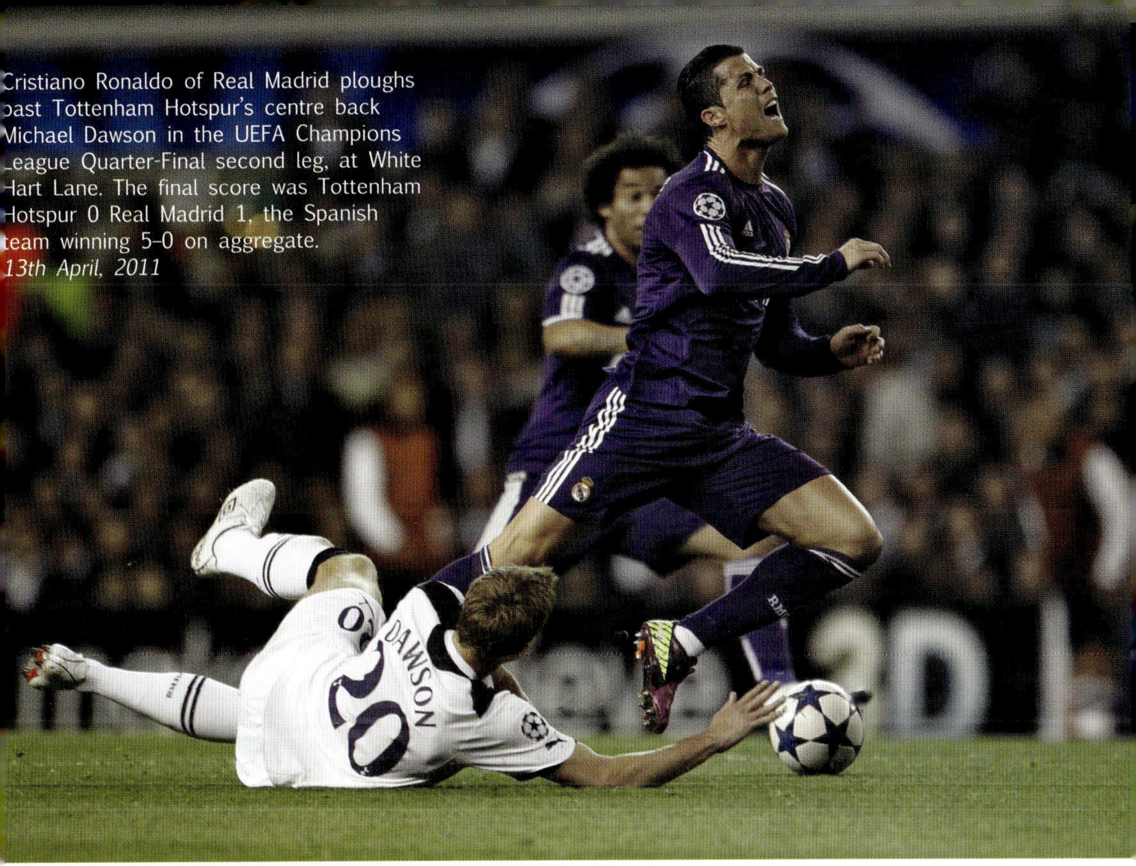

Cristiano Ronaldo of Real Madrid ploughs past Tottenham Hotspur's centre back Michael Dawson in the UEFA Champions League Quarter-Final second leg, at White Hart Lane. The final score was Tottenham Hotspur 0 Real Madrid 1, the Spanish team winning 5-0 on aggregate.
13th April, 2011

"I'm living a dream I never want to wake up from."

Cristiano Ronaldo.

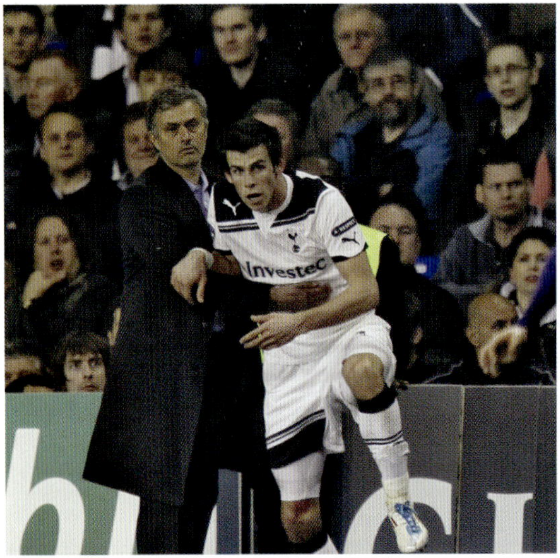
Investec

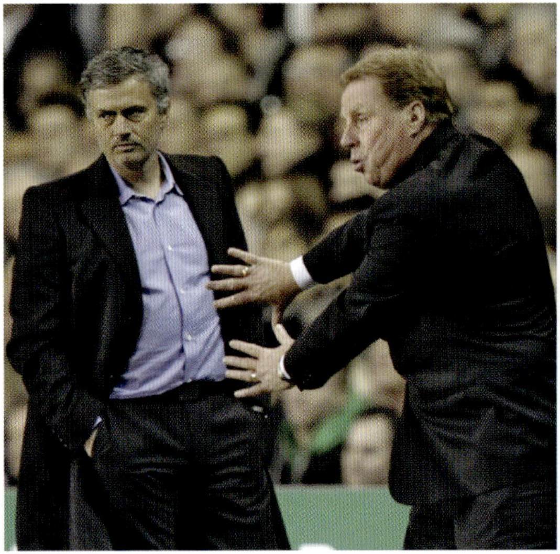

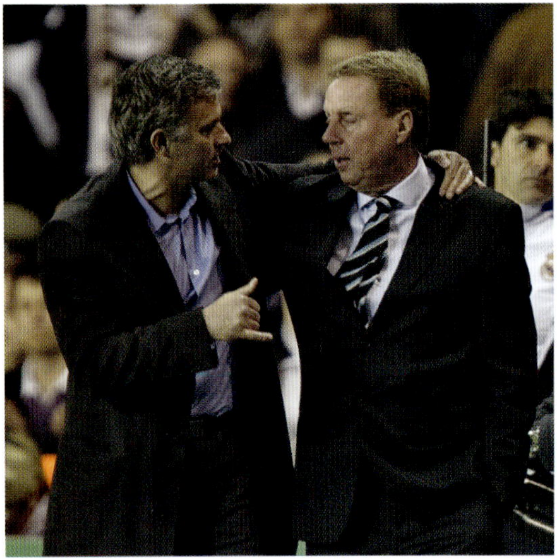

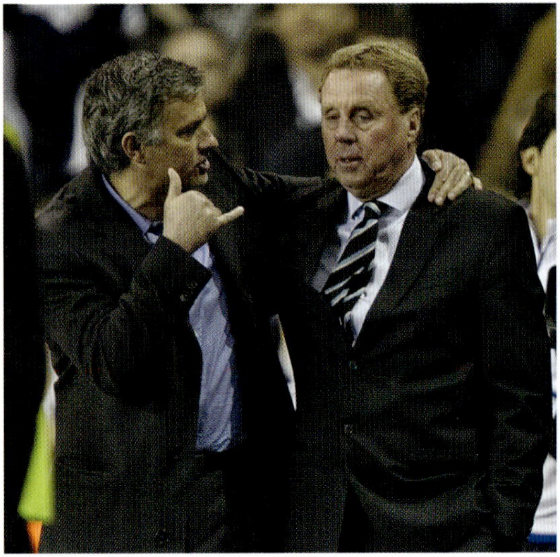

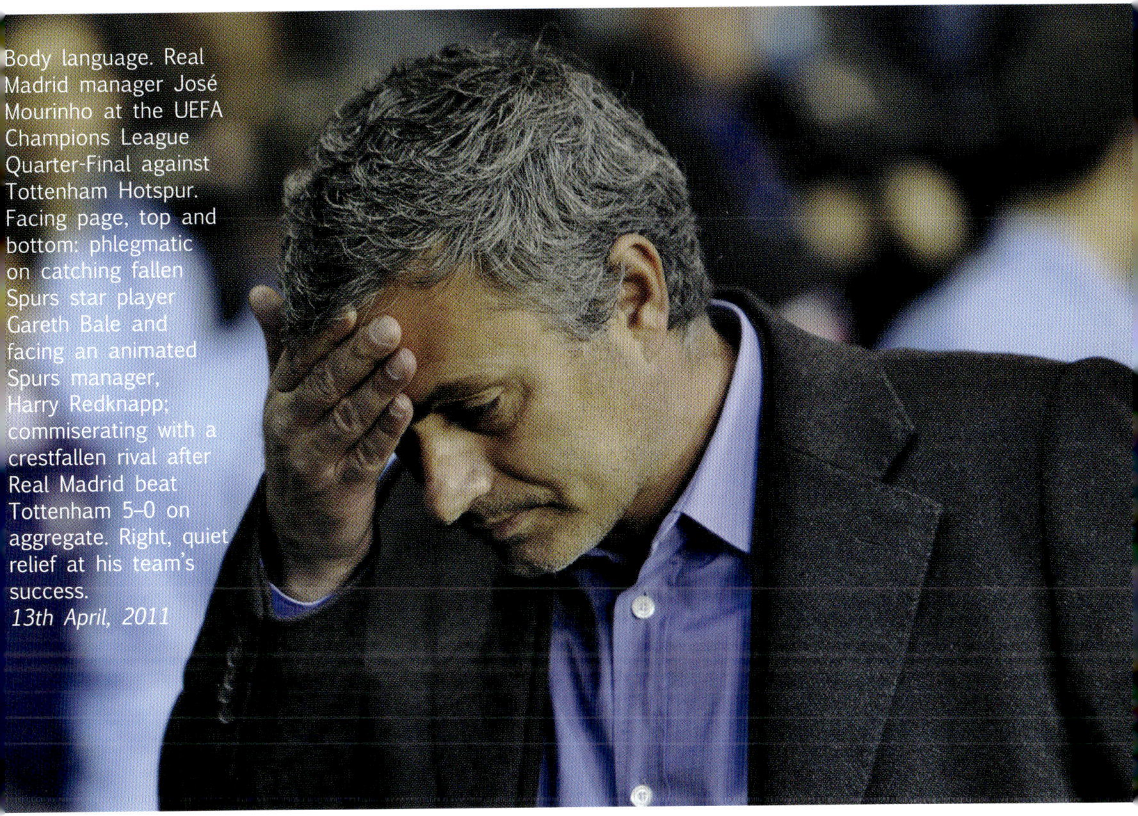

Body language. Real Madrid manager José Mourinho at the UEFA Champions League Quarter-Final against Tottenham Hotspur. Facing page, top and bottom: phlegmatic on catching fallen Spurs star player Gareth Bale and facing an animated Spurs manager, Harry Redknapp; commiserating with a crestfallen rival after Real Madrid beat Tottenham 5–0 on aggregate. Right, quiet relief at his team's success.
13th April, 2011

"I think because of the passion of every English player and every English supporter, and every English journalist for the game, most of the game is played with passion, love for football and instinct, but in football you also have to think."

José Mourinho.

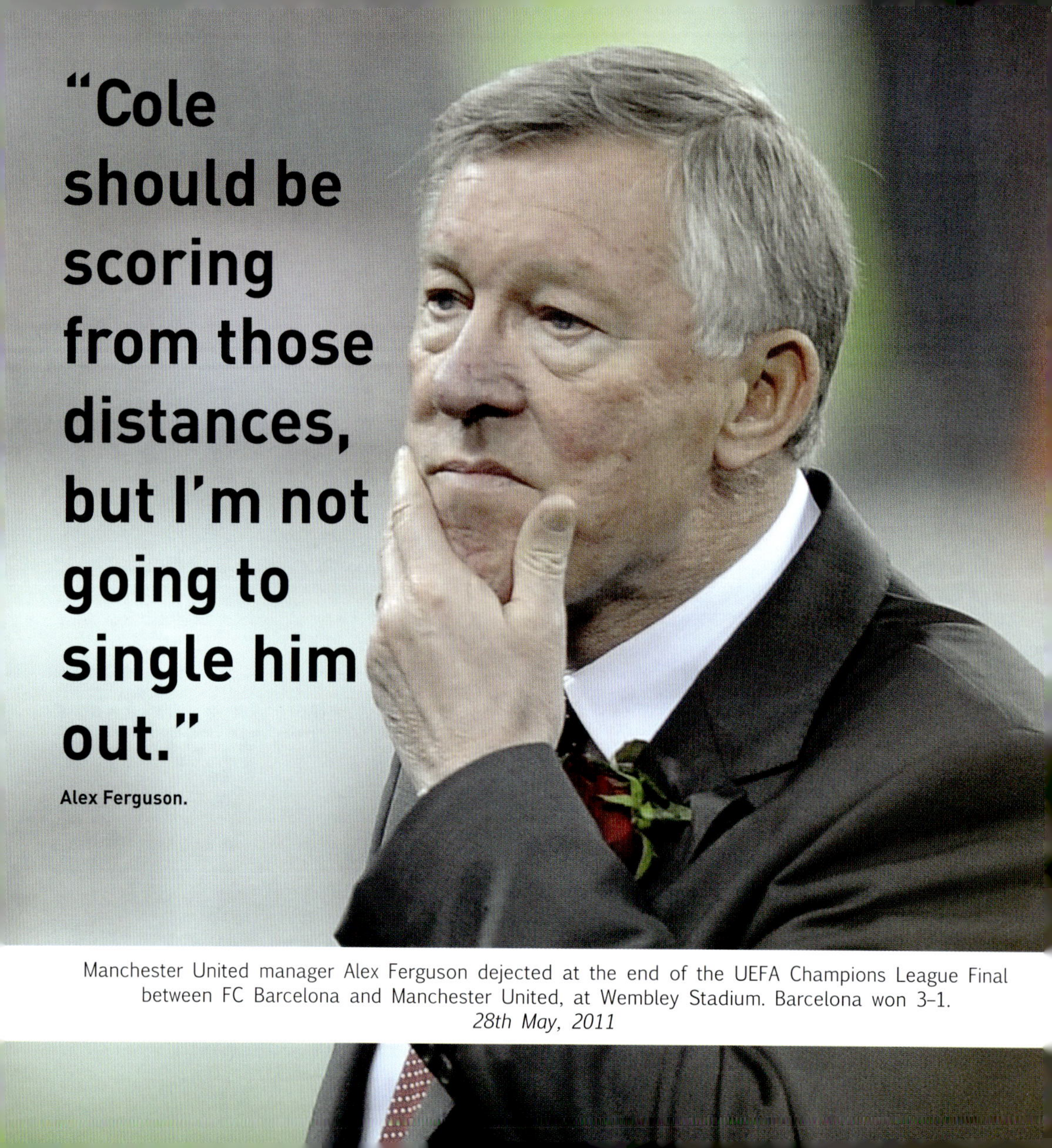

"Cole should be scoring from those distances, but I'm not going to single him out."

Alex Ferguson.

Manchester United manager Alex Ferguson dejected at the end of the UEFA Champions League Final between FC Barcelona and Manchester United, at Wembley Stadium. Barcelona won 3–1.
28th May, 2011

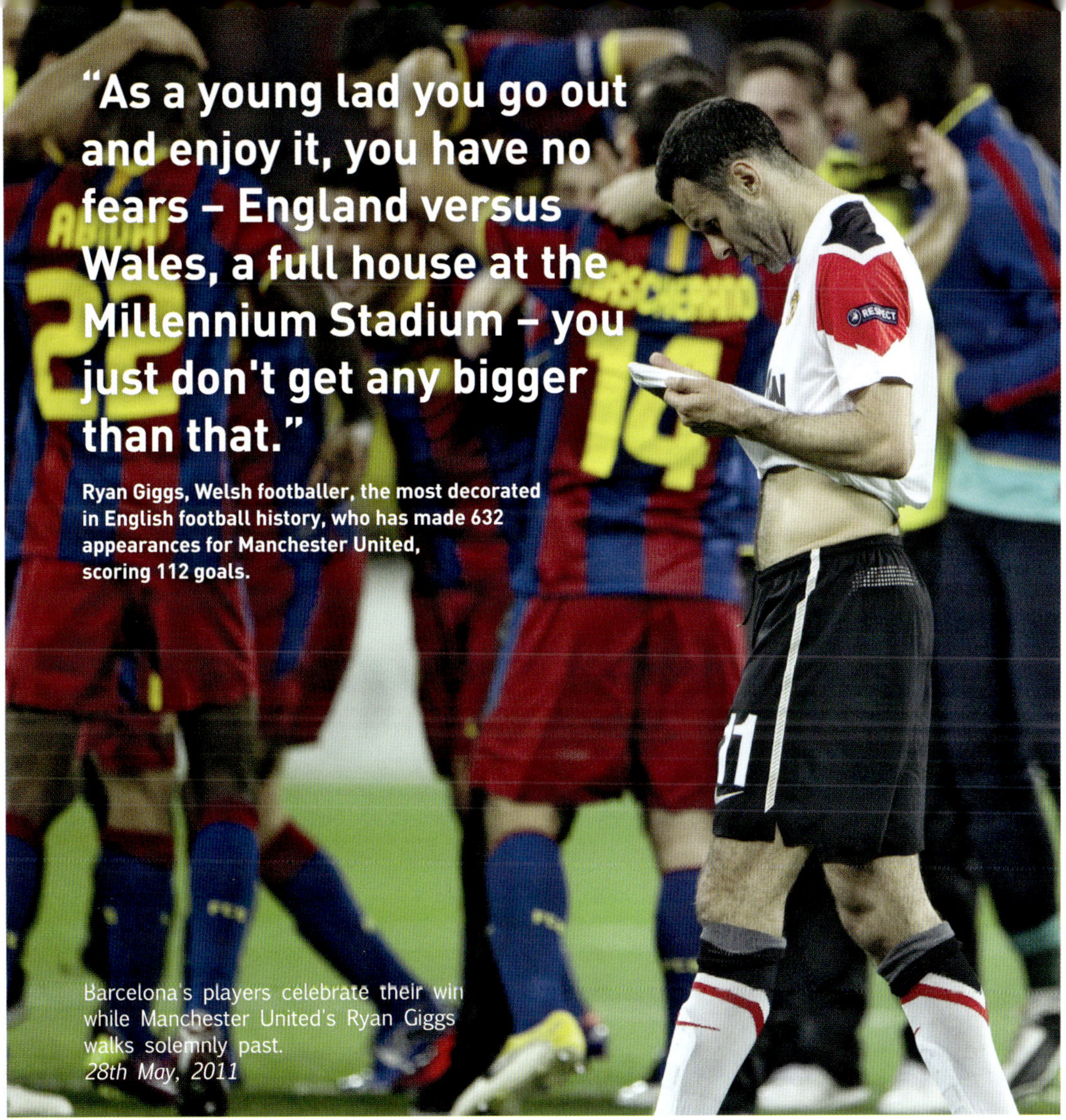

"As a young lad you go out and enjoy it, you have no fears – England versus Wales, a full house at the Millennium Stadium – you just don't get any bigger than that."

Ryan Giggs, Welsh footballer, the most decorated in English football history, who has made 632 appearances for Manchester United, scoring 112 goals.

Barcelona's players celebrate their win while Manchester United's Ryan Giggs walks solemnly past.
28th May, 2011

"England now have three fresh men, with three fresh legs."

Jimmy Hill.

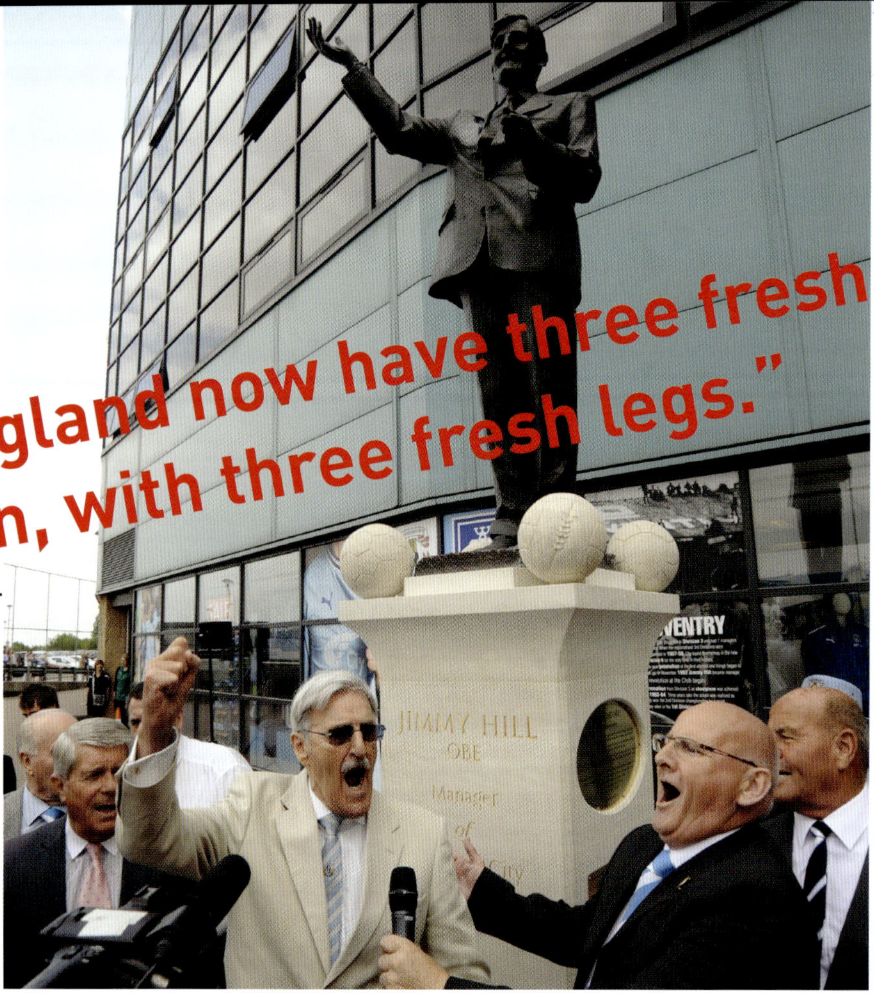

Jimmy Hill, 83, former director and chairman of Coventry City, saw how much he still means to the club, 50 years since he arrived and 30 years since he left. He wiped away a tear as the club unveiled their tribute at the Ricoh Arena, a 7ft bronze statue, its £150,000 cost paid by donations. To the delight of the crowd, the evergreen showman launched into an impromptu rendition of the *Sky Blue Song*.
28th July, 2011

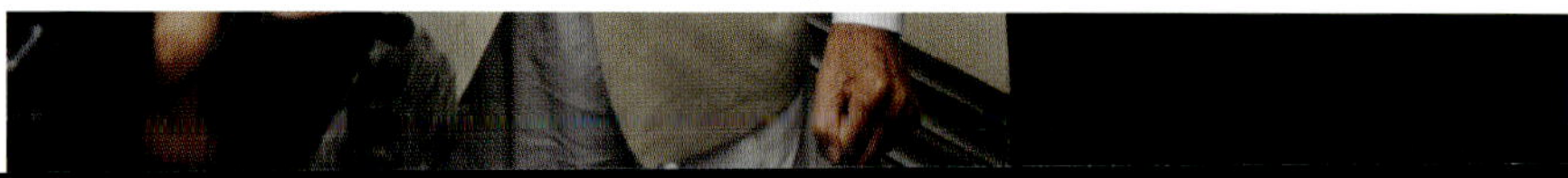

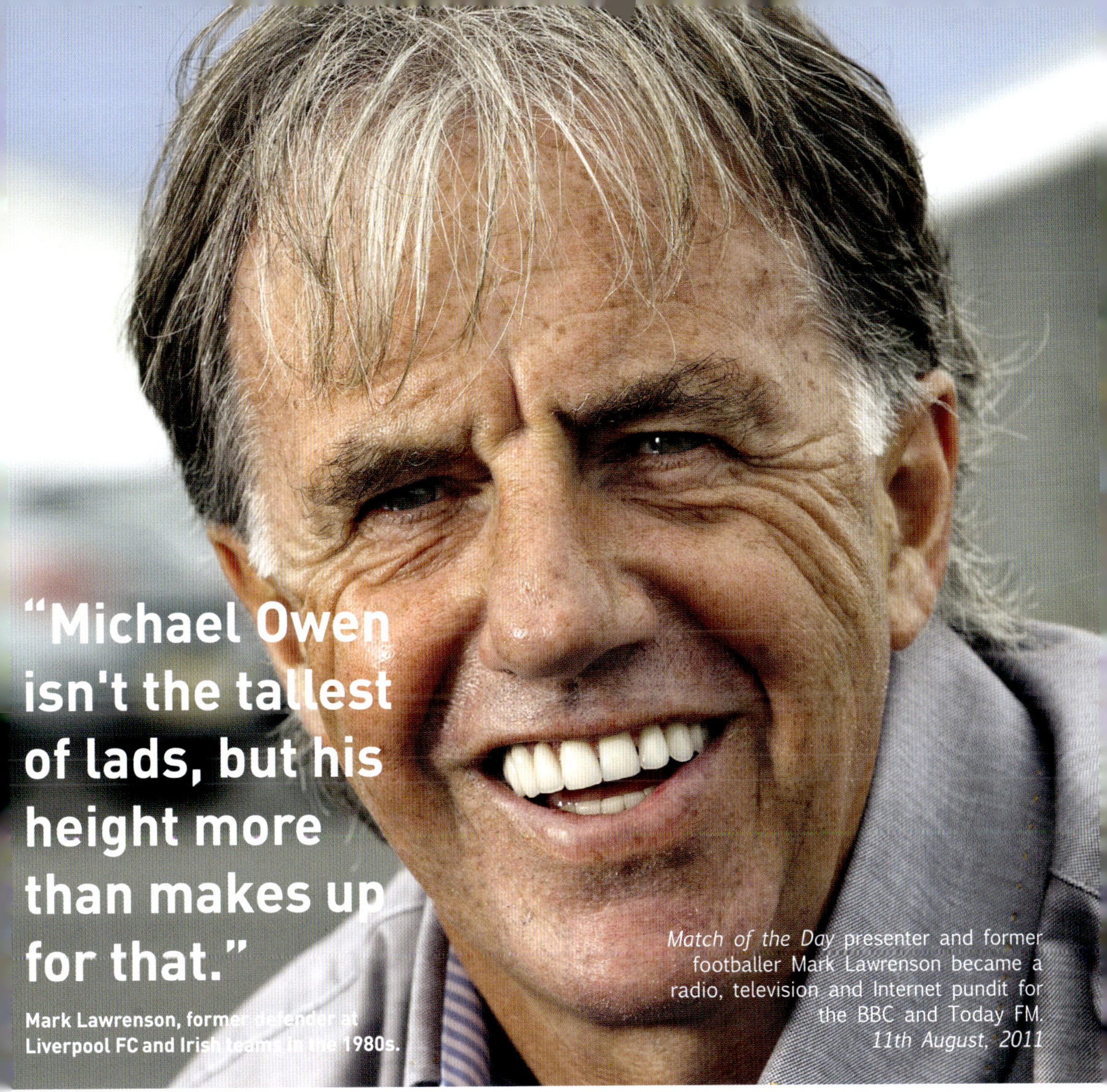

"Michael Owen isn't the tallest of lads, but his height more than makes up for that."

Mark Lawrenson, former defender at Liverpool FC and Irish teams in the 1980s.

Match of the Day presenter and former footballer Mark Lawrenson became a radio, television and Internet pundit for the BBC and Today FM.
11th August, 2011

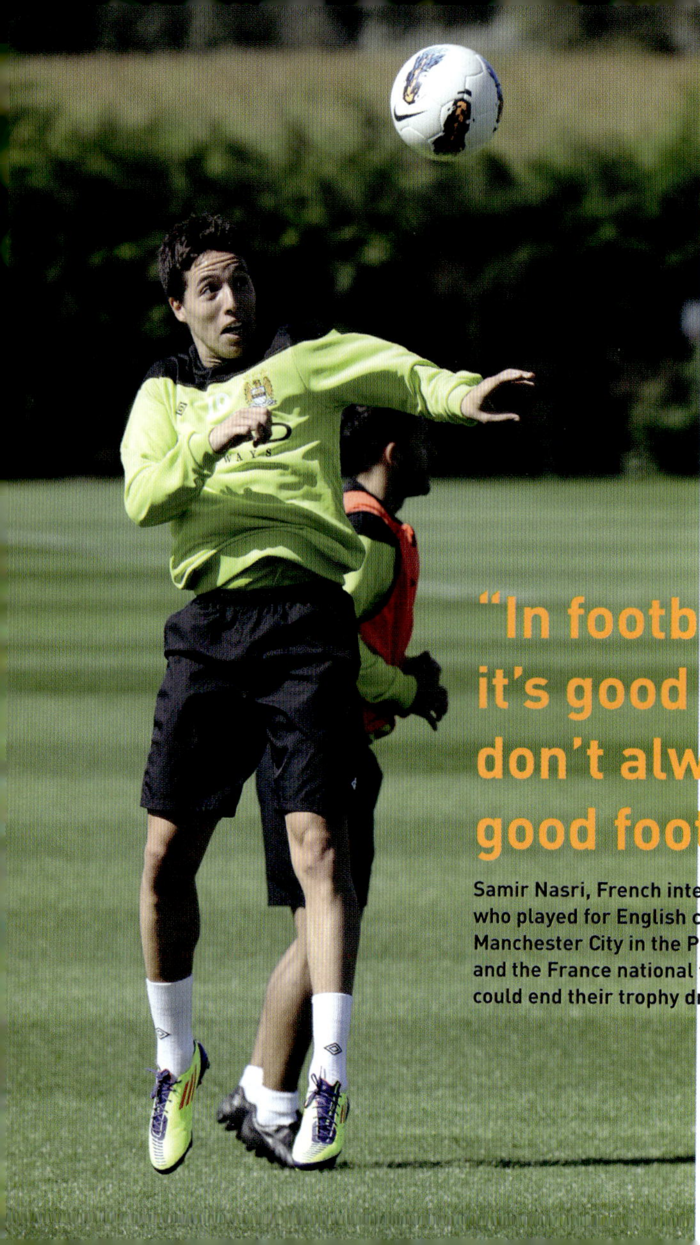

Manchester City new boy Samir Nasri on his first day at training after joining the club from Arsenal.
25th August, 2011

"In football, sometimes it's good to win ugly – you don't always have to play good football to win."

Samir Nasri, French international footballer who played for English clubs Arsenal then Manchester City in the Premier League, and the France national team, on how Arsenal could end their trophy drought.

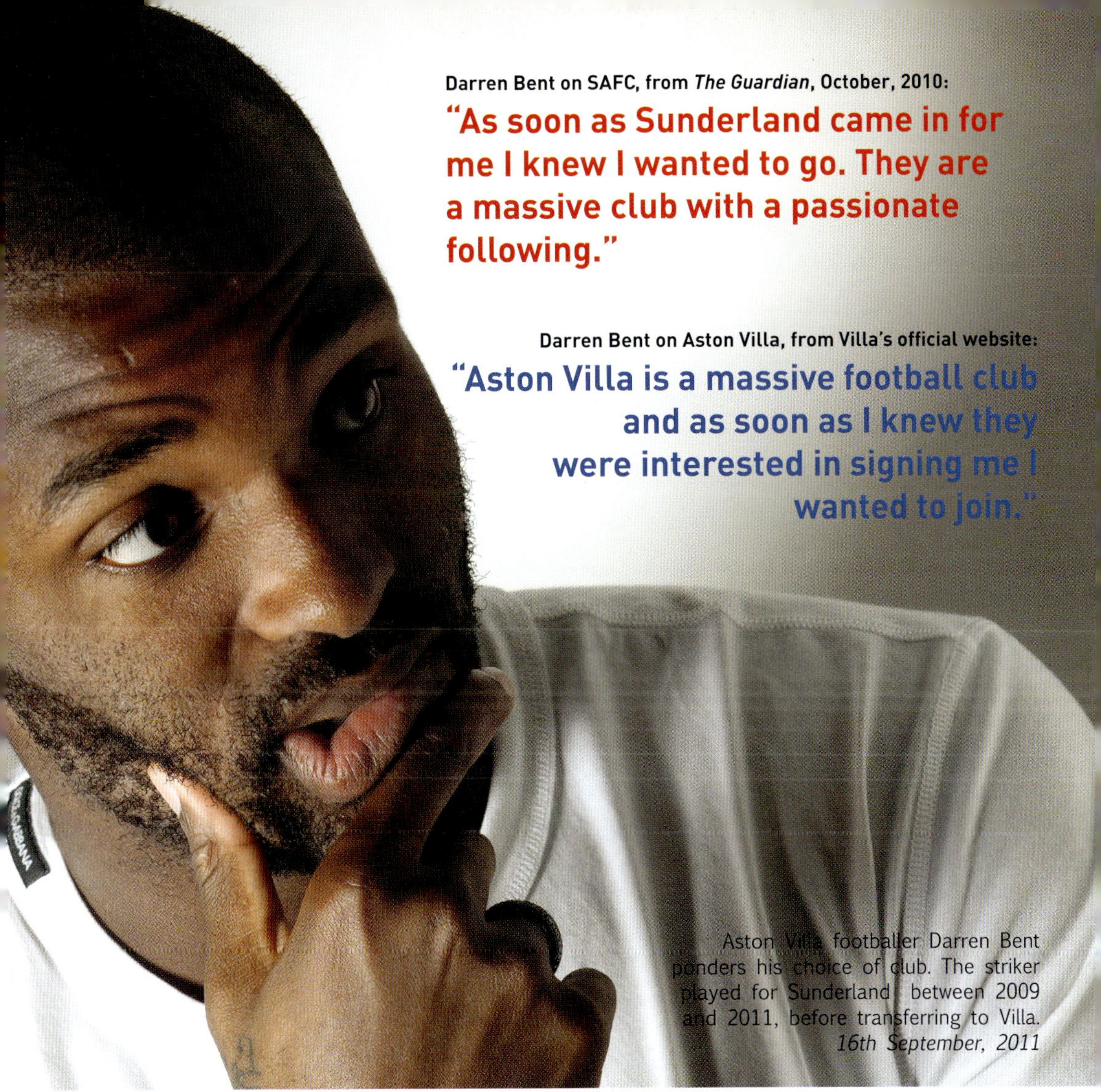

Darren Bent on SAFC, from *The Guardian*, October, 2010:

"As soon as Sunderland came in for me I knew I wanted to go. They are a massive club with a passionate following."

Darren Bent on Aston Villa, from Villa's official website:

"Aston Villa is a massive football club and as soon as I knew they were interested in signing me I wanted to join."

Aston Villa footballer Darren Bent ponders his choice of club. The striker played for Sunderland between 2009 and 2011, before transferring to Villa.
16th September, 2011

"Brucie's record with Liverpool speaks for itself, and his handling skills, his athleticism, his alert distribution and quickness off his line have all become shining examples that future Anfield goalkeepers will be hearing plenty about."

Bob Paisley.

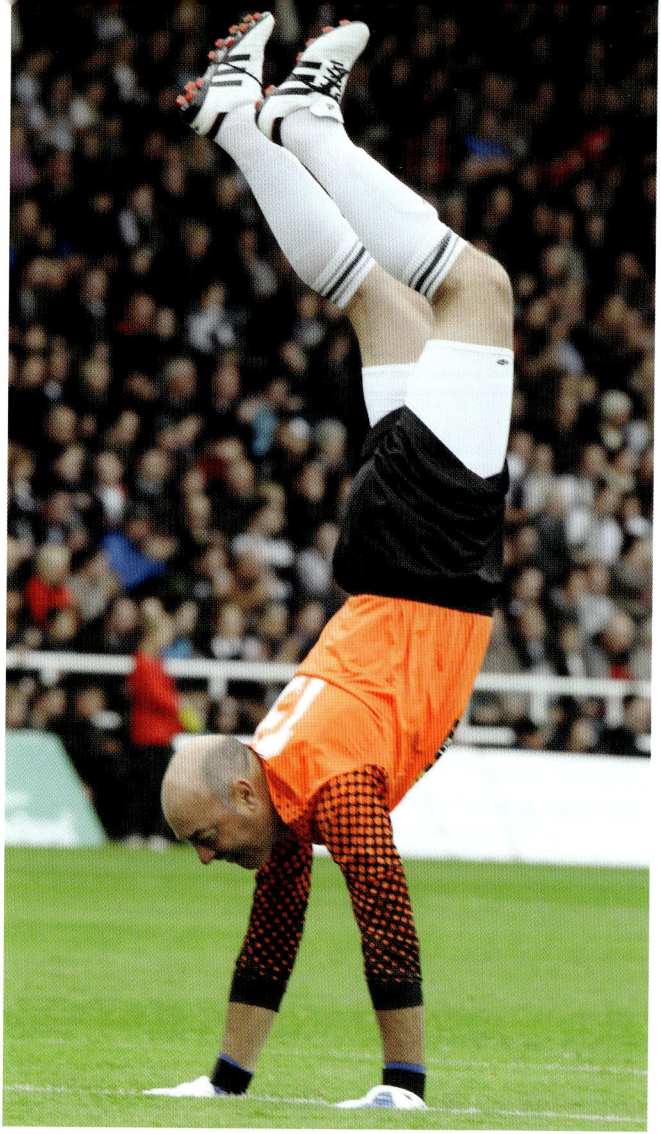

The Entertainers Charity Football Match – Newcastle United v Liverpool Legends XI – took place at Kingston Park, teams of veteran players taking to the pitch for an afternoon of family entertainment. 'The Entertainers', Newcastle United, led by Kevin Keegan, fielded a team including Ferdinand, Shearer, Lee and Srnicek, against a Liverpool team that boasted McManaman, McAllister, Rush, and the irrepressible goalie Bruce Grobelaar, who amused the crowd with his athletic antics.
9th October, 2011

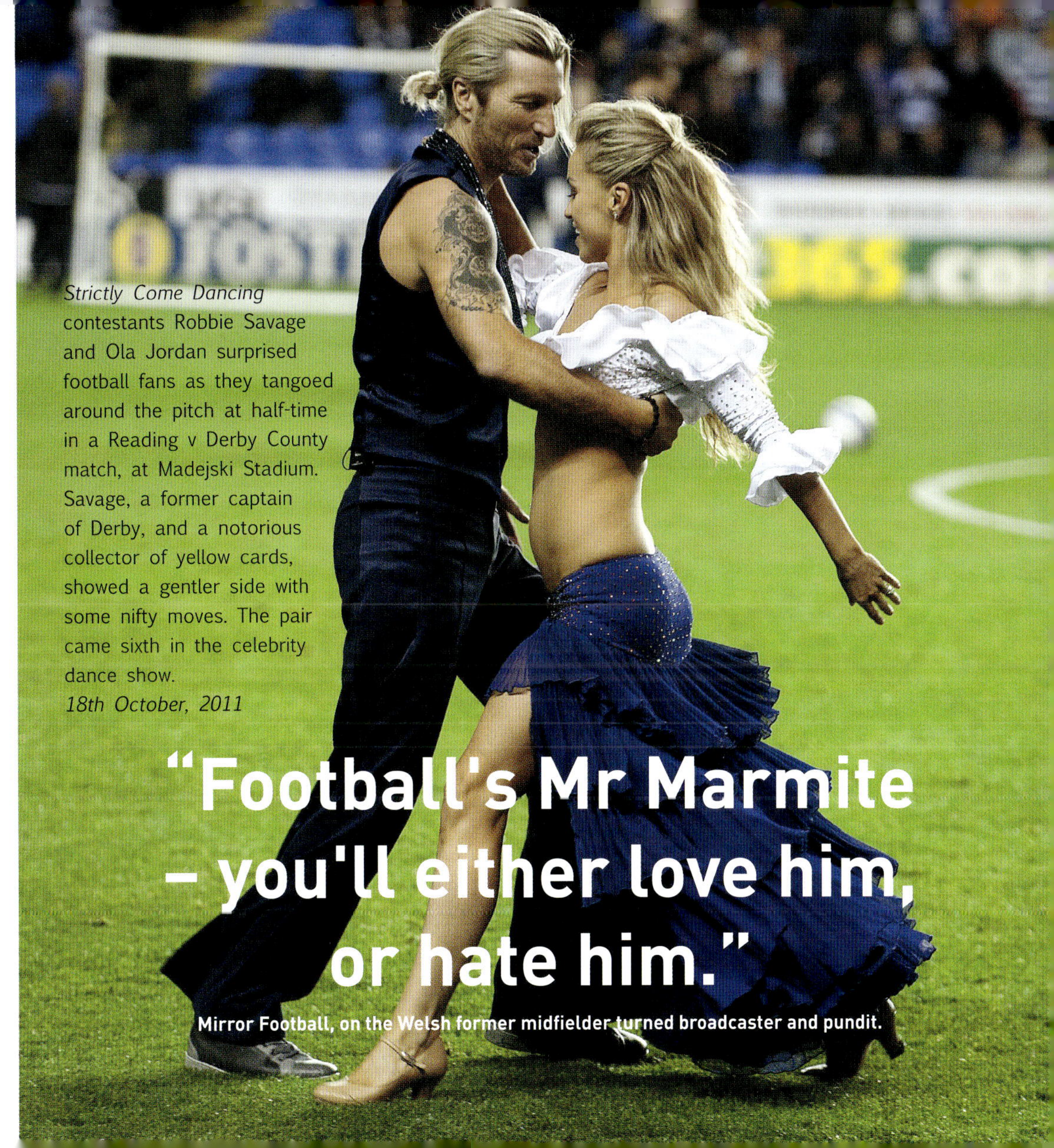

Strictly Come Dancing contestants Robbie Savage and Ola Jordan surprised football fans as they tangoed around the pitch at half-time in a Reading v Derby County match, at Madejski Stadium. Savage, a former captain of Derby, and a notorious collector of yellow cards, showed a gentler side with some nifty moves. The pair came sixth in the celebrity dance show.
18th October, 2011

"Football's Mr Marmite – you'll either love him, or hate him."

Mirror Football, on the Welsh former midfielder turned broadcaster and pundit.

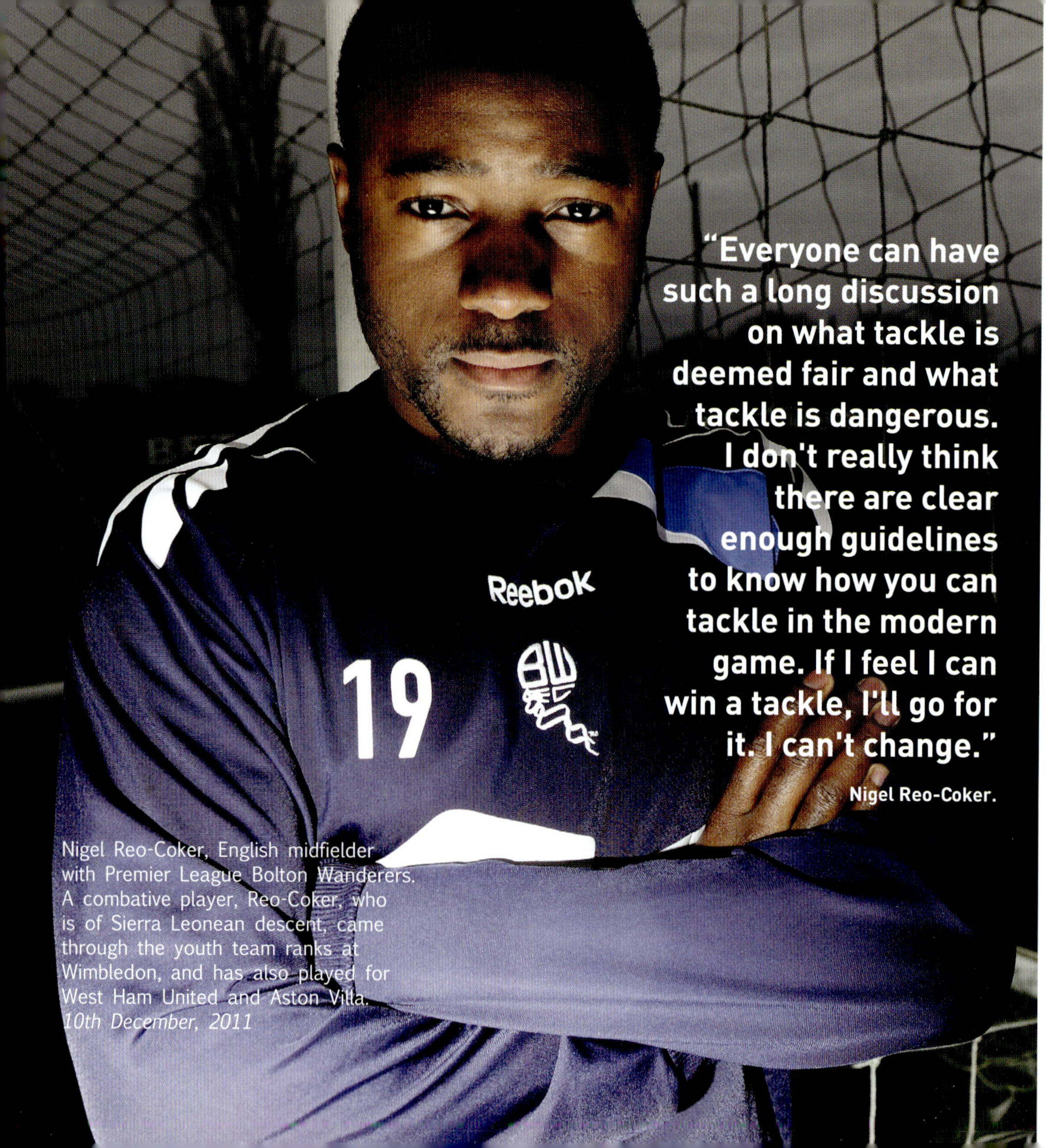

"Everyone can have such a long discussion on what tackle is deemed fair and what tackle is dangerous. I don't really think there are clear enough guidelines to know how you can tackle in the modern game. If I feel I can win a tackle, I'll go for it. I can't change."

Nigel Reo-Coker.

Nigel Reo-Coker, English midfielder with Premier League Bolton Wanderers. A combative player, Reo-Coker, who is of Sierra Leonean descent, came through the youth team ranks at Wimbledon, and has also played for West Ham United and Aston Villa.
10th December, 2011

"I love scoring goals for England and playing for England. That's one of the reasons I didn't retire – I love playing for my country."

David Beckham.

David Beckham, global ambassador for the London 2012 Olympics, brandished the Olympic torch at the launch of Samsung's London 2012 campaign in London, but was tight-lipped about his involvement in the games. In March 2012, it was revealed that he would become part of the 18-man Olympic squad, despite being, at 37 years old, more than twice the age of some of his team-mates. *13th June, 2011*

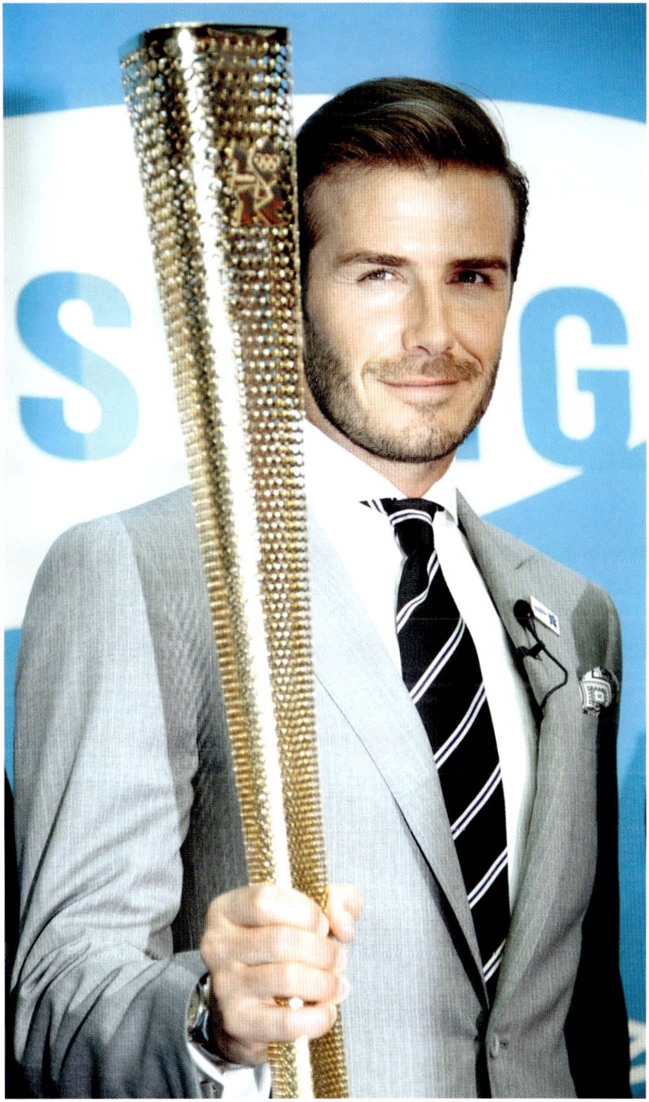

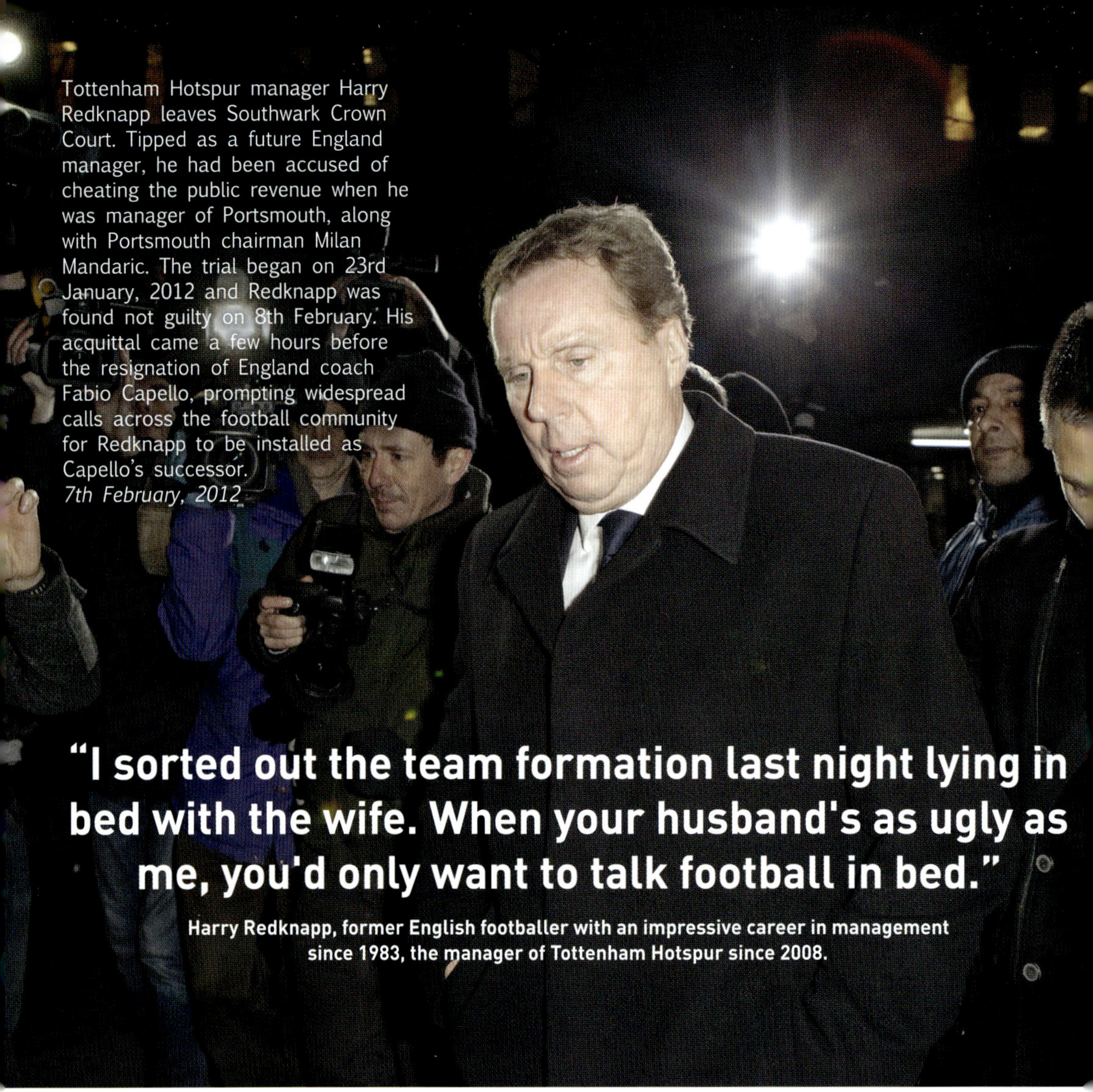

Tottenham Hotspur manager Harry Redknapp leaves Southwark Crown Court. Tipped as a future England manager, he had been accused of cheating the public revenue when he was manager of Portsmouth, along with Portsmouth chairman Milan Mandaric. The trial began on 23rd January, 2012 and Redknapp was found not guilty on 8th February. His acquittal came a few hours before the resignation of England coach Fabio Capello, prompting widespread calls across the football community for Redknapp to be installed as Capello's successor.
7th February, 2012

"I sorted out the team formation last night lying in bed with the wife. When your husband's as ugly as me, you'd only want to talk football in bed."

Harry Redknapp, former English footballer with an impressive career in management since 1983, the manager of Tottenham Hotspur since 2008.

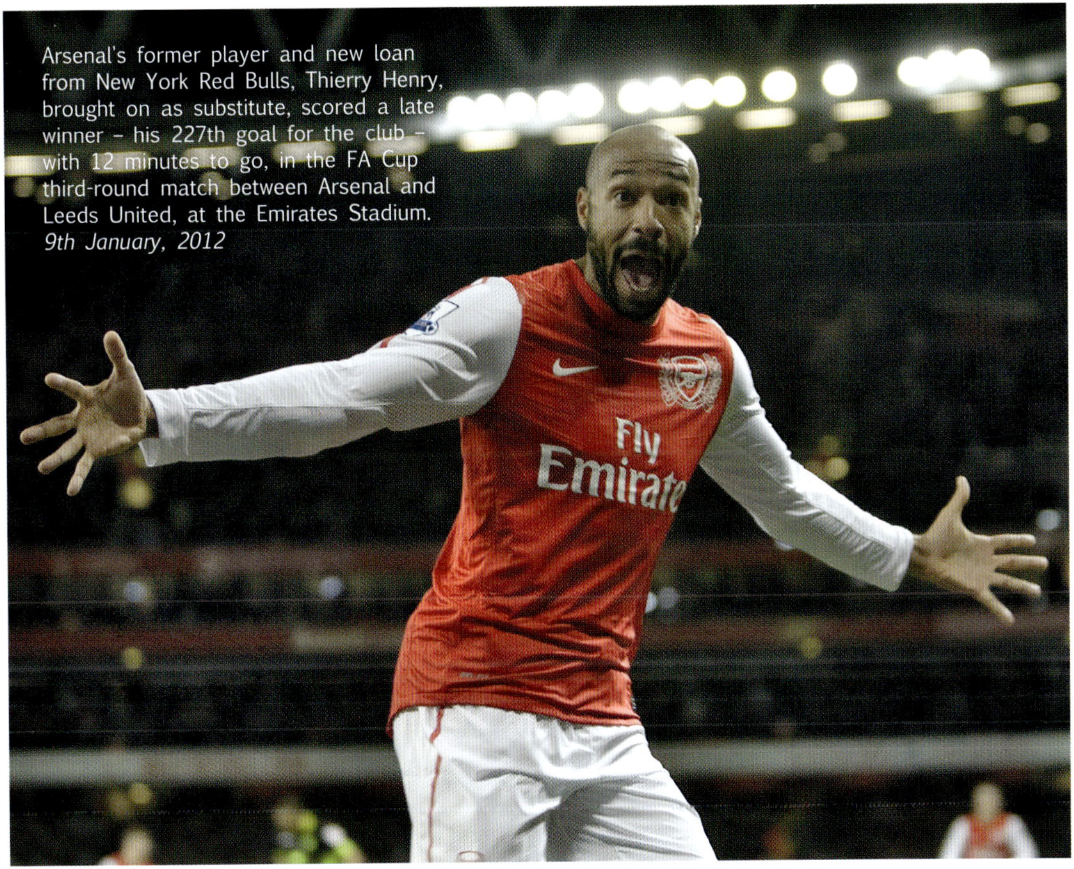

Arsenal's former player and new loan from New York Red Bulls, Thierry Henry, brought on as substitute, scored a late winner – his 227th goal for the club – with 12 minutes to go, in the FA Cup third-round match between Arsenal and Leeds United, at the Emirates Stadium. *9th January, 2012*

"Sometimes in football you have to score goals."

Thierry Henry.

The publishers gratefully acknowledge Mirrorpix, from whose extensive archives
the photographs in this book have been selected.

mirrorpix

AMMONITE
PRESS